# Pragmatism and Naturalism

# Pragmatism and Naturalism

Scientific and

Social Inquiry After

Representationalism

Edited by Matthew Bagger

Columbia University Press

New York

Columbia University Press
*Publishers Since 1893*
New York    Chichester, West Sussex
cup.columbia.edu

Columbia University Press wishes to express its appreciation for assistance given by the Columbia University Department of Religion in the publication of this book.

Library of Congress Cataloging-in-Publication Data
Names: Bagger, Matthew C., editor.
Title: Pragmatism and naturalism : scientific and social inquiry
after representationalism / edited by Matthew Bagger.
Description: New York : Columbia University Press, [2018] |
Includes bibliographical references and index.
Identifiers: LCCN 2018007540 | ISBN 9780231181884 (cloth : alk. paper) |
ISBN 9780231543859 (ebook)
Subjects: LCSH: Naturalism. | Pragmatism.
Classification: LCC B828.2 .P69 2018 | DDC 146—dc23
LC record available at https://lccn.loc.gov/2018007540

Columbia University Press books are printed
on permanent and durable acid-free paper.
Printed in the United States of America

Cover design: Milenda Nan Ok Lee

Cover art: Boston Athenaeum, USA / Bridgeman Images

*To Wayne*
*with affection and gratitude*

# Contents

## PART II

# Pragmatism and the Study of Religion

## PART III

# Pragmatism and Democracy

## PART IV

# Pragmatism and the Philosophy of Religion

# Acknowledgments

In a sense, this volume consists almost entirely of a series of acknowledgments. The desire of all but one of its authors to acknowledge publicly their indebtedness to the remaining one, Wayne Proudfoot, inspires it. Although most of the essays in the volume do not address Wayne's scholarship directly, the contributors all intend their essays to honor him by advancing the discussion of topics that reflect his scholarly interests and influence. Anyone who knows Wayne can attest that he highly values what he terms "fresh" scholarship (and disdains "potted" interpretations or arguments). I think it is fair to say that these essays not only pay tribute to Wayne but also, in their originality and insightfulness, honor his standards of scholarship.

I must thank the contributors to this volume for their patience and support over the many years it has taken me to complete the project. The Department of Philosophy at Auburn University and the Department of Religious Studies at the University of Alabama have provided congenial environments and intellectual stimulation while I worked on this volume. During the summer of 2012, Vinnie Colapietro and John Stuhr presided over invaluable conversations with the other members of Emory University's Institute for the History of Philosophy, which helped me sharpen the thinking behind my contributions to the volume. From beginning to end, Wendy Lochner at Columbia University Press bestowed her wisdom and understanding. Andie Alexander helped format the manuscript. Becky Brown compiled the index.

# Pragmatism and Naturalism

# Introduction

MATTHEW C. BAGGER

There was a time in philosophy, not too long ago, when the term *naturalism* served as convenient shorthand for "pragmatic naturalism."[1] Consider Paul Edwards's (1967) *Encyclopedia of Philosophy*. This work, which a contemporary reviewer described as "truly representative of what English-speaking philosophers are saying," provides a snapshot of the philosophical establishment's view of the discipline at mid-century (Wallace 1968, 445). Tellingly, Arthur Danto's entry on naturalism amounts to little more than a digest of the metaphilosophical positions advanced by John Dewey (1859–1952), the framer and foremost proponent of so-called pragmatic naturalism. In his bibliography, Danto (1967, 450) offers a history of naturalism that mentions precursors outside the pragmatist fold but culminates in the claim that the "best statements" of naturalism appear in works by Dewey, his collaborators, and his coauthors. The complete identification of naturalism with Dewey's philosophy of inquiry becomes strikingly clear when Danto argues that naturalism went into decline in the 1950s (because, he says, philosophers believed it did not leave distinctively philosophical problems for philosophers to tackle employing distinctively philosophical methods).

There's no doubt that Dewey's and his pragmatist followers' overt influence on philosophy waned in the 1950s (probably for the reason Danto cites). There's also no doubt, however, that naturalism's fortunes as a label with which to declare one's philosophical allegiances did not likewise wane. "Naturalism" is more prevalent than ever. It is a commonplace that most professional philosophers describe themselves as naturalists, but there is little consensus about what naturalism entails. It can no longer simply be identified with pragmatic naturalism (which did languish in the decades following Dewey's death).

In fact, since its pragmatist heyday much that goes by the name "naturalism" deviates fundamentally from the philosophical orientation that Danto describes. Whereas Dewey insisted that naturalism is not tantamount to reductive materialism, successor naturalisms have tended to be decidedly materialistic or physicalistic. Naturalisms conferring an ontological primacy on matter and its fundamental physical properties dominated late twentieth-century philosophy. Naturalist philosophers of that era generally viewed values—to single out a key case—as ontologically inconvenient, as something either to explain reductively in terms of physical properties or of whose very reality to be suspicious. As philosophers have come to acknowledge more widely the seemingly insurmountable difficulties attending reductive physicalism, debates about naturalism have intensified, with a number of philosophers recently challenging the dominance of these more materialistic or physicalistic varieties of naturalism. They argue for more "liberal," less ontologically reductive naturalisms. In this context, David Macarthur, Huw Price, and Richard Rorty have brought pragmatism back to the heart of debate about what constitutes a viable naturalism by explicitly billing the variety of pragmatism they share with Robert Brandom and Jeffrey Stout as a liberal form of naturalism.[2]

In a sense, the history of philosophical naturalism has come full circle. When Dewey and his associates adopted "naturalism" as a label for their pragmatism, they resignified an existing term. *Naturalism*, in its earlier use, took the results of the physical sciences to be paradigmatic for philosophy. It connoted a repudiation of idealism and theologically inflected philosophy, while denoting a metaphysics consisting in mechanistic materialism and determinism.[3] Because they, too, were dedicated to remaking philosophy after the image of science, Dewey and his followers retained the label *naturalism* to signal the formative influence of science on their philosophy. They hoped to exploit the term's realist and antitheological connotations, but they eschewed their predecessors' reductive materialism. Like more recent pragmatists, Dewey (and his student Sidney Hook) sought to articulate a liberal naturalism that could readily countenance the values imbuing human history, culture, and aspiration. Then and now, pragmatic naturalism retains the basic naturalist notion that science is paradigmatic for philosophy, but develops it in a distinctive fashion.

C. S. Peirce (1839–1914) and William James (1842–1910)—the other two members of the canonical triumvirate of so-called classical pragmatists—shared with Dewey the distinctive philosophical orientation that since the 1920s and 1930s has been known as pragmatic naturalism but did not refer to themselves as naturalists because they understood the word in the original signification it still bore during their lifetimes. Both began their careers as working scientists and, like

Dewey, held science in high regard. All three classical pragmatists' esteem for science prompted them to evangelize on behalf of the practices of inquiry exemplified by science and to call for their application in arenas all too often exempted from them, including philosophy (as well as religion). Although Peirce, James, and Dewey were respectful of the methods and results of the physical sciences, pragmatism finds inspiration elsewhere in science. As Brandom (2011) has argued, the pragmatists present a form of naturalism reflecting the evolutionary and statistical models of explanation revolutionizing late nineteenth-century science. The pragmatists did not, however, simply replace a metaphysics inspired by the physical sciences with one inspired by biology. Their philosophical vision, rather, grows out of careful attention to the *practice* of inquiry as well as its results.

Evolutionary theory generates a conception of nature in light of which the pragmatists viewed humans and their practices as entirely natural. They conceived of human practices as the behaviors of a social species both shaping and responding to its environment, and in the process modifying its own ethological makeup. With no intention to denigrate or devalue human cognitive achievements, the pragmatists explain them as products of the social practices of a natural creature. The science they extol, they regard as a honed and institutionalized elaboration of the mundane practices of inquiry developed and universally implemented in the course of human natural history. When the pragmatists then parse inquiry and inquire into the norms and practices of inquiry in order to explain and refine them, they well recognize that, by their own lights, they must forgo Platonism and apriorism. They must resort to the very social practices they hope to explain and can have recourse to nothing transcending the explanatory resources those practices provide.

Cheryl Misak (2013, 252) labels this project "the pragmatist's task." The pragmatist, she writes, "must try to explain our practices and concepts, including our epistemic norms and standards, using those very practices, concepts, norms, and standards." To explain human epistemic practices and the authority of their constitutive norms, the pragmatist must employ those practices and rely on the authority of their norms. For the pragmatic naturalist, science is paradigmatic for philosophy in the sense that science treats humans and their intrinsically normative practices (including their linguistic and epistemic practices) as wholly natural and capable of explanation only by employing those very practices.

From this standpoint, the pragmatists fashioned a subtle philosophy of inquiry. Pragmatism began its well-documented career as a method that, distilled from the successful practice of inquiry, could be self-consciously deployed in the service of inquiry. In its initial and most narrow definition, pragmatism refers to a technique for clarifying the specific conceptions that inform a given inquiry.

Although important disagreements differentiate their respective pragmatisms, Peirce and James both argue that attending to the bearing that the conceived effects of the object of a conception have on human practices elucidates the conception's meaning. In other words, to get clear on a conception—whether it be a conception of wine, force, reality, or God (to list some of Peirce's and James's examples)—one must identify how the conceivable effects of wine, force, reality, or God bear on human practice. In this way, the method highlights the relationships between inquiry, semantics, and other human practices. Appreciation of these relationships, in fact, characterizes the whole tradition that takes its name from the pragmatic method.

The classical pragmatists' understanding of inquiry as a practice and their theoretical integration of meaning and human practices led them to a commitment to what, in more recent parlance, is somewhat infelicitously termed *antirepresentationalism*. Macarthur, Price, Rorty, Brandom, and Stout endorse antirepresentationalism as well, and, in fact, it constitutes the pertinent conceptual connection between the classical pragmatists and the variety of pragmatic naturalism common to these latter philosophers. The philosophical strategy that they all reject, now labeled *representationalism*, attempts to explain the semantic content of intentional states (e.g., beliefs) and linguistic expressions (e.g., assertions) by recourse to what they stand for or represent. It treats objects (i.e., what is represented) as primitive and explains semantic content in terms of word–object representational relations (e.g., reference and truth). Representationalists view this capacity to represent objects as foundational to the explanation of mindedness.

Antirepresentationalism, by contrast, explains both semantic content and the representational dimension of discourse itself (i.e., that some intentional states and linguistic expressions represent objects to which they refer and to which they are responsible for their truth) in terms of human practice. Contemporary antirepresentationalists focus more intensively on the social dimensions and the linguistic type of human practice than did the classical pragmatists, but all reject the attempt to explain semantic content (and ultimately mind) as a function of representational relations between bits of language and mind-independent objects (as they are, so to say, "anyway," that is, apart from humans and their practices). Recent antirepresentationalists have improved on the classical pragmatists not only by better explaining why we conceive of reality as consisting of objects but also by explaining objectivity so as to preserve a robust respect for its difference from any possible subjectivity. Objectivity, they argue, is a structural feature of discursive practice that cannot be reduced to the subjective perspective of any or all participants in the practice. This insight into discursive practice enables them to distinguish properly between truth and justification (rather than defining the former as an ideal version of the latter, as the classical pragmatists sometimes regrettably did). In any case, antirepresentationalists view the capacity to enact and follow social norms (rather than the capacity to represent objects) as foundational to the explanation of mindedness.

To grasp the antirepresentationalism (of both the classical and the improved contemporary varieties) of pragmatism enables a more penetrating characterization of pragmatic naturalism. Antirepresentationalism lends itself to a distinctive form of naturalism that evades the dilemmas facing a naturalist in the representationalist camp. To explain the semantic content of ethical or semantic vocabulary and concepts (indeed all sorts of normative vocabulary and concepts), a representationalist must identify the mind-independent objects or properties that they represent. Despairing of finding any such objects or properties compatible with their naturalist commitments, representationalists confront the unwelcome horns of a dilemma. Either they can abandon their naturalism and posit "ontologically queer," nonnatural objects or properties for the talk to represent or they can admit that there are no mind-independent objects or properties that normative vocabulary and concepts represent, but, according to the demands of their semantic theory, this admission robs such talk of objectivity. This dilemma presents the representationalist with the counterintuitive conclusion that a commitment to naturalism deprives one of objectivity (and leaves only subjectivity or, at best, intersubjectivity). To lose the objectivity of specifically semantic vocabulary (e.g., *true*) proves especially troublesome. It throws the door wide open to global skepticism.

In the history of representationalist philosophy since René Descartes, worries about objectivity have provided a powerful and persistent impetus toward various forms of idealism or supernaturalism. In its most elemental form, the dilemma besetting representationalism recurs perennially. The fear that our intentional states and linguistic expressions might wholly misrepresent the world of objects and properties existing independently of us haunts representationalism. Failing to exorcise the specter of skepticism naturalistically, representationalist philosophers have repeatedly sought to quell their skeptical anxiety by recourse to supernaturalist or idealist metaphysics, which provide a guarantee of the adequacy of mind to world. The song remains the same: skeptical doubt looms and supernaturalism or idealism beckon. Historically, many representationalist philosophers have embraced the supernaturalist or idealist horn of the dilemma to avoid the skeptical horn.

The variety of pragmatic naturalism exemplified by Macarthur, Price, Rorty, Brandom, and Stout sidesteps the dilemma by taking naturalism to be a doctrine about the subjects using language rather than the objects to which language refers.

Like their pragmatist forebears, these philosophers view humans as natural creatures and explain ethical and semantic concepts and vocabulary as features of linguistic social practice. One need not, they argue, regard semantic vocabulary like *truth* as representing a substantive property requiring a metaphysical (but somehow naturalistic) explanation. Resisting the gravitational pull toward metaphysics exerted by representationalism, pragmatic naturalism can adopt a "broadly anthropological" strategy and explain "truth" by displaying its indispensable role in the norm-governed activity constitutive of human linguistic and epistemic practices (Macarthur and Price 2007, 101). The new pragmatic naturalists think it sufficient for a naturalistic explanation of semantic concepts and vocabulary to exhibit their uses in the social practices in which they play a part. One can, the new pragmatic naturalists insist, preserve the objectivity of normative discourse without cooking up some purportedly mind-independent objects or properties for normative concepts and vocabulary to represent.

Pragmatic naturalism achieves this more sensible account of normative concepts and vocabulary by prioritizing social practices over ontology in the order of explanation. This antirepresentationalist explanatory strategy promises a way out of even the most elemental forms of the dilemma facing representationalism. By conceiving ontology as an artifact of social practice, pragmatic naturalism historicizes and pluralizes ontology. Linguistic practice renders reality available to us in the form of objects, but different linguistic practices institute different objects. The particular ontology of objects to which we can refer and about which we can (in principle) assert truths depends on what vocabularies we deploy in our practices. Our vocabularies mutate and proliferate over time, reflecting our evolving interests. This dependence of objects on our shifting linguistic practices results in a form of ontological relativity: what there is is relative to the vocabularies we generate through our ongoing interactions with each other and the environing world.

As pragmatists have been insisting for at least 125 years, however, ontological relativity does not entail alethic relativity. Ontology depends on our practices, but the truth or falsity of what we say about the objects our practices institute depends on the way reality is. Ontological relativity nevertheless obviates the skeptical fear associated with representationalism. What there is could not wholly diverge from what we believe and assert there to be because ontology and linguistic practice are not independent of each other. Unlike representationalism, antirepresentationalism prevents the possibility of a wholesale epistemological or semantic gap between what there is and how it is described. With no threat of a gap, antirepresentationalists feel no impulsion to embrace the supernaturalist horn of the dilemma.

This ontological relativity also explains pragmatic naturalism's long-standing resistance to reductive physicalism, scientific realism, and other forms of scientism in which the methods or findings of some (usually physical) science are claimed to limn the nature of reality as it is apart from human interests. In its many guises, scientism affirms the possibility of an absolute conception of reality, a description of reality that is not relative to some human purpose or practice. An absolute conception would name what is "really real," and not what allegedly has a dubious ontological status because of its relation to human interests. Science, so scientism would have it, identifies the paradigm mind-independent objects and properties awaiting representation (as representationalism would have it) and provides descriptions of them undistorted by human perspectives. Pragmatic naturalism maintains that no vocabularies are less suffused with human interests than any others, and so no objects as (successfully) picked out by a vocabulary are any more ontologically primary (or "really real") than those (successfully) picked out by any other. "The trail of the human serpent," as James liked to say, "lies upon all." The entities and properties discovered by fundamental physics are the referents of a vocabulary that is part of a practice answering powerfully to various human interests, but, for all that, they are no more ontologically primary than the objects and properties picked out by other, less vaunted vocabularies answering to less exalted interests. The objects (successfully) referred to by the vocabulary of fundamental physics (e.g., *quark*) are no more real (in the sense of independent of human linguistic practices, interests, conventions, and perspectives) than the objects (successfully) referred to by the vocabulary of dendrology (e.g., *oak*), the vocabulary of carpentry (e.g., *desk*), or even the vocabulary of the marketplace (e.g., *commodity*).

The pragmatists recognized early on that—however counterintuitive it may seem—scientism, because of its representationalist presuppositions, forsakes the chief aspiration of naturalism. In its myriad forms, naturalism has sought to extricate philosophy (and the other disciplines) from idealism and theologically influenced metaphysics. The pragmatists have long assailed scientism on the grounds that its conception of nonhuman reality implicitly (and incongruously) endows it with mental qualities. To give priority to ontology (rather than to social practices) proposes that reality is intrinsically carved up into objects, which exert a normative authority over their proper representation in intentional states and linguistic expressions. From these representationalist presuppositions, science easily becomes scientism. It becomes the effort to force reality to divulge its own preferred vocabulary. Giving priority to ontology supposes that reality makes claims on our linguistic practices, that reality is in a sense a privileged participant in our linguistic practices, with an interest in securing a particular description of itself in a specific vocabulary. Pragmatists, at least since James, have recoiled from the implication implicit in representationalism that we inhabit, to borrow Simon Blackburn's (2005, 151) phrase, a "talking world." They have decried the way in which the idea of a world of mind-independent objects (with their purported authority over discourse) functions in philosophy as a surrogate for God.

As early as 1890, James rejected scientism (in the guise of "materialism") because he regarded its representationalist presuppositions as an unacknowledged theology. "If, without believing in a God," he wrote in *The Principles of Psychology*, "I still continue to talk of what the world 'essentially is,' I am just as much entitled to define it as a place in which my nose itches, or as a place where at a certain corner I can get a mess of oysters for twenty cents, as to call it an evolving nebula differentiating and integrating itself" (James 1950, 2:336, note). With this remark, James concludes an argument in which he contends that a scientific description of reality (in terms of objects and properties picked out by a scientific vocabulary) enjoys only the privilege that our multifarious and inconstant interests and purposes confer on it. A scientific ontology is not absolute; like any other, it is relative to human purposes and interests. The scientistic conceit that a (true) scientific description of reality is intrinsically preferable to or truer (in some sublime sense that altogether transcends human practices and purposes) than other, indefinitely various, mundane (true) descriptions depends, he argues, on something like a religious view. It requires the existence of purposes that supersede contingent human purposes. A (true) scientific description could only gain the metaphysical significance that scientism accords to it if there were an authoritative supra-empirical purpose rendering the scientific ontology absolute (relative to other vocabularies). James duly notes the profound irony inherent in the naturalism of his day: materialism denounces teleology in metaphysics while simultaneously entailing it.

This early argument sheds light on James's late, comprehensive statement of his pragmatism. In the introductory chapter of *Pragmatism* (1907), James draws a casual distinction between "tender-minded" and "tough-minded" temperaments. "Rationalism" in epistemology and a tendency toward "idealism" in metaphysics in part characterize a tender-minded temperament, whereas "empiricism" in epistemology and an inclination toward "materialism" in metaphysics characterize a tough-minded temperament. James refers back to this distinction throughout *Pragmatism*, but in its final, culminating chapters, he quietly violates the distinction's terms by treating not only absolute idealism but also materialism as an expression of rationalism. As the book progresses, James settles on *rationalism* as his label for the metaphysical and semantic assumptions that constitute representationalism. Materialism is rationalist in this sense because, like idealism, it conceives of reality as absolute. Although they are different "brands" of rationalism, both materialism and idealism preclude the ontological relativity characteristic of antirepresentationalism (James 1975, 138). Materialism, no less than tender-minded idealism (or theism), cedes authority over and responsibility for ontology to something—in this respect—superhuman. Endowed with this superhuman authority, reality makes "claims" on us, obligating us to ensure that our conceptions of it "agree" with its ontological dictates (112). By the end of the book, "rationalism" refers to any view that presupposes sources of authority that transcend human social practices. For James (as for Brandom and other contemporary pragmatic naturalists) authority is always a product of human social practice. In *Pragmatism*, rationalism serves as a foil for pragmatism's prioritizing of human social practices over ontology. To accentuate the contrast with rationalism, James adopts F. C. S. Schiller's term *humanism* as his label for pragmatist antirepresentationalism.

James's use of the term *rationalism* to designate and disavow representationalism can cloud the underlying continuities between the classical pragmatists and Robert Brandom's currently influential so-called rationalist pragmatism. Brandom styles himself a rationalist because he argues that human sapience, that is, discursive intentionality, necessarily depends on the specific social practice of giving and asking for *reasons*.[4] Their terminological (and substantive) differences notwithstanding, James and Brandom share a fundamental commitment to an antirepresentationalist order of explanation. They both give priority to social practices over ontology and maintain that "all matters of authority and responsibility are ultimately matters of social practice" (Brandom 1999, 143).

In fact, Brandom sees his "rationalism" as requisite for undermining "rationalism," in James's sense. To meet the adequacy conditions for a semantic theory, antirepresentationalism requires a defensible account of objectivity. Brandom thinks the classical pragmatists failed in this regard and that his rationalism uniquely provides a viable antirepresentationalist account of objectivity. To explain how the authority that reality wields over the truth of what we say about it "is [nonetheless] of our making," Brandom appeals to the implicit norms informing the social practice of giving and asking for reasons. He "describe[s] the special structure of social practices that consist in our granting a kind of authority over the correctness of our thinking to the things we are (thereby) thinking *about*" (Brandom 1999, 143, emphasis in original). Granting that "the idea of a rationalist pragmatism would probably have struck [Dewey] as a *contradictio in adjecto*," Brandom (2011, 31) offers his rationalism as a tactical refinement serving the classical pragmatists' antirepresentationalist explanatory strategy.

In the interest of avoiding logomachy, perhaps the point James makes with his idiosyncratically tailored terms *rationalism* and *humanism* can be stated more perspicuously: representationalism is incompatible with naturalism. Conceiving of the nonhuman world as bearing authority beyond that conferred on it by human social practices, representationalism amounts to a vestigial theology. To fully emancipate inquiry from idealist or theological metaphysical commitments, a thoroughgoing naturalism must repudiate representationalism. Later pragmatists echo and develop this insight, and one might well think of it as the defining thesis of pragmatic naturalism.

The pragmatist conclusion that representationalism is incompatible with naturalism receives support from an unlikely source. Over the past twenty-five years, contemporary philosophy's most prominent proponent of supernaturalism, Alvin Plantinga, has been refining an argument designed to show that one cannot rationally accept both naturalism and evolutionary theory. By demonstrating that "a main pillar of contemporary science" conflicts with naturalism in this way, he ultimately aims to persuade that theism comports better with science than does naturalism (Plantinga 2011, 310). Plantinga's quixotic (or bizarre, depending on your point of view) apology for theism obscures his argument's real significance for naturalism. If the argument is valid, it confirms the pragmatists' contention that one cannot erect a viable naturalism on representationalist assumptions.

Plausibly enough, Plantinga (2011, ix) defines naturalism as "the thought that there is no such person as God, or anything like God." If those who accept naturalism also endorse the theory of evolution, they cannot, Plantinga claims, sensibly think their cognitive faculties are reliable (i.e., produce mostly true beliefs). Evolutionary theory posits that natural selection produces adaptive behavior—behavior that favors reproductive success—but provides no reason for thinking that human cognitive faculties produce mostly true beliefs. Humans may be neurologically attuned to their environments in such a way as to yield adaptive behavior without the belief contents associated with their neurological states "matching" the environment (331). Whereas Christian theism, which maintains that God created humans in his image, supplies a reason for thinking that human cognitive faculties are reliable, the conjunction of naturalism and evolution leaves the probability of reliable cognitive faculties low. If, Plantinga continues, naturalists cannot sensibly think that human cognitive faculties are reliable, they have an undermining defeater for any belief produced by those faculties, including the belief that naturalism and evolution are true. Simply put, the belief that naturalism and evolution are true gives naturalists a defeater for the belief that naturalism and evolution are true. The belief that naturalism and evolution are true is self-referentially incoherent. Plantinga concludes that one cannot, therefore, rationally accept it.

In mounting this argument, Plantinga relies on the battery of representationalist assumptions that pragmatic naturalists assail. His argument turns on the possibility that human beliefs could wholly fail to "match" reality; no matter how well humans were adapted to their environment, their beliefs might not accurately represent the objects and properties composing reality. Rather than viewing truth as a constituent norm of the linguistic practice of a natural creature interacting with its environment, Plantinga conceives of truth as a substantive property naming a relation between the content of beliefs and a world whose ontology is fixed in advance of linguistic practice. This metaphysical conception of truth threatens to open an unbridgeable epistemological chasm between belief and reality. By insisting that a global skeptical doubt afflicts naturalism, Plantinga in effect proclaims his argument's representationalist pedigree.

In its essence, Plantinga's argument simply recapitulates and repurposes the perennial dilemma plaguing representationalist varieties of naturalism. His particular focus on evolution only serves to revitalize philosophical vieux jeux for an audience respectful of science. The dilemma offers naturalists a choice: they can either maintain their naturalism and thereby invite epistemologically corrosive consequences or they can relinquish their naturalism. Plantinga's argument represents but the latest instance in a representationalist legacy dating to Descartes, in which skeptical arguments provide the impetus for idealism or supernaturalism. As an apologist, Plantinga enthusiastically exploits the threat of skepticism in an attempt to render supernaturalism more appealing. The zeal with which Plantinga impales himself on the supernaturalist horn of the dilemma should not, however, distract attention from the fact that his argument is best viewed as a reductio ad absurdum. Rather than goring oneself with either horn—looming skepticism *or* supernaturalism—one ought to reject the representationalist assumptions that produce the dilemma. Despite his intention to undermine naturalism, Plantinga has actually formulated a powerful argument against representationalism. If his argument is valid, it corroborates the pragmatist contention that a viable naturalism must be antirepresentationalist.[5]

For well over a century, pragmatism has propounded a variety of naturalism in concert (not conflict) with evolutionary theory. To reprise the title of one of Rorty's essays, pragmatic naturalism conceives of humans as "just one more species doing its best." This orientation focuses philosophical attention on human social practices, including the linguistic practices that make both objects and true beliefs or assertions about them possible. The resulting antirepresentationalism equips pragmatic naturalism to navigate the Scylla and Charybdis of scientism and skepticism.

Espousing this nonreductive naturalism, dedicated to inquiry, and keenly attentive to human practices, pragmatism has, from its inception, been the source of some of the most original, critical, and insightful thought about religion. Inquiring into the relationships between religion and other human practices, the pragmatists have investigated the semantics of religious belief and have recommended revisions to the norms constitutive of religious belief and practice. Despite their naturalism, the pragmatists have not been hostile to religion per se. In fact, compared to naturalists of other stripes, they have been unusually sympathetic to religion. Peirce penned an argument for the reality of God. As I argue in my contribution to the present volume, James combined a commitment to methodological naturalism in the study of religion with a defense of supernaturalistic religious belief. Dewey, Hook, and Rorty all reject supernatural varieties of religion, but each recognizes the value of religion and defends its rightful role in human life.

Heirs to this pragmatist tradition of reflection on religion, the contributors to the present volume take stock of it. They illuminate the naturalism of their pragmatist predecessors while appraising the value of pragmatic naturalism for contemporary purposes (in many cases, discussing the work of others in this very volume). Collectively, they evaluate the contribution pragmatism can make to a viable naturalism; explore what distinguishes pragmatic naturalism from other naturalisms on offer (including cognitive science, which, like pragmatic naturalism, takes inspiration from evolutionary theory); consider the relative merits of different forms of pragmatic naturalism within the philosophy of religion, within the academy more generally, and within a democratic polity; and address the pertinence of pragmatic naturalism to methodological issues in the study of religion.

Part 1 includes three essays, each discussing one of the three classical pragmatists in some detail. Michael Raposa's "Instinct and Inquiry: A Reconsideration of Peirce's Mature Religious Naturalism" commences this section. In this essay, he provides a novel reading of Peirce's famous "A Neglected Argument for the Reality of God." Raposa concentrates on Peirce's general account of the role that instinct plays in human reasoning and hypothesis selection, and relates that general account to the specific case of religious thought and practice. Raposa argues that Peirce's views on instinct and inquiry provide a naturalism that is also informed by attention to history, politics, and society. Raposa uses Peirce as a resource for thinking about how to be naturalist as well as historicist in the study of religion.

My essay on James, "Religious Apologetic, Naturalism, and Inquiry in the Thought of William James," follows Raposa's retrieval of Peirce's naturalism. James's *Varieties of Religious Experience* is often interpreted as an apology for supernaturalism and religious faith. This view of *Varieties* is no doubt accurate, but it overshadows James's interest in establishing and contributing to a science of religions that explains religion in naturalistic terms. My essay contends that the key to an undistorted reading of James on religion lies in properly relating his apologetic interests to his naturalism. The essay achieves this end by reading *Varieties* as addressing issues raised by the response to James's earlier essay "The Will to Believe." Ultimately, I endorse James's naturalism in the study of religion (while acknowledging its shortcomings).

Philip Kitcher's essay on Dewey, "Deweyan Naturalism," concludes part 1. Kitcher examines Dewey's naturalism in *Experience and Nature* and then reconstructs the argument of *A Common Faith* in light of the earlier work. Kitcher emphasizes the capaciousness of Dewey's variety of "method naturalism" and explains how it motivates Dewey, in *A Common Faith*, to seek a substitute for the functions of doctrinal religion. The essays in part 1 anchor many of the themes running through the later essays in the work of the classical pragmatists. The relationship between a viable naturalism and historicism, the place of naturalism in the study of religion, and the effects of naturalism on religion are topics that recur throughout the volume.

Part 2 comprises two essays that discuss pragmatic naturalism as it relates to methodological issues in the study of religion. The first, Wayne Proudfoot's "Pragmatism, Naturalism, and Genealogy in the Study of Religion," represents something of a transition between part 1, which deals with the classical pragmatists, and the remaining sections, which more fully delineate and appraise pragmatic naturalism. Proudfoot's essay both illuminates all three of the classical pragmatists and identifies a way in which their method must be extended. He revisits Dewey's criticism of James's pragmatism, then compares the pragmatists' conception of inquiry to Friedrich Nietzsche's notion of genealogy in order to call for a naturalism that consists in a kind of historicism. This historicist naturalism contrasts with those varieties of naturalism (exemplified by much cognitive science) that fail to recognize the necessity of social and cultural explanations.

Like Proudfoot's, Scott Davis's essay, "Language, Method, and Pragmatism in the Study of Religion," addresses general questions of theoretical orientation in the study of religion. Davis highlights the continuity between the understanding of thought and language involved in Peirce's "pragmatic turn" and the work of Donald Davidson and Brandom. Applying Davidson's argument for "the primacy of the idiolect" in the study of language as well as Brandom's argument against artificial intelligence, Davis offers a compelling pragmatist critique of cognitive science approaches in the study of religion. The nonreductive naturalism he defends offers an antidote to essentialism and points us back to the kind of theory exemplified by Émile Durkheim, Mary Douglas, and Max Weber.

The two essays in part 3 consider the implications of pragmatic naturalism for political theory. Both concern, in particular, the topic of religion and public life. In "Reading Wayne Proudfoot's *Religious Experience*: Naturalism and the Limits of Democratic Discourse," Jonathon Kahn contrasts two forms of pragmatic religious naturalism with respect to the virtues requisite for democratic discourse and democratic life. Proudfoot's pragmatic religious naturalism compares favorably to Rorty's, Kahn claims, because Proudfoot's careful attention to the distinction between "explication" and "explanation" refines a set of virtues by which differently religiously constituted citizens can speak honestly and sympathetically to one another.

Jeffrey Stout's essay "Public Reason and Dialectical Pragmatism" follows Kahn's. Despite rejecting Dewey's criticisms of supernaturalism in *A Common Faith*, Stout endorses Dewey's naturalization of G. W. F. Hegel's account of reason. Dewey adopts Hegel's view of reason as holistic, social, and historical but divests it of Hegel's idealist metaphysics of the absolute. Stout labels the resulting conception of reasoning *dialectical pragmatism*. Probing the ambiguities and tensions between an Enlightenment conception of reason and dialectical pragmatism in John Rawls's later work, Stout argues for "an explicitly dialectical account of democratic public reasoning." Current debates in political theory about the legitimacy of controversial religious reasons in public political discourse and in the political deliberations of citizens provide the subtext for Stout's argument, in which he collapses Rawls's carefully policed distinction between public and non-public reason.

The three essays in part 4 assess the relative merits of different forms of pragmatic naturalism as a general philosophical orientation. In "The Fate of Radical Empiricism and the Future of Pragmatic Naturalism," Nancy Frankenberry courageously reassesses the radical empiricism she endorsed thirty years ago in *Religion and Radical Empiricism*. Summarizing five lines of argument found in the works of Wilfred Sellars, Davidson, and Proudfoot, she concludes that the emphasis on experience in radical empiricism has, to its detriment, largely "been overtaken by multiple developments in twentieth-century thought collectively termed the *linguistic turn*." She does, nevertheless, retain a role for experience as a reminder of "what is presently unsayable," that "unsettles" our articulate certainties. After criticizing Plantinga's argument for supernaturalism on Davidsonian grounds, she concludes the essay by envisioning a future for pragmatic naturalism in which we see ourselves not as epistemologically or semantically answerable to the nonhuman world but rather as ethically answerable to the nonhuman world on which our ecosystem depends.

Terry F. Godlove's essay "Nonconceptualism and Religious Experience: Kant, Schleiermacher, Proudfoot" follows Frankenberry's. In his nuanced discussion of the possibility of a nonconceptual element in our cognitive grasp of the world, Godlove approaches questions pertaining to pragmatism and naturalism more obliquely than the other contributors. He explores recent interpretations of Kant on the receptivity of the senses that emphasize how the forms of intuition (space and time) situate the activity of concept application in a world on which, consequently, we have a nonconceptual "grip." Revisiting Proudfoot's famous criticisms of Schleiermacher's theory of religion, Godlove compares Schleiermacher's account of nonconceptual content unfavorably to Kant's. Godlove distinguishes between causal supernaturalism, causal naturalism, and what he calls "rule-governedness." In Godlove's reckoning, the virtue of Kant's position lies in the fact that Kant explains our cognitive relationship to the world not by causal naturalism or causal supernaturalism but by an inescapable rule-governedness. Although Godlove does not pursue the issue, rule-governedness forms the basis for the pragmatic naturalism touted by Macarthur, Price, Rorty, Stout, and Brandom, but, unlike Kant, they ground the rule-governedness to which they appeal in social practice.

After a series of essays most of which laud pragmatic naturalism, the volume ends with Jim Wetzel voicing hesitation. In "The Oracle and the Inner Teacher: Piecemeal Naturalism," he expresses misgivings about a programmatic naturalism, pragmatic or otherwise. He prefers to think of naturalism as a "post-tragic realism" about the lack of a superhuman moral order, rather than as a "fully comprehensive framework of inquiry." Even so, he explains that his naturalism is pragmatic rather than principled. It serves as a reminder that some opacities are not divine mysteries but rather "mere facts of finitude." Through beautiful and insightful readings of *Oedipus Rex* and Augustine's *De magistro*, Wetzel explains the rationale for what he calls "piecemeal naturalism." Inverting the "piecemeal supernaturalism" that James endorses in the *Varieties*, he describes a position that "cedes the domain of causes to nature" but acknowledges the relative independence of goods from the causal order.

By enthusiastic and unanimous consensus of the other contributors, the present volume is dedicated to Wayne Proudfoot, our teacher, colleague, and friend. A scholar of uncommon clarity of thought and quite possibly the foremost authority on pragmatism among students of religion, his scholarship has forcefully specified what naturalistic inquiry in the study of religion requires. Despite its title, the book for which he is best known, *Religious Experience* (1985), is most perceptively and profitably understood as an argument for naturalistic explanation (of the historical and social variety) in the study of religion.[6] His insistence on naturalism has only become more explicit in ensuing publications. I am tempted to call him the pragmatist conscience of the study of religion, but that might suggest that he is something of a scold or that pragmatism has been his only interest and inspiration, neither of which is true. Wayne is a wonderfully generous and tolerant teacher, colleague, and interlocutor, and he has a wealth of interests and expertise besides pragmatism. He has, however, written incisively on the pragmatist tradition and has been uncompromising in his calls for genuine, nonscientistic, naturalistic inquiry in the study of religion. We intend the present volume to represent but a small measure of our esteem, affection, and gratitude.

## NOTES

1. Nancy Frankenberry, Jodie Graham, Alissa Macmillan, Jeffrey Stout, and Michael Watkins all commented substantively on a draft of this introduction.
2. See Macarthur and Price (2007), Price (2003, 2004), Rorty (2002), Brandom (1994), and Stout (2007).
3. The term *naturalism* has a long prior history, in which it was used to name an object of criticism. Kant, for instance, uses it this way in *Die Religion innerhalb der Grenzen der bloßen Vernunft*. Pope Leo XIII provides a more colorful example. The purported moral, social, political, as well as religious, dangers of "naturalism" feature prominently in Leo's encyclicals. I suspect that the outré contexts in which Leo lambastes naturalism—his reactionary jeremiad against political liberalism in *Libertas Praestantissimum* and his ludicrous denunciations of freemasonry (of all things) in *Humanum Genus* and *Custodi di Quella Fede*—virtually assured that the term would ultimately be used approvingly and self-ascriptively.
4. Jeff Stout urged me to include this point.
5. Frankenberry discusses Plantinga's argument more fully in her contribution to the present volume.
6. See Bagger (2017).

## WORKS CITED

Bagger, Matthew C. 2017. "Wayne Proudfoot's *Religious Experience*, Pragmatism, and the Study of Religion." *American Journal of Theology and Philosophy* 38:3–9.
Blackburn, Simon. 2005. *Truth: A Guide*. New York: Oxford University Press.
Brandom, Robert. 1994. *Making it Explicit: Reasoning, Representing, and Discursive Commitment*. Cambridge, MA: Harvard University Press.
Brandom, Robert. 1999. "Interview with Robert Brandom." *Epistemologia* 22:143–50.

Brandom, Robert. 2011. *Perspectives on Pragmatism*. Cambridge, MA: Harvard University Press.

Danto, Arthur. 1967. "Naturalism." In *The Encyclopedia of Philosophy*, edited by Paul Edwards, 5:448–50. New York: Macmillan.

James, William. 1950. *The Principles of Psychology*. 2 vols. New York: Dover.

James, William. 1975. *Pragmatism* and *The Meaning of Truth*. Cambridge, MA: Harvard University Press.

Macarthur, David, and Huw Price. 2007. "Pragmatism, Quasi-realism, and the Global Challenge." In *New Pragmatists*, edited by Cheryl Misak, 91–121. New York: Oxford University Press.

Misak, Cheryl. 2013. *The American Pragmatists*. Oxford: Oxford University Press.

Plantinga, Alvin. 2011. *Where the Conflict Really Lies: Science, Religion, and Naturalism*. New York: Oxford University Press.

Price, Huw. 2003. "Truth as Convenient Friction." *Journal of Philosophy* 100:167–90.

Price, Huw. 2004. "Naturalism Without Representationalism." In *Naturalism in Question*, edited by Mario De Caro and David Macarthur, 71–88. Cambridge, MA: Harvard University Press.

Rorty, Richard. 2002. "Cultural Politics and the Question of the Existence of God." In *Radical Interpretation in Religion*, edited by Nancy K. Frankenberry, 53–77. Cambridge: Cambridge University Press.

Stout, Jeffrey. 2007. "On Our Interest in Getting Things Right: Pragmatism Without Narcissism." In *New Pragmatists*, edited by Cheryl Misak, 7–31. New York: Oxford University Press.

Wallace, William A. 1968. Review of *The Encyclopedia of Philosophy*, edited by Paul Edwards. *Thomist: A Speculative Quarterly Review* 32:443–45.

# PART I

## The Classical Pragmatists and Naturalism

By the middle of the twentieth century, branding pragmatism as *the* American philosophy had become routine. Friend and foe alike conceived pragmatism as uniquely expressive of the American national character. Admirers argued that pragmatism bespeaks the optimism, openness, self-possession, and practical orientation of a young nation chafing at inherited forms and putting the ideals of democratic community to the test. To Henry Steele Commager (1950, 97), for instance, "pragmatism's willingness to break with the past, reject traditional habits, try new methods, put beliefs to a vote, [and] make a future to order" resulted in its becoming "almost the official philosophy of America."[1] Detractors, by contrast, feared that pragmatism's emphasis on practical results expresses the crass commercialism of a parvenu among the nations. They complained, furthermore, that pragmatism displays the overweening expectations and naïveté of a people as yet unbowed by the weight of history and the confounding complexities of human nature. During the First World War, Randolph Bourne, a student and follower of John Dewey, repudiated pragmatism, which Bourne (1917, 697) describes as "almost our American religion," because he came to believe it exacerbates America's penchant for shallow idealism and thoughtless busyness, the sources of American imperialism and bellicosity. After the war, Lewis Mumford (1926, 261) cited Bourne's critique and charges that pragmatism's deficiencies "are the deficiencies of the American scene itself." It reflects, he argues, America's overriding passion for utility and technological innovation, a passion that levels higher values and justifies Babbittry.

Dewey himself, as earnestly as anyone, identified pragmatism with the spirit of America. Responding to the critics, he dismisses "the suggestion that pragmatism is the intellectual equivalent of [American] commercialism," and, in a rare display of wit, quips that such a suggestion "is of the order of interpretation which would say that . . . the tendency of French thought to dualism [is] an expression of an alleged Gallic disposition to keep a mistress in addition to a wife." He argues, in fact, that America's commercialism "diverts" and "perverts" the quintessentially American "faith in the future, in experiment directed by intelligence, in the communication of knowledge, in the rights of the common man to a common share in the fruits of the spirit." He contends, furthermore, that America's "pragmatic faith walks in chains" forged from European links. America's heritage includes both feudal social forms and a liberal tradition that embraces "a creed as absolute, as final, as eternal as that wielded by [its] opponents." Perpetuating the feudal institutionalization of private interest and "the dogma of natural rights of the individual," Americans "tied [themselves] down to political and legal practices radically hostile to [their] native disposition and endeavor." Having hobbled their faith in experimentation, they canalize its energies into the furrows of commercialism. Dewey acknowledges, moreover, the "noisy and nauseating 'idealism,'" about which the critics complain, but explains it as Americans' reaction to their pragmatic faith's "corruption" and "paralysis." The proper action of their quiet faith impeded, Americans compensate with the "sloppy idealism of popular emotion" (Dewey 1922, 185–87). Dewey locates the source of America's spiritual rot in the people's capitulation to Old World traditions and ideological absolutes. Pragmatism serves as a prophetic reminder of America's spiritual vocation.

Dewey's view of the American spirit has a distinguished heritage. In *Democracy in America*, for instance, Alexis de Toqueville (1956, 143) reports that although "Americans have no philosophical school of their own," they do share a tacit philosophical method, a distinctive set of standards for the conduct of inquiry. Derived not from books or "speculative studies," these norms (Toqueville calls them "rules") arise organically in America's democratic society. The mobility of American society and the citizens' democratic mistrust of authority lead them to discredit received opinions and to locate "the chief arbiter of their belief within, and not beyond, the limits of their [human] kind" (147). Toqueville observes, "To evade the bondage of system and habit, of family-maxims, class opinions, and in some degree, of national prejudices; to accept tradition only as a means of information, and existing facts only as a lesson to be used in doing otherwise and doing better ... such are the principle characteristics of what I shall call the philosophical method of the Americans" (143). The success with which Americans resolve the practical problems they face, moreover, leads them, he argues, to "conclude ... that nothing in [the world] transcends the limits of the understanding." They exhibit, therefore, "an almost insurmountable distaste" for supernatural explanations of particular objects or circumstances (144). Like Dewey, Toqueville insists that the American character suffers tradition and ideology as bondage. In the 1830s, Toqueville found that "Americans have no philosophical school of their own." By the twentieth century, pragmatism supplied the lack, and Dewey saw it as explicitly expressing what both he and Toqueville describe as America's intrinsic antiauthoritarian, anti-ideological, democratic spirit.

Dewey's critics condemned pragmatism on the grounds that its very disregard for the hard-won wisdom of tradition and for the absolutes it dismisses as ideology eliminates any authoritative vantage from which to diagnose and resist the callowness, crudity, and cruelties of modern life. Without such a vantage, pragmatism can only be complicit with (or complacent before) the social, political, and economic forces imperiling human dignity and freedom, Dewey's bold talk of intelligence, discriminating social criticism, and socially useful cooperative activity notwithstanding. Intellectuals as different from one another as Bertrand Russell, Reinhold Niebuhr, Walter Lippmann, Lewis Mumford, and Waldo Frank all faulted pragmatism as insufficiently realistic. In their different ways, they insisted that pragmatism does not adequately heed the realities—whether theological, metaphysical, physical, psychological, sociological, or historical—constraining human possibilities. This heedlessness—the pragmatists' blithe lack of deference to what their opponents consider unalterably authoritative—explains why criticism of pragmatism tends to describe it as childish, irresponsible, or unhinged.[2]

Although all three of these idioms appear in Russell's evaluations of pragmatism, his most notorious critique particularly exploits the last. In his *History of Western Philosophy*, Russell (2008, 818, 828) describes pragmatism as "a form of ... subjectivistic madness" because it does not exhibit "humility" before nature's "stubborn facts." This "cosmic impiety," he cautions, increases the "danger of vast social disorder." By disdaining the "stubborn facts" that limit human ascendency, pragmatism defies the universe's authority over the human imagination, destroys the necessary basis for the very concept of "truth," fails to "check" human pride, encourages "the intoxication of power," and portends "anarchy." Russell's rhetoric in this passage depicts pragmatism as a deranged and dangerous disrespect for nonhuman authority. His comically tetragrammatonic warning about the woeful wages of "cosmic impiety" illustrates how radical and audacious pragmatism's antiauthoritarianism can seem, even to those who fashion themselves radical and audacious. For all of Russell's vaunted (and flaunted) iconoclasm, he nevertheless recoils from the thoroughgoing antiauthoritarianism he perceives at the heart of pragmatism.

Charles Peirce made this antiauthoritarian purport evident from the outset. In his canonical *Popular Science Monthly* essays on "the logic of science" (1877–1878), he prefaces his analysis of scientific method with epistemological and ontological arguments that position science as the alternative to authoritarianism. The first essay in the series of six, "The Fixation of Belief," introduces the "method of science" by contrasting it with three unsatisfactory methods of settling opinion. Of the three, only two, the "method of authority" and the "a priori method," take into account the irrepressible human social impulse, "so that the problem becomes how to fix belief, not in the individual merely, but in the community" (Peirce 1958a, 103). After initially examining them separately, Peirce ultimately concludes that the "a priori method" of believing what seems "agreeable to reason" does not differ essentially from the "method of authority," in which the powerful enforce dogma either by the threat of physical punishment or by the more subtle "moral terrorism" of social pressure. In both methods, the interests of the socially dominant and the status quo produce the prevailing standards of reasonableness. Whereas these alternatives to science suit "intellectual slaves," the scientific method emancipates the human community from the tyranny of tradition and ideological absolutes (105). Peirce presents the scientific method as the subversion of authoritarianism. Science, he argues, can authorize opinion without authoritarianism.

Peirce's much-derided, quasi-idealistic definition of "reality" in the second essay, "How to Make Our Ideas Clear," seems less perverse when viewed as his attempt to formulate science's antiauthoritarian authority. The authority (and the point) of science rests on the "fundamental hypothesis" that "there are real things" about which empirical investigation can disclose the truth (Peirce 1958a, 107). Wary of authoritarian abuse of absolutes, however, Peirce construes reality in a way that prevents it from serving authoritarianism. He defines "reality" as the object of the opinion "which is fated to be ultimately agreed to by all who investigate" using the scientific method (Peirce 1958b, 133). The real depends, he explains, on the opinions universally endorsed at the ideal end of inquiry. With this definition, Peirce deprives reality of nonhuman authority. He grounds authority in the ongoing practice of the human community as it empirically investigates the real. Because the community reaches agreement by each member employing the scientific method, egalitarianism and cooperation supplant authoritarianism in principle, until at the ideal end of inquiry they preclude authoritarianism altogether. By indefinitely postponing the end of inquiry, Peirce ensures the open-endedness of the community. No given or particular community of inquirers has absolute authority. However objectionable in other respects, Peirce's definition of "reality" preserves the authority (and point) of inquiry, while offering no foothold to authoritarianism.

Mostly for reasons pertaining to ontology, Peirce objected (petulantly, at times) to William James's version of pragmatism. He did not fail to notice that James had no use for his so-called Scotistic realism or his fundamental categories. Peirce's anti-authoritarianism, however, found in James a congenial host. James (1975, 62) emphasizes the "humanism" of pragmatism and describes pragmatism as "philosophic Protestantism" because it effects an anti-ideological, democratic "alteration in the 'seat of intellectual authority.'" Despite intramural differences among the pragmatists, the antiauthoritarian impulse persists through Dewey's era to the present. Antiauthoritarian in the sense that it accords no belief, principle, or faculty (including sense perception) final, fixed, absolute, or eternal authority, pragmatism even regards the empirical method of science as itself probationary. Eschewing metaphysical or theological touchstones, pragmatic naturalism consists in the denial of any sources of authority transcending the practices by which humans collectively, cooperatively, and fallibly authorize their beliefs and behavior.

Pragmatism's antiauthoritarianism distinguishes it from other varieties of naturalism. Most naturalisms reflect a distinctly antitheological legacy. Whether advancing substantive ontological claims or proposing methodological principles (or both), their polemical significance (at least when viewed in historical perspective) derives from the fact that they banish *Geist*. Some naturalisms set themselves in opposition to a robustly theological notion of *Geist*, others to an attenuated idealistic one. The more reductive varieties of naturalism root out the vestiges of the soul and repudiate *Geist* even in the form of individual consciousness or agency. All these naturalisms stem from eighteenth- and nineteenth-century efforts to corral (if not discredit) theology by allowing the natural sciences to survey the contours and audit the contents of the universe. Although the pragmatists likewise champion science (and do not flinch when it discredits accepted religious beliefs), their naturalism does not share this antitheological heritage. Pragmatism, rather, makes explicit a democratic, antiauthoritarian American "faith in the future." It gives expression to a practical attitude that regards tradition and ideology as nothing more than "means of information . . . and . . . lesson[s] to be used in doing otherwise and doing better." On the whole, pragmatists have not objected to God-talk. For the pragmatists, science unseats theological tradition and ideology as final "arbiter of . . . belief" (and behavior), but it does not necessarily repudiate theology altogether. Consistent with their antiauthoritarianism, the pragmatists approached religion, perhaps the most potent source of ideology, nonideologically. Their investigations of religion produced both methodological insights for the study of religion and provocative reflections about the meaning and role of religion for the individual and for society. The three essays in part 1 examine afresh the thought of Peirce, James, and Dewey, respectively, to illuminate the contributions of pragmatism's founders to its distinctive naturalistic perspective on religion.

NOTES

1. Despite his evident enthusiasm for pragmatism, Henry Steele Commager mischaracterizes it and offers a hostage to its enemies when he says that it puts beliefs to a vote. He correctly detects a democratic tendency in pragmatism (see part 3 of the present volume), but this regrettable description bolsters the notion that pragmatism does not provide an adequate account of objectivity. Bertrand Russell (1966, 106) first introduced the canard about voting in 1909: "The influence of democracy in promoting pragmatism is visible in almost every page of William James's writing. There is an impatience of authority . . . a tendency to decide philosophical questions by putting them to a vote." Commager lauds pragmatism in precisely the (inaccurate) terms that Russell had intended as sad commentary on James's supposed inability to abide hard, unyielding facts.
2. This paragraph and the next reflect the influence of Rorty (1991).

WORKS CITED

Bourne, Randolph. 1917. "Twilight of Idols." *The Seven Arts* 11: 688–702.
Commager, Henry Steele. 1950. *The American Mind: An Interpretation of American Thought and Character Since the 1880's.* New Haven, CT: Yale University Press.
Dewey, John. 1922. "Pragmatic America." *New Republic* 30 (April 12): 185–87.
James, William. 1975. *Pragmatism* and *The Meaning of Truth.* Cambridge, MA: Harvard University Press.
Mumford, Lewis. 1926. *The Golden Day: A Study in American Experience and Culture.* New York: Boni and Liveright.
Peirce, Charles S. 1958a. "The Fixation of Belief." In *Charles S. Peirce: Selected Writings,* edited by Philip Wiener, 91–112. New York: Dover.
Peirce, Charles S. 1958b. "How to Make Our Ideas Clear." In *Charles S. Peirce: Selected Writings,* edited by Philip Wiener, 113–36. New York: Dover.

Rorty, Richard. 1991. "Just One More Species Doing Its Best." *London Review of Books* 13 (July 25): 3–7.

Russell, Bertrand. (1945) 2008. *History of Western Philosophy*. New York: Simon and Schuster.

Russell, Bertrand. 1966. "Pragmatism." In *Philosophical Essays*, 79–111. New York: Simon and Schuster.

Tocqueville, Alexis de. 1956. *Democracy in America*, edited by Richard D. Heffner. New York: Mentor.

# I

# Instinct and Inquiry

*A Reconsideration of Peirce's Mature
Religious Naturalism*

MICHAEL L. RAPOSA

I

Charles Peirce's mature religious naturalism was organized around his conviction that a vague belief in God is instinctive for human beings. The development, late in his philosophical career, of an "argument for the reality of God" is more properly conceived as supplying the rubrics of a pragmatic test for the presence of such an instinct. At the same time, this argument is a specialized version of Peirce's general account of the role that instinct plays in human reasoning—more precisely, its gentle influence on the process of hypothesis selection. This chapter briefly explores that account, but its goal is ultimately prospective rather than narrowly exegetical. I contend that Peirce's understanding of the relevance of instinct for inquiry can supply the naturalist core of a pragmatic perspective that is also informed by attentiveness to the historical, political, and sociocultural factors that shape religious thought and practice. That perspective is articulated here in conversation with Peirce's classical pragmatism, toward the end of supplying resources potentially useful for the purposes of contemporary religious naturalists.

II

The word *naturalism* is a fuzzy label for a broad variety of philosophical stances, some metaphysical and others more strictly methodological, but each of them uncomfortable with any sort of talk about the "supernatural," and many of them also opposed to any sharp contrast between nature and culture. Metaphysical naturalists are committed to the view that nature is all that there is, although their understanding of what "nature" encompasses can be more or less capacious in any given case. In its more austere forms, naturalism reduces to some form of materialism or physicalism, with no aspect of nature, at least in principle, being inaccessible to the probing investigations of natural scientists.[1] In its methodological versions, naturalism embodies the claim that scientific knowing is the only way of knowing possible and that the general method of inquiry employed by scientists has universal application. But here, too, there are a variety of species under the genus, as opinions vary about exactly how the "scientific method" is to be conceived.[2]

John Dewey is most typically classified as a "naturalist," William James sometimes so, while Charles Peirce is almost always left out of the conversation about the relationship between golden age pragmatism and philosophical naturalism. In fact, Peirce has often been labeled as an "objective idealist," much like Josiah Royce and some of the nineteenth-century German post-Kantians. Moreover, he was a vague sort of theist (identifying God as the *ens necessarium*), and much of his metaphysics and evolutionary cosmology leaned heavily upon the operation of final causes. So at first blush it would seem odd to identify his philosophy, without serious qualification, as representing any kind of naturalism.

On closer inspection, however, it is interesting to note that Peirce's defense of objective idealism not only included the admission that materialism cannot "be absolutely refuted" but also further concluded that the idealistic hypothesis itself "might be called materialistic" (Peirce 1935, vol. 6, paras. 274–77). Materialism, like idealism, has the advantage of simplicity over any metaphysical theory that parses reality as consisting of some combination of matter and mind. It was conceivable to Peirce that, at least in principle, some version of materialism could be subtle and sophisticated enough to account for mental phenomena. Nevertheless, at least as he understood it in its typical nineteenth-century formulations, materialism recognizes only those explanations that employ efficient causation for their purposes.[3] And this restriction—a form of reductionism that he sometimes labeled *mechanical necessitarianism*—violated Peirce's prime directive that one ought never to "block the way of inquiry" (Peirce 1935, vol. 1, para. 135). In the 1870s, Peirce famously surveyed the various methods by means of which human beings might ease the "irritation" of doubt and succeed in "fixing belief." The last of these methods was that of science, and it easily trumped all of the others in his appraisal, most especially because they all set up obstacles to inquiry, of one kind or another. Significantly, Peirce offered perhaps his clearest description of what that method entails, thirty years later, in his article "A Neglected Argument for the Reality of God."

Peirce's commitment to leaving inquiry "open," and his devotion to the scientific method as the primary means for honoring that commitment, supply an immediate link with contemporary philosophical naturalists, at least those of the methodological variety. His worry about the narrowness of materialism resonates with the concerns of "liberal naturalists" who argue for a perspective on nature that accommodates nonreductive talk about normativity, while also incorporating insights and methods developed in the human and social sciences. In these respects, such a perspective is designed to be considerably broader than the one articulated in other, more "orthodox" accounts of naturalism.[4] Importantly, Peirce regarded the limited scope of materialism as problematic for the same reason that contemporary naturalists reject the appeal to supernatural causes and explanations: both serve to undermine human inquiry.[5] Despite his concerns about a reductionist materialism. Peirce (1935, vol. 5, para. 613) proclaimed "that the universe is all of a piece, and that we are all of us natural products, naturally partaking of the characteristics that are found everywhere through nature." This certainly sounds like a claim that a naturalist would make.

At the same time, he understood science (as his father, Benjamin, did before him) as a kind of religious vocation; scientists are best equipped to grasp some fragment of the meaning of God's "great poem" (para. 119). Now this conception of science does *not* seem to represent so happy a fit with the perspectives of contemporary philosophical naturalists, even those of a liberal sort. Of course, to determine a priori that all God-talk is meaningless would also be unscientific, in Peirce's view. Moreover, when and if it occurs, any such talk must be designated as clearly and emphatically *hypothetical*. Finally, one cannot automatically assume that the theistic hypothesis, as Peirce himself formulated it, ought to be regarded as representing some kind of supernaturalism. (It should at least be an open question whether some type of naturalism might possibly be considered religious, and if so, whether it can also be, in the vague sense that Peirce intended, theistic.)

Peirce's pragmatic philosophy underscores the ubiquity of inference in human experience;[6] even our most straightforward sense perceptions, in his view, take the form of abductive inferences or hypothetical judgments, albeit often unconscious ones and so indubitable as they occur. Peirce was an "inferentialist" of sorts, then, long before Robert Brandom made such a philosophical position popular.[7] This is not an altogether surprising fact, given both the importance of Wilfrid Sellars's ideas for the development of Brandom's thought and the clear resonance between Peirce's early attack on Cartesianism and Sellars's critique of the "Myth of the Given." (That resonance has been described with admirable clarity and detail by Richard Bernstein in a discussion to which I will gesture here with gratitude but not pause to summarize.)[8] In Peirce's account, however, there is an important role for *experience* to play in human reasoning, in contrast to Brandom's claim that there is no need or room for such a concept in his philosophy.[9] Moreover, Peirce was disinclined to reduce semiosis to its manifestation as *language*, our meaningful discursive practices extending, for him, far beyond the game of giving and asking for reasons. I suspect that even Ludwig Wittgenstein understood how language games involve much more than just the words and grammar that we use to play them. And Peirce's semiotic theory, there can be no doubt, presupposes a generously expanded sense of what it means "to give an interpretation," for creatures living in "a world perfused with signs" (Peirce 1935, vol. 5, para. 448, note 1), a widened account of where and how semiosis can occur.

These observations about language and experience are connected. In Peirce's view, experience is always already interpreted experience, always semiosis. Such experience is also ongoing, taking the form of a "dialogue" (albeit not one conducted exclusively in language) between one's present and future self, as one thought-sign follows another in time. The relation between signs is essentially inferential; Peirce regarded illation as the primary semiotic relation (vol. 2, para. 444, note 1).[10] Moreover, as already indicated, he had a broad and nuanced account of what it means to make an inference or to give an interpretation. A soldier can interpret a command or a dancer can interpret music with physical gestures and movements, for example, and artists make inferences using colors and shapes. Peirce's theory of experience-as-semiosis is organized around this basic observation concerning the ubiquity of inference (i.e., all perception and all thinking is a continuous process of sign interpretation). When he argued that every logical concept, in order to be meaningful, must enter through the gate of perception and exit through the gate of purposive action (vol. 5, para. 212), Peirce intended not only to circumscribe or indicate the "constraints" on our discursive practices but also, more generally, to situate them, to locate the roots of semiosis in sense experience and its fruits in deliberate behavior.[11]

The priority of semiosis in Peirce's view is to be carefully distinguished, however, from certain arguments for the "ontological priority of the social" that some neopragmatists have recently articulated.[12] Signs can have real (Peirce called them "dynamic") objects that exist independently of their being signified; these objects "determine" their signs in a manner that Peirce sometimes struggled to clarify but always carefully insisted upon. While objects do not "cause" their signs, they do place external constraints on the range of possible meanings that these signs can have. The encounter with such objects in experience has a brute, primordial quality for Peirce, what he called "secondness" and characterized, at least in some instances, as producing a feeling of "shock" or "surprise." This element of second-ness functions more as an "editor" than as the author of meaning, flagging *this* as a mistake, reinforcing *that* as sound judgment, and sometimes gently but often forcibly directing attention *here* or *there*. In this view, reports of or appeals made to experience, while always inevitably shaped by some community's norms and expectations, cannot be reduced to a function of "cultural politics," that is, simply to being a "matter of what a community will let you get away with" (Rorty 2002, 61).[13] Even if what we come to know is best understood as always being a product of some interpretation and not simply "given" in experience, nevertheless, "all that we can anyway know relates to experience" (Peirce 1935, vol. 6, para. 492).[14] Peirce navigated a middle path in his philosophy between the Myth of the Given at one extreme and strong versions of social constructivism or inferential-ism at the other.

My primary concern here is with the role that instinct plays in Peirce's theory of inquiry. It is insufficient to point out that Peirce regarded certain inferences as being instinctive, since the relationship between such inferences and human inquiry as a deliberate, self-controlled, communal activity still needs to be carefully explored. But first it seems necessary to argue that there is any kind of relationship at all, rather than simply a sharp contrast between them. The need to establish such a connection is a direct consequence of the canonical significance attached to Peirce's article "The Fixation of Belief," published in *Popular Science Monthly* in 1877. To observe that I thoroughly agree with my teacher, Murray Murphey, in regarding this essay as one of Peirce's weakest published performances does not belie that fact that it has been and continues to be one of his most well known and influential.[15] Moreover, in that famous account, Peirce clearly contrasted the "a priori method" with the method of science, the former being identified as problematic precisely because it appeals to human instinct as a way of fixing belief. Using this method, beliefs will be adopted principally because they are "agreeable to reason" so that "we find ourselves inclined" to embrace them. Peirce read much of the history of Western metaphysics as riding on the back of such a method. Philosophy conducted in this way, no matter how impressive it might be in certain respects, is confined to "the development of taste" and finally reduces to being nothing more than a "matter of fashion" (Peirce 1935, vol. 5, paras. 382–83).

Given the manner in which Peirce employed specific terms in "Fixation of Belief," it is important to note that the a priori method, no less than science, still qualifies as a method of *inquiry*, that is to say, as a strategy for easing the irritation of doubt and attaining belief. At the same time, Peirce admitted that "this is sometimes not a very apt designation," hardly felicitous as a label for the a priori method, even less so in the cases where it is applied to the methods of "tenacity" and "authority" (para. 374). It is just this contrast with the high level of precision that Peirce typically achieved in other writings, this "inapt" use of terms, a tendency almost to caricature, that informed Murphey's (and my own) negative judgment of the article.

Even Peirce himself seems to have been a bit self-critical (or, at the very least, nervous) in this regard. In an article published in the same series the following year, Peirce admitted that he had used words that were "too strong" for his purpose, almost as if he "had described the phenomena as they appear under a mental microscope" (para. 394). And more than thirty years later, two years after the publication of "A Neglected Argument for the Reality of God," Peirce inserted a sentence into his discussion of the a priori method, hedging his confession of its "failure" with the observation that "as long as no better method can be applied, it ought to be followed, since it is then the expression of instinct which must be the ultimate cause of belief in all cases" (para. 383). What, exactly, was he trying to say here?

The clue to an answer is embedded in the text of the "Neglected Argument." There, the discussion of instinct recurs, but this time not in order to expose it as the shaky foundation of an unscientific metaphysics but rather to explain the necessary role that it plays in all scientific reasoning. Peirce wrote, in that 1908 article, about the "proper function" of different animals, in each instance consisting of the sort of thing that it would be regarded as natural or instinctive for them to do. For "ordinary birds," Peirce explained, "flying and nest-building" constitute their proper function. But, for humans, what else can this proper function be "if it be not to embody general ideas in art-creations, in utilities, and above all in theoretical cognition?" The ultimate source of these ideas, the origin of an inclination to embrace one idea among many alternatives, is to be located in "the spontaneous conjectures of instinctive reason." Peirce proposed that "*if we knew* that the impulse to prefer one hypothesis over another really were analogous to the instincts of birds and wasps, it would be foolish not to give it play, within the bounds of reason" (vol. 6, paras. 475–76, emphasis in original).

This is the core idea underlying Peirce's "critical common-sensism," his mature philosophy of science: scientific inquiry is a process of giving certain vague but powerful human instincts "play," yet always as a prelude to critical reasoning and with the full recognition that such instinct is highly fallible. The tendency to guess wrong more often than right accounts for a significant number of mistaken inferences. Nevertheless, such guesses are correct far more often than any statistical analysis would suggest that one ought to expect them to be if they were purely random conjectures (see vol. 5, para. 173). The appeal to instinct will eventually lead the inquirer, then, not disastrously far astray but gradually closer to the truth.

And so Peirce concluded that "man's mind must have been attuned to the truth of things in order to discover what he has discovered" (vol. 6, para. 476). Humans are adapted for the purpose of effective reasoning, so that it is as "natural" for them as flying is for birds or making honey is for bees.

It is not always clear precisely what status this claim about the attunement of the human mind to nature has in Peirce's philosophy. Sometimes it seems to be an assumption, acting as a regulative principle of logic, one that must be embraced in order for there to be any real hope that human inquiry can succeed.[16] At the same time, it ought to be regarded as a hypothetical claim, not a principle asserted a priori, but one upon which a significant body of empirical evidence can be brought to bear. In this instance, as Peirce saw it, the relevant evidence is supplied by the historical and ongoing success of scientific inquiry in ascertaining the truth about nature, at a level that would be implausible without the assumption that humans are adapted to the task, so that for them it has become instinctive. This success is less apparent the more theoretically advanced science becomes. It is most pronounced at a very basic and general level of inquiry, since Peirce's hypothesis was that the instinctive guessing capacity would have evolved as a result of exigencies associated most especially with human nutritional and sexual needs. By a process of natural selection, two general areas of "common sense" would have been developed, one "founded on those instincts about physical forces that are required for the feeding impulsion and the other upon those instincts about our fellows that are required for the satisfaction of the reproductive impulse." Rooted thus in common sense, "all science is nothing but an outgrowth of these two instincts" (Peirce 1935, vol. 6, para. 500).

There are compelling historical arguments demonstrating how evolutionary theory was as important to the origins of classical pragmatism in the nineteenth century as it has been for the development of philosophical naturalism in the twentieth and twenty-first.[17] Yet one can surely be a naturalist without embracing pragmatism. It is not immediately obvious whether the reverse is true. Peirce's mature pragmaticism represents a rather interesting test case.[18] Any tentative proposal that I might make about this case is not intended, however, to supply a global answer to the question about pragmatism's naturalist presuppositions.

III

I suggest that the best way to understand Peirce's religious naturalism is to shift attention away from concerns about supernaturalism and to focus instead on Peirce's rejection of any sharp distinction or contrast between nature and culture.[19] Creating and sustaining a culture—that is to say, speaking a language, developing various social and political arrangements, creating artworks or engaging in scientific inquiry—is precisely the sort of thing that it is natural for human beings to do. Peirce's numerous discussions of a "guessing instinct" underscore the importance of instinct for inquiry. But given the ubiquity of inference in Peirce's philosophy, there is an important sense in which all of these cultural practices might be regarded as forms of inquiry (and thus somehow rooted in instinct). The embodiment of ideas in artworks or in rituals of various kinds is different from but nevertheless analogous to their embodiment in scientific reasoning.[20]

Another way to make this point is to portray the human species as *Homo symbolicus*. Without strictly limiting semiosis to the realm of human experience and activity, Peirce clearly judged humans as unique among animals in terms of the nature and extent of their semiotic capacities. Moreover, to focus attention directly on human semiosis is already to blur the line between nature and culture. Since even the most straightforward, seemingly immediate sense perception must involve a perceptual *judgment*, in Peirce's view, meaningful human experience is always to be regarded as matter of interpretation. A walk in the woods, for example, featuring a lively flood of sense perceptions, is different from but still continuous with the rigorous scientific investigation of various flora and fauna that might be discovered in such an ecosystem. To perceive any X as Y, even in cases where one is incorrect or where the label applied to X is quite vague and uninformative ("tall green tree," for example, in contrast to the specificity of recognizing something as *Araucaria columnaris*), is already to make an abductive inference. This is not yet scientific inquiry in the full-blooded sense, but it is the only possible starting point for any such investigation.

Once again, this is a bit different from saying that human experience is language all the way down, so that no experience is to be regarded as meaningful unless some linguistic community has given it license. I sometimes suspect that certain neo-pragmatist arguments, whether by design or not, have the actual effect of reinforcing a sharp nature/culture distinction while also establishing the hegemony of the latter over the former. But a Peircean pragmatic naturalist would want to say that our experiences are shaped *not only* by our membership in a particular community and our facility with its language and practices *but also* by our inclusion in a certain species, with its distinctive natural capacities, a species comprising bipeds who walk upright, with brains like ours, sexual organs like ours, hands with opposable thumbs, eyes in the front rather than on the sides of our head . . . and perhaps with behavior shaped by certain vague instincts. (Such a pragmatist would also want to insist that our experiences are to some extent "determined" or constrained by their objects.)

It becomes a crucial matter, then, to explore the relationship between "instinct" and "habit" in Peirce's account. The concept of instinct was clearly of central importance in Peirce's pragmatism, as it was in Dewey's.[21] It might seem reasonable to suggest that, while both concepts refer to some innate tendency, inclination, or disposition to behave in a certain way under certain specifiable conditions, instinct is a fully "natural" tendency, to be distinguished from habit as something acquired. Yet it would be important in making such a suggestion to recognize that, although he was clearly influenced by Charles Darwin, Peirce was also something of a Lamarckian who believed in the inheritability of acquired characteristics.[22] The plot thickens. Any rigid nature/culture contrast organized around the distinction between natural instincts and acquired habits is just not going to fit neatly within Peirce's perspective.

This is not to contend that Peirce rejected any notion of instinct as a biologically inherited tendency, ingrained in the individual as a member of the species. The "guessing instinct" is just one of this sort. Nor is it to conclude that he found no role for natural selection to play in determining which instincts would be transmitted and thus preserved (although he was certainly eager to delimit its explanatory significance). In fact, Peirce stipulated that if a habit is "some general principle working in a man's nature to determine how he will act, then an instinct, in the proper sense of the word, is an inherited habit" (Peirce 1935, vol. 2, para. 170). But he immediately proceeded to observe that "it is difficult to make sure whether a habit is inherited or is due to infantile training and tradition," so that it seemed to him permissible "to employ the word 'instinct' to cover both cases." All that I have been trying to propose *here* is that, from the point of view supplied by Peirce's pragmatic naturalism, the distinction between such cases, even when it can be ascertained, ought not to be sharply drawn.

This proposal does involve a claim about the extent to which natural instincts can be *developed*. Moreover, Peirce would allow that what has been developed in humans can be passed on to future generations, so that from his Lamarckian, admittedly idealistic perspective, the line between biological and superorganic evolution is effectively blurred. (Of course, more than a hundred years ago, Peirce could not have known what molecular biologists have since learned about genetic predispositions and the mechanisms for their transmission across generations.) That "instinct is capable of development and growth" is something that Peirce explicitly asserted, just as he concluded that "this development takes place upon lines that are altogether parallel to those of reasoning"; in fact, "it chiefly takes place through the instrumentality of cognition" (vol. 1, para. 648).

It is somewhat ironic that this discussion of instinct's development through reasoning occurred in Peirce's 1898 Cambridge Conference lectures, where, in irritated response to William James's suggestion that he address "vitally important topics," Peirce had tended repeatedly to exaggerate the distinction between theory and practice, often driving a wedge between reason and instinct.[23] But it should not be a surprise to the reader of Peirce's "Neglected Argument" that he portrayed human reason as having instinctive roots. Those roots are most clearly exposed in the initial phase of scientific inquiry, when the various hypotheses that might function as explanations for some object of inquiry are first being formulated and entertained. An open attentiveness to the thing encountered, and a cultivated indifference with regard to any practical interest that might cause the inquirer to interpret it in one way rather than another, are the keys to bringing human instinct into "play." This kind of playful thinking (and feeling) is what Peirce referred to in that article as "musement."

I have long been convinced that Peirce intended musement to be a kind of experiment and that the "Neglected Argument" is better understood as making a case for the instinctiveness of certain religious ideas than as a warm and fuzzy version of the argument from design.[24] Peirce invited the reader to engage in musement under the exact conditions that he described in order to test whether such religious ideas, perhaps not immediately but eventually, would naturally tend to suggest themselves. With regard to Peirce's (1935, vol. 6, para. 465) prediction that "sooner or later" this will in fact occur, the "later" perhaps ought to be emphasized over the "sooner." My reason for saying this is that, like all good experiments, Peirce intended musement also to be a type of practice. One is advised to engage in musement not once, twice, or occasionally but, rather, regularly and repeatedly. Such repetition is important for a number of reasons, but here I want to focus on the role that it plays in helping to hone the skills that may be crucial for the success of the experiment itself. That is to say, it may take some practice to be able mindfully to discern those habits or instincts that are gently shaping a certain thought process. And it is also through practice that "instinct is capable of development and growth."

I could perhaps invest more energy here convincing my own readers that Peirce's essay should not be regarded as a precursor of contemporary intelligent design proposals, that his "hypothetical God" was never intended as a supernaturalist alternative to some purely scientific, naturalist account of how this or that phenomenon might best be explained. In fact, he accepted David Hume's classical critique of the argument from design as compelling, and he evaluated his own hypothetical idea of God as being too vague to yield predictions that could then be put to some empirical test (Peirce 1935, vol. 6, para. 489). Providing a religious explanation for the order of nature is not the sort of project that Peirce was undertaking in the "Neglected Argument," and it is certainly not the lesson that his argument has to teach contemporary religious naturalists.

What we do learn from Peirce's pragmaticism is that human thinking, the deliberate and continuous production of thought-signs, is always partially shaped by habitual tendencies, many of which are the product of our becoming embedded in specific cultures and communities, some of which may be instinctive. It is important, to the greatest extent possible, to make such habits explicit (as Brandom has argued so forcefully, but also more narrowly than I intend to suggest here), to attempt to formulate as rules the leading tendencies that shape our inferences and guide our behavior. This suggests that a sincerely pragmatic, naturalist philosopher of religion would want to be open to and familiar with the intellectual labors of others devoted to such disciplines as anthropology, history, neuroscience, and evolutionary psychology. If my interpretation of Peirce's "Neglected Argument" is correct, it was designed to show that belief in God is "natural." This hardly warrants the conclusion that "God exists." To posit that there is a divine ideality manifested in nature (which both Charles and his father, Benjamin, believed) and that the human mind has gradually become adapted or attuned to it would indeed explain the naturalness of belief in God. But cultural anthropologists and psychologists have produced alternative explanations for such religious ideas. To rule out any of these accounts before exploring their plausibility and persuasiveness would surely be to roadblock inquiry.

If such exploration is to be considered a central task for the philosophy of religion, inquiry must be focused directly on the nature and the functioning of our human semiotic capacities. The project of evaluating religious truth claims will be logically parasitic on the more fundamental project linked to questions about what makes human beings tend to produce religious interpretations of experience, what it is in our historical and biological legacies that might explain such a tendency, how pervasive such a tendency actually is, and how we might account for its absence in certain cases. Because *both* our histories and our biology could be relevant to explaining our deepest human inclinations, there is no need to set a nuanced, liberal naturalism at odds with an historicist account.[25]

The scientific method is not something that Peirce, or any of the other classical American pragmatists, thought should be limited in its application to the natural sciences. The formulation and selection of hypotheses, the deductive explication of entailments or expectations following upon the proposal that any specific hypothesis is true, and the ongoing inductive testing of such expectations, blended all together, constitutes the only reliable method of fixing beliefs in the long run. No solitary individual can fully enact this method; rather, it must be undertaken by a community of inquiry cooperating for extended periods of time.

While the God hypothesis, at least as it arises in musement, is too vague to predict the specific design features of any world that such a deity could be expected to create, religious ideas will nevertheless exert a "commanding influence over the whole conduct of life" of those who embrace them (Peirce 1935, vol. 6, para. 490). A life lived in conformity to those ideas is the laboratory in which their meaning is gradually revealed.[26] This is something about which all pragmatists can agree. "By their fruits you will know them" (Matthew 7:16).[27]

A focused attentiveness on human sign making and interpretation should not be so narrow as to ignore either the dynamic *object* of any given sign or the deliberate, patterned behavior that constitutes its *meaning*. In trying to make sense out of our semiotic practices, Peirce realized that it was also crucial to direct attention to the flow of semiosis moving through the two "gates" of perception and purposive action. Dispositional tendencies are formed in response to what we perceive to be the case, either suddenly or gradually, as we interact with various figures, forces, and factors in the environment. Our perceptual judgments can be mistaken on any given occasion, yet the repeated encounter with any given object of experience, combined with regular communication among individuals encountering the same object, serve as correctives for such false interpretations. Once again, interpretation and inquiry were essentially communal activities, from Peirce's point of view, and their success was never to be regarded as an isolated, episodic achievement but always as something eventuating over time, "in the long run."

Our natural appetites, instincts, drives, and tendencies are then subtly transformed by what we pragmatically *do* with them, how we develop them through a self-controlled process of interpretation, embody them in artworks, rituals, and theories, temper them with critique, and balance them with other forces and factors in the building of communities. The same is true—but even more dramatically so—of those very basic habits of thought, feeling, and conduct that may prove to be the product of "infantile training and tradition." In either case, they partially determine how we perceive things and so can also greatly affect how we do things.

Here the line between nature and second nature can easily be blurred. But this blurring is hardly an obscuring if *by nature* we are best understood as semiotic creatures capable of remaking and reinterpreting ourselves through a continuous process of habit formation. Rendering our natural tendencies explicit through some practice like musement, giving them "play," while also proceeding to evaluate them with all of the resources that the natural and human sciences can bring to bear and measuring their capacity fruitfully to shape our social and moral practices—this is the best strategy for honoring Peirce's pragmatic legacy. While we might be wise to treat with some suspicion the inclination to feel, think, or do what comes naturally, we ignore it altogether at our peril. The elaborate "nests" we humans build with strands of semiosis woven together in deliberate, complex arrangements may show no obvious trace of an instinctive origin. Yet any inquiry concerning why we build them and how we propose most effectively to live in them cannot ignore the possibility of instinct having played a role in their creation and design. Such an inquiry will thus also involve very basic questions about what it means to be human, to live in a world that we can see only with human eyes, and so one "perfused" with signs and yet not composed exclusively of them.[28]

## NOTES

1.  Among contemporary religious naturalists, Robert Corrington's (2000) "ecstatic naturalism" (significantly influenced by his reading of Charles Peirce) represents a very broad view of all that "nature" might be said to include, in contrast to someone like Charley Hardwick (1996), who equates naturalism with a rigorous form of "physicalism."

2.  Opinions also vary about whether there actually is such a thing as a unified scientific method. See John Dupre (2004). But even a very sophisticated application of methodological naturalism to religious questions, like that developed by Matthew Bagger, while open to diverse forms of inquiry and not confined to employing scientific method, nevertheless rejects the appeal to entities or agencies that are not amenable to scientific investigation. See, especially, Bagger (1999).

3.  Consider Sandra Rosenthal's (1986, beginning at 114) exceptionally clear account of Peirce's thinking about this topic.

4.  Mario De Caro and David Macarthur have assembled two important volumes of essays devoted to the critique of a narrow scientific naturalism and the articulation of a more "liberal" perspective. In addition to *Naturalism in Question* (2004), see the more recent collection in *Naturalism and Normativity* (2010).

5.  A narrow, mechanical materialism infects inquiry "from below," so to speak, by rejecting out of hand any explanation of a phenomenon that does *not* involve reducing its occurrence to a causal account that originates at the level of its most basic material substrate. A supernaturalist account blocks inquiry "from above" by importing nonempirical agents and causes for the purpose of explaining human experience. Both involve the appeal to metaphysical assumptions that rule out in advance any consideration of alternative perspectives.

6.  Wayne Proudfoot (1978, 378) first used the phrase "ubiquity of inference" as an especially felicitous description of what he observed to be one of the distinguishing features of a pragmatic theory of interpretation, in his article "Interpretation, Inference, and Religion."

7.  Most notably in Robert Brandom's magnum opus, *Making it Explicit: Reasoning, Representing, and Discursive Commitment* (1994), and then more succinctly in

*Articulating Reasons: An Introduction to Inferentialism* (2000). For a comparison of Peirce and Brandom, consult Catherine Legg (2008).

8. See, especially, the prologue to *The Pragmatic Turn* (Bernstein 2010, 1–31).

9. Brandom (2011, 197) admits that he has some limited use in his philosophy for a properly rehabilitated concept of *representation* but none at all for the concept of *experience*, the latter being a word that does not even appear once in *Making It Explicit*!

10. Just as Peirce does not limit our discursive practices to linguistic ones (behavior embodying "thirdness" will be rule-governed in some sense, but it may not be possible to formulate these rules explicitly in words), "illation" for Peirce is a general sign-relation and so not necessarily linguistic (propositional) in form.

11. The constraint talk is in Brandom (1994, 330–31), appearing there as a response to the charge of linguistic idealism. Brandom's position resembles Peirce's in some important ways, yet it is interesting that Peirce talks about "gates" where Brandom talks about our discursivity being "constrained." Gates, to be sure, can and do constrain our activities, but they also can swing open. Peirce the synechist was committed to tracing the continuity of perception, thought, and action, and he did so in a manner that required semiosis to provide the thread of continuity.

12. Richard Rorty (2002) used this phrase to describe Brandom's position.

13. Despite the similarities between Peirce's pragmaticism and Brandom's neo-pragmatism, the salient differences between them might be best understood in terms of how far they were willing to follow G. W. F. Hegel's lead. For Peirce's critique of what he took to be Hegel's lack of appreciation for the irreducible importance of "secondness" in human experience, consider Peirce (1935), vol. 1, para. 368; and vol. 5, para. 91.

14. See my brief discussion in *Peirce's Philosophy of Religion* (Raposa 1989, 33).

15. In his classic study *The Development of Peirce's Philosophy*, Murphey (1961, 164) described "The Fixation of Belief," among all of Peirce's essays, as "one of the most curious and least satisfactory that Peirce ever wrote."

16. I supply a brief discussion of Peirce's treatment of certain regulative principles of reason in "Love's Purposes, Hope's Necessity, and the God of Pragmaticism" (Raposa 2002).

17. An early, classical account of this importance is to be found in Philip P. Wiener's (1949) *Evolution and the Founders of Pragmatism*.

18. It is interesting precisely because Peirce seems frequently to be an outlier in discussions of this sort concerning the classical American pragmatists. In contrast, if one's naturalism is sufficiently "liberal," there seems little reason to hesitate before classifying John Dewey as a naturalist—especially since he was perfectly blithe to classify himself that way. But if a reasonable case can be made that Peirce was also a kind of naturalist, then the connections between pragmatism and naturalism may be more subtle and numerous than previously suspected.

19. This is hardly to suggest that the question of whether Peirce was in fact a "supernaturalist" is unimportant. But that is a difficult, perhaps even an unanswerable question, given the textual evidence available, and it is not my purpose is to pursue it here. Elsewhere I have argued that Peirce was neither a straightforward supernaturalist nor a pantheist but that he is best understood as having embraced some form of

*panentheism* (Raposa 1989, 50–52). Peirce (1935, vol. 6, para. 483) waffled a bit in the Neglected Argument, affirming belief in a Creator "independent" of all three universes of experience, "or at any rate two of the three." Yet his synechistic emphasis on the continuity of all things, combined with his conviction that any God who is real must be one that humans are capable of actually perceiving, at the very least, would seem to rule out any rigid natural/supernatural contrast.

20. I have developed the case for religious ritual in "Ritual Inquiry: The Pragmatic Logic of Religious Practice" (Raposa 2004).

21. For a general assessment of the importance of the concept of instinct, see my discussion in *Peirce's Philosophy of Religion*, especially chapter 4, "Habits and Values" (Raposa 1989, 93–116). The significance of this concept for Dewey's pragmatism is most clearly illustrated in *Human Nature and Conduct* (Dewey 1983).

22. Murphey (1961), 349–50.

23. John E. Smith explains Peirce's irritation, in his analysis included in *Purpose and Thought: The Meaning of Pragmatism* (Smith 1978, 167 and accompanying note 15).

24. I proposed such an interpretation of the "Neglected Argument" in *Peirce's Philosophy of Religion* (Raposa 1989, 125–41). It is important to understand that Peirce himself distinguished between all formal philosophical arguments for the existence of God (which he classified as "argumentations") and the sort of argument that is embodied in any "process of thought reasonably tending to produce a definite belief" (Peirce 1935, vol. 6, para. 456). Musement (the "Humble Argument") is such a process, and Peirce's "Neglected Argument" explores the role that instinct plays in shaping it.

25. Wayne Proudfoot (2012) wrestles with the tension between naturalist and historicist perspectives in his brilliant article "Pragmatism and Naturalism in the Study of Religion." I see less of a tension between these two perspectives than he does, and so I am more optimistic about the significance of the natural sciences for philosophy of religion, not *apart* from the analysis of relevant historical, political, and social factors shaping human behavior but in a way that is informed by such analysis. I would affirm his conclusion that we ought to be suspicious of assumptions about the world being shaped to our interpretations "apart from what humans themselves have shaped" (199). But a healthy suspicion would not automatically lead me to conclude that the objects of the signs we produce in no manner or measure determine the nature and course of our interpretations.

26. This notion that the lives of persons living in conformity to religious beliefs and ideals might supply data that can be submitted to scientific inquiry links what I have called Peirce's "theosemiotic" with William James's attempt in *The Varieties of Religious Experience* to lay the foundation for a "science of religions." See Matthew Bagger's illuminating essay on James in the present volume. I have compared Peirce and James on this issue in an article entitled "From a 'Religion of Science' to the 'Science of Religions': Peirce and James Reconsidered" (Raposa 2006).

27. Even a neo-pragmatist like Rorty (2002, 66) would agree that the salient question to ask about God is "whether it is a good idea to continue talking about Him, and which human purposes might be served by doing so."

28. Peirce dramatically announced "that all this universe is perfused with signs, if not composed exclusively of them" (Peirce 1935, vol. 5, para. 448, note 1). I argue, in a

forthcoming book entitled *Theosemiotic: Religion, Reading and the Gift of Meaning*, that the fact that anything can be or can become a sign does not entail the conclusion that semiosis is ubiquitous in the universe. In concluding this way, I want only to emphasize that, just as not all signs are linguistic signs, not all of reality is semiosis.

## WORKS CITED

Bagger, Matthew. 1999. *Religious Experience, Justification, and History*. Cambridge: Cambridge University Press.

Bernstein, Richard. 2010. *The Pragmatic Turn*. Cambridge: Polity.

Brandom, Robert. 1994. *Making It Explicit: Reasoning, Representing, and Discursive Commitment*. Cambridge, MA: Harvard University Press.

Brandom, Robert. 2000. *Articulating Reasons: An Introduction to Inferentialism*. Cambridge, MA: Harvard University Press.

Brandom, Robert. 2011. *Perspectives on Pragmatism*. Cambridge, MA: Harvard University Press.

Corrington, Robert. 2000. *A Semiotic Theory of Theology and Philosophy*. Cambridge: Cambridge University Press.

De Caro, Mario, and David Macarthur, eds. 2004. *Naturalism in Question*. Cambridge, MA: Harvard University Press.

De Caro, Mario, and David Macarthur, eds. 2010. *Naturalism and Normativity*. New York: Columbia University Press.

Dewey, John. 1983. *Human Nature and Conduct*. Carbondale: Southern Illinois University Press.

Dupre, John. 2004. "Miracle of Monism." In *Naturalism in Question*, edited by Mario De Caro and David Macarthur, 36–58. Cambridge, MA: Harvard University Press.

Hardwick, Charley. 1996. *Events of Grace: Naturalism, Existentialism, and Theology*. Cambridge: Cambridge University Press.

Legg, Catherine. 2008. "Making it Explicit and Clear: From 'Strong' to 'Hyper-'Inferentialism in Brandom and Peirce." *Metaphilosophy* 39:105–23.

Murphey, Murray. 1961. *The Development of Peirce's Philosophy*. Cambridge, MA: Harvard University Press.

Peirce, Charles Sanders. 1935. *The Collected Papers of Charles Sanders Peirce*, vols. 1–6, edited by Charles Hartshorne and Paul Weiss. Cambridge, MA: Harvard University Press.

Proudfoot, Wayne. 1978. "Interpretation, Inference, and Religion." *Soundings* 61:378–99.

Proudfoot, Wayne. 2012. "Pragmatism and Naturalism in the Study of Religion." *American Journal of Theology and Philosophy* 33:187–99.

Raposa, Michael. 1989. *Peirce's Philosophy of Religion*. Bloomington: Indiana University Press.

Raposa, Michael. 2002. "Love's Purposes, Hope's Necessity, and the God of Pragmaticism." *Cybernetics and Human Knowing* 19:47–57.

Raposa, Michael. 2004. "Ritual Inquiry: The Pragmatic Logic of Religious Practice." In *Thinking Through Rituals: Philosophical Perspectives*, edited by Kevin Schilbrack, 113–27. New York: Routledge.

Raposa, Michael. 2006. "From a 'Religion of Science' to the 'Science of Religions': Peirce and James Reconsidered." *American Journal of Theology and Philosophy* 27:191–203.

Rorty, Richard. 2002. "Cultural Politics and the Question of the Existence of God." In *Radical Interpretation in Religion*, edited by Nancy K. Frankenberry, 53–77. Cambridge: Cambridge University Press.

Rosenthal, Sandra. 1986. *Speculative Pragmatism*. Amherst: University of Massachusetts Press.

Smith, John E. 1978. *Purpose and Thought: The Meaning of Pragmatism*. New Haven, CT: Yale University Press.

Wiener, Philip P. 1949. *Evolution and the Founders of Pragmatism*. Cambridge, MA: Harvard University Press.

# 2

# Religious Apologetic, Naturalism, and Inquiry in the Thought of William James

MATTHEW C. BAGGER

To many analytic philosophers, the legacy of pragmatism reduces to its seminal but—so they would insist—crude contributions to antifoundationalist epistemology and semantic holism as well as to its failures as a theory of truth.[1] To many other contemporary scholars, its legacy consists in the resources it bears for democratic theory and practice. These perspectives on pragmatism are not unrelated, of course, but both would have gravely disappointed the historical pragmatists, who viewed their narrowly technical theories and their enthusiasm for democracy alike as products of, and in service to, a larger philosophical appreciation of scientific inquiry. Recognizing the formative influence of science on the pragmatists makes clear their relevance to the rise of naturalism, which in its various formulations represents philosophy's twentieth-century attempt to accommodate science and a scientific outlook. Even before John Dewey and Sidney Hook explicitly espoused it, the pragmatists had forged a distinctive and appealing naturalism. The pragmatists' signal contributions to a viable formulation of naturalism constitute a legacy more congenial to their self-understanding.

In the relevant sense, the term *naturalism* appeared in the years around the turn of the twentieth century. Derived from the phrase *natural science*, it originally signified an outlook shaped exclusively by the methods and findings of the so-called natural sciences. In *The Varieties of Religious Experience* (1902), William James uses the term with this understanding. For James (1961, 404), *naturalism* signifies a cosmology limited to the "facts of physical science." Far from endorsing naturalism construed in this manner, however, James blanches at the very thought of the "curdling cold and gloom and absence of all permanent mean-ing" that he believes naturalism entails. He contrasts its bleak prospect to the "thrill" and "zest" that religion's assurance of permanent meaning confers on life (124). Indeed, much of James's philosophical oeuvre defends the right of the scien-tifically educated to demur when confronting "the sickly hotbed atmosphere" of cosmological naturalism reigning in the "philosophic-positivistically enlightened scientific classroom" and to adopt a religiously believing attitude.[2]

James's antipathy toward this sort of naturalism is not, as it is sometimes taken to be, the last word with respect to James and naturalism, however. James com-bined his defense of the right to reject cosmological naturalism with a dedication to what later came to be called methodological naturalism.[3] Even in the context of inquiry into religion, James (1961, 23) defends and resolutely practices inquiry that explains phenomena in terms of their history and "derivation from natural antecedents." This latter aspect of James's thought is almost invariably overlooked or misconstrued. In this chapter, I highlight James's methodological naturalism and elucidate its relationship to the sanction he gives to supernaturalism. Despite the fact that the later pragmatists all reject the cosmological supernaturalism so dear to James's heart, which he argues we have a right to affirm, James set the tone for the variety of naturalism so distinctive of (and explicitly espoused by) pragma-tists like Dewey, Hook, Richard Rorty, and Wayne Proudfoot. James conjoins a clear-eyed fidelity to naturalistic inquiry—conceived broadly to include biology, psychology, and history—with a deep, sympathetic awareness of the practical importance of religion to individuals. James bequeathed this unusual combination to his fellow pragmatists. For Dewey and Hook, for example, naturalism is primar-ily a methodological stance about the conduct of inquiry and the kinds of explana-tion appropriate to it, and is only secondarily a cosmological or ontological doctrine.[4] They both, furthermore, assiduously avoid scientism in their accounts of naturalism (by not defining it in terms of the protocols of the well-developed sci-ences), and they both (to differing degrees) articulate a legitimate role for religion in human life.

The claim that the pragmatists were methodological naturalists may seem unexceptionable with regard to Dewey, but making the case for James requires some argument. James's famous Gifford lectures, *The Varieties of Religious Expe-rience: A Study in Human Nature*, have been almost wholly misunderstood. They are usually read either as an argument for the truth of supernatural religion, based on the evidence of extraordinary religious experience, or as an investigation of various religious phenomena that proposes explanations of them that are only dubiously or, at best, equivocally naturalistic. In fact, as its subtitle suggests and despite its reception and subsequent reputation, James intends *The Varieties of*

*Religious Experience* to be a proposal for, defense of, and contribution to what we would designate naturalistic inquiry into religion.

In a celebrated introductory chapter arguing against what he calls "medical materialism," James draws a distinction between inquiries into the nature, causal origin, or history of a phenomenon and inquiries into the value of a phenomenon. One answers the first sort of inquiry with an "existential judgment" and one answers the second sort of inquiry with a "spiritual judgment" (James 1961, 23–24). James famously (and, it seems to me, a bit overoptimistically) claims that an existential judgment cannot undermine a spiritual judgment. He argues, in other words, that the nature, causal origin, or history of a phenomenon does not bear on a judgment about the value of the phenomenon. This chapter is usually read as James's argument against reductionism in the study of religion. James is usually thought to be trying to render toothless the threat to religion posed by science, but James is equally clearing a space for a methodologically naturalistic science of religions. He's arguing for the legitimacy of inquiry into the organic constitution, the "natural antecedents," the "causes and elements" responsible for religious phenomena, but he's trying to take the sting out of it. In this chapter, James is primarily assuaging the anxieties of his theological audience about his forthcoming methodologically naturalistic treatment of religion.[5]

Readers are not wrong, however, when they impute an apologetic ambition to James. The key to an undistorted reading of James on religion lies in keeping both his methodological naturalism and his apologetic interests stereoscopically in view and then properly relating the two. In his thought about religion, James had a dual ambition. On the one hand, he wanted to "ventilate" religion with what he called "the northwest wind of science," but, on the other hand, he wanted to encourage individuals to venture on the religious hypotheses that appeal to them (James 1956d, x). James sought simultaneously to defend religion (especially religion of a supernatural sort) and to promote and defend methodological naturalism in inquiry into religion.

Failure to identify, distinguish, and properly interrelate these dual ambitions has bedeviled commentary on James. In the last decade of his life, Richard Rorty published two essays purporting to interpret William James's most famous writings on religion. In "Religious Faith, Intellectual Responsibility, and Romance," Rorty (1997, 90) claims to "evaluate James's argument in 'The Will to Believe,'" but most of the essay "sketches" a philosophy of religion that Rorty says "is shadowed forth in much of James's work" and that Rorty believes James *should* have espoused. In "Some Inconsistencies in James's *Varieties*," Rorty (2004), without saying so, tries in essence to square the position he believes James should have espoused in "The Will to Believe" with the concluding chapter of *The Varieties of Religious Experience*.

Despite the idiosyncrasies of Rorty's interpretations, his essays raise important considerations for students of James. First, he notes that a distinction between the public and the private is central to James's discussions of religion. As Wayne Proudfoot (2002) demonstrates, Rorty's account of James's use of this distinction is deeply flawed.[6] Rorty, nevertheless, manages to call attention to this neglected theme in James's writings on religion. Second, Rorty recognizes that what Philip Kitcher has labeled the "natural reading" of the *Varieties*—the reading that sees James as adducing all those eccentric reports of the experiences of religious virtuosi in an attempt to supply sufficient empirical evidence to warrant supernaturalism—involves a departure from the theme of "The Will to Believe," in which James asserts a right to believe in the absence of evidence.[7] Rorty poses a dilemma for the interpreter of the *Varieties*: either James betrays the view he articulates in "The Will to Believe" and argues something closer to the "natural reading" or there is thematic continuity between "The Will to Believe" and the *Varieties*, but then much of the empirical detail of the *Varieties* seems superfluous, if not ill-conceived. If we reject the "natural reading" of the *Varieties*, we are left, Rorty (2004, 96) says, "wondering why we need bother with all these virtuosi—whether the twenty Gifford lectures add anything to the twenty pages of 'The Will to Believe.'"

In the remainder of this chapter, I intend to take another crack at the relationship of the *Varieties* to "The Will to Believe," a topic that has foiled interpreters of James more faithful than Rorty.[8] I hope to show that, in the *Varieties*, James does not betray the message of "The Will to Believe," nor does the empirical detail of the *Varieties* belie that message. Rather, the detail completes, elaborates, and specifies the argument of the earlier article. The reading I offer re-embeds the infamous chapter on mysticism (which, when taken out of context, has caused so much mischief by suggesting, among other misinterpretations, the "natural reading") in the larger argument of the book and pays due heed to James's intention to contribute to a public "science of religions." If "The Will to Believe" emphasizes private permission to believe within certain limits, the *Varieties* attempts a public "science of religions" that circumscribes the range of private permission. Individuals exercising their right to believe and living their private religious persuasions in public, in turn, make inquiry into religion possible. The lives of individuals, conducting themselves in accord with their faiths, become so many experimental tests of those faiths and provide sine qua non the subject matter of the science of religions. A commitment to inquiry integrates the dual poles of James's philosophy of religion. James displays a keen sensitivity to the emotional needs that religion satisfies, and he also seeks to vindicate the right to honor the leadings of personal religious impulse, but this apologetic intent forms but one element of an encompassing devotion to inquiry.

## "THE SENTIMENT OF RATIONALITY"

James displays a notable consistency in his thought about religion. As early as 1880, in "The Sentiment of Rationality," the earliest of the essays collected in *The Will to Believe*, James articulates themes around which his discussion of religion will revolve for at least the next twenty-five years: the inability of states of mystical insight in themselves to answer our metaphysical and religious questions in a way that meets the proper standards of objectivity, and the private freedom of the individual to embrace religious beliefs in the absence of sufficient evidence. In only slightly different form, these themes give the much later *Varieties* its shape.

At one point in this early essay, preparing the ground for his ultimate conclusion that investigation into the truth of religion *requires* that individuals act on their faiths, James acknowledges that mysticism can counter the "ontological wonder-sickness" that the cosmological question (Why is there something rather than nothing?) produces. Speaking of the heart and its ecstasies of ontological emotion, however, he remarks, "The erection of its procedure into a systematized method would be a philosophic achievement of first-rate importance. But as used by mystics hitherto it has lacked universality, being available for few persons and at few times, and even in these being apt to be followed by fits of reaction and dryness" (James 1956b, 74–75). James here asserts that the deliverances of mystical emotion are pertinent to inquiry, but he rues their fugitive nature. This passage contains an aspiration and an objection; both figure prominently in the *Varieties*.

In the *Varieties*, James again laments that mystical states are too idiosyncratic to serve in themselves as evidence for the truth of the insights they impart. He complains that mystical insight is neither universal nor unanimous. Contrary to the common perception of his motives in the notorious chapter on mysticism, James (1961, 337) says that he has "undermined the authority of mysticism" with respect to the objective truth of a divine presence. Mysticism is "too private (and also too various) in its utterances to be able to claim a universal authority." Mystical states, as he puts it earlier in the book, "come seldom, and they do not come to everyone; and the rest of life makes either no connection with them, or tends to contradict them more than it confirms them" (31). By calling mystical states private, James signals their divergence from the intellect. One of the phenomenological marks of mysticism that James identifies is ineffability. Mystics report that their experiences "defy expression." In this respect, he says, they are "more like states of feeling than like states of intellect" (300). The intellect, by contrast, strives for articulacy and impartial, universal assent. "To find an escape from obscure and wayward personal persuasion to truth objectively valid for all thinking men has ever been the intellect's most cherished ideal. To redeem religion from unwholesome privacy and to give public status and universal right of way to its deliverances, has been reason's task" (338). Despite undermining the authority of mysticism, James nevertheless aspires, in the *Varieties*, to redeem some universality from religious experience (broadly conceived) by an application of philosophy suitably transformed into a science of religions. He describes his Gifford lectures as "a laborious attempt to extract from the privacies of religious experience some general facts which can be defined in formulas upon which everybody may agree" (339).

From the very first, however, James also sought to stake out a space for legitimate private belief beyond the realm of universal agreement on objective truth. This aspect of James's thought is best known from "The Will to Believe," but James ends "The Sentiment of Rationality" by distinguishing the domain of universal, objective truth from a space of permission to entertain uncertain beliefs privately. Summarizing his conclusions about the character of the "ultimate philosophy," he writes, "There must be left over and above the propositions to be subscribed *ubique, semper, et ab omnibus* [everywhere, always, and by everyone], another realm into which the stifled soul may escape from pedantic scruples and indulge its own faith at its own risks; and all that can here be done [by the ultimate philosophy] will be to mark out distinctly the questions which fall within faith's sphere" (James 1956b, 110). In arguing for this conclusion, James makes it clear that the emotional needs of the stifled soul are not the only (or the decisive) consideration mandating faith's special preserve. It is, rather, the methodological requirements of inquiry that necessitate an indulgent attitude toward faith.

Science depends on individual members of the scientific community having faith enough in their unsubstantiated hypotheses to test them by conducting experiments in accord with them. In a process that can take generations, the scientific community assesses the hypotheses by evaluating the conformity of the experimental results to what the hypotheses predict. James argues that, in a precisely parallel way, the only verification to be had of hypotheses about the ultimate character of the universe taken as a whole (e.g., cosmological naturalism, or belief in a world endowed with "permanent meaning") lies in generations of individuals testing their personal faiths by acting on them "exactly as does the physical philosopher in testing an hypothesis." Alluding to the history of science, in which scientists have regularly incorporated "epicycle upon epicycle of subsidiary hypothesis" into a theory to explain unwelcome or unanticipated results, before the scientific community ultimately acknowledges the theory's failure, James allows that individuals confronting experience uncongenial to their lived religious hypotheses will inevitably concoct secondary elaborations to attempt to safeguard them (105–6). Nevertheless, James insists that, as in the case of science, the course of experience will ultimately refute or verify religious hypotheses put to the test.

In "The Will to Believe," James heeds the conclusion he reached in "The Sentiment of Rationality" and defends the right of the stifled soul to indulge its own faith at its own risk, but "The Will to Believe" gives only cursory mention of the limits to this freedom. The *Varieties*, on the other hand, while defending the realm of private permission, pays greater attention to the realm of public objective truth that frames and defines the realm of permission. James tries, in the *Varieties*, to establish some truths that emerge from the collective history of religious experimentation. When James employs the phrase "religious experience" in the title of his lecture series, he does not use it to refer solely or even primarily to episodes of extraordinary consciousness. In fact, that familiar use of the phrase (both within the academy and at large) originates from the widespread misreading of James's influential book that overemphasizes and misconstrues the mysticism chapter. James adopts the phrase from American Protestantism, where one might be asked to testify to one's religious experience, or, in other words, to one's religious autobiography (as one might, in another context, be asked to testify to one's work experience).[9] In James's intended sense, the varieties of religious experience are the varieties of religious lives—including the sources of religious conviction as well as the effects of those convictions on the individual, and the consequences of religiously inspired actions for the individual and for others.[10] Surveying the varieties of religious experience in this sense, the *Varieties* attempts, on the basis of these assorted religious experiments, to make summary judgments about truth, which limit the legitimate, fruitful avenues for further experiment. It attempts, that is, "to mark out distinctly" what "fall[s] within faith's sphere."

## "THE WILL TO BELIEVE"

James (1956c, 1) introduces "The Will to Believe" as an apology, "a defence of our right to adopt a believing attitude in religious matters." The right he defends extends to cases when the intellect cannot resolve a question. He announces as his thesis the claim that *"our passional nature not only lawfully may, but must, decide an option between propositions, whenever it is a genuine option that cannot by its nature be decided on intellectual grounds"* (11, emphasis in original). The distinction James applies throughout the essay between the intellect and "our passional nature" never receives satisfactory definition. One can, however, glean from what James does say the gist of the distinction as he uses it. In describing what he terms "the magnificent edifice of the physical sciences"—an edifice he associates with the intellect—James characterizes it as "impersonal" and portrays its creators as "disinterested." In this same passage, he labels the intellect "incorruptibly truthful" (7). After a full paragraph of fustian extolling scientific scruples, James cautions that the intellect plays only a supporting role in the fixation of belief. What James terms our "willing nature" is responsible for rendering a hypothesis live or dead. Acts of the intellect compose only part of our willing nature. James explains, "When I say 'willing nature,' I do not mean only such deliberate volitions as may have set up habits of belief that we cannot now escape from—I mean all such factors of belief as fear and hope, prejudice and passion, imitation and partisanship, the circumpressure of our caste and set. As a matter of fact we find ourselves believing, we hardly know how or why" (9). Our willing nature, which fixes our beliefs, includes deliberate volitions as well as interests, emotions, and contextual factors. James's previous work in psychology elucidates this passage. In *The Principles of Psychology*, James argues that belief and will are the same psychological phenomenon: the attention is turned to an idea, guided by interests and emotions, resulting in action. In light of this theory and what James does say in "The Will to Believe," we can take James in this context to mean by the intellect the self-conscious, deliberate, impartial weighing of evidence in the service of an impersonal theoretical interest.[11] James (1956c, 22) summarizes this account of the intellect when he calls it the "dispassionately judicial intellect." Our passional nature includes the other determinants of our attention, of which we are not necessarily aware or in control.

In "The Will to Believe," James attempts, as he did throughout his life, to offer a generic characterization of the religious hypothesis that abstracts from the specifics of one creed or another. "What do we . . . mean by the religious hypothesis?" James asks. "Science says things are; morality says some things are better than other things; and religion says essentially two things. First, she says that the best things are the more eternal things, the overlapping things, the things in the universe that throw the last stone, so to speak, and say the final word. . . . The second affirmation of religion is that we are better off even now if we believe her first affirmation to be true" (James, 1956c, 25–26). Religion proposes that the ultimate and indelible configuration of the universe harmonizes with the highest human aspirations. It proposes that the universe is congenial to our ideals and ratifies our strivings, at least to the extent that it is not indifferent to human concerns and offers some sort of shelter for our nobler hopes. Across thirty years—from 1873 through at least the publication of the *Varieties* in 1902—James repeats the same phrase to summarize his conception of religion: religion, he says, affirms that "all is *not* vanity" in the universe. The religious individual's particular sense of "the whole residual cosmos as an everlasting presence" attests that life is neither farce nor unrelieved tragedy (James 1961, 45).

James believes the jury is still out on the religious hypothesis taken in this generic way. The intellect can as yet render no verdict. He writes that religion "cannot yet" be verified scientifically and that the evidence for religion is "still insufficient" (James 1956c, 25, 27).[12] Because the intellect can render no verdict at present, James argues that it is permissible and unavoidable that our passional nature decides the issue. With regard to religion, we each believe or disbelieve as it suits our temperament, experience, and education, all the while assuming the risks, epistemic or otherwise, attending our preference.

"The Will to Believe" elicited a fair amount of criticism from his contemporaries, on the grounds that James was advocating what amounts to epistemic irresponsibility, that he was promoting a "will to make-believe."[13] Within a matter of months, Dickinson Miller, one of James's former students, became the leading spokesman for this line of criticism. In 1896, soon after the essay's initial publication in the journal *New World*, Miller wrote James a letter chiding him for effacing the "sharp" distinction between objective "evidence" and subjective "craving." An exchange of well-publicized letters on the topic ensued, followed by a session dedicated to the dispute at the annual meeting of the American Psychological Association, in December 1898. Miller's pointed criticism took final shape in an essay published early in 1899, "'The Will to Believe' and the Duty to Doubt." In this essay, Miller offers at least two uncomplimentary interpretations of James's view. Initially, he argues that James's "The Will to Believe" authorizes intellectual dishonesty:

> The Will to Believe is the will to deceive—to deceive one's self; and the deception, which begins at home, may be expected in due course to pass on to others. It is the will to hold that thing certain which now we feel to be uncertain; it says, "This thing seems to my best intelligence doubtful; but I will subject my mind to such a course of treatment; I will so tempt and beguile it by presenting this one matter for its credence and withholding rivals; I will so hypnotize it by keeping its gaze on this one brilliant object; that I shall presently find myself reposing in the peaceable possession of a full belief."
>
> (Miller 1899, 173)

Miller claims that James advocates a form of culpable self-persuasion in which one contrives to divert one's attention from countervailing evidence. In so characterizing James's position, Miller in effect accuses James of promoting precisely the kind of intellectual bad faith that William Clifford—against whose views James directed "The Will to Believe"—had castigated in "The Ethics of Belief." Clifford's initial and most memorable example of an ethical lapse in belief concerns a ship owner who surmounts his warranted doubts about the seaworthiness of his vessel (to the detriment of its doomed passengers) by carefully controlling what thoughts he will entertain.

Later in the essay, Miller suggests that James's career as a psychologist is responsible for his having championed a philosophy lacking a sufficiently robust respect for truth. James's philosophy, Miller claims, is a therapy for souls; James is not interested in objectivity. This therapeutic motivation leads James, so Miller intimates, to propound skeptical fideism (though Miller does not use the phrase). "As soon as the lights of reason are turned down we may help ourselves in the dark to what we can lay hands on. Since there is no longer a rational warrant for belief, there is no longer a rational bar to assumption; one belief is just as good in that regard as another; so that we may deal with them on the single basis of our predilections, unconfused by the introduction of any alien standard" (Miller 1899, 187–88). James degrades or disparages the notion of objective evidence, Miller asserts, in order to level distinctions in warrant and thereby pave the way for wishful thinking. Both of Miller's characterizations of "The Will to Believe" portray James as wantonly flouting objective and impartial standards of evidence and truth. Implicit, too, in the negative reaction to "The Will to Believe" that Miller's essay epitomizes is the fear that James's argument is an invitation to fanaticism and religious tyranny, especially in light of James's (1956a, 211–14) exaltation of religion's capacity to evoke what he calls the "strenuous mood."[14]

James foresaw the lineaments of Miller's criticism, and he addresses the objection briefly at the end of "The Will to Believe." He summarizes his thesis, describes what he predicts will be the negative reaction, then reiterates the limits he places on the right he defends:

> Sad experience makes me fear that some of you may still shrink from radically saying with me, *in abstract*, that we have the right to believe at our own risk any hypothesis that is live enough to tempt our will. I suspect, however, that if this is so, it is because you have got away from the abstract logical point of view altogether, and are thinking (perhaps without realizing it) of some particular religious hypothesis which for you is dead. The freedom to "believe what we will" you apply to the case of some patent superstition; and the faith you think of is the faith defined by the schoolboy when he said, "Faith is when you believe something that

you know ain't true." I can only repeat that this is a misapprehension. *In concreto*, the freedom to believe can only cover living options which the intellect of the individual cannot by itself resolve; and living options never seem absurdities to him who has them to consider.

(James 1956c, 29, emphasis in original)

James insists that the right he defends is limited to those live hypotheses about which the intellect can come to no conclusion. He does not grant a right to believe something fantastic or that the intellect deems false. Unfortunately, the way James phrases his qualification surrenders hostages to the enemy. He limits the freedom to believe to beliefs that "the intellect of the individual" leaves open. This phrase seems to open the door to epistemic anarchism, as though each is an epistemic law unto oneself. James seems to discount the impartial, normative force of cooperative inquiry. James's efforts in the *Varieties* toward a public science of religions rectify this impression.

## THE VARIETIES OF RELIGIOUS EXPERIENCE

After the initial publication of "The Will to Believe," James's first attempt in print to counter the impression that the essay holds a brief for epistemic or intellectual license appears in the preface to the book *The Will to Believe* (1897). In this synoptic statement of his philosophical and religious standpoint, James distinguishes between, on the one hand, "mankind at large," which could well stand to heed better the findings of science and exercise more caution in its religious believings, and, on the other hand, "academic audiences," whose critical and scientific scruples paralyze their "capacity for faith" (James 1956d, x). James here reprises his earliest epistolary response to Miller's criticisms of the essay. In his August 30, 1896, letter to Miller, James (1993, 163) contrasts "men at large," to whom one should "preach" hesitation in their convictions and whose "faiths" need "airing" in "the howling wilderness of nature," to "studious persons . . . whose simple-minded faith in 'naturalism' . . . need[s] airing." In print, James makes stylistic improvements to the diction of the letter, rephrasing "the howling wilderness of nature" as "the northwest wind of science," but the earlier reference to nature highlights the methodologically naturalistic character of the inquiry to which James believes we must subject religion. The earlier formulation also more precisely identifies cosmological naturalism, which James finds so enervating and stifling, as the impetus for his apologetic efforts.

After distinguishing "mankind at large," to whom he would not "preach the liberty of believing" espoused in the essay, from "academic audiences," James (1956d, xi) denies, in the preface, that even to the latter he preaches "reckless faith." He then proceeds to set the argument of the "The Will to Believe" more explicitly against the backdrop of inquiry. Echoing the argument of "The Sentiment of Rationality," he insists that acting on the religious hypotheses that tempt our will is the best way to test them experimentally and verify their truth. Competition between them, moreover, ensures that the fittest survive. With a confidence that seems almost impossibly hopeful from our perspective, he asserts that history attests to the way that religious beliefs yield when contradicted by science and experience. Mentioning the "science of religions" for the very first time in his writings, James tasks it with identifying those religious hypotheses that best comport with "a widening knowledge of the world" (xii). He proposes that the science of religions should determine which religious hypotheses prove most tenable in light of what we have come to know about our environment and ourselves. The context in which James introduces the science of religions indicates that he conceives its inquiries as continuous with the more prosaic conclusions drawn by the race in the course of history. This effort on James's part to place his argument defending private permission to believe in the context of respect for the impartial, normative force of science and inquiry finds fuller expression in the *Varieties*.

James began composing the lectures that would make up the *Varieties* in 1900, shortly after the criticism of "The Will to Believe" reached its peak, in 1899, with the publication of Miller's essay and those of others who shared Miller's point of view. The exchange with Miller unmistakably shapes the *Varieties*. Among other aims, the *Varieties* attempts to address the complaint that the will to believe doctrine is too wanton.[15] In "The Will to Believe," James (1956c, 11, 29) argues that we have permission or freedom to believe live options in questions that the intellect cannot resolve, that "cannot be decided on intellectual grounds." *Varieties* is an attempt to give the intellect its full rights in this issue. What *can* be decided on intellectual grounds? When, early in the book, James argues that consistency with our other beliefs (what he alternately calls philosophical reasonableness) as well as serviceability for our needs (what he alternately calls moral helpfulness) are the criteria that go into our judgments of truth, he evinces that he still believes that interests other than purely intellectual ones determine what we believe. The *Varieties*, moreover, simply translates James's previous talk of how our "willing nature" makes an option "live" into a discussion of how our subconscious as the repository of memories and "motives deposited by the experiences of life" explains our inarticulate "feelings of reality," the impulsive source of an individual's religious experience and convictions (James 1961, 190). In the *Varieties*, as distinct from "The Will to Believe," however, James elaborates on his distinction between what we privately have a right (permission) to believe—he calls these "over-beliefs," perhaps because they are "left over and above the propositions to be subscribed *ubique, semper, et ab omnibus*"—and what is common truth.

At the end of the chapter on mysticism, James signals an intention to move away from privacy and permission in favor of publicity and compulsion. In the next chapter, he turns to philosophy in hopes of exercising the intellect to arrive at firm conclusions regarding the truth of the religious hypothesis. Unfortunately, by the end of the chapter, he determines that philosophy as heretofore practiced is not much help. "In all sad sincerity," he writes, "I think we must conclude that the attempt to demonstrate by purely intellectual processes the truth of the deliverances of direct religious experience is absolutely hopeless" (355).

At this point, however, James proposes an alternative use of the intellect. He explicitly argues for a public, naturalistic science of religions that stands in judgment over the intellectual acceptability of religious assertions and that seeks to explain religious phenomena with *explanantia* drawn from other scientific disciplines. Subjecting religious claims to science is not an unwarranted imposition, in James's view, because the intellect has always informed articulate religious conceptions, both directly in reflection and indirectly through subconscious predisposition. His recommended science of religions would determine what is "objectively true" about religion and weed out what is false (because it conflicts with science), while framing the space of private permission to adopt and act on over-beliefs "grafted" onto or "built out" from this common truth (390, 398). James, in fact, states that he hopes the *Varieties* will make a "crumb-like" contribution to such a science.

The impartial science of religions aims to reconcile the various religious hypotheses by isolating a common doctrine amenable to science. James conceives the science of religions as the "moderator amid the clash of hypotheses, and the mediator among the criticisms of one man's constructions by another" (339). The science of religions, by explaining religion in ways consonant with the other sciences, enables a verdict as to what can be considered true in religion. The point I wish to emphasize is that James is a methodological naturalist in his science of religions. When engaged in inquiry about religion, the sciences condition our conclusions in at least three ways. First, the sciences dictate which religious beliefs or doctrines must be rejected. Far from promoting epistemic anarchy or a will to make-believe, James sharply limits the permission to believe. Second, the sciences assess to what extent religious claims can be considered true. Third, hypotheses in the science of religions must not be foreign to the other sciences—the causal agencies to which one appeals in explaining religion must keep religion "in connection with the rest of science" (395).

James presents the result of his own foray into the science of religions in the following passage: "Disregarding the over-beliefs, and confining ourselves to what is common and generic, we have in *the fact that the conscious person is continuous with a wider self through which saving experiences come*, a positive content of religious experience which, it seems to me, *is literally and objectively true as far as it goes*" (398, emphasis in original). Readers often misunderstand James's claim here. They fall victim to what Kitcher calls the "natural reading," that James here concludes that the testimonies he has presented provide evidence for the truth of supernaturalism. Rather, James has identified what he believes is common to the testimonies he has examined and to that extent has reconciled them. He has also identified a naturalistic explanation for these "saving experiences." They are incursions from the "subconscious continuation of our conscious life" (396). When he declares that the positive content he has identified is "literally and objectively true as far as it goes," he is applying the dual criteria of consistency with our other opinions and moral helpfulness. James's result is consistent with science because it explains the experiences in scientific terms, and the conclusion also includes a positive evaluation of religion's moral helpfulness. He describes the experiences as "saving," after all. As James sees it, the fact that he has identified a scientific explanation for religion that corroborates (a generic and descriptively thin synopsis of) what the religious report about the phenomenology and effects of religion, in conjunction with the serviceability of religion, especially as evidenced in the dispositions of some saints, validates it precisely to that extent.

Having offered a hypothesis in the science of religions, James continues and reveals the over-belief that he says appeals to the "whole drift of [his education]" (401). It appeals, that is, to his "willing nature." James ventures on the over-belief that supernatural forces work through the subconscious to effect regenerative change. This willingness on his part to state his own substantively supernaturalistic over-beliefs has overshadowed his commitment to methodological naturalism in the study of religion.

In what I have argued so far, one may feel that I have distorted the *Varieties* as much as those who take the chapter on mysticism out of context and adopt "the natural reading" or read the book as a treatise on the epistemology of religious experience, conceived as episodes of extraordinary consciousness. The *Varieties* consists of twenty lectures. Fully five of the lectures concern the topic of saintliness. Saintliness occupies more of James's attention than any other topic. In fact, I think it is fair to say that the chapters on saintliness are the heart and soul of the book. Heretofore I have said little, if indeed anything, about saintliness in my discussion of the *Varieties*, as if the topic were inessential. A careful look at James's discussion of the value of saintliness, however, suggests that it corroborates my interpretation of the *Varieties*. In the course of arriving at a generally strong endorsement of the saintly fruits of religion—he says they are "indispensable to the world's welfare!"—James (1961, 297) forthrightly considers some of the morally troubling manifestations or expressions of the saintly character. Among others, he considers how saintly devoutness can produce fanaticism, with intolerance and persecution in its train. In the end, James attributes these extravagances of saintliness to a deficiency of intellect.

Despite the umbrage easily taken at some of James's comments about the intellectual shortcomings of certain Catholic saints, James is not centrally deprecating the faculties of individuals. He is insisting that religion must be responsive to the intellect (as well as to our evolving social sensibilities). It is science (as well as our developing social arrangements) that enables us to recognize certain manifestations of the saintly character as vices. As he puts it with respect to some historical expressions of religion, they have "fallen below the common secular level" (262). "Science, idealism, and democracy," he says, lead us to condemn many of the older expressions of the saintly attributes (275). In his discussion of saintliness, James echoes the themes I have been emphasizing. On the one hand, he displays his ambition that, as he puts it in the preface to "The Will to Believe," "the northwest wind of science" would blow away the "sickliness and barbarism" of many conventional forms of religion. On the other hand, he is defending the argument he mounts in "The Will to Believe" about private permission to believe by countering the suggestion that his argument invites fanaticism and religious tyranny. The scope of private permission to believe is shaped and limited by the intellect (i.e., science).

As James envisions it, the science of religions is not essentially different from the evaluations of religion that have always occurred in the "drift of common life," through which the fittest faiths survive (264).[16] It depends on the same facts of personal experience, and it issues in the same kinds of judgments. The science of religions, however, inquires into the facts in a more comprehensive, directed, self-conscious, and intentional fashion. Gleaning its data from the lives of generations of individuals venturing on their faiths, it offers provisional conclusions, at any given moment in history, about truth and falsity in religion, and it shapes the space of legitimate hypotheses at that stage of the inquiry. Intensively subjecting religion to inquiry, the public science of religions exerts a salubrious influence on the private faiths of individuals. In the conclusion to the

*Varieties*, James argues at length that the impersonal science of religions cannot supplant or obviate personal conjectures (i.e., over-beliefs), which answer directly to "the pinch of an individual's destiny as he privately feels it" (387). Rather than conceiving it as a substitute for private faiths, James sees the methodologically naturalistic science of religions as a health-promoting supplement—or, better, in the argot of James's era, a tonic. It counteracts "sickliness," tones and reinvigorates religious conceptions to suit the "mental climate," and produces fit faiths (262).

As an exercise in the science of religions, the *Varieties* attempts to see how far the intellect might go in rendering a verdict on religion and where "philosophically lawful" permission to believe begins. The *Varieties* elaborates and specifies the thesis of "The Will to Believe," both the permissions and the constraints on permission. James insists that the *Varieties* is mainly descriptive and psychological (i.e., existential). In the *Varieties*, he is providing the facts against which the permissibility defended in the "The Will to Believe" is measured and limited. James adduces the wealth of empirical detail that misleads proponents of the "natural reading," not, as they suppose, to amass evidence to warrant supernaturalism but rather because it is necessary for a methodologically naturalistic science of religions, and the science of religions shapes the space of personal permission to believe. James limits the science of religions to naturalistic hypotheses in order to better distinguish those (potentially supernaturalistic) religious hypotheses about the world's ultimate character, upon which one can legitimately act, from those we can come to "know ain't true."

Freely acting on these legitimate over-beliefs, in turn, exposes them to further public appraisal. Not only does competition in the marketplace between the various religious conceptions render diffuse judgments about their relative intellectual and moral fitness but also the open, uninhibited practice of religion provides additional data for the more deliberate and focused inquiries of the science of religions. In James's view, both the methodologically naturalistic science of religions as well as conduct expressing legitimate private religious conviction advance the public cause of inquiry into the objective truth about religion. In a letter to Henry Rankin (February 1, 1897) discussing psychological explanations of religious phenomena (e.g., possession, conversion, and miracles) and the bearing of those naturalistic explanations on religious interests, James (1993, 166) declares, "I prefer an open mind of inquiry, first *about the facts*, in all these matters" (emphasis in original). A careful reading of James on religion corroborates this self-avowal about the preeminence of inquiry. From start to finish—from "The Sentiment of Rationality" through *The Varieties of Religious Experience*—the requirements of inquiry structure James's philosophy of religion and yield its abiding features.[17] An over-arching dedication to inquiry integrates James's apologetic efforts with his methodological naturalism.

## PRAGMATISM, NATURALISM, AND RELIGION

I do not endorse the specifics of James's philosophy of religion. I cannot, for instance, accept his distinction between feeling and intellect (even granting that this distinction is not as sharp for James as most interpreters make out). I do not believe that James's particular way of relating private permission in religious matters to the public study of religion is necessarily advisable, in large part because I agree with James's pragmatist descendants that cosmological supernaturalism is best reconceived. In other words I agree with Dewey, Hook, Rorty, and Proudfoot that the fittest faiths acknowledge that, in Proudfoot's words, "Any moral order, any *more* that is continuous with the higher parts of the self, any forces that might help to bring our ideals about, can be understood only as the emergent social products of the beliefs, desires, and actions of men and women" (Proudfoot 2002, 85, emphasis in original). Finally, I do not, as James does, privilege psychological explanations of religious phenomena over cultural and historical explanations.

Relatedly, I believe that James's variety of methodological naturalism may itself court scientism, in that he seems to suggest that the causal agencies to which one appeals in explaining religion must be drawn from the other sciences, rather than simply requiring that the causal agencies must be in principle amenable to themselves being investigated by science (though it all depends on exactly what James means when he says that the science of religions must be "in connection with the rest of science").[18] The agencies to which one appeals when offering a historical explanation, for example, are not drawn from the sciences but ought to be, in principle, amenable to themselves being investigated by science. (If it is claimed that they are not in principle amenable to being investigated by science, they are *pro tanto* supernatural.) Methodological naturalism should not rule out historical explanations.

I do, nevertheless, believe that James and the other pragmatists keep the right aims in view. We ought to foster respect for science and its methods and champion the idea that religion does not escape its jurisdiction. In the study of religion (or anything else, for that matter), we need to be resolutely naturalistic. By this I mean that we must unrelentingly endeavor not to shelter any aspect of religious inclination, belief, or practice, no matter how dear, from the full impact of a thoroughgoing naturalism. Our naturalism, however, should aspire to avoid scientism. We must (as I would put it) appeal in our inquiries only to entities or causal agencies in principle amenable to scientific investigation. We also, however, need to acknowledge the continuing importance of religion as a source of solace and inspiration in the lives of many of our fellow citizens. James, if nothing else, illustrates that dedication to inquiry and methodological naturalism is compatible with deep sympathy for the solace and inspiration afforded by religion. To sustain the legacy of pragmatism, we must try to devise a way to reap these benefits of religion to the individual while also preventing it from impinging on naturalistic inquiry, even into religion itself. The project to identify and defend a legitimate role for religion, without compromising the integrity of inquiry, unites the efforts of James, the self-described "crude" supernaturalist, and Rorty, the atheist. To those of us engaged in the study of religion and (therefore) aware of the role religion plays in some people's lives, the pragmatist legacy of an uncompromising methodological naturalism that is not dismissive of religion's pertinence to human hopes retains its commanding importance.

## NOTES

1. Alissa Macmillan, Amy Langenberg, Rich Penaskovic, Nancy Frankenberry, Vincent Colapietro, and Wayne Proudfoot all read a draft of this essay and offered comments that improved it. Audiences at Auburn University and Washington and Lee University heard earlier versions. Portions of two paragraphs appeared previously in Bagger (2011).

2. William James to John Jay Chapman, April 5, 1897, quoted in Perry (1935, 2:237).

3. Edgar Brightman, an admirer of James, is generally credited with coining the term *methodological naturalism* in his 1936 presidential address to the Eastern Division of the American Philosophical Association, later published as "An Empirical Approach to God" (1937). The term does not appear in the writings of the classical pragmatists.

4. Sidney Hook (1961, 185) explains that cosmological or ontological naturalism consists in "broad generalizations which are established by use of" the method.

5. In private correspondence, James wrote, "I regard the *VRE* [*Varieties of Religious Experience*] as in a sense a study of morbid psychology, mediating and interpreting to the philistine much that he would otherwise despise and utterly reject" (Perry 1935, 2:325). I understand James to mean by "mediating and interpreting" that he makes the naturalistic explanations palatable to his audience.

6. Wayne Proudfoot (2002) has shown, moreover, how far Richard Rorty's proposal for "The Will to Believe" in fact strays from James's position.

7. Philip Kitcher (2004, 99–100) labels it the "natural reading" because "it is so hard to understand what *else* James might have in mind." Nevertheless, Kitcher attempts a divergent reading because James could not possibly have been guilty of what Kitcher derides as a "blatant blunder." In his attempt to glean what *else* James might have had in mind in the *Varieties*, Kitcher, like Rorty, turns to "The Will to Believe."

8. Many scholars offer untenable interpretations of "The Will to Believe" (1896) that inhibit a clear view of the relationship between it and the *Varieties*. David Hollinger (2004, 28), for instance, argues that James seeks, in "The Will to Believe," to treat religion as a separate province from science and to protect it from "the structures of plausibility being inculcated in modern societies by science." Only in 1897, Hollinger claims, did James begin promoting the experimental verification of religious hypotheses in the same fashion as scientific hypotheses. This new strategy finds expression in the *Varieties*. In fact, however, James's longest explanation of how to verify religious hypotheses "exactly as does the physical philosopher in testing an hypothesis" occurs in "The Sentiment of Rationality," dating to 1880 (James 1956b, 105). James does not depart from this early conception in "The Will to Believe" or, indeed, ever.

   For his part, Kitcher too closely assimilates James's argument in "The Will to Believe" to Pascal's Wager and so believes it succumbs to the problem the wager faces with regard to conceivable alternative gambles with the same distribution of costs and benefits. Distinct alternative gambles with the same distribution of costs and benefits prevent any of the proposed gambles from constituting "a 'free move' that brings us a possible gain and no possible loss" (Kitcher 2004, 113). Despite James's repeated insistence that the upshot of his view consists in the claim that we have the right to choose our own risk, Kitcher misconstrues James's argument as suggesting that believing the religious hypothesis constitutes a "free move." Moreover, he ignores James's (1956c, 29) insistence that "the freedom to believe can only cover living options" that actually tempt our assent, not mere conceivables. Kitcher believes that all the empirical data James produces in the *Varieties* serves the purpose of replacing the flawed, abstract, wager-like argument of "The Will to Believe." James, he argues, intends the rich, empirical detail of the *Varieties* to demonstrate that "there are good grounds for thinking that failure to believe [the religious hypothesis] will involve us in a loss" (133).

9. James's use of *experience* in the *Varieties* forms a precedent for John Dewey's, in which he resists the empiricists' reductive conception of experience. For the "pragmatist" conception of experience, see Brandom (2011), 6–9.

10. James focuses on religious lives in which religious propensities are especially prominent.

11. See James's letter of August 4, 1907, to Ralph Barton Perry, discussing the intellectual interests and satisfactions that contribute to the "human emotional endowment." James chides Perry for interpreting *practical* too narrowly:

> How unlucky a word pragmatism has been to attach to our theory of truth. It seems to most people to *exclude* intellectual relations and interests, but all it *means* is to say that these are subjective interests like all the others, and not the sole ones concerned in determining the beliefs that count as true. . . .

You . . . use [the word "practical"] as *excluding* intellectual practice. The pragmatic test of a concept's meaning is a difference in possible *experience* somewhere, but the experience may be a pure observation with no "practical" use whatever. It may have the tremendous theoretical use of telling which concept is true, however, and that may remotely be connected with practical uses over and above the mere verification, or it may not. The "cognitive intention" . . . is an intensely peculiar part, when developed, of our human emotional endowment; involving, as it does, curiosity for new fact, insistence on non-contradiction, and on simplification of form, and love of tracing applications. You treat it as if it lay apart from all other human urgencies, whereas psychologically it is only one species of the genus human urgency. . . . You speak, again, as if the "degree of satisfaction" was *exclusive* of theoretic satisfactions. . . . My position is that, *other things equal*, emotional satisfactions count for truth—among the other things being the intellectual satisfactions.

(Perry 1935, 2:475, emphasis in original)

12. Contra Hollinger and Kitcher, James did not think that the religious hypothesis was *in principle* unverifiable.

13. It also occasioned jocularity. George Santayana (1921, 77) said of James that he "did not really believe; he merely believed in the right of believing that you might be right if you believed."

14. Ironically, James thought his argument in "The Will to Believe" serves as an impediment to religious tyranny. Answering a reader who felt that what James defends hardly amounts to faith, James writes, "The trouble about your robust and full-bodied faiths, however, is, that they begin to cut each other's throats too soon, and for getting on in the world and establishing a *modus vivendi* these pestilential refinements and reasonablenesses and moderations have to creep in" (Perry 1935, 2:237).

15. Even after the publication of the *Varieties*, however, James combated readings of "The Will to Believe" that did not heed his warning at the end of the essay. In 1904, James gently reproached L. T. Hobhouse for misreading "The Will to Believe. "My essay hedged the license to indulge in private over-beliefs with so many restrictions and signboards of danger that the outlet was narrow enough" (Perry 1935, 2:245).

16. James exemplifies the characteristically pragmatist emphasis on the continuity between "experience" (taken in a broad sense) and science.

17. Getting James's philosophy of religion right has important implications not only for our overall understanding of James but also for our histories of pragmatism. Cheryl Misak (2013), for instance, faults James for embracing a subjectivism that entails that there is no truth. This deplorable feature of James's view established a precedent, she claims, for some later pragmatist figures (e.g., Dewey and Rorty), who, together with James, made pragmatism disreputable. Misak's treatment of James largely rests on her interpretation of James's philosophy of religion, in which she espouses something like Dickinson Miller's reading of "The Will to Believe" and a version of the "natural reading" of *Varieties*. Properly understood, James's philosophy of religion provides evidence for a conclusion about James's thought that is contrary to the one

she draws. In fact, James's philosophy of religion underscores his insistence on objectivity and truth. I do not mean to suggest, however, that James's views on truth cannot be improved upon. See the introduction to the present volume.

18.　See Bagger (2011).

## WORKS CITED

Bagger, Matthew. 2011. "Dewey's Bulldog: Sidney Hook, Pragmatism, and Naturalism." *Journal of the American Academy of Religion* 79:562–86.

Brandom, Robert. 2011. *Perspectives on Pragmatism*. Cambridge, MA: Harvard University Press.

Brightman, Edgar. 1937. "An Empirical Approach to God." *Philosophical Review* 46:147–69.

Hollinger, David. 2004. "'Damned for God's Glory': William James and the Scientific Vindication of Protestant Culture." In *William James and a Science of Religion*, edited by Wayne Proudfoot, 9–30. New York: Columbia University Press.

Hook, Sidney. 1961. "Naturalism and First Principles." In *The Quest for Being*, 172–95. New York: Macmillan.

James, William. 1956a. "The Moral Philosopher and the Moral Life." In *The Will to Believe, Human Immortality*, 184–215. New York: Dover.

James, William. 1956b. "The Sentiment of Rationality." In *The Will to Believe, Human Immortality*, 63–110. New York: Dover.

James, William. 1956c. "The Will to Believe." In *The Will to Believe, Human Immortality*, 1–31. New York: Dover.

James, William. 1956d. *The Will to Believe, Human Immortality*. New York: Dover.

James, William. 1961. *The Varieties of Religious Experience*. New York: Collier.

James, William. 1993. *The Selected Letters of William James*, edited by Elizabeth Hardwick. New York: Anchor.

Kitcher, Philip. 2004. "A Pragmatist's Progress: The Varieties of James's Strategies for Defending Religion." In *William James and a Science of Religion*, edited by Wayne Proudfoot, 98–138. New York: Columbia University Press.

Miller, Dickinson. 1899. "'The Will to Believe' and the Duty to Doubt." *International Journal of Ethics* 9:169–95.

Misak, Cheryl. 2013. *The American Pragmatists*. Oxford: Oxford University Press.

Perry, Ralph Barton. 1935. *The Thought and Character of William James*. 2 vols. Boston: Little, Brown.

Proudfoot, Wayne. 2002. "Religious Belief and Naturalism." In *Radical Interpretation in Religion*, edited by Nancy K. Frankenberry, 78–92. Cambridge: Cambridge University Press.

Rorty, Richard. 1997. "Religious Faith, Intellectual Responsibility, and Romance." In *The Cambridge Companion to William James*, edited by Ruth Anna Putnam, 84–102. Cambridge: Cambridge University Press.

Rorty, Richard. 2004. "Some Inconsistencies in James's *Varieties*." In *William James and a Science of Religion*, edited by Wayne Proudfoot, 86–97. New York: Columbia University Press.

Santayana, George. 1921. *Character and Opinion in the United States: With Reminiscences of William James and Josiah Royce and Academic Life in America*. New York: Scribner's.

# 3

# Deweyan Naturalism

PHILIP KITCHER

I

The contemporary philosophical world is full of self-described naturalists, and there is probably some minimal cluster of theses on which all of us who claim this badge agree.[1] Nevertheless, as articles and books discussing naturalism typically note (or complain), in the house of naturalism there are many mansions. John Dewey, America's premier philosopher, was among the first to choose the title. My aim in what follows is to elaborate his style of naturalism so as to expose its attractions.

Because Dewey's writings range so widely, a full articulation of his naturalism that examines its development throughout his career and its influence on his treatment of all the topics he addressed lies beyond the scope of any moderately-sized essay—and beyond my own current expertise. Instead, I shall try to reconstruct the position that emerges in three significant later works. Two of these, *Experience and Nature* (*EN*) and *The Quest for Certainty* (*QC*) offer general accounts of his conception of philosophy and its proper role. The third, *A Common Faith* (*CF*), pits his naturalistic approach against a contrasting alternative, in the domain—religion—where a deviation from naturalism has been most evident historically.[2] Although I take the naturalistic approach I reconstruct to capture important aspects of these works, I shall not attempt to refute all rival interpretations of them, nor shall I consider how other parts of Dewey's corpus might favor a different reconstruction. Modesty seems appropriate; hence my title "*Deweyan* Naturalism" rather than "*Dewey's* Naturalism."

Part of the minimal cluster of theses associated with naturalism is a claim that the natural sciences are great accomplishments and unusually worthy of respect. Yet a positive attitude toward the sciences is hardly enough to distinguish a thinker as naturalistically inclined. Many of those whose approaches Dewey saw as insufficiently naturalistic not only expressed their enthusiasm for major scientific developments but also contributed to them (René Descartes and Gottfried Leibniz are notable examples). Some contemporary naturalists advocate a far more ambitious thesis. Natural science is viewed as *superseding* philosophy. Naturalists of this stripe sometimes contend that the achievements of particular areas of science—physics, neuroscience, and evolutionary psychology are prominent candidates—provide the means to answer, or to dismiss, questions with which philosophers have struggled for millennia.[3]

Many philosophical naturalists prefer a more modest approach. They suppose that the contemporary development of the natural sciences provides the means to address *some* but not all traditional philosophical questions, and they foresee future elaborations of natural science as gradually mopping up the rest. Often, the naturalist will restrict attention to a particular domain—the philosophy of mind, say—arguing that once-popular conceptions of the mind must be abandoned, given contemporary research in psychology and neuroscience, and that with their departure many of the conundrums that have occupied philosophers also vanish.[4] It seems to me undeniable that natural scientific developments sometimes undermine philosophical theses and remove issues from the philosophical agenda—that happened, for example, with respect to philosophical speculations about the nature of life and living things in the wake of discoveries in biology from the late nineteenth century to the present (particularly the molecular revolution of past decades). If this example is not salient for contemporary philosophers, that is largely because of a tendency to draw the boundaries between the philosophy and the science (or the "natural philosophy") of previous centuries in such a way that the earlier speculations are taken to be part of science, so that the replacement is seen as an instance of scientific change rather than the reformation of philosophy through scientific progress.[5]

Philosophers who decry the naturalistic tendencies of some of their colleagues typically concede that the natural sciences can make philosophical theories obsolete and reframe long-standing questions, and that they have sometimes done so. What they question is the confidence that, in time, all will be resolved and philosophy will disappear in the triumphant march of natural science. In this debate, there are firm believers, firm deniers, and agnostics. Deniers argue that certain limits on the power of scientific explanation can be identified in advance: we can recognize that *however* our understanding of the brain increases, it will never be possible to answer certain questions about consciousness (to cite a perennially popular example).[6]

In my view, the ambitious claim that future science will either answer all philosophical questions or enable us to overcome them is an optimistic conjecture, perhaps even an article of faith. But the skepticism of the deniers who claim to know in advance that particular issues must permanently resist scientific resolution embodies a limited understanding of the history of science, one that fails to appreciate the variety of ways in which philosophical perspectives and questions have been gradually displaced and that consequently insists on artificially limited forms of resolution.[7] To revert to my earlier example, we now treat as misguided formerly popular conceptions of the living world, and the questions that flowed from them, not because we have any ability to give a full physicochemical specification of the concept of a living thing but because we have learned to treat many of the functions of organisms within the framework of physicochemical theory.[8]

The versions of naturalism I have been reviewing might be dubbed *content naturalism*, in that they turn to the content of various areas of natural science in search of insights for the reform of philosophy. Dewey's naturalism is not of this type. Dewey is a *method naturalist*,[9] and his guiding idea in campaigning for a naturalistic renewal of philosophy looks to the ways of proceeding that he identifies as crucial to the success of the natural sciences.

II

Dewey begins *Experience and Nature* by suggesting that his "philosophy" might be given any one of three labels, all of which contain either *naturalism* or *naturalistic* (Dewey 1981, 10). His opening chapter is, as its title promises, devoted to the concept of experience and the identification of proper philosophical method. From the beginning, the inadequate methods of the philosophies Dewey intends to reform are contrasted with the procedures of the successful natural sciences. He offers a concise account of what distinguishes those procedures:

> He [the scientific investigator] uses reason and calculation freely; he could not get along without them. But he sees to it that ventures of this theoretical sort start from and terminate in directly experienced subject-matter. Theory may intervene in a long course of reasoning, many portions of which are remote from what is directly experienced. But the vine of pendant theory is attached at both

ends to the pillars of observed subject-matter. And this experienced material is
the same for the scientific man and the man in the street.

(Dewey 1981, 11)

It's very easy to read this passage as an informal characterization of something
many twentieth-century thinkers saw as central to scientific inquiry, the
hypothetico-deductive method, discussed in more detail by later logical empiricist philosophers like Rudolf Carnap, Hans Reichenbach, and Carl Hempel. I
maintain that this assimilation should be resisted, but, for the moment, it's worth
seeing how scientific investigations contrast with the practices of philosophers.

"The charge that is brought against the non-empirical method of philosophizing
is not that it depends upon theorizing, but that it fails to use refined, secondary
products as a path pointing and leading back to something in primary experience.
The resulting failure is three-fold" (Dewey 1981, 16–17). Dewey immediately goes
on to list the three failures: philosophers fail to "test and check," their proposals do
not enlarge and enrich the "meaning" of the things of ordinary experience, and the
refined subject matter they posit becomes disconnected, and consequently "arbitrary, aloof"—or, as Dewey charges elsewhere "isolated from life."[10]

If you concentrate on the first of these failures and ignore the second two, it's
easy to combine Dewey's diagnosis with the thought that he takes the proper practice of science to be a simple and straightforward application of the hypothetico-
deductive method to yield an equally simple and straightforward reading of his
proposal for reforming philosophy. Science works by scientists' dreaming up con-
jectural answers to questions prompted by their observations, and subsequently
testing and confirming their conjectures by using them to predict consequences
that can be observed. Philosophy should do the same. There's a common language
spoken by scientists and by ordinary people (recall the kinship of the "scientific
man" and the "man in the street"), a language that can be employed to characterize what is observed—call it the *observation language*. Scientific hypotheses are
well supported because they have consequences, statements in the observation language, that can be checked directly in experience and found to be correct. If
philosophical theses were developed to yield similar observational consequences,
they, too, would be susceptible to confirmation and philosophy could become a
form of rigorous inquiry.

This is so easy a reading of Dewey that it's hardly surprising that many of his
interpreters presuppose it, without argument or even statement. Yet it's worth
probing the assumption that Dewey is subscribing to an informal version of logical empiricism. If asked, what account of the observation language would he

provide? Apparently not the phenomenalist version, popular in the early stages of the logical positivist/empiricist project; one of the major concerns of *EN* chapter 1 is to restore the connection between experience and nature. Dewey (1981) is often forthright: "We primarily observe things, not observations" (21); experience is distorted by treating mental states as what "is primarily *given*" (24, emphasis Dewey's).[11] It seems, then, that we should interpret Dewey as supposing a "thing language," in which both scientists and ordinary folk can report their observations. In practice, the hypotheses of the sciences are tested by verifying consequences formulated in this language—and, in principle, philosophers could emulate this good example.

The connection between Dewey's program and later trends in logical empiricism can be elaborated further by fastening on his talk of "the instrumental nature of the objects of scientific knowing" and his claim that the role of physical science is to fathom connections that can be used to determine outcomes (Dewey 1981, 6). It's very natural to assimilate such remarks to the instrumentalism much discussed in philosophy of science in the 1950s. Apparently, Dewey sees the "thing language" as a privileged vocabulary, in which we can characterize objects of knowledge, and takes those parts of theoretical science that appear to talk of unobservable entities and processes as convenient devices for organizing the everyday world to which the scientist and the man in the street have access in observation. What he would then demand of the theoretical language of philosophy is that its apparent invocation of unfamiliar entities should be equally fruitful in predicting observational consequences—and that philosophical posits, like those admitted in theoretical science, should not be viewed as part of the deep structure of nature.

So understood, Dewey's program for philosophy faces an obvious rejoinder, and it's no surprise that it has been frequently dismissed for its misunderstanding of the character of philosophy. Philosophy, it is often claimed, is simply not in the business of providing theses that might be tested by observation of the world. Metaphysics isn't a special sort of physics; ethics isn't a descriptive account of human decisions and actions. To think that issues about the existence of universals could be settled by verifying observational consequences, or that principles of ethics could be tested in experiments, betrays a deep confusion about the philosophical project. Hence, for many philosophers, it hardly matters that Dewey's naturalism starts with method rather than content. In the end, he wants to do what other, more candid naturalists aim to achieve—to replace philosophy with empirical science.

In my view, Dewey is guilty of no such confusions. They are artifacts of inadequate ways of reading him. Widespread though it is, straightforward though it appears, the strategy of reading him as an instrumentalist avant la lettre is a woefully inadequate approach to his writings. The idea of a privileged observation language, whether of sense data or of physical objects and properties, is at odds with fundamental features of his philosophical perspective; perhaps because of his Hegelian background, he reaches forward to the critiques of logical empiricism offered by Wilfrid Sellars (1963) and Thomas Kuhn (1962). The straightforward instrumentalism is complicated by his claims that the sciences reach into nature's depths, by his willingness to see geology as acquainting us with objects from the remote past that we are not capable of observing directly, and by the casual remark that characteristics often dismissed as subjective are as real as "sun or electron" (Dewey 1981, 11–12, 14).

More significantly, the remarks about the need for method, in the social and human sciences as well as in philosophy, suggest that what is needed is not something that lies ready to hand, something bequeathed to us by the pioneering physicists of the seventeenth century and their successors, but something *analogous*. In his insightful essay on Charles Darwin, Dewey (1977, 7) had already claimed that proper method in pursuing human questions depended on an extension of the method of the physical sciences to cope with the phenomena of life: "But prior to Darwin the impact of the new scientific method upon life, mind, and politics had been arrested, because between these ideal or moral interests and the inorganic world intervened the kingdom of plants and animals." The thought is articulated in his later works, where Dewey (1984, 200) warns against misinterpretations of his views that suppose him to be claiming that "science is the only valid kind of knowledge." Creative work is required, if the methods of the sciences are to be extended to the human domain and to philosophy.

Yet the principal reasons for abandoning the simple reading of *EN* chapter 1 lie in that chapter itself, first in Dewey's recognition of three failures of traditional philosophizing and second in his lengthy discussions of the concept of experience. I'll take these as clues to a better understanding of his claims about philosophical method and to a more distinctive style of philosophical naturalism.

III

Philosophers go astray, Dewey (1981, 17) tells us, not only because they fail to "test and check" but also because their reasonings do not lead to "enlargement and enrichment of meaning" in the things of ordinary experience. The counterpart of this defect (Dewey's third form of failure) is the creation of an unreal world of pseudo-objects, "abstract" and "aloof," which, to the extent that it might be taken seriously, would detract from meaningful experience. Part of his self-appointed task is to defend the meaningfulness of ordinary experience against philosophical distortions and dilutions, but beyond this he seeks a mode of healthier philosophizing that will provide the same kind of enlargement and enrichment that the natural sciences have achieved for our experience of physical (and, more recently, organic) nature.

Because it isn't easy to identify exactly what Dewey has in mind when he discusses the enrichment of meaning in experience or, despite the many sentences he devotes to attempts to explain, just what his concept of experience is, there's an obvious appeal in the strategy of dismissing these murky passages, of concentrating on the first form of failure, and of settling for the straightforward reading of Dewey as a scientific instrumentalist who wants philosophy to be a branch of science, instrumentally conceived. That interpretation allows the (impatient?) reader to skip most of the pages in chapter 1 of *EN*. But patience is a virtue, and I recommend going more slowly.

Dewey recognizes very clearly that the notion of experience can be characterized in many different ways, and (as already noted) one of his major targets is the approach that identifies experiences as subjective states of cognitive subjects. Citing William James, he draws attention to two aspects of experience: the states of the world (typically the world beyond the subject) that are experienced and the way in which those states are registered in the experience (Dewey 1981, 18). From the beginning of the book, he locates experience by starting with sentient organisms and their responses to their environments. As the account of *EN* chapter 7 eventually makes fully explicit, Dewey borrows the biological notion of animals embedded in environments and introduces distinctions as they are fruitful for understanding animal activity in general, the processes of conscious activity in particular, and the very specific functions that occur in our own species. The categories of traditional philosophy are to be replaced or supported by an inquiry into what divisions are most helpful for the human purposes of understanding animal behavior and achieving the richest sense of our own lives and their possibilities.

To recognize what Dewey is about in his probing of the notion of experience, we do best to start with a theme from James. In *The Principles of Psychology*, James advances the thesis that the structured world in which we live, the world of objects divided into kinds and of processes taken to follow natural courses, is constructed out of something independent of all cognitive subjects—the world in a bare, relatively unstructured, sense. The structure introduced reflects the sensory and cognitive characteristics and capacities of the organism; the world of the bat is different from the world of the human being. In the human case, it also embodies the culturally and socially evolving interests and concerns of particular groups. Thus, we may correctly say that the worlds of different cultures are distinct and that people belonging to the same cultural tradition may inhabit distinct worlds at different stages of their history.

James (1981, 277) offers a vivid (but in some ways misleading) analogy: "The mind, in short, works on the data it receives very much as a sculptor works on his block of stone. In a sense the statue stood there from eternity. But there were a thousand different ones beside it, and the sculptor is alone to thank for having extricated this one from the rest."[12] If we suppose Dewey to be developing James's thesis that the world of experience is partially constructed by human faculties and human interests, we can make sense of his discussion of experience and of his claims about proper philosophical method.

We inherit a world of experience structured by the generations who have preceded us. All too often, those structures are simply accepted as "natural," as inevitable constituents of the world we experience. Yet it is possible to reflect on them, to stand back and inquire whether they continue to answer to present purposes and interests. One important aspect of the sciences consists in their revisions and restructurings—people come to recognize Earth as one among many planets, to see swinging stones as pendulums, to read the strata in a rock face as records of previous geological and biological events. A primary task of philosophy is to probe our inherited categories more systematically, attending especially to those that might seem to be most deeply embedded in our structuring of the world.

Dewey (1981, 40) offers a diagnosis of the pre-philosophical predicament: "There is a special service which the study of philosophy may render. Empirically pursued it will not be a study of philosophy but a study, by means of philosophy, of life-experience. But this experience is already overlaid and saturated with the products of the reflection of past generations and by-gone ages. It is filled with interpretations, classifications, due to sophisticated thought, which have become incorporated into what seems to be fresh, naïve empirical material." Simple enculturation presents a world of experience in which the residual structures of the past are taken for granted, whether or not they continue to promote the goals of those who live in that world. When the construction of the world figures as a source of constraint and limitation, people need to take up the enterprise of reconstruction—in search of "enlargement and enrichment of meaning."

At this point, we can begin to understand how the practices of the natural sciences serve as a model for philosophy. For scientists not only formulate new hypotheses and test them against the results of experiment and observation. They also refine and replace the categories they have inherited from the past. Although this sometimes results in redrawing the boundaries of objects or of modifying the standards for the normal course of processes, it is most evident in the grouping of things, states, and events into kinds: living things come to be ranked together on the basis of common descent, respiration is recognized as akin to combustion, social arrangements are related to game-theoretic equilibriums. From an ambitious realist perspective, the resultant taxonomies might be viewed as reflecting a prior and independent structure in the world, as if the scientists concerned had come to speak "nature's own language," but that is neither Dewey's perspective nor my own.[13] Dewey envisages scientific inquiry as aimed at the contingent purposes of a particular species of animal (with a particular stock of psychological and biological capacities), attempting to introduce order into parts of the environment, so that the phenomena pertinent to the goals envisaged can be understood, predicted, and controlled and so that the classifications properly introduced are those that facilitate the attainment of this ordering. I'll summarize this view by taking science to be directed toward producing *spheres of order*, well-organized parts of the world of experience that answer both to nature (how it will admit of organization) and to evolving human purposes.[14]

As my last formulation suggests, Dewey's approach is partly realist, partly constructivist. The world of experience is a construct, but the work of construction is constrained by something outside ourselves—we are by no means free to postulate entities as we fancy. One way to present the point is to distinguish two senses of *world*. In the bare sense, the world is everything independent of the thinking subject; it is that to which subjects of experience respond. So conceived, the world is relatively unstructured. There is no privileged division of it into objects with well-demarcated boundaries, no privileged groupings of objects into natural kinds, no privileged standards for the normal course of processes. All that is our work. We select certain parts of the world (in the bare sense) to count as objects, we group them into kinds to facilitate the building of spheres of order, and we set the standards for the normal course of processes (as, for example, when we come to view swinging stones as imperfect pendulums). So we produce the world of experience, a world containing living things and physical objects, parts of which we can enumerate and measure. To say that the world is finite (for example) can only be to make a claim about this constructed world, the world of experience.[15]

Notice that the discussion in the previous paragraph depends on making a particular categorical division, in separating a thinking subject from the independent material to which that subject responds. Language must deploy categories, and so, even when you try to gesture toward the independence of the world (bare sense), some minimal construction is presupposed. In principle, the categories used in formulating the picture, in distinguishing the two senses of *world*, might themselves be scrutinized and replaced by a different construction. They are simply part of a fallible, indeed recognizably inadequate, means for presenting the background picture against which the Deweyan idea of construction proceeds.[16]

At this point, we can return to the critique of traditional philosophy offered in *EN* chapter 1. Science, as we have seen, responds to the need for creating or extending spheres of order by developing new categories, reconstructing the world of experience so that the needed organization is produced—and its novel hypotheses and "thought objects" are validated by revealing just how they are effective in yielding that organization. The social and human sciences would ideally emulate this pattern by developing methods for generating similar results. So, too, for philosophy. Dewey sees philosophy as focusing on pervasive categories and reacting to points at which the categorical organization inherited from previous generations no longer serves important human purposes. Traditionally, philosophers have been moved to respond to some problems that call out for reconstruction, and have built new systems inspired by the difficulties they have perceived, but they have not returned to life experience and embedded their proposed categories in analogues of the scientific spheres of order. In consequence, they have failed to deliver the enlarged and enriched meaning that is the whole point of reconstruction and have offered, instead, abstract systems that float free of life experience, offering brilliant scholars opportunities for speculative play—but nothing more.

If you read Dewey in this way, it becomes abundantly clear why he writes the kinds of books he does. The central philosophical work lies in reforming human thought—and consequently human practices, human material products, and human institutions—in regions of the inherited world of experience where the traditional categories are no longer adequate, so that new and liberating ways of going forward in those regions are achieved. *Art as Experience* seeks to reorganize thought and practice with respect to the arts, so that art will no longer be divorced from most of human life; *The Public and Its Problems* aims to reorganize political thinking and political practice so that citizens of complex democratic societies will lead lives that are richer and freer; *Democracy and Education* reorganizes thought about education so that future educational practice will allow for richer and more meaningful lives; and, as we shall see in the next section, *A Common Faith* reacts to the breakdown of literalist religions with a new set of categories for continuing the liberatory and enriching functions that religion has traditionally served. In all these instances, Dewey is doing highly specific work, reacting to problems he diagnoses in the lives of people in his own times. He is proposing to reconstruct the world of experience in ways that we may test—first by imagining what it would be like to live under the new forms of organization he recommends, and then by engaging in social experiments to try them on for size.

*EN* and *QC* supply the general framework and the tools for the particular projects and activities that constitute, in Dewey's view, the primary work of the philosopher. By interpreting them as I have suggested, we can understand the connection among the various, apparently disconnected characterizations of philosophy scattered through his major later works. Thinking of philosophy as "the general theory of education" or as "seeking to clarify men's ideas as to the social and moral strifes of their own day" or as "criticism in its generality" or as "a liaison officer between the conclusions of science and the modes of social and personal action through which attainable possibilities are projected and striven for"—all of these are ways of focusing on different facets of the process of reconstruction I've seen as central to Dewey's thought and to his practice.[17] To pursue the general theory of education is to ask for categories that are apt for unfolding human lives so that they will develop as richly as is possible; to clarify ideas about social and moral strifes is to seek ways of organizing thought that will resolve the conflicts that limit human lives; criticism in its full generality scrutinizes the most prevalent conceptions and methods that frame our lives; and the "liaison officer" attempts to build on our best available picture of the world to enlarge the opportunities for living.

I'll close my account of Deweyan reconstruction by looking briefly at a puzzle that emerged briefly in considering the interpretation of him as a scientific instrumentalist. As I noted, Dewey is often quite happy to suppose that scientific inquiry extends our reach, connecting us with parts of nature inaccessible to ordinary observation, and he sometimes writes in an unabashedly realist vein about particular scientific posits: "It is as much a part of the real being of atoms that they give rise in time, under increasing complications of relationships, to qualities of blue and sweet, pain and beauty, as that they have at a cross-section of time extension, mass, or weight" (Dewey 1981, 91). On the other hand, there are many passages suggesting that scientific theorizing should be viewed as providing tools for organizing and connecting events and states we detect with our unaided senses. Although I have pointed toward the "realist passages" as challenges for the instrumentalist reading, it would be perfectly legitimate to demand that my own account should make sense of the emphasis on viewing theorizing in terms of the provision of tools (Dewey 1984, 152–53, represents one among many such discussions).

Our knowledge of the things of experience is always incomplete; we identify particular aspects of them and can sometimes use those identifications to advance our ends. If I come to know enough about the various kinds of mushrooms that grow in the local woods, I can engage in profitable gathering without risk of injuring those for whom I cook. Relying on the inquiries of others, I create a sphere of order that helps me achieve some of my ends. Nevertheless, the mycological insights guiding my successful expeditions would fall far short of exhausting all that is known about these fungi, and even the sum total of human knowledge in this area is inevitably extraordinarily selective. Nobody would be tempted to equate the mushrooms with schematic entities that have all and only the properties I could ascribe to them.

With respect to the posits of scientific theory, however, that temptation can easily arise. The scientist hypothesizes an abstract atom or an abstract electron, conceived as having all and only the properties in a specified set, and, on this basis, is able to organize particular phenomena (e.g., chemical reactions or radioactive decay). Conceived as model, the posit is a useful tool. When the success of the positing becomes sufficiently pronounced, scientists often regard themselves as having discovered a new constituent of reality, and, in his realist moments, Dewey is happy to follow them in this.[18] What disturbs him is the supposition that these constituents have *exactly the properties ascribed to them in the scientist's model and no more*. For that conjures up a world of allegedly "fundamental" constituents, one that displaces the qualities rightly ascribed to everyday things. *EN* and *QC* are intent on resisting the remaking of reality in the image of theoretical models, but that does not in any way preclude Dewey from supposing that macroscopic things are made up of microscopic constituents, constituents that *include* among their properties those ascribed in the abstract description. Those constituents also have the properties of giving rise, under the appropriate conditions, to the manifest qualities ("blue," "sweet," and so forth). Dewey (1984, 191) can, quite consistently, assert that the macroscopic table is "the only table"—denying the existence of something made up of the abstract posits of the model—while affirming that that sole real table is made up of tiny constituents, whose interactions generate its familiar properties and which have among their properties the qualities the model ascribes to them.

The error that gives rise to Arthur Eddington's supposed problem of the two tables is a *philosophical* mistake (although it is one of which scientists may be guilty). It is already diagnosed in Dewey's third failure of standard philosophizing, in which reflection, "aloof" from experience, generates a "realm of its own"—and becomes lost in it (Dewey 1981, 17).

## IV

The "method naturalism" I have outlined can be seen at work in Dewey's Terry Lectures, where he proposes to reform our usage of such concepts as *religion* and *God*. Dewey begins by describing the controversy about religion as it played itself out in the early 1930s in the United States. He characterizes the debate as involving two principal factions, one of which takes religion to be indissolubly linked to beliefs in something supernatural and another which sees the "advance of culture and science" as completely discrediting the supernatural (Dewey 1986, 3).[19] At the beginning of the second lecture, he implicitly offers a verdict on this opposition, referring to a "crisis in religion" (Dewey 1986, 21). After arguing that science is to be conceived in terms of its method, he draws the conclusion explicitly: "Scientific method is not only adverse to dogma but to doctrine as well" (27).

So far, it appears that Dewey is drawing the same conclusions about religion as those trumpeted by many naturalistic thinkers from his time to ours. The distinctive move in his naturalism, however, consists in his "study, by means of philosophy, of life-experience" (Dewey 1981, 40). The starting point for that study is the type of experience to which friends of religion appeal in attempting to defend their beliefs about the supernatural. He tells us that "there is much talk, especially in liberal circles, of religious experience as vouching for the authenticity of certain beliefs" (Dewey 1986, 9). Because of his understanding of the varieties of religious doctrine and of the ways that people who accept (or who know about) particular doctrines characterize very similar parts of their life experience, using the categories of those familiar religions, Dewey is rightly skeptical about the "vouching." He sees the hypotheses about particular supernatural causes, or, indeed, *any* supernatural cause, of the doctrines heralded as religious as being a gratuitous addition to the phenomena. These are, one and all, speculations about *different* supernatural features of the world, and none of them is in any way privileged over the others. To recognize that fact is not to abandon the notion of the "religious elements of experience" (9). But some reconceptualization is in order.

We err, Dewey thinks, in treating religious experience as if it were a category of experience akin to aesthetic or scientific or political experience (9). We should conceive the religious quality in experience as something that can attach to any of these types of experience. He recommends that we focus on this religious quality, wherever it is to be found, and that we do so not because experiences with this quality point us toward some important cause but because of the effects they have within human lives.[20] When the religious quality is present, the result is "an adjustment in life, an orientation, that brings with it a sense of security and peace"

(Dewey 1986, 10). Instead of worrying about, or squabbling about, which experiences are "genuine" in the sense of properly pointing to the supernatural as it really is, we ought to concentrate on the class of experiences that can yield this important effect. Dewey equates religious experience with the production of that effect: "The actual religious quality in the experience described is the *effect* produced, the better adjustment in life and its conditions, not the manner and cause of its production. . . . If the reorientation actually occurs, it, and the sense of security and stability accompanying it, are forces on their own account" (11).

He goes on to offer a more detailed phenomenology of the transformation accomplished. The subject of experiences with a religious quality undergoes a psychological restructuring, one that may prove permanent.[21] The change consists in a "harmonization of the various elements of our being," one that brings a voluntary acceptance of the external conditions of our life (Dewey 1986, 12–13).[22] Through an analysis whose details are not easy to follow, Dewey then elaborates this harmonization of the self as an imaginative projection of an ideal, one that yields a unified self from the fragments of our being and that conceives the universe as an "imaginative totality" (Dewey 1986, 14).[23] The crucial feature of this (to my mind, shaky) connection is the introduction of the notion of an ideal, for this concept enables Dewey to see the product of the transformation as an orientation of conduct. Ideals have authority over what we do, and this makes room for faith—now conceived as the product of the transformation that has been wrought—as *moral* faith (Dewey 1986, 15). The joyful acceptance of self and universe, generated by the experience with religious quality, consists in a determination to make the world and the self as they *should be*. The subject becomes oriented toward what is valuable.

The analysis just presented prepares the ground for a crucial move in Dewey's second lecture. There he considers what sense, if any, can be retained for the most prominent term in American religion: What could we mean by *God*? Dewey (29) states, "On one score, the word can mean only a particular Being. On the other score, it denotes the unity of all ideal ends arousing us to desire and actions. Does the unification have a claim upon our attitude and conduct because it is already, apart from us, in realized existence, or because of its own inherent meaning and value?"

The structure of the argument developed in the previous pages, with the sustained undercutting of supernatural entities supposedly manifested in religious experience, as well as the epistemological opposition to timeless objects of knowledge, articulated throughout *EN* and *QC*, leave no doubt about what Dewey's answer must be. A few pages on, he provides us with his preferred definition:

This idea of God, or of the divine, is also connected with all the natural forces and conditions—including man and human association—that promote the growth of the ideal and further its realization. We are in the presence neither of ideals completely embodied in existence nor yet of ideals that are mere rootless ideals, fantasies, utopias. For there are forces in nature and society that generate and support the ideals. They are further unified by the activity that gives them coherence and solidity. It is this *active* relation between ideal and actual to which I would give the name "God."

(34)

Plainly, by replacing talk of "religion" with references to the transformation wrought by the religious quality in experience, by seeing this as potentially available in a wide range of contexts and effected without any belief in some supernatural aspect of reality, by identifying the transformative effect with a projected unification of the self and a corresponding unification of the world, by interpreting the projected unification in terms of an orientation toward conditions recognized as valuable but as not yet realized, Dewey has prepared the way for substitutes both for the concept of faith and for the idea of God, apparently scheduled for elimination once the thought of anything supernatural has been abandoned. Faith is now viewed in terms of commitment to realizing what is valuable—possibly including the hope that such realization is possible. The active work that flows from that commitment becomes the replacement for the traditional conception of the deity.[24]

The principal goal of the third (and final) lecture is to reconceive the religious community as a locus and a vehicle for the active pursuit of ideals. The ideals Dewey has clearly in mind are centered on human well-being.[25] Although he recognizes the human good that traditional religions have often done, he supposes that liberation from the false devotion to the supernatural will make the projects undertaken by communities moved by "the religious element in experience" even more wide ranging and powerful. His objection to the emphasis on conventional doctrines is not merely the expression of ontological parsimony or of epistemological rigor; he thinks the supernatural blocks important endeavors: "The objection to supernaturalism is that it stands in the way of an effective realization of the sweep and depth of the implications of natural human relations. It stands in the way of using the means that are in our power to make radical changes in these relations" (Dewey 1986, 53).

From this perspective, there is no need to eliminate some of the social institutions that have been central to religious life. Dewey speaks of "churches," but his remarks apply equally to mosques, synagogues, temples, or any other place at which people come together, bound by faith and directed toward joint attempts to realize shared goals. Once you have made the transformations he commends, once supernaturalist doctrine gives way to the new conceptualizations he has proposed, the activities of religious communities are liberated. "The fund of human values that are prized and that need to be cherished, values that are satisfied and rectified by *all* human concerns and arrangements, could be celebrated and reinforced, in different ways and with differing symbols, by the churches. In that way, the churches would indeed become catholic" (54–55, emphasis in original). That is to say, the churches would become focused on the most prevalent human problems—such as war and economic injustice.

*CF* closes with one of Dewey's most eloquent passages (unlike James, he is hardly notable for the stylistic elegance of his prose), a passage in which Dewey connects his entire line of argument to the thoughts about enrichment of life expressed in *EN*'s account of well-conducted philosophy: "The things in civilization we most prize are not of ourselves. They exist by grace of the doings and sufferings of the continuous human community in which we are a link. Ours is the responsibility of conserving, transmitting, rectifying, and expanding the heritage of values we have received, that those who come after us may receive it more solid and secure, more widely accessible and more generously shared than we have received it" (57–58). The philosophical analysis of life experience thus leads to a conceptual transformation that, if it were implemented in the reform of individual attitudes and social institutions, would provide "enrichment and enlargement of meaning," in the concrete sense that human lives would contain a greater variety of valuable aspects and that more of them could be expected to share in this increase of values.

All I have attempted to do here is to provide an analysis of what I take to be the central line of thought in *A Common Faith*. It would be possible—and worthwhile—to look more closely at some of the concepts Dewey employs and some of the transitions in which they figure (such as, for example, the notion of unification and its elaboration in terms of ideals). Even more, it would be worth considering ways in which Dewey's proposals might be implemented in small-scale "experiments of living" (to use Mill's famous phrase), contemporary analogues of Robert Owen's New Lanark community, in which the framework Dewey constructs would be tried on and assessed.[26]

These are projects I hope to pursue elsewhere. My aim in this chapter, however, is to illustrate a Deweyan version of naturalism by seeing its conception of philosophy as exemplified in *CF*. Dewey starts, as *EN* recommends, from life experience, specifically from those experiences that religious people often take to validate their doctrines. He then embarks on a chain of reasoning intended to free our existing modes of categorizing this area of experience from dubious presuppositions. New ways of figuring the notion of "religious experience" are proposed, and the novel concepts are articulated and connected to other concepts—unification, ideals, faith, God—that form a new framework for thinking about what we are and what we do. Finally, Dewey points the way to implementing that framework, in our individual attitudes and in our social organization. The concepts and theses of *CF* can be led back to experience (as Dewey 1981, 17, demands that they should be). They are not simply a new field for detached philosophical speculation—a recreational facility in which philosophers can play—but a blueprint for change. Dewey thinks that, if we make that change, values will become "more solid and secure, more widely accessible and more generously shared" (Dewey 1986, 58). His naturalism accords with the fundamental idea of pragmatism—it is intended to make a difference.

If a particular society, or the entire human population, were to follow Dewey's proposal, the world—the world of experience—would change. That is not because a character who once existed, the supernatural deity, would have vanished from the scene. Our powers of world making do not extend that far. In the traditional sense of the term, God never existed. Dewey began from the powerful arguments that exposed the falsehood of all the substantive doctrines of all the world's religions. Rather, the reconstruction of the world consists in the reconceptualizations Dewey provides, in the new accounts of the religious aspects of experience, of faith, and of God. As those new concepts are embedded in our thinking, and as they guide us in remaking the physical environment and the social world, becoming instantiated in new places and artifacts, new social groups, new customs, and new forms of social interaction, the world of daily experience becomes very different. According to Dewey, this brave new world would be a better place, one deserving celebration for the rich lives of the people in it. Perhaps it would be worth experimenting to find out if he was right.

Surely the most prominent versions of naturalism on the contemporary philosophical scene are forms of the content naturalism with which I began. Initially, attempts to articulate method naturalism appear to lead back to content naturalism after a dispensable detour. I hope to have shown that some of Dewey's writings suggest a different naturalistic approach, an alternative species of method naturalism, one concordant with his frequent emphasis on reconnecting philosophy with life. I also hope to have shown that this rival species of naturalism might be worth taking seriously.

NOTES

1.  I'm delighted to dedicate this essay to Wayne Proudfoot, in gratitude both for his friendship and for all that I have learned from him. Matthew Bagger and Nancy Frankenberry offered me insightful comments on an earlier draft, and I am very grateful to both of them.

2.  I refer to *Experience and Nature* as *EN*, *The Quest for Certainty* as *QC*, and *A Common Faith* as *CF*. Page references are to the splendid editions published by Southern Illinois University Press (Dewey 1981, 1984, 1986).

3.  Distinguished scientists sometimes formulate this judgment extremely clearly; Stephen Hawking and E. O. Wilson are obvious examples. A philosopher who presents and defends the thesis is Alexander Rosenberg (2011).

4.  See, for example, Churchland (1986).

5.  Many critics of philosophy respond to historical episodes in which philosophers have paved the way for later scientific advances by arguing that the insightful innovators were practicing science all along. A counterpoise is the tendency of some philosophers to offer a retrospective account in which the displacement of philosophical theories by developments within science is reconceived as a change internal to the sciences. Intellectual historians and historians of science rightly take both lines of response to be misguided and consider the projection of sharp categories from the present into the past to be methodologically naive.

6.  The most eloquent presentation of the limits of those sciences to which the most ambitious naturalists point is found in the writings of Thomas Nagel. See, for example, *Mind and Cosmos* (Nagel 2012).

7.  Charles Darwin (1871, 2) is less gentle than usual when he maintains that "it is those who know little, and not those who know much, who so confidently assert that this or that problem will never be solved by science."

8.  I have expanded on this point in a discussion of Nagel's arguments in *Mind and Cosmos*, in "Things Fall Apart," in the *New York Times* (Kitcher 2013).

9.  In his important book *Naturalism Without Mirrors*, Huw Price (2011) also distinguishes two types of naturalism: *object naturalism* and *subject naturalism*. My content naturalism embraces both Pricean forms of naturalism, since it looks to science as the source of information about both subjects and the cosmos with which they interact. Yet Price's subject naturalism might be seen as the key to articulating the method I ascribe to the Deweyan naturalist, so that, in an obvious sense, the naturalistic approaches we prefer would be akin. To sort out this kinship would require exploring our divergences with respect to representational states—and that would lead very far from the central issues of this chapter.

10. The list is given in *Experience and Nature* (Dewey 1981), 17. The accusation that (traditional) philosophy is cut off from life is articulated in *The Quest for Certainty* (Dewey 1984), 204.

11. As might be expected from someone who cut his philosophical teeth on G. W. F. Hegel, John Dewey is no great fan of the "given." In an uncharacteristically testy footnote, he distinguishes his own view from the subjectivism to which his critics have assimilated it (Dewey 1981, 24, note 3).

12. The analogy is potentially misleading in its ability to favor the idea of sense data as epistemologically fundamental.

13. I articulated a strong version of realism in *The Advancement of Science* (Kitcher 1993), but abandoned it in *Science, Truth, and Democracy* (Kitcher 2001) and (more thoroughly) in *Preludes to Pragmatism* (Kitcher 2012)—chapters 3, 4, and especially 5, of *Preludes* further articulate the approach I outline here. The phrase "nature's own language" is due to Richard Rorty (1982).

14. Dewey sees spheres of order as the objects of scientific knowledge, elaborating this conception in Dewey (1981, chap. 4) and in Dewey (1984, chap. 4, especially beginning at 69). As I understand him, he anticipates the concept of a "nomological machine," developed by Nancy Cartwright (1999).

15. The position outlined in this paragraph seems to me to be central to the pragmatist tradition, from the work of William James on. Its roots lie in *Principles of Psychology*, and it receives its Deweyan development in both *EN* and *QC*. It surfaces in the writings of later philosophers sympathetic to the pragmatist tradition, in Rorty's (1982) *Consequences of Pragmatism*, in Hilary Putnam's (1983) "Why There Isn't a Ready-Made World," and perhaps most obviously in Nelson Goodman's (1978) *Ways of Worldmaking*.

16. At this point, it is worth addressing a charge leveled against my account of Dewey's position in an illuminating recent article, "Dewey and the Question of Realism," by Peter Godfrey-Smith (2013). Godfrey-Smith points out that Dewey's preferred term is *reconstruction* rather than *construction* and concludes that Dewey must presuppose a prior structuring of the independent world (in the bare sense). But I think Godfrey-Smith misreads here. Dewey talks of reconstruction precisely because what is of most interest to him are the ways in which later generations respond to the constructive efforts of their predecessors. The picture is not of a reality-with-prior-structure that people reconstruct but of a reality-with-relatively-little-prior-structure that human beings have always been in the position of structuring and which we constantly reconstruct so as to answer our evolving needs. Godfrey-Smith is using *reconstruction* with the wrong contrast in mind.

17. The passages cited are from *Democracy and Education* (Dewey 1980), 338; *Reconstruction in Philosophy* (Dewey 1982), 94; *Experience and Nature* (Dewey 1981), 298; and *The Quest for Certainty* (Dewey 1984), 248.

18. Some of the most distinguished contemporary pragmatists would doubt whether Dewey has *any* "realist moments." Following Rorty, and emphasizing both Dewey's explicit concerns about "representationalism" (in a much-quoted letter of 1905), his 1909 "A Short Catechism Concerning Truth" (Dewey 1978), and the frequent characterizations of theories as instruments in his later works (in particular *EN*), both Huw Price (2011) and Robert Brandom (2011) hail Dewey as a foe of a correspondence account of truth. I suppose that, like James before him, Dewey is attempting to *understand* the correspondence of signs and things, not to *reject* the whole idea. See Kitcher (2012), chapter 5; and, for Dewey's echoing of James, Dewey (1978), 5–6. Price (2011) helpfully analyzes his own position with respect to Rorty and Brandom, seeing Rorty as occupying one end of a line, Brandom another end, and positioning himself between them. This conception views Brandom as more

sympathetic to the idea of representation than Price, and Price as more sympathetic than Rorty. We might extend the line by adding Godfrey-Smith and me: the trend to realist-representationalist involvement would then go Rorty, Price, Brandom, Kitcher, Godfrey-Smith. In future work, I hope to defend both the particular position I favor and the thesis that this position is Dewey's own considered place.

19. The situation Dewey describes is not so different from that obtaining today. In my own Terry Lectures, I follow him in regretting the simple opposition that dominates contemporary discussion (see Kitcher 2014). As I read him, Dewey and I also agree on categorically denying the existence of supernatural beings, and, as Nancy Frankenberry pointed out to me, we thus diverge sharply from the kinds of descriptions religious people would use in characterizing religion. Our dismissal may seem too blunt (or perhaps *my* dismissal and *my* reading of Dewey are too blunt?). An alternative approach would be to acknowledge that religion is focused on doctrines putatively referring to supernatural beings and to propose a different semantic treatment of those doctrines.

20. This plainly recapitulates the emphasis on the "fruits for life" that pervades James's *Varieties of Religious Experience*.

21. Dewey describes this psychological restructuring as "enduring" and as persisting through a variety of internal and external changes. This is, I think, a mistake. The change may be dissipated under the action of other causal conditions. The important thing is that, while it lasts, it is a large-scale restructuring of the self.

22. Dewey's characterization of the contrast between the voluntary acceptance he has in mind and the "mere Stoical resolution" seems to recapitulate James's contrast between joyful "acceptance of the universe" and stoicism in lecture 2 of *The Varieties of Religious Experience*.

23. As Matthew Bagger pointed out to me, the line of argument is easier to understand if Dewey is read against the background of James's *Varieties*. If we think of Dewey as endorsing the Jamesian thesis that religion unifies the self with the imaginative totality of the universe, we can view the transition in these pages as accomplished by replacing the thesis that the unification depends on psychological attitudes toward some supernatural being with the claim that it is accomplished by projecting ideals—a claim not so far from James's own frequent proposals that the religious believer identifies with the ultimate values. A detailed reconstruction of Dewey along these lines is something I hope to pursue elsewhere.

24. I should note that, immediately after the passage I have quoted, Dewey explicitly points out that he doesn't insist on retaining the old terminology. As I read *CF*, he is evidently sensitive to the charge that continuing to deploy parts of traditional religious language can easily foster confusion and allow for slippage back into the supernaturalist positions he intends to leave behind. See, for example, Dewey (1986), 34–35, and the earlier worry that his approach will seem "a timid halfway position" (4).

25. This is thoroughly in line with the account of ethics as growing "out of the very conditions of human life" (Dewey [and James Tufts] 1985, 308). In *The Ethical Project* (Kitcher 2011), I attempt to provide a detailed elaboration of the type of humanism I suppose Dewey to have had in mind.

26. We might see the development of Jewish Community Centers as a partial experiment along Deweyan lines. Mordecai Kaplan, who played a prominent role in the Jewish Community Center movement, was much influenced by Dewey.

## WORKS CITED

Brandom, Robert. 2011. *Perspectives on Pragmatism*. Cambridge, MA: Harvard University Press.

Cartwright, Nancy. 1999. *The Dappled World*. Cambridge: Cambridge University Press.

Churchland, Patricia. 1986. *Neurophilosophy*. Cambridge, MA: MIT Press.

Darwin, Charles. 1871. *Descent of Man*. London: John Murray.

Dewey, John. 1977. "The Influence of Darwinism on Philosophy." In *John Dewey: The Middle Works, 1899–1924*, vol. 4, *1907–1909*, 3–14. Carbondale: Southern Illinois University Press.

Dewey, John. 1978. "A Short Catechism Concerning Truth." In *John Dewey: The Middle Works, 1899–1924*, vol. 6, *1910–1911*, 3–11. Carbondale: Southern Illinois University Press.

Dewey, John. 1980. *John Dewey: The Middle Works, 1899–1924*, vol. 9, *1916: Democracy and Education*. Carbondale: Southern Illinois University Press.

Dewey, John. 1981. *John Dewey: The Later Works, 1925–1953*, vol. 1, *1925: Experience and Nature*. Carbondale: Southern Illinois University Press.

Dewey, John. 1982. *Reconstruction in Philosophy*. In *John Dewey: The Middle Works, 1899–1924*, vol. 12, *1920*, 77–202. Carbondale: Southern Illinois University Press.

Dewey, John. 1984. *John Dewey: The Later Works, 1925–1953*, vol. 4, *1929: The Quest for Certainty*. Carbondale: Southern Illinois University Press.

Dewey, John. 1985. *John Dewey: The Later Works, 1925–1953*, vol. 7, *1932: Ethics*, 2nd ed. Carbondale: Southern Illinois University Press.

Dewey, John. 1986. *A Common Faith*. In *John Dewey: The Later Works, 1925–1953*, vol. 9, *1933–1934*, 1–58. Carbondale: Southern Illinois University Press.

Godfrey-Smith, Peter. 2013. "Dewey and the Question of Realism." *Noûs* 50:73–89.

Goodman, Nelson. 1978. *Ways of Worldmaking*. Indianapolis: Hackett.

James, William. 1981. *The Principles of Psychology*. Cambridge, MA: Harvard University Press.

Kitcher, Philip. 1993. *The Advancement of Science*. New York: Oxford University Press.

Kitcher, Philip. 2001. *Science, Truth, and Democracy*. New York: Oxford University Press.

Kitcher, Philip. 2011. *The Ethical Project*. Cambridge, MA: Harvard University Press.

Kitcher, Philip. 2012. *Preludes to Pragmatism*. New York: Oxford University Press.

Kitcher, Philip. 2013. "Things Fall Apart." *New York Times*, http://opinionator.blogs.nytimes.com/2013/09/08/things-fall-apart.

Kitcher, Philip. 2014. *Life After Faith: The Case for Secular Humanism*. New Haven, CT: Yale University Press.

Kuhn, Thomas S. 1962. *The Structure of Scientific Revolutions*. Chicago: University of Chicago Press.

Nagel, Thomas. 2012. *Mind and Cosmos*. New York: Oxford University Press.

Price, Huw. 2011. *Naturalism Without Mirrors*. New York: Oxford University Press.

Putnam, Hilary. 1983. "Why There Isn't a Ready-Made World." In *Realism and Reason: Philosophical Papers*, 3:205–28. Cambridge: Cambridge University Press.

Rorty, Richard. 1982. *Consequences of Pragmatism*. Minneapolis: University of Minnesota Press.

Rosenberg, Alexander. 2011. *The Atheist's Guide to Reality*. New York: Norton, 2011.

Sellars, Wilfrid. 1963. "Empiricism and the Philosophy of Mind." In *Science, Perception, and Reality*, 129–94. London: Routledge Kegan Paul.

# PART II

## Pragmatism and the Study of Religion

In America, the study of religion largely grew out of liberal Protestant dissatisfaction with historical Christianity.[1] Although a few orthodox Calvinists cataloged the idolatries and superstitions of the world's benighted heathens—providing "no small entertainment" for voyeurs, as well as information (purportedly) useful to missionaries—the main impetus for the study of religion did not emanate from this quarter.[2] It emerged, rather, among nineteenth-century Unitarians and transcendentalists whose contempt for orthodox Calvinist doctrines distanced them enough from historical Christianity to regard other religions as potential sources of inspiration and instruction. These theological liberals investigated the texts, histories, and social circumstances of other religions chiefly to edify themselves and their audience, not to display and diagnose the spiritual impoverishment of the globe's outer darknesses. Convinced that principled comparison could refine and elevate theology, Unitarians and transcendentalists scoured non-Christian sources (Asian "sacred books," in particular) for intimations of the wisdom they believed orthodoxy's moral and intellectual coarseness had all but effaced from Christianity.[3] William James's pragmatist classic *The Varieties of Religious Experience* (1902) diverges from these earlier theological investigations in crucial respects, but it took shape against the background of the precedents they set. The American study of religion, to which James's book represents the first major contribution, took root in sod broken by Unitarianism and its rebellious child, transcendentalism.

For most of the nineteenth century, Unitarianism remained predominantly a New England phenomenon associated with Harvard University. An oft-cited contemporary jape illustrates Unitarianism's connotation as a regional peculiar-ity. James Freeman Clarke, the Unitarian author of the most widely read nineteenth-century American work of comparative theology, *Ten Great Religions: An Essay in Comparative Theology* (1871), also composed a well-known Unitar-ian "counterpart" to the five canons of Calvinism ratified at the Synod of Dort (1618–1619), "The Five Points of Calvinism and the Five Points of the New Theol-ogy" (Clarke 1886, 10).[4] As this title suggests, Clarke presents Unitarian theology in five cardinal doctrines in order to underscore by comparison its departures from orthodoxy. The first three proclaim "the fatherhood of God," "the brotherhood of man," and "the leadership of Jesus." Parodying Clarke, some now forgotten wit cari-catured Unitarianism by reducing it to a bathetic trinity: the fatherhood of God, the brotherhood of man, and the neighborhood of Boston.

For all his cosmopolitanism, William James resided culturally and intellectu-ally in the neighborhood of Boston. *The Varieties of Religious Experience* reveals his familiarity with European developments in the study of religion, but James took his bearings from Unitarian and transcendentalist approaches to religion. Boston theology environed him from childhood. James's domineering father, a frustrated theologian, had as a young man listened admiringly to William Ellery Channing's Unitarian sermons and later insinuated himself into transcendental-ist circles by cultivating Ralph Waldo Emerson. At his father's suggestion, James courted Alice Howe Gibbens at meetings of the Boston Radical Club, a gather-ing of Unitarian intellectuals who seem to have lived up to their club's name.[5] Julia Ward Howe (1899, 282), a more conventional Unitarian, sniffs that the mem-bership manifested a "disposition to seek outside the limits of Christianity for all that is noble and inspiring in religious culture, and to recognize especially within these limits the superstition and intolerance which have been the bane of all religions." Presumably less "pained and irritated" than Howe by the club's meetings, James and Gibbens eventually married. A Unitarian minister con-ducted the service.

At times, James explicitly accounted himself a representative of Boston's theo-logical nonconformism and an heir to Harvard's liberal legacy. In the first para-graph of "The Will to Believe" (1896), for instance, James (1956d, 1) addresses his Yale audience by playfully contrasting "our Harvard freethinking and indiffer-ence" with the catechism "we are prone to imagine" occurs at "your good old orthodox College." James alludes here to the history of theological and institu-tional conflict between Unitarians and Calvinists. One of the two nouns by which he characterizes Harvard's theological atmosphere, *indifference*, served in nineteenth-century American apologetics as a denunciation of Unitarianism specifically. This use of the term dates to the so-called Unitarian Controversy, a polemical exchange between William Ellery Channing and Samuel Worcester in 1815. Worcester (1815, 13) charged that the liberals' emphasis on conduct, character, and community rather than on creeds, and in particular their tolerance for differences of metaphysical opinion about Jesus, evinces "cold and lofty indifference [about] who the saviour of the world is!" Although James's jest lampoons both Harvard and Yale, he does pronomially align himself with Unitarianism's legacy of scorn for canonical doctrine.

In private correspondence, James expressed his allegiance to the neighborhood of Boston more bluntly. Writing to Frances Morse, a family friend, James describes the composition and circumstances of his impending Gifford lectures, which ultimately became *Varieties*. He recounts meeting a certain Scottish woman and bemoans their ensuing conversation: "No talk but evangelical talk. It seemed assumed that a Gifford lecturer must be one of [D. L.] Moody's partners, and it gave me rather a foretaste of what the Edinburgh atmosphere may be like. Well, I shall enjoy sticking a knife into its gizzard. . . . Blessed be Boston—probably the freest place on earth, that isn't merely heathen and sensual."[6] In this letter, James vents his contempt for the doctrinaire obscurantism of evangelical Protestantism, celebrates Boston's liberal religious and intellectual ethos, and anticipates that his lectures will deliver a coup on behalf of broad-mindedness.

Despite his appreciation for the intellectual climate they helped introduce, James did not identify with Unitarianism or transcendentalism specifically, nor did he regard them uncritically. They feature prominently in the intellectual landscape, nevertheless, and as landmarks orient James even when he strikes out in new theoretical directions. In the same letter to Frances Morse, James summarizes his project in *Varieties*:

> The problem I have set myself is a hard one: *first*, to defend (against all the prejudices of my "class") "experience" against "philosophy" as being the real backbone of the world's religious life—I mean prayer, guidance, and all that sort of thing immediately and privately felt, as against high and noble general views of our destiny and the world's meaning; and *second*, to make the hearer or reader believe, what I myself invincibly do believe, that, although all the special manifestations of religion may have been absurd (I mean its creeds and theories), yet the life of it as a whole is mankind's most important function.
>
> (James 1993, 187, emphasis in original)

Commentators on James sometimes cite these remarks as evidence that James intends to locate religion's essence in some inaccessible interior realm. Such an interpretation, however, not only ignores James's effort in *Varieties* to convey the "asininity"[7] of essential definitions of religion but also implausibly proposes that, when theorizing religion, James forsakes his fundamental pragmatist conviction that if a mental phenomenon has "positive significance at all," its meaning consists in the difference it makes to conduct (James 1961, 347). A more promising reading attends to James's intellectual and social location in the neighborhood of Boston. In this letter to Morse (herself a Unitarian), James declares his intention to deviate from the approaches to the "world's religious life" prevailing among Boston's urban elite. When James dichotomizes "experience" and "philosophy," he does not mean to lodge religion in a prelinguistic or precultural preserve. He protests, rather, against Unitarian and transcendentalist myopia.[8] To confine inquiry to the contributions non-Christian sacred books can make to an elevated religious philosophy, James claims, fails miserably to account for "the world's religious life." To describe and explain the world's religious life more adequately, inquiry should instead focus on the idiosyncratic (and in that sense "private") moral careers of those who understand their lives in relation to "whatever they may consider divine" (James 1961, 42).[9] Like other members of his "class," James did in fact believe that the world's religious life bears philosophical significance, but he urges a more empirical, social scientific approach to the study of religion.

James's predilection for empirical inquiry distances him especially from the leading transcendentalists of his formative years. Tasked with commemorating Emerson, James delivered a marvel of barbed encomium. In his "Address at the Emerson Centenary in Concord" (1903), James piously cements the revered sage's reputation as a spiritual "seer" and "prophet" as well as verbal "artist." The "music" and "nobility" of Emerson's prose, James (1912, 34) proclaims, will earn his writings a "place among the Scriptures of humanity." Divested of their music, however, Emerson's "thoughts . . . would be trivial" (21). Not his "mental gifts," therefore, but the "harmony" of Emerson's personality accounts for his influence. "Rarely," James explains, "has a man so accurately known the limits of his genius or so unfailingly kept within them" (20). James intimates that empirical inquiry lay beyond the limits of Emerson's genius. Although he carefully observed empirical "facts" (so to glimpse the absolute, shining through them), Emerson unfailingly "kept within the limits" of his vocation as a metaphysical litterateur. James cautions that one should not expect "too rigorous a consistency" from a seer whose "mission culminated in his style," and he commends Emerson's "sublime pages" as the "hearteners and sustainers of our *youth*" (22, 26, 32, italics added). These equivocal pleas on behalf of Emerson's oracular art betray James's intellectual dissatisfaction with it. Although Emerson kept up with the science of his day, he did not share James's inclination to submit inspiration to inquiry, the seer to the scientist.

In intellectual outlook, James more closely resembles Unitarian Christians like Channing than romantic transcendentalists like Emerson, despite having, like Emerson, "grown" out of the Christian "prejudices of [his] infancy."[10] Channing regards empirical facts principally as grounds of inference rather than conduits for inspiration. Religion's authority derives, he argues, from human judgments. Humans infer God's existence and moral character from the known facts about human nature and the observable order pervading both the animate and inanimate universe.[11] These inferences establish God as exemplar and object of aspiration. "All religion," Channing (1844, 195) writes, "supposes and is built on judgments passed by us on God and on his operations." Whatever authority the Bible enjoys, it too rests on rational inferences drawn from empirical facts. When reading the Bible, moreover, one should "distrust every interpretation, which after deliberate attention, seems repugnant to any established truth" (Channing 1849, 64). Channing insists that all Christians (not just Unitarians) interpret the Bible governed by their idea of the truth—even those who deny that they do. This inescapable hermeneutical fact freights inquiry with decisive theological significance. Newly "established" truth carries theological consequences. Widely accepted "revolution[s] of opinion" attending "the progress of the human mind" produce new theologies. "Such is the power of public opinion and of an improved state of society on creeds," Channing argues, that Christians can forgo the dated, degrading, Calvinist portrait of God as a vain, cruel despot and instead recognize him as a loving father (Channing 1844, 188–89, 201–2).

Despite attesting to the "revolution[s] of opinion" that accompany intellectual "progress," Channing would not entertain the possibility that *his* religious inferences would in time lose their empirical grounds. His untroubled confidence in Christianity's invulnerability to future inquiry seems, in retrospect, almost tragic. Alexis de Tocqueville's notebooks record a conversation with Channing dated October 2, 1831. Addressing orthodox Protestant disapproval of Unitarianism, Channing states, "The issue between them and us is whether the seventeenth century can be revived, or has disappeared forever. . . . We insist that human reason has made progress and that what people believed in a century of crudeness and corruption is no longer tenable in the enlightened times in which we live now." Tocqueville asks, in response, "Don't you and your friends fear . . . that in seeking to purify Christianity you will end up draining it of its substance?" Channing's reply reveals his blindness to the lessons of his own historicism: "I believe . . . that there is little reason to fear such an outcome. Man needs positive religion, and why would he ever abandon Christianity? The evidence for the Christian religion can withstand the most serious intellectual scrutiny" (Tocqueville 2010, 245).

Despite himself, Channing fails to appreciate the contingency of the "evidence" for Christianity.

In important respects, the *Varieties* exhibits striking continuity with Channing's thought. In the spirit of Channing, James (1961, 22) adduces a "descriptive survey" of empirical facts pertinent to religion, on which grounds to judge its intellectual admissibility and moral fitness. Although James eventually proposes a new "science of religions" that, among other tasks, would pass judgment on religious beliefs that contradict empirical fact, he insists that humans have always judged religion by what he calls the "empiricist criterion"—even those who deny that they do. They credit (and confer authority upon) only those gods whose existence and nature are warranted by their conception of the facts. Intellectual and moral advance, therefore, inevitably bring theological change.

> Nothing is more striking than the secular alteration that goes on in the moral and religious tone of men, as their insight into nature and their social arrangements progressively develop. After an interval of a few generations the mental climate proves unfavorable to notions of the deity which at an earlier date were perfectly satisfactory.... Today a deity who should require bleeding sacrifices to placate him would be too sanguinary to be taken seriously. Even if powerful historical credentials were put forward in his favor, we would not look at them. Once, on the contrary, his cruel appetites were of themselves credentials.
>
> (James 1961, 262–63)

Like Channing, James argues that any religion's authority over belief and behavior ultimately rests on human judgment. To gain credence, religious ideas must in some way or other suit prevalent conceptions of the moral and intellectual good. Transformations in what Channing refers to as "public opinion" and the moral or political "state of society" alter the grounds for judging religious notions. Wittingly or not, James even reproduces the thesis of Channing's "Moral Argument Against Calvinism" to illustrate his point:

> Few historic changes are more curious than these mutations of theological opinion. The monarchical type of sovereignty was, for example, so ineradicably planted in the mind of our own forefathers that a dose of cruelty and arbitrariness in their deity seems positively to have been required by their imagination. They called the cruelty "retributive justice," and a God without it would certainly have struck them as not "sovereign" enough. But today we abhor the very notion of eternal suffering inflicted; and that arbitrary dealing-out of salvation and damnation to selected individuals, of which Jonathan Edwards could persuade

himself that he had not only a conviction, but a "delightful conviction," as of a doctrine "exceedingly pleasant, bright, and sweet," appears to us, if sovereignly anything, sovereignly irrational and mean.

(James 1961, 263–64)

As human standards evolved, James observes, the credibility of Calvinism waned. Judging it "irrational and mean," Protestants no longer invest Calvinist theology with authority over belief and behavior. The authority of religion, James argues, depends on human judgments that apply socially established "values" and "ideals," whose authority in turn derives from the human community's ongoing "experience, if we take it in the largest sense." James resolves superhuman authority into the historically contingent norms of human social practice. "The gods we stand by," he writes, are "the gods whose demands on us are reinforcements of our demands on ourselves and one another" (264).

When James stresses the sovereignty, ubiquity, and historical contingency of human judgment in religious matters, he echoes, but also sublates, Boston Unitarianism. In James's hands, this mainspring of Unitarian theology undermines Unitarian theology. To borrow the Nietzschean (and broadly Hegelian) formula, "the lawgiver himself eventually receives the call: 'patere legem, quam ipse tulisti' [Submit to the law you yourself proposed]" (Nietzsche 1967, essay 3, section 27). For James, the empirical facts pertaining to the human mind and the material universe no longer warrant the inferences on which Channing stakes theology. Late nineteenth-century science affords no inference establishing God's existence and exemplary nature. Natural theology, James writes in 1895, "has suffered a definitive bankruptcy in the opinion of a circle of persons, among whom I must count myself, and who are growing more numerous every day. For such persons the physical order of nature, taken simply as science knows it, cannot be held to reveal any one harmonious spiritual intent. It is mere *weather*, as Chauncey Wright called it, doing and undoing without end" (James 1956a, 52, emphasis in original). As a scientist in the post-Darwinian age, James could no more accept the judgments on which Channing's Unitarian Christianity depends than Channing could accept those on which Edwards's Calvinism depends. The human community's "experience, if we take it in the largest sense," had produced empirical standards that undermine the credibility of Channing's inferences. If contemporary empirical norms undermine the inferences supporting a divine father, a fortiori they undermine the Unitarian version of providence. The fifth of Clarke's five points of Unitarianism heralds "the *Continuity of Human Development in all Worlds*, or the *Progress of Mankind* onward and upward for ever" (Clarke 1886, 15–16, emphasis in original). To justify this doctrine, Clarke offers a teleological inference based on an anthropic interpretation of geologic and bio-logical history, "the advancement of civilization" to date, and continuing improvement in the human intellectual, social, as well as spiritual condition. "The one fact which is written on nature and human life," he writes, "is the fact of progress, and this must be accepted as the purpose of the Creator" (17). From James's perspective this kind of argument for cosmic optimism whistles past the graveyard. It blithely ignores (or distorts) the best recent geology and biology and relies on a partial—in both senses—account of human history.[12] Sober assess-ment of the results of empirical inquiry reveals no such "fact of progress written on nature and human life."

For James, the Darwinian revolution bankrupts not only the Unitarian infer-ences based on "the physical order of nature" but also those based on human intel-lectual and social progress. Darwin argues (despite some rhetorical backsliding) that biological fitness obtains relative to particular and changing environments, not to some absolute standard toward which evolution advances. James under-stands progress analogously. Progress occurs relative to the purposes and ideals of historically situated human communities, not to some absolute standard toward which (in the famous words of the transcendentalist Theodore Parker) the "arc" of the universe inexorably "bends" (Parker 1853, 85). James propounds this Darwin-ian conception in the very first sentence of *Some Problems of Philosophy* (1911): "The progress of society is due to the fact that individuals vary from the human average in all sorts of directions, and that the originality is often so attractive or useful that they are recognized by their tribe as leaders, and become objects of envy or admiration, and setters of new ideals" (James 1911, 3). Ideals, James argues, get their value from their usefulness or attractiveness in a particular context of purposes and norms. As early as 1891, he disparages as "superstitious" the view that ideals and norms derive their value from their approximation to a set of abso-lute standards inhabiting "some sublime dimension of being" that transcends historically situated human societies (James 1956b, 195). When Clarke infers "the purpose of the Creator" from human intellectual and social progress, he relies on just such a "superstitious" understanding of value. He presupposes that a meta-physical standard external to the historical "weather"—the endless "doing and undoing" of situated social actors—provides the normative yardstick for human strivings. Without this presupposition, the empirical fact that human societies *sometimes* progress relative to their *own* ideals, purposes, and norms lends no sup-port to Unitarian inferences. In Channing's era, Unitarian theology had distin-guished itself by its empiricist scruples. After half a century of "alteration" of the "mental climate," Unitarian inferences seemed to require the suppression of empiricist scruples.

James's religious investigations in the *Varieties* revive the empiricist and historicist impulse that propelled Boston theology in the first half of the nineteenth century. Like his Unitarian forebears, he argues that developments in science and society bear directly on "metaphysics" (James 1961, 17). Emerging scientific as well as moral or political norms, in other words, set the conditions for a viable religious philosophy. James's "empiricist criterion" and "science of religions" preserve the Unitarian aspiration to elevate religious conceptions (and practice) by making empirically informed judgments.[13] He innovates, however, by reconceiving the empirical grounds for judgments about religion. Convinced that empirical investigation of nature and the history of human progress afford no inference establishing God's existence or nature, James redirects the focus of empirical inquiry. He investigates religion itself—particularly how it variously shapes and takes shape in individuals' lives—to establish empirical grounds for judgment. The causes and consequences of individuals' religious behavior become the target of inquiry. Instead of attempting to infer the true religion from empirical facts about the natural and social world, he attempts to establish empirical facts about religious lives from which to propose inferences about the truth and value of religion.

In the author's preface to the *Varieties*, James relates that he initially planned to address two topics equally: first, the psychology of "man's religious appetites," followed by what he calls "their satisfaction through philosophy," or the religious philosophy he believed the empirical facts about religion could warrant. In writing the lectures, however, he found that the empirical "description of man's religious constitution" grew until it filled the entire course of lectures. Lacking sufficient space to pursue both topics, he could only "suggest" his "philosophical conclusions" (James 1961, 17). The completed work comprises two methodological lectures (lectures 1 and 2); twelve lectures dedicated to rendering "existential judgments" on the empirical causes and constituents of *"the feelings, acts, and experiences of individual men . . . so far as they apprehend themselves to stand in relation to whatever they may consider the divine"* (lectures 3–13, 19); six lectures offering "spiritual judgments" on the spontaneous appeal, intellectual admissibility, and moral fitness of religion so conceived and explained (lectures 14–18, 20); and a postscript "suggesting" a justifiable religious philosophy (42, emphasis in original).

From the time of its publication, the *Varieties* has enthralled, but also confounded, its readers. In surpassingly beautiful prose, James both pioneers a methodologically naturalistic, social scientific approach to explaining the empirical facts of religion and indulges theological extrapolations from the empirical facts. James's inclination to make theological hay out of his empirical study of religion has tended to consternate scholars less indebted than he to nineteenth-century Boston's Unitarian milieu.[14] His Janus-faced religious investigations have seemed to them muddled or incongruous. In a 1904 review essay on the *Varieties*, for instance, Swiss-born James Henry Leuba (1904, 329, 337) praises James's comprehensive "naturalistic" explanations of religious phenomena but feels driven to call him a "prestidigitator" because "ghosts pop out of the very places that he has just shown you to be empty." Most contemporary scholars of religion likely share Leuba's exasperation with the *Varieties*. Aggravating matters, James's empirical theories have come to seem as antiquated as his religious yearnings.

Even so, the *Varieties* provides a distinctive (and distinctively American) template for the social scientific study of religion. James fashions a democratic, nonideological naturalism with which to explain religion's causes and consequences in history. Because he construes belief by reference to conduct, James focuses inquiry not chiefly on doctrinal statements but rather on the dynamics mutually engendering religious actors and their behavior. Since, moreover, he follows Peirce (1958, 107–9) in thinking that the "experience" of "every man" ought to bear on inquiry, James ranges beyond elite theology and canonical texts to adduce testimonies and life experiences originating among the relatively humble or unsung. Perhaps most significantly, James exhibits the clarity about normativity that has come to distinguish the pragmatist tradition in religious studies. Much contemporary naturalistic theory of religion—whether scientific or historicist—cannot account satisfactorily for the normative character of its own conclusions. When cognitive science of religion, for example, relies on a general account of concepts or intentional states that is purely causal, it jeopardizes the normative authority of the reasons for adopting the account. More conspicuously, the styles of critique descending from Karl Marx and Michel Foucault tend to terminate in self-referential incoherence (as well as bad faith attempts to obscure it); theories that comprehensively explain norms as ideology or an effect of power undermine the normative force of whatever conclusion they produce. Pragmatism, by contrast, both naturalizes and historicizes normativity while preserving its authority. James and subsequent pragmatists explain normativity as a pervasive, historically variable, irreducible, and ineluctable product of evolved human behavioral capacities. Antiauthoritarian in the sense that it denies any sources of normativity transcending the historically contingent norms informing the social practices constitutive of human language and action, pragmatism makes it possible to critique ideology and the effects of power in good conscience.

The essays in part 2 examine the legacy of pragmatism in the study of religion. They identify naturalistic methodological principles associated with pragmatism and evaluate them relative to alternative paradigms in the study of religion, including Nietzschean genealogy and cognitive science.

NOTES

1.  See Turner (2011). In Europe, of course, colonial administration, inter alia, played a major role in the origins of the study of religion.

2.  Charles Goodrich, *Pictorial and Descriptive View of All Religions* (1842), quoted in Turner (2011, 34).

3.  The twentieth-century ubiquity of Ralph Waldo Emerson's ponderous poem "Brahma" in high school literature curricula has made the transcendentalist attitude toward Asian religions passingly familiar to generations of Americans and has exaggerated its centrality to nineteenth-century American culture.

4.  Often arranged under the mnemonic acronym TULIP, the five Calvinist canons are *T*otal depravity, *U*nconditional election, *L*imited atonement, *I*rresistible grace, and *P*erseverance of the saints.

5.  Speakers included James Freeman Clarke, Ralph Waldo Emerson, and William Henry Channing (the transcendentalist nephew of William Ellery Channing).

6.  Letter to Frances Morse, April 12–13, 1900 (James 1993, 187–88).

7.  Letter to James Henry Leuba, March 25, 1901 (Perry 1935, 2:347).

8.  He intends to combat idealism as well. James writes to Josiah Royce, his Harvard colleague and a leading American idealist, "When I compose my Gifford lectures mentally, 't is with the design exclusively of overthrowing your system, and ruining your peace" (James 1993, 192). Unlike James and the Unitarians, however, Royce had little interest in exploring the diversities of actual religious thought or practice.

9.  Erving Goffman, the coiner of the term *moral career*, read William James avidly.

10. Letter to James Henry Leuba, April 17, 1904 (Perry 1935, 2:351).

11. From a contemporary standpoint, Channing's famous sermon "Likeness to God" (1828) comes across like a theological reading of Ludwig Feuerbach married to eighteenth-century deism.

12. James permits (at one's own risk) beliefs that run beyond the empirical evidence, but not those that contradict the empirical evidence. See chapter 2 of the present volume.

13. The "northwest wind of science," he wrote in 1896, should "ventilate" popular religions and "blow away their sickliness and barbarism" (James 1956c, x).

14. Scholars less subject than James to paralyzing post-Christian cosmic angst have also found his theologizing irksome.

WORKS CITED

Channing, William Ellery. 1844. "The Moral Argument Against Calvinism." In *The Works of William Ellery Channing in Six Volumes*, edited by Joseph Barker, 3:185–202. London: Chapman.

Channing, William Ellery. 1849. "Unitarian Christianity." In *The Works of William E. Channing, DD*, 11th ed., 3:59–103. Boston: George G. Channing.

Clarke, James Freeman. 1886. "The Five Points of Calvinism and the Five Points of the New Theology." In *Vexed Questions in Theology: A Series of Essays*, 9–18. Boston: George H. Ellis.

Goodrich, Charles. 1842. *A Pictorial and Descriptive View of All Religions; Embracing the Forms of Worship Practiced by the Several Nations of the Known World, from the Earliest Records to the Present Time*. Hartford, CT: Sumner and Goodman.

Howe, Julia Ward. 1899. *Reminiscences 1819–1899*. Boston: Houghton, Mifflin.

James, William. 1911. *Some Problems of Philosophy: A Beginning of an Introduction to Philosophy*. London: Longmans, Green.

James, William. 1912. "Address at the Emerson Centenary in Concord." *Memories and Studies*. London: Longmans, Green.

James, William. 1956a. "Is Life Worth Living?" In *The Will to Believe, Human Immortality*, 32–62. New York: Dover.

James, William. 1956b. "The Moral Philosopher and the Moral Life." In *The Will to Believe, Human Immortality*, 184–215. New York: Dover.

James, William. 1956c. Preface to *The Will to Believe, Human Immortality*, vii–xiv. New York: Dover.

James, William. 1956d. "The Will to Believe." In *The Will to Believe, Human Immortality*, 1–31. New York: Dover.

James, William. 1961. *The Varieties of Religious Experience*. New York: Collier.

James, William. 1993. *The Selected Letters of William James*, edited by Elizabeth Hardwick. New York: Anchor.

Leuba, James Henry. 1904. "Professor William James' Interpretation of Religious Experience." *International Journal of Ethics* 13:322–39.

Nietzsche, Friedrich. 1969. *On the Genealogy of Morals* and *Ecce Homo*, translated by Walter Kaufmann and R. J. Hollingdale. New York: Vintage.

Parker, Theodore. 1853. "Of Justice and the Conscience." In *Ten Sermons of Religion*, 66–101. Boston: Crosby, Nichols.

Peirce, Charles S. 1958. "The Fixation of Belief." In *Charles S. Peirce: Selected Writings*, edited by Philip Wiener, 91–112. New York: Dover.

Perry, Ralph Barton. 1935. *The Thought and Character of William James*. 2 vols. Boston: Little, Brown.

Tocqueville, Alexis de. 2010. *Alexis de Tocqueville and Gustave de Beaumont in America: Their Friendship and Their Travels*, edited by Oliver Zunz. Translated by Arthur Goldhammer. Charlottesville: University of Virginia Press.

Turner, James. 2011. *Religion Enters the Academy: The Origins of the Scholarly Study of Religion in America*. Athens: University of Georgia Press.

Worcester, Samuel. 1815. *A Third Letter to the Rev. William E. Channing on the Subject of Unitarianism*. Boston: Samuel T. Armstrong.

# 4

# Pragmatism, Naturalism, and Genealogy in the Study of Religion

WAYNE PROUDFOOT

I

The word *naturalism* is used in many different ways in contemporary philosophy. For some, it has required that a properly naturalistic account appeal only to what is countenanced by the natural sciences, but there have been a number of recent attempts to formulate more liberal approaches to naturalism that allow for natural accounts that recognize the normative character of beliefs, practices, actions, and institutions.[1] A certain priority is rightly given to the sciences in the sense that, as Huw Price (2004) has put it, science tells us that humans are natural creatures and any naturalistic approach should honor that.

But that doesn't mean that the only, or even the best, accounts must be couched in terms of the natural sciences. Quite the contrary, much of the most discerning and critical recent scholarship on religion has come from the humanities, especially historical and literary criticism, and from the social sciences. Methods of research from the natural sciences can be helpful, but they are often used in ways that lose sight of the phenomena they claim to study. Historical, philosophical, and social criticism are not only permissible but also necessary for a naturalistic approach to the study of religion. An important component of any such approach requires historicizing what has been naturalized, or identifying and critically examining concepts, beliefs, practices, and institutions that are so taken for granted that subjects are not aware of their constitutive and normative roles in thought and action.

We can distinguish between *naturalistic* accounts of beliefs and practices as products of humans regarded as natural creatures and the *naturalizing* of concepts, beliefs, and practices in a way that assumes them to be naturally given and occludes their social and historical origins and development. These are two very different matters, but they are related. Any viable naturalistic account of religion requires historicizing what has previously been naturalized. In *Gender Trouble*, Judith Butler (1990, 2) writes that the law "produces and then conceals the notion of a 'subject before the law' in order to invoke that discursive formation as a naturalized foundational premise that subsequently legitimates that law's own regulatory hegemony." She makes that premise explicit and so available for critical reflection.

Attention to the work of the classical pragmatists might help to clarify the relation between naturalism and the study of religion. William James and John Dewey regard the idea of an unseen moral order as central to religious belief and practice. Each brings his pragmatic account of inquiry to bear in critical reflection on that idea and its philosophical implications. Both are instructive for thinking about religion and naturalism, for clarifying religious concepts and claims, and for asking what difference it would make if those claims were true. Neither goes on to historicize the ideas of a moral order and related institutions and practices in the way that is done by the most interesting contemporary studies of religion. Inquiry directed to historicizing what has been naturalized is important for developing an adequate naturalistic account of religion, and it is better suited for that purpose than is direct application of the tools of natural science to religion. Friedrich Nietzsche's genealogical method is the source of much of this attention to historicizing what has been naturalized. This approach should be regarded not as an alternative to the pragmatic theory of inquiry but rather as an extension of it, one that contributes fruitfully to recent discussions of the relation between pragmatic inquiry and truth.[2]

If priority is given at the outset to natural scientific explanations of religion, cultural and social practices are likely to be ignored and the important background roles they play will escape critical scrutiny. Much recent work in the so-called cognitive science of religion and in the neuroscience of religion is of this sort.[3] It yields results that are easily pressed into service for either reductive or apologetic agendas. Justin Barrett, a cognitive scientist at Oxford, claims to show that humans are "naturally endowed with cognitive faculties that stimulate belief in the divine," including what he calls a "hyperactive agent detection device" (Clark and Barrett 2011). Richard Dawkins cites this work as evidence for a Darwinian account of belief in God that undermines its epistemic value, while Barrett himself interprets it, with help from Thomas Reid and Alvin

Plantinga, as evidence of a natural and therefore reliable belief that can be used to justify religious claims.

Such accounts not only fail to give an adequate explanation of theistic belief but also serve to naturalize it in a sense of the term that is quite different from, and is in fact opposed to, the search for an acceptable naturalistic account of religious belief and practice. For a very different example, even a sophisticated historical theologian who is well informed about current work in evolutionary biology can appeal to a natural fit between the "cooperation" and self-sacrifice discovered in the world of genetics and some doctrines of Christian theology (Coakley 2013).

Scientific studies of religion are often used to naturalize religious experience and practice in the problematic sense. For example, Richard Davidson, a neuroscientist at the University of Wisconsin, has conducted a number of studies to understand the pursuit and attainment of compassion through the practice of meditation in Tibetan Buddhism (Davidson 2002). Such studies have been done before, but Davidson and his colleagues claimed to take more seriously than his predecessors had the content of the doctrines and practices of the subjects they were studying.

Davidson surveyed research on emotion and remarked that psychologists have identified distinctive facial expressions across cultures for negative emotions, but not for their positive counterparts. The only basic classification of positive emotions that correlates with biological data, according to Davidson, is one between pregoal attainment and postgoal attainment affect, between eager anticipation and satisfaction. So he decided to focus on this division rather than on distinctions within the emotion lexicon that don't have biological correlates.

That may be a reasonable research decision, but it substitutes a simple bipolar classification for a much larger set of emotion terms, each of which has its own grammar and criteria of application. For example, within the category of postgoal attainment positive affect, we can easily distinguish between the meanings of the terms *contentment*, *pride*, *enthrallment*, and *relief*. The choice of which of these terms is appropriate in a given situation requires knowledge of context, background assumptions, and reference to relevant norms.

Davidson and his colleagues compared Buddhist monks who had been training in Tibetan traditions for at least fifteen, and in some cases forty, years with control subjects who had undergone just one week of meditative training. During the study, both long-term practitioners and control subjects were asked first to "let their minds be invaded by a feeling of love or compassion" toward someone they cared about, and later to "generate unconditional loving-kindness and compassion toward all sentient beings without thinking about anyone in particular" (Lutz et al. 2004, 16369). The researchers recorded electroencephalo-graphic (EEG) activity and found that the monks had induced in themselves high-amplitude EEG gamma oscillations and phase synchronization during the nonreferential compassion meditative state. This kind of synchronization, David-son writes, may reflect attention and affective processes and is consistent with the idea that these are flexible skills that can be trained.

This study may be valuable for training subjects to control their affective states, but it doesn't tell us anything about the Buddhist notion of compassion or its pur-suit. Traditional Buddhist texts on meditation distinguish between *calming* (achieving a stillness of mind and body) and *discernment* (insight).[4] The first is considered preparation for the second. Davidson's EEG study may measure calm-ing, but it leaves discernment unexplored—in this case, discernment of Bud-dhist teaching about compassion and its application to oneself or others.

Instructions to "generate a state of loving-kindness and compassion toward all sentient beings" must have been understood very differently by the Buddhist monks and by members of the control group. The monks had undergone years of training in debating skills that are a large part of Tibetan scholastic pedagogy. They had cultivated practices that include not only techniques for the control of mental and physical states but also criteria for the proper use of terms like *com-passion* and *sentient beings*. They must have understood these terms quite differ-ently from the control subjects, who had trained for a week in an admittedly superficial way.

Georges Dreyfus (2002), a scholar of Tibetan Buddhism, notes, in response to the study, that there is no Tibetan word for *emotion*, and he asks whether com-passion is an emotion. He cites a distinction drawn, both in texts and in prac-tice, between beginners who *feel* compassion (they are saddened by the sufferings of others and moved to wish them relief) and advanced bodhisattvas who attain compassion with equanimity without being themselves moved.

Is compassion then a trait? The difference between a state and a character trait is not only one of endurance over time. We call someone "loving" or "kind" not on the basis of what we take her to feel, either on the basis of her self-report or some other evidence, but because we take the term to capture something of her character. We ascribe kindness to her by observing how she acts in response to different situations over time. Similar observations and attempts at discernment are at work in my reflections on my own character, though usually clouded by bias in my favor. To understand Buddhist compassion meditation, one would have to explicate the criteria that govern the way the monks themselves use that term in their own self-reflection, and that would require careful attention to detailed teachings in their monastic tradition. Were Buddhist practitioners to agree to

conditions under which they would be given feedback on their gamma band oscillations and phase synchronization during meditation, it might be possible for
them to manipulate those variables more directly, but that would have no bearing on their judgment, or anyone else's, about the extent to which they were on
the path to compassion.

This study not only fails to give an account of Buddhist compassion but also
serves to naturalize it, in the problematic sense of that term. It assumes that it is
possible to identify compassion without recourse to grammar, doctrine, spiritual practices, institutions, or other components of culture. The antidote to this
kind of naturalization is to historicize it, to elaborate the meanings that inform
the thought and practice of the monks and of members of the control group. A
historical account of the meaning of *compassion* in the Tibetan tradition would
contribute more to a critical and adequate naturalistic account of religion than
this attempt to naturalize it by identifying it in terms that can be measured by
an EEG detector. This is not to say that neuroscience cannot inform the study of
Buddhist meditation. It can, but it must itself be informed by careful attention
to the history of the practice and to the concepts by which practitioners understand what they are doing and what is happening to them.

Religious concepts and practices have sometimes been vehicles by which ethical
concepts, norms, practices, and institutions have been naturalized or represented
in such a way as to render invisible the fact that they are contingent products of
human society and culture. But, as these examples show, scientific study of religion
can be used for the same purpose. Much of the best recent work in the study of
religion and in the study of culture generally has been devoted to historicizing
what has previously been naturalized. Categories, practices, and institutions that
were regarded as natural have been shown to be contingent products of particular
interests and forces that can be described and made available for inquiry and for
critical reflection by a combination of historical, literary, philosophical, and social
analyses.

Michel de Certeau's (1992) genealogy of the term *mystique* and the "knowledge" and practices associated with it in late sixteenth- and early seventeenth-
century French Catholicism is an example of such work. From Caroline Bynum's
(1987) *Holy Feast and Holy Fast* to Patricia Dailey's (2013) *Promised Bodies*, scholars have historicized conceptions of gender and the body in medieval Christian
writings by and about women. Robert Sharf (1995) and Bernard Faure (1991) have
each written illuminating studies of the rhetoric of meditation and immediacy
in Chan Buddhism, both in the tradition and in modern scholarship. In *Theorizing Myth*, Bruce Lincoln (1999) analyzes theories of myth and the ways in which
they serve to naturalize ideologies. Tomoko Masuzawa (2005) shows how the idea

of religion, the list of world religions, and the characterization of particular religious traditions, were naturalized in European writings between the late eighteenth and the early twentieth centuries.

II

The concept of inquiry is central to pragmatism. Charles Peirce argued that genuine inquiry must be elicited by actual doubt, in contrast to what he took to be the feigned doubt of René Descartes that led him to reinstate immediately what he had professed to doubt. Taking a cue from science, Peirce (1992c) proposed that an idea be clarified in part by asking what difference it would make if it were true. This attempt to discover what is at stake in a particular debate and to demystify disputes that were merely verbal was intended to counter what Peirce took to be the empty or frictionless speculation of much contemporary metaphysical idealism. Pursuit of genuine inquiry informed the work of James and Dewey, also, and led each to be attentive to concepts or practices that had been naturalized in such a way as to block inquiry.

Richard Bernstein (2010, 51–52) points out that Peirce should be regarded as the father of pragmatism, as much for his anti-Cartesian essays of 1867 and 1868 as for his later formulation of the pragmatic maxim for clarifying ideas and his reflections on fixing belief. Peirce's arguments in those early essays, "Questions Concerning Certain Faculties Claimed for Man" (Peirce 1992d, 1:11–27) and "Some Consequences of Four Incapacities" (Peirce 1992e, 1:28–55), are thorough and convincing criticisms of foundationalism and of what Wilfrid Sellars (1997) was later to call the "Myth of the Given."

The faculties about which Peirce raises questions are those of intuition. None of our cognitions, he argues, is self-standing, if that is taken to mean that it is independent of or undetermined by previous cognitions. Intuitions, in Peirce's sense, are conclusions of inference and judgment that have been naturalized. Insofar as an intuition is purported to be an immediate cognition, Peirce argues that we have no such thing. To claim that a perception, or a conception of self, is unmediated is to naturalize it and to occlude the linguistic capacities and beliefs that it presupposes. Peirce shows by example and argument that perceptions are judgments. What seem to be direct sensations of sound and touch, for instance, take time and require comparison and inference. To recognize the pitch of a note, I need to detect the frequency of the sound, and to feel the texture of a piece of cloth, I must move my finger slightly across the fabric

(Peirce 1992d, 1:15). Peirce draws out the implications of this critique of intuition for understanding language, emotions, and the self as well as for our conception of knowledge. In these early papers, he clearly articulates the fallibilism that is central to the pragmatist tradition. Nothing is certain in a sense that precludes future doubt and inquiry concerning it.

Peirce argued that the best method for settling opinion and removing doubt is the method of science, in contrast to appeal to tradition or dogma, to consensus, or to what seems to be the case after careful reflection. In "The Fixation of Belief," he wrote that the method of science requires settling belief by having it caused by "something on which our thinking has no effect."[5] James appropriated Peirce's doubt-belief theory of inquiry and his rule for clarifying the meaning of ideas, but he drew on Peirce's early work to argue that belief could never by fixed by something independent of thought. Thoughts and interests always shape inquiry and its conclusions. Peirce and James each tried to combine a conception of inquiry that can be affected by its object, and thus serve the aim of getting things right, with a rejection of foundationalism.

Peirce's critique of intuition is aimed at historicizing what has been naturalized. James and Dewey often make similar criticisms. James (1981, 195) says that a psychologist is subject to the fallacy that arises from her confusing her own standpoint with that of the mental fact she is trying to describe. In the introductory chapter to *The Varieties of Religious Experience*, he writes that experiences cannot be accurately described or explained by reference only to what we might learn about the brain (James 1985c, 11–29). Dewey (1984b, 239–43) claimed, throughout his work, that the chief error of idealism was to convert the results or aims of inquiry or action into antecedently existing objects. Each of these points, like Peirce on intuition, is intended to restore the object of inquiry to a context in which it can be reexamined and reevaluated. James (1985b, 32) later wrote that pragmatism "unstiffens all our theories."

## III

James (1985b, 49) identifies religion by contrasting it to naturalism or materialism, which he takes to be identical. In one of his earliest articles, he writes that the radical question of the universe is whether this is "at bottom a moral or unmoral universe," whether it is congruous with our spontaneous powers (James 1979, 70, 84). He uses the term *intimacy* to refer to the sense that reality is congruous in this way with human powers, and at the end of his career he proposes intimacy as a criterion for any acceptable metaphysics (James 1979, 75; 1977, 16–21). The religious question, for James, is whether there is some unseen order that is continuous with our highest ideals, an order to which we can strive to adjust ourselves and that provides some basis other than that of our work and the work of our fellow humans for hope for improvement of the world as we find it. This is an issue articulated by Matthew Arnold, in 1873, when he depicted the biblical idea of God as that of "an eternal power, not ourselves, that makes for righteousness" (Arnold 1902, 46). Religion, for James, assumes a theodicy, or at least the possibility of one, and naturalism, as he uses the term, precludes it.

James's most vivid depiction of what he took naturalism to entail comes in the chapter on the "sick soul" in the *Varieties*. With regard to naturalism, he says, mankind is in the position of people living on a frozen lake, surrounded by insurmountable cliffs and knowing that the ice is melting and the day is nearing when they will be ignominiously drowned. The happier they are, the sadder and more poignant is their plight (James 1985c, 120).

In his 1898 lecture in Berkeley, "Philosophical Conceptions and Practical Results," James introduces Peirce's pragmatic criterion of meaning. The meaning of a concept, Peirce writes, can be clarified by reference to the practical effects we would expect the object of the concept to have. James uses this criterion to clarify the significance of the distinction between theism and materialism. The idea of God, he says, "guarantees an ideal order that shall be permanently preserved. . . . Materialism means simply the denial that the moral order is eternal, and the cutting off of ultimate hopes; theism means the affirmation of an eternal moral order and the letting loose of hope." The need for such an eternal moral order, James writes, is "one of the deepest needs of our breast" (James 1985a, 264).

James later revised his view, arguing that the religious pragmatist does not require a guarantee but only that such an ideal order is possible and that there are forces in addition to us and our fellow humans working toward that end. "I simply refuse," James wrote, "to accept the notion of there being *no* purpose in the objective world" (James 1992, 5:195). It is this contrast between a naturalism that is blind to our ethical ideals and a religion that offers some hope beyond what we ourselves can achieve that leads James to write, in the preface to *The Meaning of Truth*, that applying the pragmatic test to the concepts of *God, freedom*, and *design* shows them all to mean the same thing, the presence of "promise" in the world. "'God or no God' means 'promise or no promise,'" and this, he writes, is not a subjective question but an objective one about the character of the cosmos (James 1978, 6).

In a review of *Pragmatism*, shortly after it was published, Dewey endorsed James's use of Peirce's proposal that the meaning of an idea be clarified by attending to the consequences that can be inferred from it, but he commented on what he took to be an ambiguity in the way James employed it. The issue was sufficiently important, Dewey wrote, that until it was resolved he couldn't decide whether or not to regard himself as a pragmatist. Dewey asked:

> Does Mr. James employ the pragmatic method to discover the *value* in terms of the consequences of life of some formula which has its content, its *logical* meaning, already fixed; or does he employ it to criticize and revise and, ultimately, to *constitute* the proper intellectual meaning of the formula? If it is the first, there is danger that the pragmatic method will be employed only to vivify, if not validate, doctrines which in themselves are pieces of rationalist metaphysics, not inherently pragmatic. If the last, there is danger that some readers will think old notions are being confirmed when in truth they are being translated into new and inconsistent notions.
>
> (Dewey 1908, 90, emphasis in original)

Here and in his 1925 article "The Development of American Pragmatism," Dewey (1984a) argues that James uses the pragmatic method to examine the significance of concepts whose meaning is fixed in advance, rather than actively reconstructing them in a way that would reflect current knowledge and enable him to do something with the concepts. In this respect, he writes, James operates more as a teacher than as a pragmatic philosopher. In contrast to Peirce, James was interested, Dewey says, not in clarifying the logic of a term but in showing what might be at stake in traditional philosophical concepts and debates that others had dismissed as empty and sterile. This is important for understanding those debates, but it is not itself active inquiry, just as history of science is not actual science.

The concept under discussion here is the concept of God. In the article in which he introduces the pragmatic criterion of meaning, Peirce (1992c, 1:133–36) uses the idea of force as an illustration of how to make our ideas clear. The concept of force, he writes, was developed early in the seventeenth century from the crude idea of a cause and has been continually improved since then. Its meaning is given by the rule for compounding and resolving accelerations by the use of a parallelogram of forces. Fixing the term in that way was crucial for the development of modern science. Dewey argues that James, by characterizing the idea of God as one that "guarantees an ideal order that shall be permanently preserved" (James 1985b, 55), is not fixing the concept in a new way but is explicating and adopting a traditional conception. While he had not yet developed the full naturalism that emerges in his works of the late 1920s, Dewey was already wary about tying the significance of the term *God* to some moral order that was independent of human thought and action.

Dewey sets out in *A Common Faith* to do what he thought James had failed to do. He criticizes and tries to reconstruct the term *God* so as to bring it into accord with what we have come to know and to connect it with actual effects in the world. He wants to liberate what he takes to be a genuinely religious attitude or quality of experience from claims about the supernatural. Aims as ends of action, duties, virtues, and criteria for moral judgment are all the result of the intelligent and imaginative shaping of human action.

Citing the *Oxford English Dictionary*, Dewey begins with a Jamesian description of religion as recognition of and reverence for an "unseen higher power" and asks what idea of the unseen would remain if the religious quality in experience could express itself free from historical encumbrances. Such powers have been conceived differently across religious traditions, he notes, and we are actually quite selective in our ways of thinking of them. For instance, we value reverence shown by a free human being over servile obedience to an arbitrary power. This kind of selectivity is not new. We ought to acknowledge it, Dewey (1986, 6) writes, and embrace it. What conception of unseen powers, he asks, would be "consonant with the best achievements and aspirations of the present"? Like James, Dewey thinks of religion as devotion to unseen powers that are congenial to our ideals and that help us to make progress toward achieving them. He agrees with James that some conditions for the development of our ideals exceed the capacity of any individual and that they depend on further resources in nature and in human association. In this sense they are "not ourselves," but they need not be thought to be beyond the realm of natural inquiry and explanation.

The religious, as Dewey thinks of it, is an attitude or a quality of experience that is distinguishable from the institutions and doctrines of the religions. It is a new unification of self that is unusually deep-seated, enduring, and inclusive. This enduring unification of self is quite similar to the idea of conversion at the center of James's *Varieties*. Dewey proposes to detach this effect from the subject's interpretation of it—for instance, from his or her explanation of it in supernatural terms. He here assumes that critical inquiry into the causes of the experience will alter the interpretation but leave the effect intact. This is almost certain to fail to identify the experience under the description assumed by the person whose experience it is, and therefore to fail to capture the experience.[6]

This harmonizing of self with universe is an ideal that is a product of the imagination, though it can't be obtained by conscious deliberation and often seems to come from beyond the self. Wherever this unification takes place, Dewey says, we have a genuinely religious quality of experience, with its source in conditions of nature and human association that elicit it and that provide support through periods of disappointment and despair and other obstacles to the realization of our ideals.

Dewey (1986, 17) argues that the philosophical idealist errs by converting ideals for action into a system of beliefs about antecedently existing realities, and that religions have often attached themselves to such a view. The unseen power from which the religious element in experience emerges is the attractive power of an ideal. Stability traditionally sought for in knowledge of antecedently existent ideals, he says, can come only from experimental inquiry and intelligent action directed toward particular ends. Friedrich Schleiermacher was right to describe the religious as a sense of dependence, but it is dependence on contingent goods of nature and of social relations.[7]

Dewey cites the phrase "natural piety," from William Wordsworth, in recognition of this dependence. Action on behalf of one's ideals serves to unify them and contributes to conditions required to bring them about. "It is the *active* relation between ideal and actual," Dewey writes, "to which I would give the name 'God.'" He doesn't insist on the term, but he thinks he has captured its meaning. This "*function* of such a working union of ideal and actual," he writes, "seems to me to be identical with the force that has in fact been attached to the conception of God in all religions that have a spiritual content; and a clear idea of that function seems to me urgently needed at the present time" (Dewey 1986, 51–52, emphasis in original). Dewey doesn't insist on this term, but he rejected suggestions from some of his colleagues that he dispense altogether with the idea of God. He is not just explicating what he takes to be the significance of the idea but is also endorsing the need for something like it. He wants to distinguish his position from aggressive or militant atheism.

Dewey must have appreciated the dual resonance in Wordsworth's phrase, of both piety toward the natural world and piety as natural rather than artificial. But, for Dewey, no normative authority accrues to piety because it is natural in the latter sense. Just as knowledge is the product of intelligent thought and directed action and virtue is the result of imaginative and intelligent shaping of aims and habits, the piety Dewey commends must be the result, in part, of reflection on experience and action in the world.

## IV

During the 1880s, while James was raising the question of whether this is a moral or unmoral universe, Friedrich Nietzsche also wrote about the idea of an eternal moral order. In the *Genealogy of Morals*, he characterizes the idea of God as "some alleged spider of purpose and morality behind the great captious web of causality," and he observes that people can endure suffering but find it much more difficult to accept meaningless suffering (Nietzsche 1989, essay 2, section 7; essay 3, section 9). In *The Anti-Christ*, he refers to "the lie of a moral world order" (Nietzsche 1968, 38). Nietzsche recognized a deep need for such an order, but he thought that both the need and the idea were suspect. He worked to identify what was at stake in that need, to inquire how it came to exert such a hold on us, and to begin to gain some critical distance from it.

Nietzsche thought critical reflection on the need for a moral order required a new kind of inquiry. In the preface to the *Genealogy*, he calls for an actual or realistic history of morals, in contrast to those that assume the concepts and practices to be explained (Nietzsche 1989, essay 7). He situates ideas of free will, conscience, moral guilt, and asceticism in the context of the Christian doctrines and practices that inform European conceptions of morality, and he examines how they shape and express current affect, normative judgments, and social practices. Nietzsche rejects any single narrative in favor of brief descriptions of multiple practices and concepts that might have served different interests as they were taken over, appropriated, redescribed, and given new meanings. The appropriate kind of inquiry is not best modeled by the scientific experiment but requires close reading and reflection on moral concepts and practices and on the standard narratives we use to justify them.[8] He constructs a form of inquiry that will provide traction, identify resistance, and connect with actual motivations and consequences but that avoids any kind of foundationalism.

Pragmatists since Peirce have sought to provide an account of inquiry that is both fallible and sensitive to evidence. In the triadic system of categories he developed, Peirce designated *secondness* as the compulsive component or the resistant in experience.[9] Secondness is the element in perception that consists in "our knocking up against it," and, he writes, a "hard fact is of the same sort" (Peirce 1992a, 1:249). Actual perceptions and recognition of facts are judgments that are informed by language and inference, but secondness designates the element of the resistant. Peirce recognized that G. W. F. Hegel had criticized claims for immediacy and argued against uninterpreted cognition in much the same way that Peirce had, but he thought Hegel had given insufficient attention to secondness and that he "almost altogether ignores the Outward Clash" (Peirce 1992b, 1:233). As Misak (2013, 254) writes, pragmatists in the Peircean tradition call for revision of beliefs in such a way that they are able to withstand rational reflection and are not overturned by argument or recalcitrant experience. *Experience* here does not mean immediate experience, nor must it privilege sensory perception or the kind of first-person accounts James considers in the *Varieties*. Rather, it refers to the learning from experience that informs realistic views of human psychology and social relations as well as of nonhuman nature. Peirce (1992a, 1:256) comments that, by overlooking secondness, Hegel "committed the trifling oversight of forgetting that there is a real world with real actions and reactions." Peirce invoked the logic of science in order to criticize ineffectual inquiry in philosophy and to connect change of belief with actual experience. Nietzsche also devised a kind of inquiry that he thought could begin to do justice to actual history or realistic reflection on experience.

Nietzsche's genealogical method constitutes a new way of getting in touch with the recalcitrant or realistic components of experience. The kind of realistic history he calls for yields a secondness, a clash, that is different from the resistant component in sense perception. His close attention to particular concepts and practices in modern moral philosophy, and his reflections on the motivations they reveal, are intended to elicit and to analyze resistance that arises from conceptions of self and world that distort, are counterproductive, and impede self-knowledge. Resistance is not always a mark of the actual or the real, but Nietzsche calls for and provides tools for recovering awareness that there is a real world with real actions and reactions and for reflecting on its implications for moral philosophy.

Peirce initially invoked the example of science to provide an account of inquiry that differed from that of the idealists of his day and from their speculative approach to philosophy, which he thought lacked secondness and was friction free. Nietzsche aims to construct a method of reflection that will not be overturned by the kind of self-knowledge that comes from recognizing complex and perhaps unwelcome motives, inequalities of power, and social forces that help to account for how we interpret the world and how we act. Inquiry should be accountable to experience in the sense of what we can learn about ourselves and the world. Nietzsche's method does not contradict, but extends, the scope of pragmatist inquiry and offers additional resources for an adequate naturalism.

In "The Fixation of Belief," Peirce wrote that genuine inquiry begins when a problem disrupts habits of thought and action. Dewey (1984b, 79–84, 98–99) calls particular attention to the fact that problems don't always present themselves as such. Indeterminate situations require reflection to turn them into problems so that inquiry can be directed appropriately. Nietzsche goes further in the same direction. He poses questions that are not experienced as problems but that provoke resistance and often denial. He criticizes assumptions, norms, and interests that are deeply entrenched in habits of action and thought. This requires a method of inquiry that disrupts complacency and that can be pursued in the face of strong resistance. In the *Genealogy*, he examines a concept of free will that he takes to be assumed by ascriptions of blame and responsibility, as well as current conceptions of conscience, ascetic life and practices, and the institutions associated with them. While these are familiar topics, Nietzsche argues that they are more problematic than they might appear to be. The first task of inquiry is to problematize them and to display their oddity against the background of actual experience. His genealogical method is intended to accomplish that.

Dewey offers two developmental accounts that might appear to be genealogies. In *The Quest for Certainty*, he traces a search for a secure foundation for knowledge and value from the Greeks through the seventeenth century and shows how it is motivated by social and economic causes of insecurity that vary across different periods. He uses this history to illumine his critique of metaphysical idealism, of religious thought and theologies that have associated themselves with it, and of its legacy in contemporary philosophy. In *Human Nature and Conduct* (Dewey 1983), he sets out a philosophical reconstruction of how moral aims and practices might have developed from natural and social resources that don't assume any distinctively moral concepts. In each of these, Dewey argues that contingent aims of knowledge and action have been idealized and represented as having an antecedent existence. So, in each, he is historicizing something that he takes to have been naturalized.

But neither of these is a genealogy in Nietzsche's sense. Both are relatively continuous narratives along a line that is understandable from the perspective of our own purposes. Nietzsche (1989, essay 2, section 12) says that our purposes are the last things to employ in seeking the origin of moral concepts or social practices. He calls for actual or more realistic history that recognizes the ways in which concepts and practices are taken over, reinterpreted, and redirected toward different ends.

Nietzsche examines specific concepts and representations of modern European moral thought, with particular attention to the ways in which they have been shaped by Christian theology and religious practice. For example, he criticizes the idea of a will that is prior to and independent of its actions. His critique is directed not so much against the idea of will, or of free will, but against a radical notion of freedom that he takes to be in the service of a language and practices of accountability that have developed with and sustain a moralized, peculiarly Christian conception of self and its relation to the universe. This conception and these practices, Nietzsche argues, have become so ingrained, so naturalized, we might say, that we are unaware that they might be the product of contingent events and interests that, if known, would weaken or undermine our confidence in them. Christian doctrines of sin and redemptive love that inform even secular European moral thought and practice may have arisen not from primitive impulses of regret and fellow feeling that have been honed and cultivated over time but from resentment and a propensity to ascribe blame for misfortune or suffering.

Nietzsche's point is not to retrieve some original meaning but to show motivations that may conflict with one another and with the stated meaning of the doctrine or practice being examined. Even when Christianity and its concept of God is subject to doubt or is relinquished, its shadow survives in the ways in which it has shaped moral concepts and practices. Something so deeply entangled with our ways of understanding ourselves and the world can be revealed and made available for critical reflection only by careful dismantling, by posing alternatives, by imaginative thought experiments, historical inquiry, and whatever else might help to illumine these issues and advance self-knowledge.

Nietzsche is not necessarily committed to a minimalist moral psychology, as Bernard Williams (1993a) has argued, but to a naturalistic account of psychology, in contrast to the moralized and naturalized one he criticizes in the *Genealogy*. He writes that the concepts and practices that contribute to the sickness produced by Christianity also make humans interesting in a distinctive way and open up new possibilities. After distinguishing the concept of *good*, which he attributes to nobility, from its inversion by the reactive reinterpretation of the priestly class, Nietzsche writes, "It was on the soil of this *essentially dangerous* form of human existence, the priestly form, that man first became *an interesting animal*, that only here did the human soul in a higher sense acquire *evil* and become *evil*—and these are the respects in which man has hitherto been superior to the other beasts" (Nietzsche 1989, essay 1, section 6, emphasis in original).

Later, Nietzsche likens to pregnancy the illness brought about by the internalization of instincts to produce "bad conscience." It was here, he says, that man first developed what was later called his soul. "Let us add at once that . . . the existence of an animal soul turned against itself, taking sides against itself, was something so new, profound, unheard of, enigmatic, contradictory, and *pregnant with a future* the aspect of the earth was essentially altered" (essay 2, section 16). This "illness from which humanity has never recovered" is the source of possibilities that distinguish humans from other animals. Nietzsche is not proposing to eliminate the idea of conscience but to naturalize it in a way that contributes to self-knowledge. He wants to call attention to what he calls the moralization of will, conscience, and the ascetic life while recognizing their value for ethics (essay 2, section 21).

In *Shame and Necessity*, his examination of ethical concepts and practices in ancient Greek tragedy, Williams (1993b, 163) proposes that we ask "whether or not a given writer or philosophy believes that, beyond some things that human beings have themselves shaped, there is anything at all that is intrinsically shaped to human interests, in particular to human beings' ethical interests." In the light of this question, he writes, Plato, Aristotle, Immanuel Kant, and Hegel are all on the same side, "all believing in one way or another that the universe or history or the structure of human reason can, when properly understood, yield a pattern that makes sense of human life and aspirations." Sophocles and Thucydides, by contrast, are alike in leaving us with no such sense. "Each of them represents human beings as dealing sensibly, foolishly, sometimes catastrophically, sometimes nobly, with a world that is only partially intelligible to human agency and in itself is not necessarily well adjusted to ethical aspirations."

This question of whether there is anything intrinsically shaped to human beings' ethical interests that humans themselves have not shaped is a version of James's question of whether this is "at bottom a moral or unmoral universe," whether it is congruous with the "higher part" of ourselves (James 1979, 84; 1985c, 400). It is also related to Dewey's criticism of philosophical idealism and theology for reifying ideals that are aims for action and ascribing to them an existence antecedent to human thought and action. James and Williams both pose their questions rhetorically, but that doesn't mean that it is an empty question. Their rhetoric points in opposite directions. James writes that he refuses to accept that there is "no purpose in the objective world," and he makes *intimacy*, his term for a congruity between the universe and ethical interests, a criterion of any adequate metaphysics (James 1977). Williams poses the question as a critical tool by which to inquire into the ways in which moral interests have been naturalized and tacitly continue to structure our conceptions of the cosmos and of history, reason, and psychology.

The aim is not to purge moral reflection and experience from conceptions of history, mind, and cosmos. It is to contribute to self-knowledge and knowledge of the world by coming to understand the extent to which norms and ideals are products of human social practices. Much of what goes under the name of genealogical criticism consists of inquiry into the histories by which normative concepts, practices, and institutions have developed and have been reinterpreted, redirected, and naturalized. In the study of Buddhism, for example, Bernard Faure (1991, 1996) and Robert Sharf (1995) have each critically examined modern conceptions of Buddhist meditation, showing how they emerged and reexamining classical texts with careful attention to their historical and literary contexts. Though Faure and Sharf work on Chan Buddhism in China rather than on Tibet, this kind of analysis is more fruitful than the work of Davidson and his colleagues and is, in any case, necessary for understanding the concepts and practices they set out to study.

Nietzsche's genealogy and the work of scholars in the humanities and social sciences to historicize what has been naturalized are not in opposition to scientific study of humans as natural creatures. They contribute to that study. Claims by neuroscientists, cognitive scientists, and others to provide accounts of religion that circumvent culture and social practices are suspect for that very reason. They are often used uncritically to provide support for or opposition to religious beliefs and practice in a way that impedes rather than aids the development of an adequate naturalistic account. Genealogy contributes to the kind of inquiry that pragmatism calls for, with a more critical attention to history than the classical pragmatists actually practiced.

## NOTES

1. See, for instance, De Caro and Macarthur (2004, 2010).
2. Misak (2004). See also Misak (2007); Bernstein (2010).
3. It is ironic that *cognitive science* has come to refer to work that deliberately excludes reference to the thoughts of the people being studied. Cognitive psychology in the mid-twentieth century was a reaction against behaviorism precisely because behaviorists excluded attention to thinking. See, for example, Bruner (1956); Miller, Galanter, and Pribram (1960).
4. See Gimello (1978).
5. Charles Peirce (1960, 5:384, note) later changed *caused* here to *determined*. Belief need not be fixed by the object alone, and perception is not the only kind of experience by which beliefs are tested.
6. The identification of an experience as religious, even from the subject's perspective, often assumes that the experience cannot be fully explained in naturalistic terms. See Proudfoot (1985), especially chapter 5.
7. John Dewey (1984b, 244) cites Friedrich Schleiermacher on the sense of dependence, in *The Quest for Certainty*.
8. In his preface, Friedrich Nietzsche (1989, section 8) calls for rumination on his aphorisms, like a cow chewing its cud.
9. For Peirce's three categories of *firstness*, *secondness*, and *thirdness*, see, for instance, "A Guess at the Riddle" (Peirce 1992a, 1:247–56).

## WORKS CITED

Arnold, Matthew. 1902. *Literature and Dogma*. New York: Macmillan.

Bernstein, Richard. 2010. *The Pragmatic Turn*. Cambridge: Polity.

Bruner, Jerome. 1956. *A Study of Thinking*. New York: Wiley.

Butler, Judith. 1990. *Gender Trouble*. New York: Routledge.

Bynum, Caroline. 1987. *Holy Feast and Holy Fast*. Berkeley: University of California Press.

Certeau, Michel de. 1992. *The Mystic Fable*. Translated by Michael Smith. Chicago: University of Chicago Press.

Clark, Kelly James, and Justin L. Barrett. 2011. "Reidian Religious Epistemology and the Cognitive Science of Religion." *Journal of the American Academy of Religion* 79:639–75.

Coakley, Sarah. 2013. "Evolution, Cooperation, and Divine Providence." In *Evolution, Games, and God*, edited by Martin A. Nowak and Sarah Coakley, 375–85. Cambridge, MA: Harvard University Press.

Dailey, Patricia. 2013. *Promised Bodies*. New York: Columbia University Press.

Davidson, Richard. 2002. "Toward a Biology of Positive Affect and Compassion." In *Visions of Compassion*, edited by Richard Davidson and Anne Harrington, 107–30. New York: Oxford University Press.

De Caro, Mario, and David Macarthur, eds. 2004. *Naturalism in Question*. Cambridge, MA: Harvard University Press.

De Caro, Mario, and David Macarthur, eds. 2010. *Naturalism and Normativity*. New York: Columbia University Press.

Dewey, John. 1908. "What Does Pragmatism Mean By Practical?" *Journal of Philosophy* 5:85–99.

Dewey, John. 1983. *John Dewey: The Middle Works, 1899–1924*, vol. 14, *1922: Human Nature and Conduct*. Carbondale: Southern Illinois University Press.

Dewey, John. 1984a. "The Development of American Pragmatism." In *John Dewey: The Later Works, 1925–1953*, vol. 2, *1925–1927*, 3–21. Carbondale: Southern Illinois University Press.

Dewey, John. 1984b. *John Dewey: The Later Works, 1925–1953*, vol. 4, *1929: The Quest for Certainty*. Carbondale: Southern Illinois University Press.

Dewey, John. 1986. *A Common Faith*. In *John Dewey: The Later Works, 1925–1953*, vol. 9, *1933–1934*, 1–58. Carbondale: Southern Illinois University Press.

Dreyfus, Georges. 2002. "Is Compassion an Emotion? A Cross-Cultural Exploration of Mental Typologies." In *Visions of Compassion*, edited by Richard Davidson and Anne Harrington, 31–45. New York: Oxford University Press.

Faure, Bernard. 1991. *The Rhetoric of Immediacy*. Princeton, NJ: Princeton University Press.

Faure, Bernard. 1996. *Chan Insights and Oversights*. Princeton, NJ: Princeton University Press.

Gimello, Robert. 1978. "Mysticism and Meditation." In *Mysticism and Philosophical Analysis*, edited by Steven Katz, 170–90. New York: Oxford University Press.

James, William. 1977. *A Pluralistic Universe*. Cambridge, MA: Harvard University Press.

James, William. 1978. *The Meaning of Truth*. Cambridge, MA: Harvard University Press.

James, William. 1979. *The Will to Believe*. Cambridge, MA: Harvard University Press.

James, William. 1981. *The Principles of Psychology*. Cambridge, MA: Harvard University Press.

James, William. 1985a. "Philosophical Conceptions and Practical Results." In *Pragmatism*, 257–70. Cambridge, MA: Harvard University Press.

James, William. 1985b. *Pragmatism*. Cambridge, MA: Harvard University Press.

James, William. 1985c. *The Varieties of Religious Experience*. Cambridge, MA: Harvard University Press.

James, William. 1992. *The Correspondence of William James*, edited by Ignas Skrupskelis and Elizabeth Berkeley. 10 vols. Charlottesville: University of Virginia Press.

Lincoln, Bruce. 1999. *Theorizing Myth*. Chicago: University of Chicago Press.

Lutz, Antoine, Lawrence Greischar, Nancy Rawlings, Matthieu Ricard, and Richard Davidson. 2004. "Long-Term Meditators Self-Induce High-Amplitude Gamma Synchrony During Mental Practice." *Proceedings of the National Academy of Sciences* 101:16369–73.

Masuzawa, Tomoko. 2005. *The Invention of World Religions*. Chicago: University of Chicago Press.

Miller, George A., Eugene Galanter, and Karl Pribram. 1960. *Plans and the Structure of Behavior*. New York: Henry Holt.

Misak, Cheryl. 2004. *Truth and the End of Inquiry*, expanded paperback ed. Oxford: Oxford University Press.

Misak, Cheryl, ed. 2007. *New Pragmatists*. New York: Oxford University Press.

Misak, Cheryl. 2013. *The American Pragmatists*. Oxford: Oxford University Press.

Nietzsche, Friedrich. 1968. *The Anti-Christ*. Translated by R. J. Hollingdale. New York: Penguin.

Nietzsche, Friedrich. 1989. *The Genealogy of Morals*. Translated by Walter Kaufmann. New York: Vintage.

Peirce, Charles Sanders. 1960. "The Fixation of Belief." In *The Collected Papers of Charles Sanders Peirce*, edited by Charles Hartshorne and Paul Weiss, 5:358–87. Cambridge, MA: Harvard University Press.

Peirce, Charles Sanders. 1992a. "A Guess at the Riddle." In *The Essential Peirce*, edited by Nathan Houser and Christian Kloesel, 1:245–79. Bloomington: Indiana University Press.

Peirce, Charles Sanders. 1992b. "An American Plato: Review of Royce's *Religious Aspect of Philosophy*." In *The Essential Peirce*, edited by Nathan Houser and Christian Kloesel, 1:229–41. Bloomington: Indiana University Press.

Peirce, Charles Sanders. 1992c. "How to Make Our Ideas Clear." In *The Essential Peirce*, edited by Nathan Houser and Christian Kloesel, 1:124–41. Bloomington: Indiana University Press.

Peirce, Charles Sanders. 1992d. "Questions Concerning Certain Faculties Claimed for Man." In *The Essential Peirce*, edited by Nathan Houser and Christian Kloesel, 1:11–27. Bloomington: Indiana University Press.

Peirce, Charles Sanders. 1992e. "Some Consequences of Four Incapacities." In *The Essential Peirce*, edited by Nathan Houser and Christian Kloesel, 1:28–55. Bloomington: Indiana University Press.

Price, Huw. 2004. "Naturalism Without Representationalism." In *Naturalism in Question*, edited by Mario De Caro and David Macarthur, 71–88. Cambridge, MA: Harvard University Press.

Proudfoot, Wayne. 1985. *Religious Experience*. Berkeley: University of California Press.

Sellars, Wilfrid. 1997. *Empiricism and the Philosophy of Mind*. Cambridge, MA: Harvard University Press.

Sharf, Robert. 1995. "Buddhist Modernism and the Rhetoric of Meditative Experience." *Numen* 42:228–82.

Williams, Bernard. 1993a. "Nietzsche's Minimalist Moral Psychology." *European Journal of Philosophy* 1:4–14.

Williams, Bernard. 1993b. *Shame and Necessity*. Berkeley: University of California Press.

# 5

# Language, Method, and Pragmatism in the Study of Religion

SCOTT DAVIS

For the last quarter of a century, pragmatism has been something of a contested notion in philosophy generally. What I intend to call the "pragmatic turn" in the study of religion refers primarily to the thought of Charles S. Peirce, and specifically to his understanding of inquiry.[1] For Peirce, inquiry begins when a question or a puzzle presents itself with enough force to disrupt the stability of the beliefs that have, up to that point, accounted for our actions, practices, and policies. For example, according to a well-known story, Louis Pasteur was approached by a winemaker who wanted to know why a certain percentage of his product failed to ferment properly. In the course of his investigations, Pasteur confirmed the germ theory and laid the foundation for microbiology and modern medicine. Peirce, as a practicing scientist steeped in the history of the sciences, could recognize in the work of Pasteur the common pattern of discovery and progress in our quest for justified true beliefs about the world.

As a practicing philosopher, Peirce found the accounts of how we acquire this knowledge—justified true belief—put forward by René Descartes, John Locke, and their various followers to be based on incoherent premises. Descartes, for example, begins with the idea that we establish a foundation through examining the contents of our minds and then use that foundation to build up the edifice of knowledge. But, Peirce (1992, 1:31) insists, "we have no power of Introspection." Locke, and the tradition of British empiricism generally, believes that we can start with the content of the senses and build science on that, but this requires unmediated access to the content of our experience and "we have no power of Intuition." Why does Peirce repudiate introspection and intuition? In an argument that would be developed in more detail by Ludwig Wittgenstein, he maintains that "all knowledge of the internal world is derived by way of hypothetical reasoning from our knowledge of external facts" and that we "have no power of thinking without signs."

Descartes and Locke, for all their differences, share the model of thinking that Wittgenstein identifies with Augustine at the very beginning of *Philosophical Investigations*. But humans are not born thinking beings, with a language that allows us to interpret and, in doing so, learn the language of our elders. Language is a product of human societies, which have evolved over a very long period of time and have developed this sort of behavior as part of our repertoire of problem-solving skills. This is what Wittgenstein means when he writes that "the verbal expression of pain replaces crying, it does not describe it" (Wittgenstein 1953, section 244). At some point in our evolution, our predecessors developed forms of verbal behavior that made it much easier for them to solve important coordination problems than their competitors in the field. They were able to impart this behavior to their progeny, who have made language a powerful and constantly evolving human skill, capable of dealing with and giving rise to ever more complicated social and cultural practices, such as Pasteur's microbiology.

So pragmatism, as I understand it, combines a particular view of the practice of science with a closely related view of the philosophy of science. It rejects Cartesian rationalism—not much of a contemporary player in any case—as well as the empiricist tradition from Locke through the Vienna Circle and its heirs. Peirce, if I were going to tell that story, is the heir of Aristotle and G. W. F. Hegel and the progenitor (despite their family squabbles) of Karl Popper, N. Russell Hanson, Stephen Toulmin, Paul Feyerabend, Thomas Kuhn, and Bas van Fraassen.

But I'm not going to tell that story. Instead, I'm going to follow another strain in Peirce's thought, which rejects any hard-and-fast distinction between the natural and the social sciences. Any question can provoke inquiry, and the pursuit of justified true beliefs about human beings, whether individuals or groups, is as natural and potentially fruitful as similar inquiry directed at the reproductive cycle of wasps. And, specifically, I'm going to ask what this pragmatic turn, and the understanding of thought and language it involves, reveals about a family of currently trendy approaches to the study of religion.

It is, I suppose, important to get clear on one thing at the outset: studying religion is not the same thing as doing theology. Theologians, as I understand them, are involved in interpreting the meaning and implications of a commitment to a tradition for the members of that tradition. Karl Barth and Stanley Hauerwas would be examples. Students of religion, believers or not, study one or more traditions with an eye to what was said and done, by whom, when, and for what reasons. Émile Durkheim and Mircea Eliade would seem to qualify here. And some scholars do both, perhaps none so famously, in the last century, as Rudolf Bultmann.

But for my pragmatist, believer or not, inquiry requires holding the student of religion to the same standards of evidence and argument found in analogous areas of inquiry. In the case of religion, this means biology, psychology, history, sociology, and anthropology, together with their ancillary fields. Insofar as biology is important, this means nothing more than a basic commitment to the best available version of Darwinian evolution. Whatever else we are, we are creatures of the natural world, and any approach to studying us that makes us alien to that world cannot be a credible foundation for inquiry. This makes the connection to psychology. In the ongoing dispute between the partisans of nature and the partisans of nurture, my pragmatist embraces both, though perhaps not in equal measure. While this is not the place to argue the point, I'm inclined to say that nature is in charge through the endocrine system and its workings, and then it's nurture the rest of the way up. Pathologies that inhabit the gray area in between are best left to Oliver Sacks.

Peirce's is a nonreductive naturalism. He believes that causality is best understood in terms of habits, as opposed to mathematics. Even if, pace Pierre-Simon Laplace, we knew all the weights, angles, and velocities, there still would be no determinate way that things would happen. There would be only higher and lower probabilities. Another way to put this would be to say that, for Peirce, probability is not a function of the experimenters' ignorance but a fact about reality. Human beings and lumps of coal are part of a continuum in a world where everything is made up of the same sort of stuff; it's just that the best explanation of how that stuff behaves is based on the well-observed workings of ordinary human beings. To think otherwise is understandable, given the hold that empiricism has exerted over much of the scientific and philosophical world, but to insist on it dogmatically, as Wittgenstein said, is to be held captive by a "picture" of how things must be (Wittgenstein 1953, section 115). Part of the Darwinian moral, to which Peirce and I both subscribe, is that there is no way things *must* be. Inquiry is about how the things that happen to be came to be. I plan to hold inquiry into religion to Peirce's standards. And this takes me back to the question of language.

## DONALD DAVIDSON ON LANGUAGE AND THOUGHT

Donald Davidson stands foursquare in the tradition that goes from Peirce through Willard V. O. Quine, though none of the three thought of himself as a "pragmatist." In a watershed essay of 1986, Davidson writes that "there is no such thing as a language, not if a language is anything like what many philosophers and linguists have supposed. There is therefore no such thing to be learned, mastered, or born with." From this, he concludes, "We must give up the idea of a clearly defined shared structure which language-users acquire and then apply to cases" (Davidson 2005a, 107). A few years later (1994), Davidson acknowledged that "this is the sort of remark for which one can expect to be pilloried" (Davidson 2005c, 109). Nevertheless, the argument is sound and its implications reach far beyond the philosophy of language. For, rightly understood, it renders problematic not a few trendy projects in the philosophical study of human beings, including a currently influential one in the study of religion.

The object of Davidson's attack is well characterized by David Lewis (1975, 3), who describes language as, "something which assigns meanings to certain strings of types of sounds or of marks. It could therefore be a function, a set of ordered pairs of strings and meaning. The entities in the domain of the function are certain finite sequences of types of vocal sounds, or of types of inscribable marks."[2] Language, construed *this* way, is unabashedly formal, "a set-theoretic entity which can be discussed in complete abstraction from human affairs" (Lewis 1975, 19). There are all sorts of reasons to study language in this sense, just as there are for studying logic, but the problem comes when students of these artificial languages attempt to draw substantive conclusions about communication, thought, and action. For if these set-theoretical entities are artificial, what Lewis calls "rational reconstructions" (35), then it's hard to see what role they could play in any but a very narrow slice of human behavior. And this, in turn, makes it hard to see what role they could serve in our studies of that behavior.

Davidson asks us to consider Archie Bunker's "We need a few laughs to break up the monogamy," or Goodman Ace's "We're all cremated equal." While it doesn't flag Archie's line, Microsoft Word does insert a wiggly blue line under Ace's, indicating that it doesn't recognize this as standard usage. "What is interesting," writes Davidson, "is the fact that in all these cases the hearer has no trouble understanding the speaker in the way the speaker intends." These and other "mistakes," intended or not, threaten the formal account of language because "the intended meaning seems to take over from the standard meaning" (Davidson

2005a, 90–91). Languages, in Lewis's sense, produce well-formed sentences that are interpretable given the grammar, vocabulary, and universe associated with them. For formal languages, as John Burgess (2009, 10) puts it, should be "the *number* of elements in the domain of the model, and the *pattern* of distinguished relations among them" (emphasis in original).

For natural language users, however, what Davidson calls "first meaning . . . will be what should be found by consulting a dictionary based on actual usage" (Davidson 2005a, 91). On most ordinary occasions, the normal "way to distinguish first meaning is through the intention of the speaker. The intentions with which an act is performed are usually unambiguously ordered by the relation of means to ends" (92). So "Close the door" would normally register my intention that someone close the door, and "John has already closed the door" will be true, spoken by a particular individual at a particular time and place, if and only if John has already closed the door.

When characterizing what a speaker and hearer share that allows communication to succeed, we typically say, "a system which makes possible the articulation of logical relations between utterances and explains the ability to interpret novel utterances in an organized way" (93). At the very least, Davidson continues, it would seem that any such system must conform to the following "three plausible principles":

1. *First meaning is systematic* . . . there must be systematic relations between the meanings of the utterances.
2. *First meanings are shared.* For speaker and interpreter to communicate successfully and regularly, they must share a method of interpretation of the sort described in (1).
3. *First meanings are governed by learned conventions or regularities.* The systematic knowledge or competence of the speaker or interpreter is learned in advance of occasions of interpretation and is conventional in character (Davidson 2005a, 93).

Unfortunately, the plausibility of each principle is undermined by the fact of linguistic innovation, of which malapropisms are but one example. When Archie substitutes *monogamy* for *monotony*, he violates the first meaning in a way that the theory (and MS Word) must flag as unintelligible. But it isn't; "the interpreter adjusts his theory so that it yields the speaker's intended interpretation." The same is true of names, catchphrases, descriptions—in short, "there is no word or construction that cannot be converted to a new use by an ingenious or ignorant speaker." And from this Davidson concludes that "learning to interpret a word that expresses a concept we do not already have is a far deeper and more interesting phenomenon than explaining the ability to use a word new to us for an old concept. But both require a change in one's way of interpreting the speech of another, or in speaking to someone who has the use of the word" (Davidson 2005a, 99–100).

Given these facts, it turns out that principle 1 is, at best, woefully incomplete. If (1) is incomplete, then (2) must be false, at least for a substantial number of linguistic performances. And (3) is simply false. Even the most skilled and thoughtful language user will encounter cases that cannot be specified in advance. "The theory we actually use to interpret an utterance," Davidson concludes, "is geared to the occasion" (101).

Even if we continue to be interested in studying formal systems, the upshot of Davidson's argument is that the "idiolect," the way of talking, writing, and thinking associated with an individual, is "conceptually primary"(Davidson 2005c, 109). Why does this make a difference? Consider a view of mind popularized by such thinkers as Steven Pinker. "According to Pinker, Jerry Fodor, and a number of others," writes Davidson, "the extraordinary ease with which language develops, added to the apparent existence of linguistic universals, shows that what is innate—that is, genetically programmed—is an internal language, the which they call the language of thought, or mentalese" (Davidson 2005b, 132). On this view, "mentalese" is hardwired into the brain. When the infant learns the language into which he is born, he translates between mentalese and what will become his home language. The details of that home language, and of all natural languages, must, therefore, be constrained by the structure of mentalese. Since our thoughts are articulated in language, mentalese sets the parameters for what we can think, and studying the brain can provide insight into the biological constraints on human thought. Wittgenstein is wrong.

This sounds pretty exciting, but "the arguments for the existence of a language of thought," thinks Davidson, "are feeble." Davidson is perfectly willing to embrace "the idea of inborn constraints on syntax, for which [Noam] Chomsky has argued so vigorously," but, "there is no reason to suppose that ideas, concepts, or meanings are innate" (Davidson 2005b, 133–34). Ideas, concepts, and meanings are matters of semantics; syntax, even with a comprehensive dictionary, cannot yield semantics (Davidson 1984b). The meanings of words are inseparable from their uses, and uses must be learned. The notion of a "language of thought" is doing no work, unless it is a highfalutin way of saying that so-and-so speaks English. Of course, individuals with some physical or psychological pathology may not be able to become language users, but this is beside the point. If we hadn't evolved the way we did, we might never have become language users, but how much specialized hardware do we need to impose between the functioning body and the healthy mind?

If you start with your basic baby, the only thing that's really essential is a well-disposed, language-using adult. Babies babble, at some point, in an environment characterized by adult speech. And there seems to be something like an instinct to mimicry. The adult produces sounds and the baby produces sounds. When the product sounds sufficiently like the input to the adult, she laughs and smiles and says "Yes!" and repeats. "By the time he is two, the baby learns to form rudimentary sentences. He makes innumerable errors, of course . . . But, like calling an orange 'ball,' his errors tend to be understandable" (Maurer and Maurer 1988, 203). Like Pavlov's dogs, the baby can be trained to respond differentially, so that *ball* comes to be associated with various inedible round things and *orange* with a particular kind of edible roundish thing.

Of course, real languages being messy, he is also being trained to differentiate among *orange*, *blue*, and the like, but eventually the toddler can be counted on to produce unprompted noises very similar to the ones his teacher is likely to produce under similar circumstances. "By three years," writes Davidson (2005b, 131), "most children glibly generate sentences, and have the basic grammar of their environment right." At this point, according to Davidson, only two more components need to be added in order to attribute thought to children. "The first is the concept of error, that is, the appreciation of the distinction between belief and truth" (141). The making of mistakes, when they are recognized as such by the agent, sets up the distinction between what he is initially inclined to say and the way things are. When he understands error, we get the second component of thought: he is in a position to understand "truth" and its cognates. Syntax, semantics, error, and truth: "The primitive triangle, constituted by two (and typically more than two) creatures reacting in concert to features of the world and to each other's reactions, thus provides the framework in which thought and language can evolve."

Becoming a successful language user requires no knowledge of set theory or linguistics, as interesting as they may be, much less any knowledge of the human brain and the neurochemical events that take place there. The standard-issue baby, inserted into a minimally functional family, will master, in a few short years, the basics of the local dialect. In the process, the adults around him impart their norms and standards, which he will perhaps modify in the process of maturing. By the time the youngster is ready to strike out on his own, he has an idiolect capacious enough to identify the components of his world, rank them hierarchically for a variety of purposes, and make plans for the future. He and his mother, while speaking the same dialect, may have different purposes, preferences, and desires for the future, because at every stage they have adjusted their ways of communicating to be recognizably similar to each other's. As they move out into the wider world, they encounter fellow beings who have developed in pretty much the same way. It is natural to treat them all as speaking the same language and sharing the same beliefs, even though it is unlikely that anyone speaks or believes exactly the same things in exactly the same ways. This is Davidson's point about the conceptual primacy of the idiolect. While there is no objection, and some good reasons, for studying languages as abstract entities, in complete isolation from what people actually do, it's rarely going to help us discern why the individuals who inhabit a particular community do what they do.

## PRAGMATISM, LANGUAGE, AND RELIGION

Here, I think, we can see the possible fruitfulness of the pragmatic approach for studying religion. Imagine treating religions as languages, in Lewis's sense, and do a simple substitution experiment. You get something like this: What is a religion? Something which assigns meanings to certain strings of types of sounds or marks. A religion associates certain strings with certain sanctioned forms of behavior and then sorts those pairs (string and behavior) to more or less clearly defined groups of individuals at coordinates defined by a calendar (time and place).

Just as attempting to understand the relations between sentences containing modal terms such as *could*, *possible*, *impossible*, and *can't* led to the development of modal logics (see Burgess 2009, beginning at 40), somebody might, with enough effort, construct a set-theoretical entity sufficiently elaborate to be called a formal representation of religion X. In fact, there have been more than a few attempts to formulate at least part of such a language, most notably by E. Thomas Lawson and Robert McCauley, Harvey Whitehouse, and their colleagues. Pascal Boyer's *Religion Explained*, for example, opens with the claim that "the explanation for religious beliefs and behaviors is to be found in the way all human minds work . . . because what matters here are properties of minds that are found in all members of our species with normal brains"(Boyer 2001, 2).

For all its aspirations, however, *Religion Explained* doesn't deliver much. The bulk of the book relies on anthropology and the history of religions to deploy a variety of beliefs and rituals for analysis. The analyses depend on the claim that the mind "comprises lots of specialized explanatory devices, more properly called *inference systems*, each of which is adapted to particular kinds of events and automatically suggested explanations for these events" (17). These devices are instantiated in the brain and apparently process the raw data delivered through the senses to produce explanations of events. The programs for these devices, if we're to take seriously his endorsement of Pinker, are written in mentalese and have evolved along with the rest of the human organism (331). But the proof is in the pudding, and rather than rehash the arguments against inference systems, which are merely the latest version of Peirce's *introspection* and *intuition*, we should look at the theory in action.

An important example of how the cognitive approach is supposed to work comes out in Boyer's discussion of imitation:

> The fact that an infant can imitate adults' facial gestures (sticking out the tongue, pursing the lips, frowning, etc.) shows that the newborn's brain is equipped with highly specialized capacities. To imitate, you need to match *visual* information from the outside with *motor* control from inside. Infants start doing all this before they have ever seen their own faces in mirrors and before parents react to that behavior. The child does not learn to imitate but uses imitation to learn.
>
> (110)

Maybe Jimmy Fallon goes through something like this when he works up a caricature of Neil Young: identify the cadence of the voice, shift pitch, exaggerate facial or bodily characteristics, and so forth. But babies aren't like that, except in television commercials. Sticking out your tongue is an intentional act, and intentions require basic natural language ability. The behaviors we might attribute to intentions in a mature agent are, in the baby, no different from that of a newborn puppy. To interpret his reactions as if he were a mature language user doesn't explain any more than attributing them to instinct. The benefit of instinct language is that it doesn't tempt us into the fallacy of Boyer's final sentence, which attributes complex intentional action to a being for which we have, at this point, no evidence for intentionality.

That, I think, is the real issue. When academics enter the lists of argument, we accept certain burdens of proof. In this particular battle, "instinct" is the baseline. It registers the belief that a certain form of behavior is the unlearned, non-intentional, perhaps hormone-induced product of the evolution of the critter. It may be a precondition for developing language, thought, and intentional behavior, but these come later. We pragmatists and naturalists assume that, like everything else, it requires some sort of biochemical structure, but that doesn't go very far toward explaining the individual bit of language, thought, and intentional behavior that we care about. In particular, it doesn't go very far in explaining the religious beliefs and behaviors around us. That's why thinkers from Edward Tylor to the present have offered interpretive projects that purport to explain the puzzling bits of belief and behavior we gather under the rubric of *religion*. Boyer is entering into this battle, and the burden of proof is high. In particular, since his claims for cognitive science are designed to vanquish the tradition of Tylor et al., he is not entitled to smuggle an intentional mechanism into the works.

But Boyer has already begun that, in the discussion of mimicry, and he continues it in the section on innateness. "Loose talk of 'innateness,'" he writes, "seems to imply that we will find in infants the *same* concepts that we observe in adults. But the actual study of developing minds reveals something more complex—a series of skeletal principles, initial biases and specialized skills that result in adult concepts, if the child is provided with a *normal* environment" (Boyer 2001, 113). But what grounds do we have for ascribing any concepts to infants at all? To talk of inference systems outside of the context of communication, which involves the practices of asserting, making mistakes, and judging propositions, is Pickwickian at best. All of these practices are learned in the process of acquiring a language. As Davidson (2005c, 124) puts it, "A grasp of the concept of truth . . . depends on the norm that can be provided only by interpersonal communication." Boyer (2001, 118) tries to skip this step by identifying inference systems with "evolved responses to recurrent problems in ancestral conditions." We seem to have gone from the Pickwickian to the Lamarkian.[3] Boyer (2001, 135) moves to treat "information" on the analogy of nutrition, which is supposed to license the claim that "religious concepts are probably successful to the extent that they activate inference systems." This broadly epigenetic account of innate ideas seems to be what provokes the social Darwinist account of religion in the last three-fifths of the volume, concluding with the hope that we can "better understand many fascinating features of our mental architecture by study the human propensity toward religious thoughts" (330).

I am skeptical, but perhaps we should give Boyer the benefit, at least temporarily, of the doubt. So let's go back to the suggestion that an ambitious theorist might be able to create a formal account of a particular religion, as practiced at a particular time and place. On the epigenetic argument, generations of humans, having developed religion as a survival mechanism, did not alter human DNA but have created a biophysiological environment in which contact with the external world triggers a response that favors the creation and practice of religion.

This can be split into two questions. It might have been the case that at some early point our instincts led our particular group to develop its practices, but what about the second generation? Since the survival situation has been changed for the better by their parents' creation of religion, the trigger isn't pulled and that generation adopts the religion under the pressure of its elders, so now the "information system" model doesn't seem to have anything to do. From here on up, we study the tradition in familiar Durkheimian ways.

Or it might be claimed that the development of religion in the current generation is overdetermined, that even if the elders had not come out with their version, the current generation would come up with something recognizably similar. That would be a strong claim, amounting to the thesis that human beings are highly complicated machines in which the evolved systems can be compared to computer programs that have the capacity to revise or augment, without changing the original program—in this case, our DNA. On this model, we might think that, under stress, program H wrote and installed program R, which will, in subsequent generations, trigger R' as part of its survival protocol. We could, in theory, trace the formal account of R' back to R, and then back to H, without any necessary recourse to the language of intention.

Assuming that the formal reconstructions can be made as coherent as the various systems of modal logic, this would still face serious obstacles. For this would commit us to saying that the current generation could be understood as a machine, instantiating the formal language. Unfortunately, notes Daniel Dennett (2000, 99), "as every programmer learns, it is essential to 'comment' your 'source code.' Comments are lines of ordinary language, not programming language, inserted into the program between special brackets." This is important because "without the handy hints about how the programmer intended the process or state to function, the very identity of the state entered when a computer executes a line of code is often for all intents and purposes inscrutable." A moment's thought on this "epistemological version of Original Sin" makes it clear that any complex of inference systems adequate to even a single agent, much less an entire community, depends on the scrutiny and interpretation of a mature natural language user. Given Davidson's earlier argument for the primacy of the idiolect over the set-theoretical model of language, this implies that the computational account of the mind is grossly inadequate. The information systems were supposed to explain the language and the religion, but it looks like it needs to be the other way around.

## DOXASTIC UPDATING AND RELIGIOUS CHANGE

Boyer might complain that it is unfair to pin so much on an admittedly popular introduction to a complicated field. But the more formal we get, the greater the technical problems become. One way to think of the computational model is in terms of the set of programs that need to be written in order to attribute intelligence to a robot. Even more elegant than Dennett's is the version of this argument laid out by Robert Brandom in *Between Saying and Doing: Towards an Analytic Pragmatism.* "Very crudely," he writes, artificial intelligence "is the claim that a computer could, in principle *do* what is needed to deploy an autonomous vocabulary, that is, in this strong sense, to *say* something." This claim requires, in turn, that "there is some program (some algorithm) such that anything that runs that program (executes that algorithm) can pass the Turing test, that is, can deploy a vocabulary in the sense which any other language-users do" (Brandom 2008, 70).

If this were true, then whatever was running the program would be able to carry on a conversation indistinguishable from the sorts of conversations we normally have with each other. And if this were so, then there would be no good reason *not* to attribute "sapience" to our conversation partner. We would, in other words, be forced into admissions such as "That's one ugly machine, but it sure knows what it's talking about," even if we still had qualms about what counted as "sentience" (see 71–74). And if this were true of the homely machine across the table, then why shouldn't it be true of you or me?

If, in other words, the complex routines that we use to talk and write can be decomposed into simpler algorithms and programmed into a machine that meets the Turing test, then we would have good reasons for thinking that babies are like basic machines, to which we progressively add those simple algorithms until they begin to talk like us. And since we all started out as babies, there would be good reasons to think the same of ourselves. Or, as Brandom puts it, "there just is no point in insisting that something that is genuinely indistinguishable (including, crucially, dispositionally counterfactually) from other discursive practitioners . . . should nonetheless not be counted as *really* talking, so thinking (out loud), and deploying a meaningful vocabulary" (74, emphasis in original).

On this model, Boyer's language could be cleaned up and freed from its intentional shorthand. We could, in principle, decompose the language of a particular Buddhist community into its subroutines, connecting its language of beliefs to that about practical activities, specific Buddhist rituals, talk about other traditions, and the like. We could then compare this community to, let's say, other Sri Lankan Theravada communities and perhaps identify those programs that seem to be most characteristic of Sri Lankan Buddhism in general. From here we could move on to make comparisons with other Theravada traditions, between Theravada and Mahayana, and so on. This would be to set comparative religion on a truly scientific footing.

The problem comes with what Brandom calls "doxastic updating." One of the important features of a mature human being, if it is around long enough, is that it will need to recalibrate its beliefs. For example, I spent most of my childhood around the computers at Stanford, but, almost a year before I met him, my friend Peter's friend Bill at SRI received the first ARPANET transmission from UCLA. If Peter had told me about it—which, for all I remember, he did—then I would have had to revise my beliefs about what could be done with computers. As it is, I've had to revise those beliefs on a regular basis for the past forty-some years, as computers have transformed not only academic life but also the life of almost everyone on the planet. The same with mobile phones. Put the two together and we have information-gathering and -sharing capacities that have required most of us to revise our beliefs about what we can know, when, and where. In the past, perhaps, revision wasn't so frequent, but it was still the prerequisite for intellectual and practical progress. Now add to this all the other revisions we make as a result of innovation, discovery, and personal experience. Learning, in short, is a matter of doxastic revision, and we are learning all the time.

Why might this prove a problem for the artificial intelligence model? For that model to be viable, the ability to update must itself be algorithmically decomposable. This, Brandom thinks, is a problem. "The key point," he writes, "is that the updating process is highly sensitive to collateral commitments or beliefs. The significance of undertaking a new commitment (or relinquishing an old one) depends not just on the *content* of *that* commitment, but also on what *else* one is already committed to" (Brandom 2008, 80, emphasis in original). Updating, in other words, isn't just a matter of adding new beliefs about the facts to a particular doxastic system. Most beliefs added will require some change in other beliefs, which may in turn require modifying some of the inferences you are committed to drawing about the shape of your world. Some of those changes are going to be relevant to your day-to-day activities, while some are not. And at some point you will need to decide which beliefs about which things should be modified and which you can ignore; thus, "updating requires exercising what turns out to be a crucially important but easily overlooked cognitive skill: the capacity to *ignore* some factors one is capable of attending to." This requires deciding what to ignore. "Dealing with objects as knowers and agents," Brandom continues, "requires the ability to *privilege* some of these respects of similarity and difference—to sort the myriad of such respects into those that *are* and those that are *not* relevant or significant" (81, emphasis in original). Since what makes a difference will be unpredictable for different individuals at different times and places—dependent, we might say, on the idiolect at a particular moment—it will be implausible, at best, to claim that an algorithm can be written to predict where the change will happen.

Suppose, to take a famous example, that you are an observant Jew in the first century of the Common Era. Having heard reports of some guy being crucified, who some people now believe to have returned and been revealed as the Messiah, you might wonder what to think. You might just chalk it up to the unsettled times and keep going about your business. Or you might seek out more information and decide to join the Jesus movement. On the other hand, you might find the whole business blasphemous and make it your business to persecute the movement. And at any point in the subsequent chain of events, there may well be further choices to make. Saying that God knows *what* choices *which* people will make won't do much for the advocate of artificial intelligence, since writing a god's-will function into your program is the equivalent of giving in to the unpredictable, or at least the nonalgorithmic.

When Edward Slingerland writes that we are "robots designed not to believe we are robots," he is failing to take seriously what it would mean to be a full-fledged robot, as opposed to a human being with lots of habits and needs that render its behavior often easy to predict. And when he continues that our being robots renders "firmly entrenched ideas such as *soul, freedom, choice,* and *responsibility . . .* in some sense, an illusion" (Slingerland 2008, 394–97, italics in original), he is making a claim that he can't sustain. Beliefs are, for the pragmatist, fallible, but doxastic updating, if it can't be done algorithmically, requires freedom, choice, and responsibility in exactly the ordinary senses of those terms.

This doesn't mean, however, that the alternative is Cartesian dualism or the embrace of ineffable mystery. Peirce, Davidson, and I can remain good Darwinian naturalists without embracing reductive materialism. When Davidson admits that his anomalous monism renders mental events supervenient on physical ones, he need only be taken to mean that, because the mental is anomalous, mental events will not figure into whatever turns out to be the best scientific account of the brain. To call this "epiphenomenalism," as some of his critics do, means only that desires and beliefs will not be terms that figure into that final theory of human neurophysiology.

## PRAGMATISM AND THE PROSPECTS FOR COMPARATIVE RELIGION AND ETHICS

If Brandom's problem of doxastic updating supports Davidson's anomalous monism, as I think it does, this needn't be taken as some sort of death knell for the systematic study of comparative religion or ethics. In fact, I think it points to a particularly promising way of imagining such comparisons. I'll end this discussion with some rough suggestions about how to combine the tradition of Brandom and Davidson with that of Durkheim and Max Weber in ways that may, for those inclined to work them out, point toward, in a phrase I do not fear will be repeated or stolen, positive pragmatic comparativism.

John Kelsay has recently taken me to task for being unreasonably averse to theory in the comparative study of religion and ethics. Kelsay writes, "Davis concludes, in a brief discourse on (or really against) method: '. . . If the pursuit of method short circuits the history and ethnography, by providing categories and cubbyholes in which to file and dismiss the counterintuitive, it is a positive danger to good work'" (Kelsay 2012, 590, quoting Davis 2008, 398). Not unfairly, he wants to know how my generally positive remarks about Durkheim and Weber square with this dismissal of theory.

When I say bad things about "theories," I usually identify them with "algorithmic" approaches to interpreting texts and phenomena, which present themselves as keys to interpretation, providing what, to my mind, are ready-made accounts of people, beliefs, and events. In this chapter, I have been out to get those who are inclined, for whatever reasons, to turn to the cognitive sciences, but Freudians, postmoderns, and others often fall into this category. They, too, bring to bear vocabularies, usually derived from elsewhere, that attempt to persuade us that it would be not only mistaken but naive to lend much, if any, credence to what the objects of our inquiry say about themselves, their practices, and their world. Perhaps the single most important thing about Weber's *Protestant Ethic* is his insistence on the centrality of ideas as instigators of action. Weber's critique of Karl Marx revolves around the fact that you cannot understand why Germans and Americans in the eighteenth and nineteenth centuries developed the sort of work ethic they did, without understanding the theological ideas that shaped their imaginations and patterns of action. Ideas aren't the only factor, but they cannot be ignored.

In the work to which Kelsay refers, I endorse Mary Douglas's chastened Durkheimianism as an important improvement on what has been, for a century, the most fecund approach to interpreting religions. She wants to understand, not dismiss, what the Lele of the Kasai and the authors of the Hebrew Bible were up to and what ideas are implicit in their thought about themselves and their worlds (see Davis 2012, 62–73). At the same time, my defense of Clifford Geertz is an embrace of Weber. What I take Geertz to be doing in *Islam Observed* is showing how the Weber of *Protestant Ethic* created an approach to diachronic change in religious life. Where Weber asked how ethics and religion were transformed in Christian Europe and North America between the fifteenth and nineteenth centuries, Geertz asks about similar transformations in Morocco and Indonesia, into the twentieth century. Part, at least, of Geertz's project is to illustrate a Weberian approach to comparative work. If we want to call Durkheim and Weber theorists, then fine, but we should distinguish the traditions of inquiry that flow from them, from more "algorithmic" approaches, such as those advocated by Boyer and Slingerland.

When Davidson forces us to attend to the idiolect, what he's doing, in pragmatic terms, is insisting that there is no generic language to be learned. We learn linguistic behavior at our parents' knees, and then we identify the behavior of other people, a bit further removed, as closely enough related to call them speakers of our language. But if this is true of language, it's also true of religion. We learn certain ways of talking and behaving in our local communities, and then it turns out that other people call this being a Christian or a Buddhist. There is no language of Christianity or Buddhism that counts as the *essence*, or the original message, of the tradition. If you can trace things back far enough, there might—and I emphasize the *might*—be something that would count as the earliest version, delivered by so-and-so, but even your report of that version would be subject to discussion and criticism.

This is the moral we should have taken from Walter Bauer's *Orthodoxy and Heresy in Earliest Christianity*, and it should have been extended to the study of religions generally. Bauer argued that scholars do not have access to the original message of Jesus, whatever that might have been. But they do have evidence for the early dissemination of various messages that competed for adherence. And so he attempts, for example, to reconstruct the debate between Antioch and Rome. Put in very simplified form, scholars have no grounds for assuming an original orthodoxy, in response to which various heresies develop, only to be opposed by the carriers of the original, orthodox message. What we have is the evidence for various communities practicing what they eventually called Christianity. As these communities encountered other groups and individuals calling themselves Christians, they were faced with the need for doxastic updating, which could go in any of a number of ways. Over time, in Bauer's assessment, the beliefs and practices of the community at Rome became dominant, and those groups that did not "update" in a direction that tracked developments in Rome became heresies.

Such an argument was bound to trouble those who had a stake in claiming the original and unsullied message of Jesus (Bauer 1971, appendix 2, particularly 291–92), but to an outsider interested in method in the study of religion, the argument seems exemplary. If the community at Antioch, for instance, doesn't provide us with evidence that a particular doctrine was taught there, then we have no reason to believe that it was an issue important to that community. We can't assume that they *must* have cared about a doctrine just because it mattered to what became orthodox. Where critics complain about Bauer's "argument from silence"

(290), I'm inclined to see a judicious restraint in refusing to go beyond the evidence. And to attribute orthodoxy to "a kind of Christian common sense" (302) seems to verge on theological imperialism. To apply a similar argument to Buddhism or Islam would likely elicit similar objections, but this is all to the good, for it makes it clear where history and theology intersect, and it makes it possible to identify why a particular reading of the history of a tradition makes a difference to the life of a contemporary community.

What Brandom gives us is a hint about where to look for those moments in the development of a tradition that are likely to lead to what I'll call *branching*. If we think of languages as evolving local ways of talking, then, at any point where a doxastic update seems to be called for, we are likely to see different bits of the population heading in different ways. Think, for example, of the rapid branching of radical reformation communities in the late seventeenth and the eighteenth centuries. As a community updates its beliefs about what the faith demands, disagreements emerge that may fracture the community, leading to the development of more ways of talking, realized in new communities. It might be possible, using Mary Douglas's development of "grid" and "group," to characterize the different sorts of communities that emerge as a result of this doxastic updating. It might turn out that some communities are high grid, high group, and that this has predictive value for the likelihood of their survival over multiple generations. Or not. Either way, it might tell us something about what kinds of communities were likely to develop in the social world of the seventeenth century, or that of the early twenty-first. To add Geertz's reading of Weber to this mix might help us identify the moment and the context in which a particular style appeared within a tradition, be it Islam or medieval Christianity.

But all these enticing possibilities must be left for future workers in the comparative garden. As long as we attend to the facts of semantic innovation and doxastic updating, human languages will, at their most important junctures, not be decomposable into algorithms adequate to programing a robot genuinely indistinguishable from a mature human interlocutor. Not only this, but also the programs that will be available will lack any compelling explanatory or predictive power. Such formal reconstructions, if that's what we want to call them, will be purely retrospective and descriptive. They will, in other words, be no better, and probably less informative, than the most creative readings, based on the best available history and ethnography and informed by the theoretical traditions of Durkheim and Weber, that students of religion and ethics have been producing for the past hundred years. There is nothing antiscientific about this, at least not if we follow Peirce and the pragmatic tradition in interesting ourselves in the ways that real scientists and citizens have inquired into the world and have attempted to arrange their findings as systematic sets of justified true beliefs about themselves and their world.

## NOTES

1.  The discussion of Peirce draws on Davis (2012), chapter 2. In fact, this paper goes back to a lecture from 2007, parts of which found their way into chapters 5 and 6 of that volume. The bulk of the essay, however, is new and is dedicated with gratitude to Wayne Proudfoot. I see my work here as, in many ways, a continuation of the approach to the study of religion pioneered by Proudfoot in *Religious Experience* (1985), and I hope it is worthy of both his work and his friendship over many years.
2.  Donald Davidson cites this article in various places, usually in order to identify David Lewis as the sort of philosopher of language against whom he is arguing. The earliest mention seems to be from 1982 (see Davidson 1984a). In fairness, it should be said that Lewis acknowledges the social practice aspect of language from the very beginning and goes on to argue that both the formal approach and the social practice approach are full partners in the philosophy of language. But that's not the interesting point here.
3.  I mean the reference to Jean-Baptiste Lamarck to be taken seriously. Recent interest in epigenetics has tempted some thinkers, among whom I would rank Pascal Boyer, to revive the Lamarckian idea of the inheritance of acquired properties. Popularly written volumes such as Francis (2011) encourage something of this, but when we get beyond journalism to something closer to the hard science, such as in Carey (2012), the mechanisms begin to look more like the lock-and-key mechanisms of biochemistry. While environmental stress may lead to methylation at cytosine sites on the genome, which are passed down in subsequent generations, leading to distinctive developmental propensities, it's hard, as Davidson might put it, to see how you get anything "semantic" out of this. Audrey Hepburn's physique may have owed something to the Dutch Hunger Winter of 1944–1945, but her acting stemmed from her history and training. Some early hominid stress may have led to the biochemistry of social instinct, but this is both speculative and tells us nothing interesting about, for instance, the masked rituals of the Dogon (see Carey 2012, 2).

## WORKS CITED

Bauer, Walter. 1971. *Orthodoxy and Heresy in Earliest Christianity*. Mifflintown, PA: Sigler.

Boyer, Pascal. 2001. *Religion Explained*. New York: Basic Books.

Brandom, Robert. 2008. *Between Saying and Doing: Towards an Analytic Pragmatism*. Cambridge, MA: Harvard University Press.

Burgess, John. 2009. *Philosophical Logic*. Princeton, NJ: Princeton University Press.

Carey, Nessa. 2012. *The Epigenetics Revolution*. New York: Columbia University Press.

Davidson, Donald. 1984a. "Communication and Convention (1984)." In *Inquiries Into Truth and Interpretation*, 265–80. Oxford: Clarendon.

Davidson, Donald. 1984b. "Truth and Meaning (1967)." In *Inquiries into Truth and Interpretation*, 17–36. Oxford: Clarendon.

Davidson, Donald. 2005a. "A Nice Derangement of Epitaphs (1986)." In *Truth, Language, and History*, 89–108. Oxford: Clarendon.

Davidson, Donald. 2005b. "Seeing Through Language (1997)." In *Truth, Language, and History*, 127–42. Oxford: Clarendon.

Davidson, Donald. 2005c. "The Social Aspect of Language (1994)." In *Truth, Language, and History*, 109–25. Oxford: Clarendon.

Davis, G. Scott. 2008. "Two Neglected Classics of Comparative Ethics." *Journal of Religious Ethics* 36:375–424.

Davis, G. Scott. 2012. *Believing and Acting: The Pragmatic Turn in Comparative Religion and Ethics*. Oxford: Oxford University Press.

Dennett, Daniel. 2000. "The Case for Rorts." In *Rorty and His Critics*, edited by Robert Brandom, 91–100. Malden, MA: Blackwell.

Francis, Richard C. 2011. *Epigenetics*. New York: Norton.

Kelsay, John. 2012. "The Present State of the Comparative Study of Religious Ethics: An Update." *Journal of Religious Ethics* 40:583–602.

Lewis, David. 1975. "Languages and Language." In *Language, Mind, and Knowledge*, edited by Keith Gunderson, 3–35. Minneapolis: University of Minnesota Press.

Maurer, Daphne, and Charles Maurer. 1988. *The World of the Newborn*. New York: Basic Books.

Peirce, Charles Sanders. 1992. "Some Consequences of Four Incapacities." In *The Essential Peirce*, edited by Nathan Houser and Christian Kloesel, 1:28–55. Bloomington: Indiana University Press.

Proudfoot, Wayne. 1985. *Religious Experience*. Berkeley: University of California Press.

Slingerland, Edward. 2008. *What Science Offers the Humanities*. New York: Cambridge University Press.

Wittgenstein, Ludwig. 1953. *Philosophical Investigations*, 3rd ed. Translated by G. E. M. Anscombe. New York: Macmillan.

# PART III

## Pragmatism and Democracy

Of all the pragmatists, John Dewey most readily springs to mind as a theorist of, and advocate for, democracy. Throughout his impossibly long and prolific career as a scholar, public intellectual, and political actor, he tirelessly promoted democratic norms and institutions. Dewey undeniably engaged the problems of democracy more directly and more relentlessly than did his pragmatist predecessors, but his life's work accentuates a democratic imperative intrinsic to the movement they birthed. Dewey perceived early on that Charles Peirce's and William James's pragmatisms constitute an embryonic philosophy of democracy, and for more than half a century he distilled, elaborated, and propounded the democratic consequences of their principal ideas.

Consider Peirce's early essay "The Fixation of Belief." It alone lays much of the groundwork for Dewey's vision of democracy. Taking inspiration from Alexander Bain and Nicholas St. John Green, Peirce conceives of beliefs as habits of action. A belief, he argues, is a disposition to act in certain ways, should various circumstances obtain. To believe that baseballs are potentially injurious, for instance, consists in the disposition to perform specific actions (e.g., donning a helmet) in response to various sets of circumstances involving baseballs (e.g., batting). Writing retrospectively almost thirty years later, Peirce (1958b, 183–84) describes his approach as the "recognition of an inseparable connection between rational cognition and rational purpose" and declares it "the most striking feature" of his pragmatism. Although notorious for his arrogance, Peirce may actually understate the case when he deems this feature of pragmatism "strik-ing." By recognizing the "inseparable connection between rational cognition and rational purpose," Peirce effectively collapses the traditional (Kantian as well as Aristotelian) distinction between the theoretical employment of reason (to form true beliefs) and the practical employment of reason (to choose good ends and the actions that successfully attain them).[1] His pragmatism entails that questions concerning what one ought to believe become equivalent to questions concerning what habits of action one ought to establish in light of one's pur-poses. Methodological questions about the best way to govern assent in order to attain truth become equivalent to questions about the wisest way to govern hab-its of action in order to attain ends. Peirce (1958a, 103) argues, furthermore, that because of an ingrained social impulse in humans to consider the opinions of others, "the [methodological] problem becomes how to fix belief, not in the individual merely, but in the community." For Peirce, therefore, methodological questions pertaining to the pursuit of true beliefs take on the character of politi-cal questions about how best to govern actions in a community to meet needs and fulfill hopes.[2] Put simply, in "The Fixation of Belief," Peirce implicitly poses the question "What kind of political norms best serve a community?"

By the same token, Peirce's conclusion in "The Fixation of Belief"—that the antiauthoritarian, experimental, scientific method most reliably produces true beliefs—carries the consequence that antiauthoritarian, democratic political norms best enable a community to meet challenges posed by the natural or social environment. When Peirce (1958a, 107–9) contends that the scientific method depends in principle on the independent "experience and reason" of "every man," or "any man," who undertakes to resolve a given doubt, he invokes an ideal democratic community of free and equal inquirers. To function optimally, the experimental method of inquiry requires that individual inquirers enjoy the freedom to test their hypotheses and broadcast the results. The method also requires an ethos of equality among inquirers, because inequities of power or authority inevitably produce distorted or prejudiced evaluations of research pro-grams and their results. Finally, as a cooperative (even if competitive) endeavor, empirical inquiry presupposes common purposes in light of which inquirers devise experiments and evaluate their results relative to the findings of other inquirers. In sum, the scientific method generates the ideal of a community of individuals possessing freedom, equal authority, and shared purposes. Although Peirce does not draw the conclusion explicitly, "The Fixation of Belief" provides the premises from which one can infer that the ideal political community embod-ies the democratic conditions to which more specialized communities of inquiry aspire: *liberté*, *égalité*, and *fraternité*. Peirce's pragmatism suggests that democratic norms govern a community best because they sustain the conditions most conducive to the satisfaction of human ends.

Unlike Peirce, who leaves the link between empirical inquiry and democracy as subtext, James sometimes draws explicit attention to it. In "The Will to Believe," his famous defense of religious commitment, James argues for the intellectual right to believe—and act—in advance of sufficient evidence. His argument turns on the idea that individual lives constitute just so many experiments, which furnish empirical results pertinent to resolving the religious question (see chapter 2 in the present volume). Inquiry into religion depends, he claims, on individuals acting freely on their religious convictions. Immediately before he concludes the essay with a quotation from Fitzjames Stephen, James exhorts his audience to practice democratic virtue. One could easily dismiss the passage as a lapse into bombast, but in fact it closely tracks the theme of the essay, and James echoes its sentiments elsewhere. "We ought . . . delicately and profoundly to respect one another's mental freedom: then only shall we bring about the intellectual republic; then only shall we have that spirit of inner tolerance without which all our outer tolerance is soulless, and which is empiricism's glory; then only shall we live and let live, in speculative as in practical things" (James 1956, 30). In this Ciceronian peroration, James lauds the spirit of individual freedom and mutual tolerance that characterizes an ideal community of empirical inquirers. He contends, moreover, that it forms the soul of democracy, sine qua non. Democratic institutions are lifeless, he suggests, unless vivified by the "intellectual republic," in which the independent "experience and reason" (to borrow Peirce's formulation) of every person bear on the questions of the day. In a vital democracy, science's antiauthoritarian norms radiate throughout society and thereby amplify their power to enhance human welfare.

A decade later, James dedicated *Pragmatism* (1907) to J. S. Mill, declaring that he "first learned the pragmatic openness of mind" from Mill (James 1975, 3). In *On Liberty* (1859), his most sustained defense of "openness of mind," Mill justifies liberal social and political norms solely by their consequences for human welfare. He announces in the introduction that he will "forgo any advantage which could be derived to [his] argument from the idea of abstract right as a thing independent of utility" and will argue instead that freedom and tolerance promote the "interests of man as a progressive being" (Mill 1978, 10). Without dilating on Mill's exact position in the pragmatists' intellectual genealogy, suffice it to note that their commitment to democracy resembles Mill's defense of a liberal society. Peirce, James, and Dewey endorse democratic norms for no other reason than their beneficial consequences for human welfare.[3] The classical pragmatists make no appeal to natural rights or any other source of authority transcending human practice. Forsaking ideological absolutes, they offer an entirely naturalistic the-ory of democracy, proposing that humans can best meet their needs and improve their condition collectively, cooperatively, and democratically. The pragmatists justify democratic norms in the same way that an experimental scientist corrob-orates a hypothesis, and in the same way that Peirce justifies the scientific method of fixing beliefs itself: by the fact that they, as Peirce (1958a, 111) puts it, "carry us to the point we aim at and not astray." In short, the founders of prag-matism view democracy as an experiment, the success of which depends on how well it solves problems and ameliorates the human condition.[4] Drawing on sources beyond the classical pragmatists, the essays in part 3 consider the resources that pragmatic naturalism offers for democratic discourse and democratic practice, particularly in a religiously diverse society.

### NOTES

1. As both Charles Peirce and John Dewey note, Peirce also effectively collapses the Kantian distinction between the *praktisch* employment of reason to formulate unconditional moral ends and the *pragmatisch* employment of reason to serve con-ditional, prudential ends. See Dewey (1984), 4.
2. Dewey (1922, 58) writes that pragmatism "makes for a fusion of the two superlatively important qualities, love of truth and love of neighbor."
3. Unlike the pragmatists, however, Mill prizes individuality as a value intrinsic (and not merely instrumental) to human flourishing. Autonomy, over and against tradi-tion or custom, Mill (1978, 54) asserts, is "one of the principle ingredients of human happiness."
4. See Hook (1944) for an excellent summary and defense of the pragmatist theory of democracy as it stood in the middle of the twentieth century.

### WORKS CITED

Dewey, John. 1922. "Pragmatic America." *New Republic* 30 (April 12): 185–87.
Dewey, John. 1984. "The Development of American Pragmatism." In *John Dewey: The Later Works, 1925–1953*, vol. 2, *1925–1927*, 3–21. Carbondale: Southern Illinois University Press.
Hook, Sidney. 1944. "Naturalism and Democracy." In *Naturalism and the Human Spirit*, edited by Y. H. Krikorian, 40–64. New York: Columbia University Press.
James, William. 1956. "The Will to Believe." In *The Will to Believe, Human Immortality*, 1–31. New York: Dover.
James, William. 1975. *Pragmatism* and *The Meaning of Truth*. Cambridge, MA: Harvard University Press.

Mill, J. S. 1978. *On Liberty*. Indianapolis: Hackett.

Peirce, Charles S. 1958a. "The Fixation of Belief." In *Charles S. Peirce: Selected Writings*, edited by Philip Wiener, 91–112. New York: Dover.

Peirce, Charles S. 1958b. "What Pragmatism Is." In *Charles S. Peirce: Selected Writings*, edited by Philip Wiener, 180–202. New York: Dover.

# 6

# Reading Wayne Proudfoot's *Religious Experience*

## *Naturalism and the Limits of Democratic Discourse*

JONATHON KAHN

Nicholas Wolterstorff, in his famous exchange with Richard Rorty on the place of religion in democratic public discourse, presents what he calls a "more just arrangement" for conducting political discussions: "letting people say what they want to say on political issues and letting them argue for their positions as they think best to argue for them, provided they conduct themselves with the requisite virtues" (Wolterstorff 2003, 135). In many ways, this one sentence captures the past twenty years of debate over the expression of religious reasoning in the public sphere. Wolterstorff's arrangement—in contrast to Rorty's, who continued to hold that the expression of religious reasons was corrosive to public discourse—has largely ruled the day among contemporary political philosophers and religious ethicists. The work of Jeffrey Stout, Charles Taylor, and William Connolly, among many others, has replaced an early Rawlsian secular liberalism with what some call the "postsecular,"[1] or what I like to call the "new secular," in which religious reasoning is no longer excluded but accepted in democratic contexts. It may be ironic, but religious voices have achieved a newfound vigorous acceptance in many corners of the so-called secular academy.

Yet it is important to notice that Wolterstorff's sentence is only half about opening up the conditions of democracy to allow us to come as we are—with our differing passions, concerns, and sacreds expressed in whatever language we find most familiar. We should not lose track of that final clause: "with the requisite virtues." For his part, nowhere does Wolterstorff elaborate or clarify what he means by the phrase, or what these virtues are. Moreover, with this phrase, Wolterstorff introduces limitations on religious expression in public places. For even though there are few legislative or epistemological grounds by which to restrict any of us from voicing concerns in whatever terms we feel fit, democratic conditions still contain tempering moral and political grounds.[2]

What are those tempering moral and political grounds? What, after all, are the requisite virtues for conducting conversations with those of potentially radically different religious orientations? Most crucially, what do these conversations look and sound like if we understand conflicts between at least some of these passions, concerns, and sacreds as, in fact, irremediable in Isaiah Berlin's sense of irreducible value pluralism? As far as making clear the appropriate role of religion in public affairs, the new secular, one might say, has thrown us from the frying pan into the fire; the secular that sought to expunge religion from its midst now faces a cacophony of voices and styles with little more than "semblances of virtues" to guide us (Herdt 2008, 4).

Wayne Proudfoot's classic work *Religious Experience* may seem like a strange place to think through these questions, since *Religious Experience* is not a text about religion in the public square. It is a text—the most rigorous one we have—about how best to interpret religious experience naturalistically, which is to say, as necessarily involving the experiencer's concepts, beliefs, culture, social position, and history. But look more closely and I think that the central moves of the text—first, religious experience must be *explicated* from the perspective of the religious adherent; and second, religious experience must be *explained* from the perspective of the analyst—approximate in interesting ways the postsecular dynamics of the public square. On the one hand, Proudfoot's hermeneutics allow for (and even give a certain primacy to) the public expression of the language of the religious adherent, while, on the other hand, they subject that language to critique. In other words, inhering to Proudfoot's hermeneutics of explanation and explication is a potential ethics of democratic religious dialogue. Might explication and explanation be thought of as examples of the requisite virtues for democratic life?

In this chapter, I want to explore just how far these hermeneutic virtues take us. Through a reading of Proudfoot, as well as a substantial engagement with the work of both Stout and William Hart and his "misfit" "Christian naturalism" (Hart 2008, 198; 2012), I examine how the virtues of explication and explanation are necessary but not sufficient for current secular conditions. I read Proudfoot's *Religious Experience* as both a model and a warning to all of those naturalists who assume that their naturalism is part of what makes up their democratic bona fides. Proudfoot (1985, 219) expresses a certain "optimism" that the tools of explication and explanation will allow radically differently situated subjects to come to understand each other: "There is no reason, in principle, to despair about the possibility of understanding the experiences of people and communities that are historically remote from the interpreter." But, as Proudfoot himself might acknowledge, there is no reason why we should optimistically conclude that these naturalistic forms of deliberative understanding are capable of navigating deep and lasting tensions in religiously motivated conflict.

In the second part of the chapter, I consider Stout and Hart, via a reading of Jason Springs's work on religious conflict, as examples of democratic engagement that do not rely exclusively on deliberative modes of explication and explanation. As a way of addressing persistent disagreement, they seek to expand democracy's discursive terrain beyond the deliberative and conversational and into the realm of what Springs (à la Connolly) calls the visceral and the affective. I see both Stout and Hart as examples of how naturalism can contribute to modes and practices of democratic engagement, modes that alight the passions and the viscera as much as they engage the careful and rational exchange of reasons.

## EXPLICATION AND THE POLITICS OF RECOGNITION

The core of Proudfoot's *Religious Experience* is its devotion to thinking through religious experience as a matter of hermeneutics. The question at its heart is as follows: What is a religious experience if we understand it as a product of interpretation—an interpretation of both the person who experiences it as well as outsiders who read and hear accounts after the fact? This insight structures his entire account of how religious experience should be accounted for. On the one hand, Proudfoot's recognition that religious experiences emerge out of the adherent's interpretation directs any and all accounts of religious experience to the adherent's terms. The adherent's terms must be "explicated," which is to say that if anyone, including the adherent herself, is to understand the experience, the experience must be described in terms that would make sense to her. On the other hand, Proudfoot insists that religious experiences also are subject to others' interpretations—he calls these "explanations"—the terms of which may very well be foreign to the adherent. Both perspectives are critical to Proudfoot's naturalistic interpretation of religious experience.

What needs to be pointed out is that Proudfoot is attempting to cultivate religious experience as necessarily a site of conflict between two different hermeneutical stances. And it is precisely this effort to position the interpretation of religious experience as a site of contest—in fact, his efforts are better understood as an attempt to *foment* contest over religious experience—that represents the true imaginative achievement of the work. It might be said that Proudfoot offers explication and explanation in the hope that radically different subjectivities—the adherent's and the analyst's—might be able to talk and listen to each other. *Religious Experience* is at heart a dialogic text. *Religious Experience* suggests that adherent and analyst, though often strangers, need not see each other through a glass darkly.

In this section and the next, I want to take a closer look at whether Proudfoot's notions of explication and explanation warrant optimism about improving these sorts of exchanges. The question before us is whether Proudfoot's naturalistic hermeneutics can mediate deep differences between those who have religious experiences and those who do not.

Let's take a closer look at Proudfoot's account of explication to better understand how this hermeneutic functions toward this end. As if banging on a drum, Proudfoot (1985, 233) repeatedly asserts that explication embraces the central insight of the "hermeneutical tradition": "Religious experience, emotion, action, belief, and practice must each be identified under a description that is available to and can plausibly be ascribed to the subject of that experience, the holder of that belief, or the agent. To identify an experience from a perspective other than that of the subject is to misidentify it. That is the insight."

It is important to understand matters correctly here. It would be easy to get the impression that Proudfoot's deeply subject-centered account of explication expresses a type of political or ideological sympathy with the religious adherent. It would be easy to assume that Proudfoot privileges the adherent's perspective because he thinks it sets up the right sort of power relations for productive dialogue between the religious adherent and the analyst—as if Proudfoot's primary worry is to protect the religious adherent from the analyst's tendency to dismiss religious experience as mere delusion. Indeed, the imperative of explication always forces the analyst to distance himself from his own perspective and become fluent in a language other than his own: "I must describe those deeds and ascribe to him intensions, desires, and motives in terms that would have been available to him. In order to do that, I must understand the concepts and the grammar that were constitutive of his views of himself and his world" (Proudfoot 1985, 73).

But none of these reasons speak to why Proudfoot so resolutely begins his project with this notion of explication. Instead, Proudfoot's hermeneutical turn should be seen more simply as his attempt to steady and fix what he is interested in studying. The crucial question is an epistemological one: How do we know what a religious experience is? Proudfoot's answer—"It is an experience that the subject apprehends as religious" (181)—simply reflects the epistemological insight that in order for a religious adherent to have a religious experience, she has to identify and judge the experience to be religious in nature. And for her to do this, Proudfoot insists, she must recur to sets of complex social and linguistic contexts that inform the very notion of religion, and she must make inferences about those contexts. In other words, to allow that a religious experience is what its subject calls religious is to insist on the absolute critical importance of the subject's language, concepts, and contexts to the religious experience itself. The adherent's perspective is privileged epistemologically, not politically.

This should not minimize, however, the potential politics of this epistemology. Explication demands taking the language of the adherent seriously. Attention must be paid. Indeed, it strikes me that a passionate core moment of *Religious Experience* comes in Proudfoot's defense of Sigmund Freud against D. Z. Phillips's claim that Freud ignores the conceptual worldview of Maori tribespeople: "Freud does not say that it is a waste of time to listen to the reasons of the tribesman . . . One of the most important lessons Freud has taught us is to listen carefully to everything, even and especially to what appears to be trivial and unimportant" (202). At heart, the epistemological demands of explication function as a normative imperative to grant what Charles Taylor (and others) call "recognition . . . not just [as] a courtesy we owe people. It is a vital human need" (Taylor 1994, 26).

On this view, explication becomes a politics of recognition. Explication disallows the analyst the ability to dismiss prima facie accounts of religious experience. Explication allows that religious experiences are limitless and capacious; any experience holds the potential to be a religious experience, depending on how the subject refers to it. The variety and richness of religious experience is likely much greater and richer than perennialists—"those who claim that a single experience of the numinous or sacred . . . underlie all the diverse reports in different traditions" (Proudfoot 1985, 219)—suggest. In fact, Proudfoot finds the resistance to opening up the logic and categories of the adherent—in the name of protecting her from criticism and inquiry—a most patronizing form of charity, "charity with a vengeance" (206). These protective strategies are vengeful because they keep the religious adherent from being understood.

And yet, despite the strong ethics of recognition that seems implicit in the notion of explication, *Religious Experience* is at times read as doing exactly the opposite, as undermining and delegitimizing the religious adherent.[3] G. William Barnard's scathing review of *Religious Experience* is a great example. Barnard (1992, 236, 252) takes Proudfoot to task for what he calls a "presumptuous" lack of "methodological humility" that effectively devalues the religious adherent's experience in a number of ways. In particular, Barnard is alarmed by what he sees as Proudfoot's dogmatic denial of the possibility that supernatural realities exist, his explanation of religious experiences by reducing them to other natural causes, and his inability to engage in an "ethical assessment of the *pragmatic* value of spiritual transformation" (247, emphasis in original). On Barnard's view, Proudfoot's reductionism is raw, his ear for religion unmusical, and his view of those who practice religion is that they are little more than dupes who "mindlessly adopt that belief system that undergirds that practice, not because they have had any real religious experiences, or have decided that this particular belief system seems the most coherent, but because they are cognitively and socially pressured to make sense of their own strange behavior. From Proudfoot's perspective, it appears that the practice of spiritual disciplines is, at best, naive, and at worst, a case of fraudulent manipulation and hurtful self-deception" (238).

What interests me about Barnard's comments is not that I think he is right. Indeed, as we will see, I do not, on any of these counts. Rather, what interests me is how it is possible, given the imperative Proudfoot places on explication, that Barnard could have come to the conclusion that, in effect, Proudfoot is being disingenuous when he avows his desire to learn "what is distinctive about the experience for the one who undergoes it" (Proudfoot 1985, 175).

In a response to Barnard, Proudfoot (1993, 802) offers an explanation of sorts: "I am sorry that a rhetorical style intended to provide a clear and forceful statement of my thesis was taken by Barnard to contrast with [William] James's methodological humility, and to impede rather than contribute to the ongoing conversation about religion and religious experience." Indeed, rhetoric may be an important element to consider. Proudfoot's prose is unusually direct and his critical jabs are bruising at times; certain claims by Friedrich Schleiermacher, James, or D. Z. Phillips are pronounced "erroneous" or "inadequate" (Proudfoot 1985, 164, 204).[4]

Most important, I think, is Proudfoot's (1985, 219) claim, central to his notion of explication, that language, concepts, and contexts are *constitutive* of a religious experience. It is the claim that rankles critics like Barnard, prompting his cascade of criticisms that amount to the sense that Proudfoot thinks religious believers are deluded and foolish. What Proudfoot is taken to mean in this vein is that religious experience is made up of *nothing but* language, concepts, and contexts. For example, Stephen Bush (2012, 114) has recently urged Proudfoot to acknowledge that "concepts and beliefs do not *exhaustively* constitute experiences" (emphasis added), and he brings up the example of a person taking a powerful hallucinogen, such as LSD, to illustrate how a person's experience is not wholly dependent on "the experiencer's conceptualization."

But there is nothing in *Religious Experience* to lead us to conclude that Proudfoot would resist recognizing that LSD is a nonconceptual physiological force that causes hallucinations. He might even concede, for the sake of argument, that the drug could induce the exact same sorts of hallucinations— "walls melting, cracks appearing in people's faces, eyes would run down cheeks, Salvador Dali–type faces . . . a flower would turn into a slug" (Bush 2012, 113)—in everyone, regardless of their particular sociolinguistic context. In other words, Proudfoot allows that experiences very much develop out of interactions with external phenomenon. Proudfoot's deeper point about the way language constitutes religious experience does not deny this.

What Proudfoot is trying to say about the constitutive nature of language and religion is that even if two people have the same hallucination induced by an external force, each of these people still needs to make the judgment on some level that this experience has religious meaning. After all, one person on LSD might experience the melting walls as religious and one may not, and that's the point; the subject's beliefs and concepts about religion are required to name an experience as religious. It is in this sense that language is constitutive of religious experience for Proudfoot. It is not that language is all there is to religious experience, and it is not that Proudfoot would fundamentally deny that the experience might, in fact, be caused by something external to the subject's concepts—whether chemical or supernatural. It is, however, the case that to call an experience religious requires the language and concept of religion, and the very application of that language is constitutive of the experience itself. Indeed, in Proudfoot's view, the person who has a religious experience on LSD is having a different experience than the person who takes LSD and simply has a wild trip.

The crucial point is this: In this reading, naturalistic explications of religious experience need not be understood as wholly incompatible with an acknowledgement of the possibility of supernatural entities. If the goal is explication— illuminating the terms by which the experience is construed—nothing rides on the naturalist's explicit denial, or, for that matter, her affirmation, of transcendental causes. In this view, James's own famous affirmation of "the more" should be seen as deeply biographically interesting but less central to his work of interpreting how religious practices and beliefs cohere. By the same token, it is not clear to me what good Proudfoot's own need to critique James's account of an "unseen order" does for the project of explicating religious experience: "James is right to identify belief in an unseen moral order as central to theism, and even to religion more broadly. But he is wrong to think that this order can be located outside of the social products of human history and culture. We do inhabit a pluralistic moral order, but there is nothing in the cosmos that is intimate, social, or morally productive except what we have put there" (Proudfoot 2000, 62). It is not that I think Proudfoot needs to keep this hidden. Instead, what I am suggesting is that even as Proudfoot might admit his own strict naturalism, he should also make clear, or at least more clear, that this naturalism does not require the wholesale refusal of the possibility of the supernatural entities—at least when it comes to explication.

At the very least, this admission would extend the politics of explication. Indeed, one reason why I think Barnard does not hear Proudfoot's notion of explication as a form of recognition is that Proudfoot does not emphasize the potential compatibility of explication and supernaturalism. As I read it, there is nothing about explication that makes its terrain solely that of the naturalist. Supernaturalists can and do engage in explication as much as naturalists if they are willing to decipher the social and historical nests in which their language resides. This acknowledgement is completely compatible with the view that the ultimate source of those nests is supernatural. For a naturalist to make a point of recognizing that supernaturalists, too, engage in explication would be to acknowledge the emotional or visceral register of religious experience. And it might allow someone like Barnard to see a form of recognition in the naturalist's own explications.

## IS THERE A DIALOGIC VALUE TO EXPLANATION?

For Proudfoot, *explanation* refers to the reasons that an analyst uses to account for someone else's religious experience. In Proudfoot's case, these reasons are naturalistic, which is to say that they exclude supernatural reasons and may include psychological, sociological, physiological, and historical reasons. Regardless, the heart of explanation is the claim that an analyst has what can only be called the right to interpret the religious experience of another in whatever terms he thinks are persuasive, which may very well be radically foreign to the experiencer herself: "It need not be couched in terms familiar or acceptable to the subject . . . *Explanatory reduction* consists in offering an explanation of an experience in terms that are not those of the subject and that might not meet with his approval. This is perfectly justifiable and is, in fact, normal procedure" (Proudfoot 1985, 195, 197, emphasis in original).

There are a couple of notable things about this statement. Most obvious is that Proudfoot uses the term *reductionism* unapologetically, without tears, as it were.[5] Proudfoot seems entirely comfortable not only with what seems to be a necessary element of conflict but also with the notion that this conflict may very well be irresolvable. Explanation, or at least explanatory reductionism, is not interested in finding the terms by which the explainer and the explainee might come to talk.

This raises a host of questions about the relationship between explication and explanation. At the end of the day, why go through all the effort of becoming fluent in the language of the adherent if explanatory reductionism defies those very terms? Are explication and explanation two distinct activities? Is explication, in effect, a hoop that the analyst must pass through simply to justify his explanation? Even if explanation can be justified as an imperative, how is Proudfoot prepared to deal with the very real fact that these terms, even if not intended to be hurtful, will surely be alienating? Proudfoot (1985, 220) knows this: "Those who report religious experiences typically take them to be independent of and more fundamental than beliefs or theories." And if this is true, is optimism warranted when it comes to conversations between different subjects about religious experience?

The second interesting part of this statement is the phrase "normal procedure." It invites the question, Normative to what? What are the norms that Proudfoot sees as necessarily demanding explanation in the terms that he presents it? Said slightly different, if explanation amounts to a right, then rights have contexts, and to effectively claim explanation as a right requires understanding the context in which explanation rises to the level of an imperative. For what purposes does Proudfoot think that naturalistic explanations of religious experience can justifiably account for the experience in terms unrecognizable to the adherent?

I want to return to Barnard's essay again to help think through these questions. In many ways, Barnard's outrage is in response to Proudfoot's account of explanation. For Barnard, Proudfoot's willingness to give an explanation of religious experience in terms alien to that of the adherent blocks out the sun. Proudfoot's explanatory reductionism becomes synonymous, first, with the denigration of religious adherents and their experiences, and second, with the conversation-stopping powers of explanatory reductionism. Barnard (1992, 251, note 9) would have it that this is the force of explanation at work in *Religious Experience*: "unscientific dogmatic assertions that, in effect, stop the discourse, rather than tentative, open-ended additions to the conversation."

On the first count, Barnard's criticisms are misguided. Like James, Proudfoot is well aware and appreciative of the value of religious experiences, spiritual transformations, religious practices, and modes of religious discourse. What is at issue here, however, is that, unlike James, the efficacious aspects of religious experience are not Proudfoot's main concern. As Proudfoot (1993, 796) says in his response to Barnard's essay, *Religious Experience* in part is "aimed at theorists who understand these experiences as radically independent of language, practice, and culture." This is the polemical edge of Proudfoot's book. Proudfoot is trying to establish the philosophical and epistemological right to make explanations, against those who say that these are inherently illegitimate.[6] It is true that, in these moments, Proudfoot can sound defiant of the religious adherent, expressing little interest in how the religious adherent will hear an explanation that is entirely strange and potentially hostile. But it is a category mistake to think that explanatory reductionism necessarily devalues the efficacious power of religion.

The second count is more complicated and interesting. Barnard's severe claim is that the mode of explanation that Proudfoot practices is wholly monologic, uninterested in engaging the adherent. But, as Barnard presents it, these claims stay at the level of accusation. I can't find any clear account of how Proudfoot's explanation refuses these engagements. What I think is true is that at the moments when Proudfoot emphasizes explanatory reduction as a right, as something that is critical to free inquiry, he can sound defiant of the religious adherent. He expresses little interest in how the religious adherent will hear an explanation that is entirely strange and potentially hostile. Explanatory reductionism in this key becomes, in effect, largely tone deaf to the adherent and rather undialogic, uninterested in a conversation except on terms of its own. In this mode, explanation functions much like the pins that hold an insect in place under a magnifying glass.[7] And when this happens, I think it is fair to say that the relationship between explication and explanation is severed.

But the more difficult and important question is whether this is the only mode of explanation at work in Proudfoot. That is, it is obvious enough why explanation might alienate an adherent. The more powerful question is whether there is any evidence in Proudfoot of explanation operating in a way that engages the adherent. Are explication and explanation mutually edifying activities? In fact, a more capacious reading might acknowledge the way in which Proudfoot understands the two as connected. One of the most important and subtle points Proudfoot (1985, beginning at 226) makes about explanation is that it is not a mode of inquiry that is foreign to the religious adherent herself: "Interest in explanations is not an alien element that is illegitimately introduced into the study of religious experience. Those who identify their experiences in religious terms are seeking the best explanations for what is happening to them."

Proudfoot is arguing that explanation sits at the core of the religious experience when seen from the adherent's point of view. An adherent's account of her religious experience is not simply a phenomenological description. When an adherent describes what is happening, she is making implicit claims about why the experience is happening. In this sense, an adherent's explication of an experience is also her explanation of the experience. That is what Proudfoot (218) means when he says "explanatory comments are assumed in the identification of an experience as religious." Explanation is a "normal procedure" for the religious adherent of the religious experience itself. Here we have an important sense of explanation, one that is not reductive in the sense that it is entirely foreign to the adherent.

With this, a more cooperative relationship between explication and explanation comes into better view, one that, pace Barnard, allows for tentative and open-ended moods. To be sure, I've had to do a decent amount of work to draw it out of Proudfoot's text. Yet it is there, at least nascently. In this version, explanation does not represent the attempt to pull the rug out from under the religious adherent and shame her into recognizing her own self-deception. This account of explanation places at its center not reduction but the acknowledgement of interpretive uncertainty—the common project of trying to figure out just what is going on. This model would comfortably acknowledge that explanations are most often partial. Mostly, it would recognize that something of the dialogic is part of any explanation. Adherent and analyst are both engaged in projects of explanation. Explanations are not simply limited to translations of the other's experience for ourselves but also include ways we translate our experiences for ourselves. To say this is not to put a brake on the legitimacy of interpretations that use terms alien to those interpreted. But it is to acknowledge, or include in the practice of explanation, a less dichotomous account of its workings. On this, Barnard would be correct to say that Proudfoot says very little.

## EXPLICATION, EXPLANATION, AND
## IMMANENT CRITICISM

Up to this point, I have been trying to draw out the dialogic ethics in Proudfoot's naturalistic accounts of explication and explanation. And I have been doing this as a way to begin to think about whether Proudfoot's hermeneutics demonstrate the right sort of virtues for democratic exchanges. In particular, I have been trying to press the question of the degree and the ways that Proudfoot's naturalism engages nonnaturalistic dispositions and frameworks. This need for naturalists to engage nonnaturalists represents the operating conditions of the "new secular," where democratic conditions allow political actors to speak in their voice and their vernacular.

And what I have wanted to suggest is that, while Proudfoot's explication and explanation would seem to have all the markings of the needed conditions for democratic discussion of religion in the public square, questions remain. Explication, in particular, would seem to be a basic democratic virtue; understanding the terms of the other is surely crucial. Yet the practice of democratic discourse requires spelling out more exactly the ends and interests that explication serves. Is explication simply a way for the naturalist to coldly decipher his subject? Is the politics of recognition inherent in explication effective enough for productive exchanges? Explanation, on its face, would seem to be more combative, particularly when reductive. Yet I have emphasized some neglected dialogic tendrils of explanation, ones that may be currently undertheorized and call for further development.

In this section, I want to try to translate Proudfoot's notions more explicitly for questions about the public square. To do this, I want to see whether it is possible to map Proudfoot's notions of explication and explanation onto Jeffrey Stout's influential account of the way religious reasons might function in public political argument.

Stout argues against the Rawlsian notion of a public that requires a comprehensive consensus on public reasons. In fact, Stout imagines the democratic public as incapable of relying on comprehensive reasons; this necessary diversity is in part what makes a public. Instead of reasons in common, public exchanges depend upon what Stout calls "immanent criticism." The practice of immanent criticism involves one side of an exchange learning the terms and views of the other. For Stout (2004, 73), immanent criticism signals a "real respect for others" in "tak[ing] seriously the distinctive point of view *each* other occupies" (emphasis in original).

I would hasten to point out that learning vocabulary immanently entails explication as Proudfoot understands it. Immanent criticism requires taking the time to learn the language of the other. The immanent critic, of course, does not need to share the beliefs that underlie that language. His goal is to understand the way concepts are constellated and fit together to create meaning. In this view, the fact that the immanent critic, if he's a naturalist, attributes these concepts to a set of social and historical causes and reasons that the adherent might deny, is actually unimportant to the practice of learning a language immanently.

Of course, immanent criticism does not stop there. The purpose of immanent criticism is the exchange of reasons, which is to say their contest and disputation: "As immanent critics, they either try to show that their opponents' views are incoherent, or they try to argue positively from their opponents' religious premises" for or against a certain proposals (Stout 2004, 69). Clearly, immanent criticism is not a docile affair. To be sure, learning the language of another does demonstrate real respect. But we should not minimize the combativeness in Stout's model. Immanent criticism stokes differences by using the language of the other to change her mind: "I draw you into a Socratic conversation on the matter . . . and make a concerted attempt to show how *your* idiosyncratic premises give *you* reason to accept my conclusions" (72, emphasis in original).[8]

Is it right to say that this more interrogatory work of the immanent critic resembles Proudfoot's model? Indeed, there are real similarities. Like the immanent critic, Proudfoot is unafraid of the contested exchange of ideas and reasons. This is the point of his hermeneutics. And like the immanent critic, Proudfoot's full account of explication is not limited simply to learning the vocabulary and the grammar of the adherent. Proudfoot is also deeply invested in showing the adherent a fuller range of implications, things the adherent may have overlooked or not been aware of, in her own vocabulary and grammar. Explication in its fullness is explanatory. And it is explanatory precisely in the same way as the immanent critic seeks to explain to the other the way her own terms lead to positions she was not aware of or prepared to accept. Indeed, to practice Stout's immanent criticism is to build a connecting bridge between Proudfoot's notion of explication and explanation. At its best, perhaps, one might say that immanent criticism is the democratic practice of explication and explanation.

But as I have suggested, there is another sense of *explanation*, a more severe form of explanatory reduction that does not speak or even try to speak in the terms of the other. Here is where the resemblances to immanent criticism break down. It is hard to see how explanatory reduction, in its refusal to speak immanently, allows the conversation to continue. It is important to remind ourselves, against the suggestions of those like Barnard, that there is nothing in these sorts of explanations that is *inherently* derisive or debilitating to the religious adherent. And there are contexts in which this approach is perfectly justified—indeed, the religious studies classroom may be one of them. But if the context is the democratic public square and if the goal is the productive exchange of ideas and reasons to keep the conversation going between differently situated actors, then it is not clear to me what good explanatory reduction does. When we need to interact with members of different communities, we need to think about whether the reasons we give are ones that will be listened to. It seems worse than far-fetched to me to think that either side is going to have much luck convincing the other on the basis of arguments that doubt the other's basic epistemology. In this context, we very well may need to put aside our naturalistic explanatory reductions.

Still, I think there are further questions that need to be raised about this model of immanent criticism. Stout's immanent criticism seems underwritten by a certain confidence that we are right and they are wrong and all we need to do is to figure out a way to make their wrongness convincingly clear to them. At least Stout does not talk about immanent criticism that takes a form different from desiring to change the other's view. But this would seem to be only one outcome of immanent criticism. We all cannot all be Socrates, which is to say that as we begin to argue on others' premises, we may well find that we cannot convince them of our view. This may be because of our limitations or because their view is in fact rational, given their premises. We may learn that, in their terms, their position is right. Just as likely, and perhaps more importantly, is that immanent criticism redounds back on our own position. For when we speak in a different tongue, we might find out what is wrong with ours. We need to hold open the possibility that the dialogic nature of immanent criticism is deep and will affect our own discourse, and we should let it do this where it can.

On this model, immanent criticism still remains evaluative, but we might stop thinking of its success in terms of whether we can persuade our interlocutors of our rectitude. We might use immanent criticism to evaluate ourselves. We might use immanent criticism to make more explicit our debts and dependencies on nonnaturalistic vocabularies and ways of being. And this may make it more possible to express the shocks of insight that interactions with adherents of the supernatural are capable of producing. In this way, immanent criticism might be less about decoding an other's language for the purposes of testing whether it is watertight. Immanent criticism might be more about sussing out and establishing terms for admitting the mysteries and uncertainties in all of our languages.

We might think of this as a shift in emphasis away from a model of immanent criticism that is solely concerned with the rational and cogent exchange of reasons to one that seeks other registers of exchange for democratic life. In other words, while Stout's account of immanent criticism and Proudfoot's model of explanation and explication clearly are crucial for democratic discourse, I suggest that the terms by which these exchanges are conceived also feels limited and narrow. Immanent criticism, explanation, and explanation all stand against a Rawlsian rational frame in the sense that they do not rely on a set of comprehensive consensuses of reasons. But I find myself wondering whether Stout's and Proudfoot's continued emphasis on testing the cogency and coherence of reasons exchanged ends up reproducing in democratic contexts some of the very same problems they critique in Rawls.

To be clear, I am not trying to suggest that the exchanges of reasons is not crucial to democratic discourse. What I am interested in is whether there are ways of thinking about the value of those discursive exchanges in terms other than evaluating whether their terms can be fully explicated and cogently held. I turn to these concerns in the concluding two sections.

## PRAGMATIC NATURALISM IN THE PUBLIC SQUARE

Part of what made Rorty's secularism—with its hopes to prune the expression of public religious commitments to the nub—such compelling theater was the way it put him, the father of the late twentieth-century revival of pragmatism, at odds with the pragmatist tradition. Indeed, Wolterstorff earns critical points in this debate by, in effect, citing Rorty's own pragmatist commitments back to him.[9]

As we know, pragmatism, from its classic to its contemporary forms, has long been marked by a deep affinity and genuine philosophical interest in religion. Pragmatism might well be characterized as the most important tradition of philosophical thought to exhibit sympathy and confer epistemological legitimacy on religious beliefs and practices. *Naturalism* is the term that is often used to describe the version of interest and sympathy that these pragmatists exhibit toward religion. Pragmatism is the crucial philosophical tradition that informs the more recent attempts to formulate a "liberal naturalism." Liberal naturalisms try to "widen the realm of the natural" to include aspects of human experience that cannot be known under scientific laws (De Caro and Voltolini 2004, 76). As Proudfoot (2012, 185) writes, "In order to study this particular kind of natural creature, we must study its language and its culture."

Pragmatic naturalists potentially can hold different views on the existence of supernatural and theological realities, but what they all share is the view that the only way to get access to what anyone calls "religious" is through studying humans in their finitude, through the grammatical, symbolic, and material systems humans themselves create. Pragmatic naturalism expresses the view that "humans create religions just as surely as spiders spin webs, bees make honey, and birds build nests. The cultural-performative-semiotic activity of religion-making is no less natural" (Hart 2012, 149).

Consider the seemingly ready open-mindedness of these sorts of claims and it is understandable that pragmatist voices have played such an important part in opening up the public square to religious voices. Folks such as Stout, Cornel West, Eddie Glaude, Richard Bernstein, and William Connolly have explained in pragmatism's terms why, to steal Connolly's phrase, they are not secularists. It becomes easy to think that it is the pragmatist's naturalism that functions as the crucial tonic against secularist antireligious fervor. It becomes easy to assume that what's required to convert the public square from implacable contest to mutual cooperation are generously conceived naturalistic descriptions of religious beliefs and practices.

For example, this model underpins Mark Cladis's work on religion in American public life, in which he makes the case for the "religious studies classroom to serve in some degree as a national, civic model for public engagement with religion" (Cladis 2008, 3–4). That classroom work, as Cladis describes it, is effectively the work of immanent criticism, explication, and explanation. The implicit logic is as follows: the more pragmatic naturalism in the public square, the less will the square be a place of implacable battles and the more will we be able to keep the conversation going as long as possible. The assumption is that pragmatic naturalism—because it enables us to have conversation about religion, because it enables us to make ideas (ours and our neighbors') clearer and more coherent—becomes democracy's leaven.

We need to rethink this story. It is a quirk in the historiography of late nineteenth- and twentieth-century American secularism that pragmatism goes largely unmentioned, and this despite the example of Rorty.[10] We rarely consider that when the reach of pragmatic naturalism, even if disposed favorably toward religion, is limited to discursive exchanges that emphasize rationality, it can become a version of the sort of secular liberalism it is trying to critique. Too rarely does pragmatic naturalism question its own assumption that explication, explanation, and immanent criticism are actually what account for and effect successful democratic exchanges between citizens of different religious orientations. We need to consider that these same virtues may in fact alienate the supernaturally and theologically inclined as much as any form of militant atheism. This, in fact, is the lesson of Barnard's review of Proudfoot's *Religious Experience*: pragmatic naturalism, no less than a militant secularism, functions as a conversation stopper when it comes to religion, too.

Jason Springs's recent work on the limits of democratic dialogue for addressing religious conflict makes this point very effectively. Springs (2011, 331) is interested in thinking through the moments when democratic conversation breaks down, when sides are no longer able or interested in the "cultivation of deliberative virtues by which fellow citizens hold one another accountable for the validity of their inferences through the measured exchange of reasons."[11] Springs's deliberative virtues are essentially versions of explication, explanation, and immanent criticism. Springs's point is not that these virtues are not important. They are, of course, necessary. But they can quickly exhaust themselves. Even a cursory look at the current American political landscape reveals deep conflicts that will not be budged through debate employing the means of immanent criticism, explication, and explanation. Limiting ourselves to these means for navigating conflict—where conflict is deemed healthy solely by the cogency and fluidity of rational exchange—we actually find ourselves bereft of needed models for navigating these specific conflicts.

Instead, Springs (2011, 327) proposes a different account of "'healthy conflict,' where volatile—even apparently intransigent—disagreements are confronted in an attempt to creatively transform the oppositional frames that hold those disagreements in place." The transformations that this account of healthy conflict envisions "press us to go beyond analyses of democratic deliberation" (341). In these moments, something like William Connolly's "visceral registers"—the affects and passions like anger, disgust, and happiness—are necessary, expanding the discursive field. In other words, certain democratic spaces and moments may require expressions other than the temperate and the deliberative. Springs's point is that the viscera—"the guts"—do discursive work: "Though they may well up quickly—and overflow and grasp one in ways that are unruly—they are, nonetheless, discursively nested" (335).

Their discursive efficacy, however, is not in their precision or their ability to secure cognitive agreement from differing viewpoints. No, in these moments and contexts, the point of democratic discourse may be more to secure a version of basic recognition. We express the viscera to learn whether our interlocutor is willing to act in such a way that will harm our loved ones, our community, or our sacred. We express the viscera in order to determine whether our interlocutor is capable of acknowledging our distress. And we may express the viscera to learn whether we can build a coalition, not on common philosophical coherences but on, as Anthony Appiah suggests, our getting used to each other and learning to do things together.[12] What I suggest here is that this focus on the viscera shifts the frame of democratic discourse away from deliberation and toward action and practice. The democratic question becomes not, How well do we understand and talk to each other? The question becomes, What are we willing to work together on? This is what I take Springs (2011, 336) to mean when he talks of an "expanded recognition of the variety of registers in which political engagement occurs."

Ironically, I take this lesson—that explication, explanation, and immanent criticism do not represent the solitary heart of democratic practice and exchange—from Stout's latest work, *Blessed Are the Organized*. I say this is ironic because, from a certain angle, *Democracy and Tradition* and *Blessed Are the Organized* provide contrasting models of democratic exchange. Where *Democracy and Tradition* teaches immanent criticism, *Blessed Are the Organized* teaches the art of coalition building—developing relationships between sympathetic neighbors and then using those relationships to demand and effect material changes. What is striking is the lack of a role that immanent criticism plays in this account of democratic practice. Instead, anger—the visceral—sits at the heart of *Blessed Are the Organized*. A crucial passage reads:

> The public *expression* of anger is of paramount importance in political life . . . What expressed anger does . . . is to put the other party on notice that the terms of the relationship will have to be respected, or perhaps redrawn, if the relationship is going to continue . . . A community that does not have expressed anger in its symbolic repertoire is one that lacks one of the central communicative means of restoring significant relationships to equilibrium and, when necessary, redefining the roles and expectations that constitute them.
>
> (Stout 2010, 67, emphasis in original)

Of course, a great deal more can and needs to be said about Stout's account of anger, how it works, and, most importantly, how he distinguishes it from rage. But what I want to emphasize here is the way in which anger communicates, even while refusing the deliberative virtues. Anger does not require making one's point in the terms of the other; anger communicates in one's own language. Anger does not communicate discursive justifications. Anger does not require a full deliberative exposition of reasons. Nor does anger, to be effective, require that the other eventually come to agree with my reasons. Anger does something more basic: it stakes a claim and announces that something crucial, something of "sacred value," is being violated. For Stout, the democratic sacred is the freedom from domination, and so anger in democratic exchanges reflects a claim to being the victim of domination. Anger simply demands that the other be able to recognize what dignity and domination look like. And there is no necessary relationship between naturalistic modes of explication and explanation and the ability either to express or to respond appropriately to this sort of anger.

Again, I am not trying to suggest that the rigorous practice of exchanging and holding each other accountable for our reasons is not valuable and necessary. Following Springs, I am suggesting that other discursive registers are required in facing the conditions of the new secular, conditions that not only are marked by radically contested claims but also, as George Shulman (2008, 246) describes, are "the absence of a public in which such claims can be contested." If we do not, in fact, have functional public venues for such exchanges, then we need to get creative and seek out other possible publics and other possible modes of exchange. What Stout and Springs encourage us to do is to imagine and open ourselves to public moments and settings that engage a wider range of affective and rhetorical modes, in particular, modes that more fully engage the viscera. How might naturalism supplement or even extend itself beyond its modes of explication and explanation to engage the viscera?

We need, I think, to have an eye out for these examples. Stout's *Blessed Are the Organized* may be one, though it is not clear how his naturalism actually plays a role in his account of anger. Springs's work gestures toward a model but, in the end, leaves out specifics. Naturalists need to admit that we in fact do not know a great deal about what naturalistic models of visceral engagement look like. I'd like to conclude this chapter with such an example.

## THE "ODDBALL" AND "MISFIT" PRAGMATIC NATURALISM OF WILLIAM HART

For the past fifteen years, while writing on topics such as Edward Said, secularism, and the study of African American religious thought, Bill Hart has, in bits and pieces, been disclosing and working through his own religious orientation, what he describes as "naturalistic Christianity."[13] This has been a project in autobiography, an account of his own "Afro-Eccentricity": "ways of 'being black' that are off-center, 'off-color,' and outside the statistical if not 'the' axiological norm" (Hart 2008, x).[14] His Christian naturalism is a black Christian naturalism, which, for Hart (2008, 198–99), places him within and without, "on the border of the Black Church . . . in a permanent liminality": "In that context, I am an oddball, a misfit, a coldwater fish in a hot tub. I stick out like a sore thumb, a 'hard on,' an inflamed pimple on someone's ass."

What is important to hear here—beyond a certain type of candidness—is that his naturalistic Christianity sits in proximity to—which at times means literally sitting in the pews of—the Black Church. Though a misfit, he finds himself physically present, and thus Hart's black Christian naturalism sits in literal relation to black Christian supernaturalism. That relation, as Hart makes clear, is abundantly agonistic, marked by profound ambivalences, strong-worded criticisms, and discomfort. He makes it clear that he believes that "there is no transcendent, holy, or sacred object of devotion independent of nature" (Hart 2012, 160). Yet Hart does not intend these to be fighting words. Instead, he says that he is "bound to the church" through these agonisms (Hart 2008, 199). He knits a naturalistic Christianity that borrows from and plays with language and concepts—what he calls "critical elaboration" (Hart 1998, 166)—that find refuge within the Black Church's supernaturalism. This bond means that Hart's naturalism is contrapuntally indebted to and dependent on the Black Church's supernaturalism; the bind demands that his naturalism has to find some way to speak that expresses its critical debt to supernaturalism.

Hart develops this discourse in two primary ways. The first might be thought of as a mode of explication. Most centrally, Hart retains a notion of "transcendence," which he translates naturalistically: "Naturalistic transcendence is the notion that immanence has innate powers of *self*-overcoming, which entails going beyond the normal space and time of quotidian experiences. Immanence is inherently uncanny and magical" (Hart 2012, 157, emphasis in original). In moves like this, Hart does not simply seek common ground with supernaturalism. He is pushing his naturalistic self to be transformed by supernaturalism. In Hart's view, supernatural transcendence, even if epistemologically mistaken, rejects a Nietzschean "amor fati" and pushes humans to wrestle with possibilities that our existence might be otherwise.

Hart's naturalistic transcendence drinks from this well. Through his gods, he seeks and opens himself up to ways of being, beyond the normative, "a marvelous way, perhaps even a miraculous way, of discovering our own capacities and expanding our world in indeterminate directions" (163). His naturalistic transcendence even produces what Proudfoot would surely call religious experiences: "But there are other moods as well where the Trinitarian God whispers in my ear. How crazy is that? Like Montanus, I hear the Holy Spirit speaking directly to me, qualifying, resignifying, and even superseding anything written in a sacred text or anything that my church or tradition might hold as true" (Hart 2008, 201). Clearly, his analytical goals are not to disenchant naturalism of its magic. Instead, Hart's naturalistic explication of transcendence works to instill an ensorcelled mood.

The second way that Hart develops a discourse with the supernatural Black Church is performative. For while he claims that he does "not have a Pentecostal or charismatic bone in my body . . . my religion does not make me want to shout," he finds himself, at moments, engaging in what one can only call Pentecostal performative or experiential modes: "The blue notes especially move me. To paraphrase Emerson, sometimes a cry, shout, or moan is better than a thesis, sermon, or explication of sacred doctrine" (197, 200). Naturalistic Christianity may be, as he acknowledges, an "elite formation," not practiced by the vast numbers of African American Christians. Yet Hart's version seems to require not simply the presence of nonnaturalistic African American

Christians but also the ability to follow their steps: "One engages fully in the ceremonial, ritual, and performative life of the tradition: dancing, singing, and shouting" (Hart 2012, 165). The discursive modes of this naturalism include practices and actions that are obviously affective and visceral. These soften any temptation to draw a stark division with supernatural practice, actions, and affects.

At the same time, Hart is not making the mistake of re-creating W. E. B. Du Bois's (1986, 493) characterization of black religion as a "Pythian madness, a demoniac possession." It is important to remember that Hart always engages as an "oddball" and a "misfit." Nowhere does he say that when he is shouting he feels like anything other than a critic. In fact, Hart's (2012, 165) insistence that his performances occurs in the key of "*disillusioned*—again, not to be confused with disenchanted—festive irony" (emphasis in original) should make us realize that what transpires for him is not a version of mystical or racial oneness. His participation in these liminal moments does not make him any less critical of the Black Church, "a lethargic beast that has to be stung into action by prophetic gadflies," with clergy too often "monarchical, antirepublican, antidemocratic . . . [who] too often operate, as kings do, by decree and acclamation" (Hart 1998, 155; 2008, 198). Given these words, we should also assume that his supernatural brethren would do well to keep a wary eye on him.

Springs might say that a version of "healthy conflict," one in which differences are both important and stubbornly present, characterizes Hart's relationship to the Black Church. This is as Hart would want it. Still, work remains. Hart's naturalistic Christianity is not yet fully formed. He has not sustained a fuller account of the how the differences and conflicts play themselves out—what gets addressed through "patient, conversational modes of engagement" (Springs 2011, 336) and what gets addressed through more visceral modes. Were he to provide this account, he might help us to further reconceive of naturalism's approach to religion conflict.

What Hart suggests is a model of naturalism that funds both a critical analytical approach as well as one that is more embodied or affective. In other words, Hart's naturalism leads him to be critical of the supernatural, and Hart's naturalism takes place, as it were, in the supernatural Black Church. What we do not know enough about is what this naturalism that "takes place" in this way is more fully like. Might we hear more of the way in which his naturalism engages the passions in ways that promote a variety of discursive exchanges with supernaturalists? Are there examples of the way he—with his naturalistic black Christianity—and his fellow congregants—with their supernatural black Christianity—have mediated persistent conflicts?

We have reason to hope that the spirit of this naturalism—one that requires equally the sharing of reasons and explanations *and* the sharing of common actions and practices—might offer newly creative forms of democratic living. The hermeneutic virtues of explication and explanation are very much needed for naturalists to find their feet in situations of conflict and uncertainty; if we naturalists are to understand what they, the supernaturalists, are saying, what they mean by what they say, and what we think of what they are saying, we need to interpret deliberatively. The requisite virtues do include explication and explanation. But these forms of deliberative interpretation do not exhaust naturalism.

With Hart, we naturalists find an example of a naturalism that seeks affective hooks with other natural forms of being human, even when these forms speak supernaturally. These engagements are not only clinical or analytical but also participatory and dialogic. And that we all—naturalists and supernaturalists alike—should find ourselves, yet again, wondering anew about the requisite set of virtues for conducting ourselves in these sorts of democratic conditions—where we would seek more detail from Hart's affective bond with those with whom he is epistemologically different—is to squarely wrestle with the challenge of our times.

## NOTES

1. See, for example, Gorski et al. (2012).
2. In this light, Richard Rorty's (2003, 143) desire to shame citizens who recur to homophobic biblical passages might be understood as a legitimate and vociferous appeal to the virtue of justice. I thank Matt Bagger for helping me see this point.
3. For example, see Robert Friedrich (1987). Also displaying these tendencies is Robert Forman (1996).
4. Here's a particularly tough sentence on D. Z. Phillips: "The characterizations of religious belief offered by Phillips are as inadequate as his accounts of the theories of others" (Proudfoot 1985, 204).
5. See Ivan Strenski (1994).
6. In these terms, William Barnard's criticism that Wayne Proudfoot's concerns are "almost exclusively on the rational *veracity* of the descriptions of mystical experience" are not as devastating as Barnard seems to think (Barnard 1992, 246, emphasis in original). Proudfoot does indeed hold that those who describe their experiences as sitting outside of natural contexts are wrong. He doesn't think that their *description* of religious experience is rationally possible. But that position is a far cry from

denying either the rational veracity or the deep value of religious experiences themselves. Thinking that someone may be mistaken in some way in her account of her own experience does not imply an inability to appreciate, respect, and even admire the ethical or psychological value, or even the rational veracity, of that experience.

7. I've often wondered if Proudfoot ever regrets making, in *Religious Experience*, explanation essentially synonymous with explanatory reduction. In his subsequent work, I've noticed that Proudfoot's rhetoric around explanation changes, and he stops using the word *reduction* to modify *explanation*. See, for example, Proudfoot (2000, 2012).

8. For example, Jeffrey Stout is tremendously compelled by Eugene Rogers's work on homosexuality and Christianity because Rogers provides theologically rigorous Christian arguments that license same-sex marriage; this gives Stout tools with which to talk immanently to conservative Christians about homosexuality. Stout (2003, 180) writes, "If this conclusion can be made in plausible terms on an intramural basis, it can also be made to serve the purposes of immanent criticism by interested fellow citizens who would like to see same-sex marriage legally recognized for their own non-religious reasons."

9. See the opening paragraphs of Wolterstorff (2003).

10. For example, consider the absence of pragmatism in Susan Jacoby's (2004) *Freethinkers: A History of American Secularism* or David Sehat's (2011) *The Myth of American Religious Freedom*.

11. Also see Springs (2012).

12. See Appiah (2006), 72–78.

13. See "Cornel West: Between Rorty's Rock and Hauerwas's Hard Place" (Hart 1998), *Edward Said and the Religious Effects of Culture* (Hart 2000), and "Naturalizing Christian Ethics: A Critique of Charles Taylor's *A Secular Age*" (Hart 2012).

14. Also see *Afro-Eccentricity: Beyond the Standard Narrative of Black Religion* (Hart 2011).

## WORKS CITED

Appiah, Kwame Anthony. 2006. *Cosmopolitanism: Ethics in a World of Strangers*. New York: Norton.

Barnard, William G. 1992. "Explaining the Unexplainable: Wayne Proudfoot's *Religious Experience*." *Journal of the American Academy of Religion* 60:231–56.

Bush, Stephen S. 2012. "Concepts and Religious Experiences: Wayne Proudfoot on the Cultural Construction of Experiences." *Religious Studies* 48:101–17.

Cladis, Mark S. 2008. "The Place of Religion in the University and American Public Life." *Soundings* 91:389–416.

De Caro, Mario, and Alberto Voltolini. 2004. "Is Liberal Naturalism Possible?" In *Naturalism and Normativity*, edited by Mario De Caro and David Macarthur, 69–88. New York: Columbia University Press.

Du Bois, W. E. B. 1986. *The Souls of Black Folk*. In *Writings*, edited by Nathan Huggins, 357–548. New York: Library of America.

Forman, Robert. 1996. "Of Heapers, Splitters, and Academic Woodpiles in the Study of Intense Religious Experiences." *Sophia* 35:73–100.

Friedrich, Robert. 1987. Review of *Religious Experience*. *Sociological Analysis* 48:179–80.

Gorski, Philip S., David Kyuman Kim, John Torpey, and Jonathan Van Antwerpen. 2012. *The Post-Secular in Question: Religion in Contemporary Society*. New York: New York University Press.

Hart, William David. 1998. "Cornel West: Between Rorty's Rock and Hauerwas's Hard Place." *American Journal of Theology and Philosophy* 19:151–72.

Hart, William David. 2000. *Edward Said and the Religious Effects of Culture*. New York: Cambridge University Press.

Hart, William David. 2008. *Black Religion: Malcolm X, Julius Lester, and Jan Willis*. New York: Palgrave Macmillan.

Hart, William David. 2011. *Afro-Eccentricity: Beyond the Standard Narrative of Black Religion*. New York: Palgrave Macmillan.

Hart, William David. 2012. "Naturalizing Christian Ethics: A Critique of Charles Taylor's *A Secular Age*." *Journal of Religious Ethics* 40:149–70.

Herdt, Jennifer A. 2008. *Putting on Virtue: The Legacy of the Splendid Vices*. Chicago: University of Chicago Press.

Jacoby, Susan. 2004. *Freethinkers: A History of American Secularism*. New York: Henry Holt.

Proudfoot, Wayne. 1985. *Religious Experience*. Berkeley: University of California Press.

Proudfoot, Wayne. 1993. "Explaining the Unexplainable." *Journal of the American Academy of Religion* 61:793–812.

Proudfoot, Wayne. 2000. "William James on an Unseen Order." *Harvard Theological Review* 93:51–66.

Proudfoot, Wayne. 2012. "Pragmatism and Naturalism in the Study of Religion." *American Journal of Theology and Philosophy* 33:185–99.

Rorty, Richard. 2003. "Religion in the Public Square: A Reconsideration." *Journal of Religious Ethics* 31:141–49.

Sehat, David. 2011. *The Myth of American Religious Freedom*. New York: Oxford University Press.

Shulman, George. 2008. *American Prophecy: Race and Redemption in American Political Culture*. Minneapolis: University of Minnesota Press.

Springs, Jason. 2011. "'Next Time Try Looking it Up in Your Gut!!': Tolerance, Civility, and Healthy Conflict in a Tea Party Era." *Soundings* 94:325–58.

Springs, Jason. 2012. "On Giving Religious Intolerance Its Due: Prospects for Transforming Conflict in a Post-Secular Age." *Journal of Religion* 92:1–30.

Stout, Jeffrey. 2003. "How Charity Transcends the Culture Wars: Eugene Rogers and Others on Same-Sex Marriage." *Journal of Religious Ethics* 3:169–80.

Stout, Jeffrey. 2004. *Democracy and Tradition*. Princeton, NJ: Princeton University Press.

Stout, Jeffrey. 2010. *Blessed Are the Organized: Grassroots Democracy in America*. Princeton, NJ: Princeton University Press.

Strenski, Ivan. 1994. "Reductionism Without Tears" In *Religion and Reductionism: Essays on Eliade, Segal, and the Challenge of the Social Sciences for Study of Religion*, edited by Thomas A. Idinopulus and Edward A. Yonan, 95–107. Leiden: Brill.

Taylor, Charles. 1994. "The Politics of Recognition." In *Multiculturalism: Examining the Politics of Recognition*, edited by Amy Gutmann, 25–74. Princeton, NJ: Princeton University Press.

Wolterstorff, Nicholas. 2003. "An Engagement With Rorty." *Journal of Religious Ethics* 31:129–39.

# 7

# Public Reason and Dialectical Pragmatism

JEFFREY STOUT

John Dewey spent much of his career pondering the implications of G. W. F. Hegel's critique of Enlightenment rationalism. What Hegel had demonstrated, from Dewey's point of view, was the need to shift philosophical attention away from *reason*, understood as an innate faculty governed by timeless laws and principles, to *reasoning*, understood as a kind of purposive activity in which individuals and groups engage. In this chapter, I consider the implications of such a shift for one of the most important legacies of Enlightenment rationalism, the notion that important political issues ought to be settled by appeal to what Immanuel Kant called "public reason."

There is no doctrine of public reason in Dewey's pragmatism. He did, of course, affirm the centrality of public *reasoning* in democratic culture. It is something he sought to understand and ameliorate. But, in his view, the Kantian doctrine of public reason was too individualist and ahistorical to provide the sort of understanding and guidance he sought. Hegel was right to interpret reasoning holistically, socially, and historically—in a word, dialectically. Unfortunately, Hegel had left the impression that agreeing with him on this topic would commit us to a highly implausible metaphysics of absolute spirit. Rather than trying to criticize Hegel's idealism in detail, Dewey extracted Hegel's dialectical account of reasoning from the arcane vocabulary in which Hegel had expressed it. The result is what I shall call *dialectical pragmatism*, a translation of Hegel's holistic, social, and historical conception of reasoning into down-to-earth English.

Dewey was also a Darwinian naturalist and a grassroots democrat. He used the account of reasoning he extracted from Hegel to make sense of scientific inquiry and democratic contestation—two practices he ranked among the most valuable in modern culture. It is not always clear how the various strands of

Dewey's thinking are supposed to fit together.[1] Much of my own work, including the present chapter, continues the project of integrating dialectical pragmatism with an affirmative account of grassroots democracy.

Like Dewey, I distinguish grassroots democracy from the excessive trust in intellectual and bureaucratic elites that many latter-day liberals, from Walter Lippmann to Richard Rorty, have in common with Hegel.[2] I am, however, more interested than Dewey was in examining the roles that religious groups have played in democratic social movements and broad-based citizens' organizations. Some of the dissenters I most admire, religious or not, appear to be too passionate and too conceptually innovative to qualify as reasonable by Kantian standards. The question arises whether the dissenters or the standards are faulty. While Dewey's dialectical pragmatism has proven helpful to me in responding to this question, the version of naturalism he defends in *A Common Faith* has not. I basically agree with Dewey's Darwinian ontology and his praise for natural piety and democratic faith, but in that book he assumes, without much argument, that supernaturalism is inherently antidemocratic (Dewey 1934, 29–58; Stout 2004, 31–33). That assumption is an essentialist prejudice. It does not survive exposure to the full range of relevant historical examples.[3]

It is not my purpose here to examine Dewey's attempts to clarify and synthesize the various strands in his pragmatism. I shall be working further downstream in the pragmatist tradition, with John Rawls as my focal point and with Dewey, Hegel, and Kant visible in the background. My main purpose is to expose a tension between Rawls's account of political theorizing as an evolving reflective equilibrium and his account of public reason as a model of how citizens should deliberate. The notion of an evolving equilibrium shows the influence of Dewey's dialectical pragmatism and thus of Hegel's critique of Kant. The account of public reason is Kantian in inspiration. I suspect that these two strands in Rawlsian political theory cannot finally be made to cohere. The present chapter develops my grounds for suspicion.

Assuming that dialectical pragmatism is as hard to square with the doctrine of public reason as I take it to be, one could, of course, resolve the tension in more than one way. I am disposed, as Dewey apparently was, to drop the latter doctrine and to develop an explicitly dialectical account of democratic political reasoning. Such reasoning is public in two senses. First, it pertains to matters of public importance, such as war, domination, poverty, exploitation, environmental degradation, basic liberties, and constitutional design. And second, it is carried out among citizens in forums that involve no expectation of confidentiality.

When Rawls speaks of public reason, he has in mind a quite narrow sense of the term *public*, according to which only one mode of reasoning and only one kind of forum qualify as public. He says interesting things about other modes of reasoning in which citizens engage, but he does not regard the other modes as public in his technical sense. His distinction between public and nonpublic reasoning is sharp, and needs to be if public reason is to play the role he assigns to it. Explaining why it strikes me as too sharp is the second purpose of this chapter. Here, too, the influence of Dewey's Hegelianism is at work. One of his primary strategies for improving on Enlightenment ideas was to socialize and historicize them. Another was to take Enlightenment dichotomies and soften them up.

I can imagine two main avenues of resistance to my conclusions. The first would be to argue that I have misunderstood Rawls, particularly by taking his account of public reason to be less holistic and dialectical than it actually is. I grant that there are passages one can point to in support of this objection. There are, however, other passages in which public reason is made to appear relatively static, in conformity with an Enlightenment metaphor of the social contract. And we must keep in mind, throughout, that Rawls employs the distinction between public reason and nonpublic reasoning in order to place a strict limit on a kind holistic reasoning. The apparently static aspect of public reason is motivated by a concern with stability. The restriction on holistic reasoning is motivated by a concern with legitimacy.

The real issue, then, is whether Rawls and his followers can embrace a more holistic and dialectical account of public reason without abandoning central objectives of political liberalism, as he understood it. I am raising the possibility that political liberalism faces an unpleasant dilemma: either the doctrine of public reason is as holistic and dialectical as Dewey would want it to be or it isn't. If it is, it appears to require relinquishment of a Rawlsian construal of stability and legitimacy. If it isn't, it offers an implausibly rigorous standard of acceptable public reasoning. To evade the apparent dilemma, one has to either break one of its horns or slip between the horns. Mere citation of passages in which Rawls sounds like a dialectical pragmatist does not resolve the issue.

The doctrine turns out, on close examination, to be surprisingly murky. I shall be speaking of the "vagaries of public reason." These pertain to what counts as a public reason, how the approved modes of inference and justification are supposed to work, and how someone engaging in public reason is supposed to reach determinate conclusions. The suspicion expressed in the unpleasant dilemma I have posed is that these matters cannot be made fully clear without undermining either the interest or the plausibility of the doctrine. Rawls's account of public reason, like certain other features of his theory of justice, became exceedingly complicated over the years. It is therefore possible that I, being someone outside the guild of full-time Rawls specialists, have interpreted one or more of his distinctions and qualifications incorrectly. If so, I welcome correction and clarification from his defenders.

That being said, as a grassroots democrat, I must confess that the increasingly scholastic character of Rawlsian political theory is one thing that arouses my suspicion of it. The more baroque the theory has become, the more assistance an ordinary citizen has needed from professional exegetes to understand its practical implications. This result is especially ironic as it bears on the doctrine of public reason. The doctrine seeks to instruct ordinary citizens on how they should think and behave. It purports to do so without taking philosophically controversial assumptions for granted. How, then, is public reason to perform its intended political function if advanced training is required to understand its demands and rationale?

The second avenue of resistance to my conclusions would be to grant that there is a tension between the pragmatist and Kantian strands in Rawls, while claiming that the pragmatist strand is the one to drop. The reasons for taking that course would have to do, again, with why Rawlsians want an account of public reason in the first place. While I will indicate what those reasons are, I will not say much against them here, aside from voicing my suspicion that Rawlsian political theory places a greater burden on the idea of public reason than it can be made to bear.

In his first book, *A Theory of Justice*, Rawls (1999c, 42–46) sounds like a dialectical pragmatist when he describes the reasoning of political theorists as a continuing search for reflective equilibrium. The default starting point for the theorist's reasoning comprises all of his or her considered judgments. The theorist moves back and forth between particular intuitions and general principles, adjusting both, if need be, in order to bring them into congruence. As someone reflecting in this holistic and dialectical way, Rawls constructs *the original position* as the theoretical model best able to explain the bulk of our considered intuitions about justice.

According to the model, individuals select basic principles behind a veil of ignorance, without knowledge of their own distinguishing characteristics as individuals, including their various full-blooded conceptions of the divine and the good. The principles such individuals would accept codify the conception of justice Rawls calls "justice as fairness." What justice requires of society, according to this conception, is adoption of a basic framework in accord with principles thus chosen. A citizen, when exercising her or his public powers, reasons properly when guided strictly by these principles, rather than by the considerations that come into view when the veil of ignorance is lifted. In *A Theory of Justice*, the citizen's reasoning appears to be much more constrained than the theorist's reasoning. The citizen's reasoning is constrained by what the theorist discovers when engaging in the relatively unconstrained pursuit of reflective equilibrium.

Reflecting further on his own theoretical reasoning, Rawls ultimately decides that *A Theory of Justice* itself relies excessively on his own partisan philosophical assumptions, which reflect a kind of Kantianism. When justice as fairness is defended in a way that relies on such assumptions, it begs the question against opposing reasonable views. Rawls is now unable to shake the intuition that a conception of justice based on any set of partisan philosophical or religious assumptions cannot *fairly* be proposed, as the basis of public life, to reasonable people committed to other such sets of assumptions.

*Political Liberalism* is Rawls's attempt to resolve this problem. In it, the theorist of political liberalism and the reasonable citizen are both said to have *a duty of civility* to conduct their reasoning in accord with the values and standards of public reason. These are the values and standards that all reasonable people could (or would) accept, and they constitute the approved starting point for the reasoning of theorists and citizens alike. The duty of civility specifies what the default starting point of their reasoning needs to be in order to qualify as properly public. Citizenship is a public office. Public reasoning is ultimately required of citizens when they are performing their most important deliberative and justificatory functions as citizens. Such reasoning is restricted to the specified basis, which is held to be freestanding (Rawls 2005, xxx–lxii, 212–54, 435–90).[4]

I will be asking whether the resulting account of public reason in *Political Liberalism* is sufficiently dialectical and whether Rawls's distinction between public and nonpublic reasoning is too sharp. By relinquishing his technical sense of the term *public* and developing his sketchy remarks about three forms of discourse he officially classifies as nonpublic, we can begin to see what a thoroughly dialectical account of public reasoning would look like. I do not mean to disparage the sort of reasoning to which Rawls attributes uniquely public importance, but rather to make explicit the public implications of the other sorts of reasoning he mentions.

Once the Rawlsian dualism of public and nonpublic is jettisoned, *public reasoning* can be defined simply as whatever citizens think when deliberating on matters of political importance and whatever they say, apart from contexts where confidentiality is expected, when giving reasons to one another and challenging one another's commitments on matters of political importance. The dialectic of public reasoning is an interactive process in which individuals sometimes change their minds, and change one another's minds, by taking considerations of various kinds into account. Like any interactive process, it needs to be understood socially and diachronically.

## PUBLIC REASON AND ITS REASONS

According to Rawls, the reasons that matter *essentially* when we perform the most important justificatory and deliberative tasks of citizenship are *public reasons*. He describes these reasons somewhat differently in different contexts. They are said to be (1) reasons that "we are to share and publicly recognize before one another as grounding our social relations," (2) reasons that "all citizens as free and equal may reasonably be expected to endorse in light of principles and ideals acceptable to their common human reason," and (3) considerations that reasonable people view "as reasonable for everyone to accept and therefore as justifiable to them" (Rawls 2005, 49, 53, 137).[5] Because genuinely public reasoning restricts itself to this basis, according to Rawls, I shall refer to such reasoning as satisfying the public reason restriction (PRR).

Rawls uses the PRR to constrain how individual citizens may *deliberate* when deciding how to vote. When discussing this topic, Rawls is concerned with reasoning in the sense of a process of thinking. He also uses the PRR when discussing what citizens owe to one another when *justifying* proposals about "constitutional essentials" or "questions of basic justice" in the "public political forum" (Rawls 2005, 442–43). When applying the PRR in this second way, he is concerned not with a mode of thinking but with a form of discourse. The public forum (paradigmatically, a presidential or legislative debate) is distinguished from the "background culture" (for example, a symposium in a university or church, or a conversation around the dinner table).

The freestanding basis is supposed to be the set of reasons that all citizens could use, and would use if they were reasonable, when performing the genuinely public tasks of deliberation and justification. It is supposed to be sufficient for fulfilling these purposes fairly. According to what Rawls calls the "proviso," a citizen is permitted, when justifying a proposal, to rely initially on considerations outside the freestanding basis, *provided* that he or she is *able* to justify the proposal strictly on the basis of public reasons and *stands ready* to justify the proposal in this way.

When addressing one another in the public forum on basic matters, citizens ultimately owe one another justificatory arguments proceeding from the freestanding basis. Citizens who cannot justify their conclusions in this way to their fellow citizens, according to Rawls, are treating those citizens unfairly. Justifying a conclusion is an activity in which one person addresses an argument to one or more other people. An argument is public, according to the PRR, only if it appeals strictly to public reasons and only if the mode of inference involved in reaching the conclusion is itself something all reasonable people could accept. *Justifying-to* appears to be a "success" concept. Trying to justify a proposal to someone is not necessarily to succeed in justifying it to someone. The justificatory argument must not only appeal strictly to public values; it must also succeed relative to public standards.

Constitutional essentials and questions of basic justice pertain to how the state uses coercion on the citizenry. For that coercion to count as fair, Rawls thinks, it needs to be *justifiable to* citizens on whom the coercion might be brought to bear. There will always be some people who reject even the best justificatory arguments, so Rawls narrows his attention to what reasonable people could accept. The arguments are good enough, according to Rawls, *only if* all *reasonable* people *could* accept both the reasons being appealed to and the mode of inference being employed.

It might be that Rawls wishes to apply a more rigorous standard when a proposal pertains to the most basic questions, so that an argument qualifies as adequate only if all reasonable people *would* accept the reasons being appealed to and the transition from reasons to conclusion. He is not very clear on such matters but appears to need the more rigorous notion when distinguishing reasonable conceptions of justice from unreasonable conceptions. He seems to have the more permissive standard in mind in contexts where the reasonableness of a conception or a proposal is said to be a matter of degree.

This apparent permissiveness is puzzling when viewed in relation to the concern about legitimacy and coercion. Suppose I am reasonable and an argument is addressed to me that I could, in some counterfactual scenario, reasonably accept. But, for additional sound reasons of my own, I do not in fact accept the argument. It is not entirely clear why, in Rawls's view, such an argument would be sufficient to resolve the legitimacy of coercive measures subsequently taken against me when the proposal is enacted and enforced, especially if my justification for a counterproposal is much stronger, all things considered, than the argument in question. The common practice of standing back to evaluate the relative merits of the arguments for competing proposals receives little attention from Rawls when he is directly discussing the PRR.

Suppose I *could*, in some counterfactual scenario, reasonably accept an argument for P but do not in fact accept that argument as a *sufficient* case for P and would not be *epistemically entitled* to do so, *all things considered*, in my actual epistemic circumstances. Then what? This question, to which I will return, brings to the fore holistic and dialectical considerations often neglected in discussions of public reason. It also highlights the importance of distinguishing the moral and epistemic elements in Rawls's notion of reasonableness.

In a footnote, Rawls (2005, 49, note 2) says that his conception of the reasonable is "closely connected with T. M. Scanlon's principle of moral motivation." This is the view that "we have a basic desire to be able to justify our actions to others on grounds they could not reasonably reject—reasonably, that is, given the desire to find principles that others similarly motivated could not reasonably reject." Rawls does not explain the connection further, but this remark appears to tilt toward an especially rigorous notion of the values in the freestanding basis—closer to the "would accept" formulation than to the "could accept" formulation. He does not sort through the relationships among reasons that no reasonable person could reasonably reject, reasons that reasonable people would accept, and reasons that reasonable people could accept. Neither does he say how inclusive the range of counterfactual scenarios implied by the modal auxiliary verbs is supposed to be. Which of the many possible worlds that include me, and in which I am reasonable, are at issue here?

Rawls's conception of the reasonable is complicated to the point of being obscure. Reasonableness is a mixture of moral elements and epistemic elements related to justification. The moral elements have to do with the motivational concerns just mentioned, in particular, the desire to cooperate with others who are similarly motivated, on terms that they could or would accept. These terms, in Rawls's view, need to include shared principles, because these are needed to resolve the problems of legitimacy and stability. The shared principles are meant to function as a sort of social contract—not an actual contract consented to at a particular time by morally and epistemically fallible agents but a hypothetical contract constructed theoretically among all reasonable people. This explains Rawls's heavy reliance on (shifting) modal auxiliary verbs and (rather vaguely specified) counterfactual conditionals.

It is not enough for the principles to be shared among all actual people who wish to cooperate with one another in some setting and happen to agree on some set of principles. Utilitarianism and libertarianism are excluded from the class of reasonable conceptions because they do not qualify, according to Rawls, as reasonable interpretations of the basic public reasons. Each of these two positions rejects something that he takes to be acceptable to all reasonable people. So the notion of reasonableness is morally substantive and anything but uncontestable.

Any conception that does not recognize and prioritize the rights, liberties, opportunities, and provisions Rawls takes to be acceptable to all reasonable people is ruled out as unreasonable. While it can be hard for a reader to determine what moral or epistemic factors Rawls has in mind in a given case, the most important factor for his doctrine of public reason appears to be the criterion of reciprocity, which is what requires the basic reasons to be acceptable to all reasonable people in the first place (Rawls 2005, li). Each citizen owes each other citizen the same sort of justifications, founded on a *single* basis they too can accept as reasonable people.

However, justice as fairness, Rawls's own preferred conception of justice, is said to be one of several reasonable conceptions. It is, he claims, the most reasonable of those conceptions. It is the most reasonable of the reasonable conceptions, I take it, by virtue of being the one that a reasonable person surveying all of the options would be most entitled to accept. What a reasonable person is *entitled* to accept needs to be decided in light of *everything* that a *reasonable* person would want to *know* about the *relative* strengths and weaknesses of the competing conceptions.

Notice the complicated blend of moral and epistemic elements here, as well as the introduction of holistic and dialectical considerations that had not been highlighted initially. In one natural reading, such considerations are supposed to remain circumscribed by the PRR. As a reasonable person doing my best to discern the strongest of the reasonable conceptions, I am permitted to assess their relative merits in light of various considerations and arguments but not in light of everything I happen to believe, everything I happen to be epistemically entitled to believe, or even everything I happen to be obliged to believe, given my epistemic circumstances. I am still restricted to relying on considerations that *all* reasonable people could accept—including, presumably, the reasonable people I have good reason to view as significantly worse off than I am, epistemically or ethically. It is not perfectly clear, however, that this reading is correct, because this is where the tension between the theorist's evolving reflective equilibrium and the demands of public reason begin to become evident.

## THE COMPLETION OF PUBLIC REASON

Rawls holds that justice as fairness "completes" public reason. Justice as fairness is needed for this task and restricts itself to public reason when fulfilling the task. This is the point in Rawls's work at which the reasoning of the political theorist and the reasoning of the citizen appear to merge completely. Samuel Freeman helpfully explains what the completion of public reason means and why it is needed:

> The *completeness* of public reason is its capacity to fully interpret public politi-
> cal values and determine their relative significance, in order to resolve all signifi-
> cant political questions regarding constitutional essentials and matters of basic
> justice in terms of public reason. Public reason must be complete in some man-
> ner if society is to avoid appealing to comprehensive religious, philosophical, and
> moral doctrines to decide these crucial issues. If appeal to comprehensive doc-
> trines is needed to interpret and decide conflicts among political values, then to
> that degree the criterion of reciprocity and the principle of political legitimacy
> are violated; citizens are being subject to laws that they cannot reasonably be
> expected to accept in their capacity as democratic citizens.
>
> (Freeman 2007, 405, emphasis in original)

Let us step back for a moment and reconstruct the steps taken so far. Rawls, as a theorist pursuing reflective equilibrium, distinguishes public from nonpublic reasons. The former are reasons any reasonable person could or would accept. Reciprocity is among the values that qualify as a public reason. This value, inter-preted in light of concerns about legitimacy and stability, gives rise to a *criterion* of reciprocity. This criterion implies that citizens must rely essentially on public reasons when deciding how to vote or when justifying proposals in the public forum. The public reasons are the freestanding basis of public reason. Public rea-son must also provide an approved way of reasoning *from* the basis *to* a particular configuration of institutional arrangements and norms, including the practices of public reason itself. And it must somehow do this without appealing, even implicitly, to nonpublic reasons, because such an appeal would itself violate the reciprocity criterion, as Rawls understands it.

Now we have a crucial addition to the argument. Public reason needs, finally, to be *completed* by a determinate political conception of justice because, other-wise, the freestanding basis is too lacking in determinacy to permit resolution of the crucial issues on that basis by a process of reasoning that itself qualifies as pub-lic. This need for completion is fulfilled by political liberalism's philosophically nonpartisan interpretation of justice as fairness. The completion of public reason is required in order to give the freestanding basis sufficient content to do for polit-ical society what it is tasked with doing, namely, *settling all of the basic issues without surreptitiously going nonpublic.*

Political liberalism, as Rawls understands it, places the theorist and the citi-zen under the same restriction, the duty of civility. Both theorist and citizen are instructed to rely essentially only on public reasons when fulfilling their most important role-specific tasks. The theorist needs to do so, above all, because a single best political conception of justice is needed to complete public reason. That need casts the theorist of political liberalism in an essentially public role—indeed, an especially authoritative one. It also clearly brings the pursuit of reflective equilibrium into the domain of public reason while raising the stakes with regard to its conclusions. If the theorist pursuing reflective equilibrium does not settle on a most reasonable conception of justice, public reason is left incomplete and the concern about indeterminacy is not met.

The overall project is looking exceedingly ambitious. First, the public reasons need to be identified, in accordance with a rigorous, if counterfactual, standard of reasonableness. Second, an approved way of reasoning on the basis of those reasons needs to be specified, again in accordance with the rigorous standard. In fulfilling these first two tasks, there can be no equivocation or question begging on the matter of what reasonableness and reciprocity involve. That is a very big *if*, because both of these notions are plainly subject to multiple interpretations.

When deciding in favor of his own conceptions of reasonableness and reciprocity, Rawls is resolving tensions among differing intuitions about what reasonableness and reciprocity involve. Theorists who resolve those tensions differently need not take themselves to be turning against these values. Reflective equilibrium itself appears to be rather more permissive than the doctrine of public reason needs it to be at the crucial moment when interpretations of reasonableness and reciprocity are being decided. The doctrine of public reason represses the thought that theorists might well be entitled to a good deal of leeway at this juncture.

The upshot of the approved way of reasoning needs, however, to be a set of determinate solutions to the crucial issues. The solutions Rawls proposes are determinate enough. What is much less clear is whether he arrives at them in a way that is both perfectly public by *his* standards and acceptable at each step to *all* reasonable people. It is not obvious that the selection of basic values and standards of reasoning can be completed without introducing considerations that some reasonable people—in a non–question begging sense of *reasonable*—would be entitled to reject.

Among the values Rawls places in the freestanding basis are a number of basic liberties, several sorts of equality, and a set of political virtues, including reasonableness itself. Freeman admits that no complete list is given. Assuming that the value of reciprocity does belong to the freestanding basis, what Rawls calls the "criterion of reciprocity" is only one of many ways of interpreting what it demands. As for the approved way of reasoning on the basis of these values, Rawls mentions a number of "guidelines," including norms of evidence and inference, without shedding much light on how the reasoning is supposed to work (Rawls 2005, 225; Freeman 2007, 387). Later, I will try to determine how his brief treatment of non-public forms of reasoning bears on this question. But the whole picture is too sketchy for a reader to be certain that arbitrariness is not entering in. It is as sketchy as it is complicated. Its complication can create the illusion that it is not sketchy, that Rawls has the entire picture filled in.

The basic values and standards of public reason are declared incompatible with unreasonable views but are also said to leave room for multiple reasonable views. Crucially, any view according to which reasonableness is not best understood in terms of public reasons is declared unreasonable. Reasonable people are said to reason from the basic values somewhat variously, but they all acknowledge the same values and they reason from them in accord with the same mutually agreeable guidelines of reasoning.

In Rawls's view, which values and standards count as fundamental is not subject to reasonable disagreement, but what follows from those values and principles is subject to reasonable disagreement. This admission opens the door to the worry that the freestanding basis lacks sufficiently determinate content to settle the crucial issues it is meant to settle without resort to nonpublic reasons. Justice as fairness completes public reason by vindicating one reasonable conception of justice as more reasonable than the others. It does so, Rawls assures us, without appealing to anything nonpublic.

Exactly how holistic the reasoning can be without violating the criterion of reciprocity is something to which we shall return repeatedly in this chapter. Presumably, reasonable people want to adopt, and should adopt, the most reasonable available proposals about the crucial issues. So justice as fairness seems to have been implicit in the freestanding basis after all. It just needed the right philosopher to make it explicit and then complete it, making use only of what already belonged to it. The philosopher of reasonableness first rules out some views as inherently unreasonable, then makes room for multiple reasonable views, and finally arrives at one view, his own, which is most reasonable.

What a complicated structure, with so many apparently controversial elements and technical components, this turns out to be!

The fine print includes the introduction of the proviso, the distinction between the public forum and the background culture, the distinction between questions that are basic or constitutional and other sorts of questions, the could/would/might ambiguities about which reasons are public reasons, the obscure mixture of moral and epistemic factors implicit in the notion of reasonableness, the incompleteness of the list of basic values, the vagueness of the description of approved modes of inference, the apparent indeterminacy of the values in the freestanding basis, the resulting need to interpret those values in one or another way, and the admission that a contestable conception of justice is needed to resolve the problem of indeterminacy. Once we have taken all of these matters into account, the public reason doctrine must be admitted to be a rather baroque and yet unfinished theoretical construct.

There is something deeply ironic about the doctrine's architectonic structure and complexity, given that the topic is public reason, which is supposed to be maximally accessible and transparent to everyone, and given that one goal of *Political Liberalism* is to free its conception of justice from partisan philosophical assumptions. There certainly are philosophical assumptions at work here. Whether they are partisan assumptions will itself be subject to dispute. Philosophers who deem the assumptions nonpartisan are likely to be the ones who share Rawls's intuitions about what a reasonable person is like, about what it is to have a reason for something, about what it is to justify a proposal to someone, and about what reciprocity amounts to.

It is far from obvious that most ordinary people are implicitly committed to all of the assumptions at work in the elaborate edifice of public reason. One wonders how much theoretical training a citizen would need in order to assure himself that he was acting in accordance with the ideal of public reason as Rawls understands it. Critics who raise doubts about it are often told that they have missed the point or content of a subtle distinction, or the moment at which Rawls changed his mind about something or introduced a qualification. If critics persist in expressing suspicion, they are liable to be warned that their doubts are evidence of something worse than inattention to the fine print, such as unreasonableness or incivility.[6]

Taken broadly, a *reasonable* person is someone committed to cooperating appropriately with others, who are similarly committed to cooperating, in the task of establishing and maintaining acceptable basic societal arrangements. If we want to capture the epistemic connotation of the term in ordinary language, we can add that a reasonable person is someone appropriately responsive to relevant evidence and arguments. Cooperativeness and epistemic responsibility are all that the ordinary person's conception of a reasonable person comes to. So far, nothing has been said about what the terms of cooperation need to be like or about what appropriate responsiveness to relevant evidence and arguments would involve.

Taken narrowly, a reasonable person is someone committed to relying essentially *on public reason, as Rawls understands it, under the circumstances Rawls specifies.* The narrow conception of a reasonable person is part of what Rawls needs to vindicate when defending the PRR. Equivocating on the notion of a reasonable person can create the misleading impression that Rawlsians are the only reasonable people in the broad sense, the only individuals truly disposed to cooperate appropriately in pursuit of acceptable basic relationships.

The broad notion of a reasonable person leaves room for a good deal of disagreement about what liberty and equality should be thought to involve and thus what sorts of basic societal relationships would qualify as acceptable and how the cooperative pursuit of such relationships should be conducted. A person can qualify as reasonable in this sense if she finds the PRR dubious or incorrect. In contrast, a reasonable person in the narrow sense is committed to Rawlsian assumptions about what the freestanding basis is and to the assumption that rejecting the PRR would be unreasonable.

The question about indeterminacy of content that Rawls addresses when speaking of the need to complete public reason is reminiscent of Hegel's and Dewey's critique of Kantian rationalism. Let me now raise three additional questions with a similar pedigree. First, are the reasons that belong to the freestanding basis fixed or changeable? Second, are they reasons that all reasonable people, *regardless of dialectical circumstances*, would accept, or reasons that all reasonable people in *a given dialectical setting* would accept? Third, are the proposals that qualify as justified on the basis of those reasons themselves fixed or are they subject to change?

While Rawls does not say very much in direct response to the first question, some of what he says about public reason makes sense only if we take him to be assuming that the default starting point of *all genuinely public* reasoning is a *fixed* set of reasons inferred from the genuinely public values of political liberalism, above all liberty and equality. His answer to the second question is harder to make out, but he seems to grant that the very notion of a reasonable person comes clearly into view only in the wake of the religious wars and in societies where a kind of pluralism is found. Genuinely public reasons are the ones that any reasonable person, in any time and place, could or would accept. But the project of identifying those reasons and using them inferentially to construct a shared basis for society is something that emerged under particular historical circumstances.

As for the third question, Rawls's answer is clear, albeit undeveloped. He holds that the proposals justified on the basis of public reason can change:

> Political liberalism, then, does not try to fix public reason once and for all in the form of one favored political conception of justice. That would not be a sensible approach. . . . Even if relatively few conceptions come to dominate over

time, and one conception even appears to have a special central place, the forms of permissible public reason are always several. Moreover, new variations may be proposed from time to time and older ones may cease to be represented. It is important that this be so; otherwise the claims of groups or interests arising from social change might be repressed and fail to gain their appropriate political voice.

(Rawls 2005, 451–52)

In a footnote, Rawls adds the following, without further argument: "Thus, Jeremy Waldron's criticism of political liberalism as not allowing new and changing conceptions of political justice is incorrect" (452, note 30).

Here, it seems to me, Rawls is being uncharacteristically unresponsive to an apt criticism. Waldron (1993) is simply working with the bare-bones conception of public reasoning Rawls has presented.[7] According to this conception, genuinely public reasoning appears to move in one direction, from an apparently fixed basis to conclusions that are supposed to settle the crucial issues. By moving in that direction, from public reasons to proposed solutions to the issues, the reasoning produces a justification of those solutions, and it does so without recourse to anything but the reasons in the freestanding basis and the approved means of reasoning. If it relies on anything else, it appears to stray out of the severely delimited domain of the public.

Waldron is asking, in effect, how reasoning could both be genuinely public, in the sense just specified, and yet incorporate new claims arising from social change. This is an excellent question. Rawls cannot make it go away simply by asserting, without further explanation, that public reason accommodates change. We need to be told how significant change can be accommodated in an *apparently* unidirectional model of reasoning. One way of doing that would be to show in some detail, rather than merely asserting, that the model is *not* actually unidirectional. But this would involve demonstrating that, once the model's holistic and diachronic features are fully understood, it remains capable of solving the problems it is intended to solve. To accommodate change, the model needs to be somewhat dialectical. To solve the problems it is meant to solve, however, the model cannot be entirely holistic, because that would be to erase the line between public and nonpublic reasoning.

The model is designed with the problem of legitimacy in mind. Reasoning directed toward that problem is assumed to have a certain pattern. That is why the model appears unidirectional. If the public reasoning of citizens can move in the opposite direction, the model needs to be more holistic and to exhibit various patterns. And that is likely to put pressure on the doctrine's prohibition of appeals to nonpublic reasons (when deciding how to vote, when reasoning in the public forum, and so forth). It might be that the line between public and nonpublic reasons becomes much fuzzier than the defender of public reason wants it to be.

A thoroughly dialectical model of public reasoning would take reasoned consensus among cooperative people on important political questions to be something that changes over time in response to various forms of experience, action, and reasoning, including forms of reasoning that challenge a prior consensus rather than arguing from it. Pragmatists prefer the term *reasoning* over the term *reason*, in this context, because *reasoning* clearly refers to an activity, and thus to something that unfolds over time and might even change radically over time, whereas *reason* embodies at least a residual commitment to Enlightenment assumptions about reason as a faculty governed by fixed laws. I will later argue that if a thoroughgoing dialectical model of reasoning is correct, the rationale for thinking that reasoning qualifies as public only when it *proceeds from* a fixed basis is threatened. But if that conclusion is correct, then the metaphor of the social contract is no longer as apt as it once seemed and Rawls's account of nonpublic forms of reasoning becomes puzzling.

## REFLECTIVE EQUILIBRIUM AND DIALECTICAL REASONING

Defenders of Rawls will insist that he is plainly committed to a dialectical model of reasoning. His conceptions of reflective equilibrium and constructivism, they will say, are definitive evidence of this commitment (Rawls 1999b; 1999c, 42).[8] When constructing and revising his theory of justice, Rawls seeks reflective equilibrium among considered pre-theoretical judgments and his principles of justice, adjusting each, over time, with an eye toward overall coherence. The process is constructive in the sense that it involves the creation and modification of models, ideas, ideals, and principles. These are components of a theory, and they are ultimately justified by virtue of having been brought reflectively into equilibrium with considered pre-theoretical judgments and with reasonable comprehensive views of the good. The principles have practical import. They are meant to guide action.

At any moment in the reflective process, the theorist takes his or her current principles, considered intuitions about cases, and empirically grounded assumptions as a default starting point for further inquiry. The reasoning involved in such inquiry is holistic and dialectical. It involves adjusting principles in light of intuitions, intuitions in light of principles, and both in light of changes in historical experience and empirical inquiry. But the reasoning is not initially constrained by the PRR. Endorsements of the idea of public reason and of the ideal of public reason are, after all, products of the dialectical process of theoretical construction by which Rawls claims to achieve reflective equilibrium. There *is* no PRR to constrain the theorist of justice until the theorist constructs it and justifies it.

The PRR implies that citizens qua citizens are obliged to adopt as the starting point of their public reasoning a highly restricted subset of the considerations they would be entitled to take into account when deciding, as individuals, how to live well or when deciding, as theorists, what principles of justice to endorse. The process of reasoning that Rawls initially employed as a theorist thus appears to be more permissive and more holistic than the process of reasoning he came to consider obligatory for citizens. The two processes involve different starting points. The rationale for a restrictive starting point for the citizen is twofold: a commitment to reciprocity, understood as requiring agreement on a shared basis of reasons, and the need for stability in a society where reasonable people differ on topics such as the existence and nature of God and what it would be to live truly well.

The reasoning in which the theorist engages when seeking reflective equilibrium is dialectical. What one is entitled to accept when theorizing, according to Rawls, is determined in part by how the process of theoretical reasoning has gone so far. It is also determined in part by how political history has gone so far. Historical considerations are prominent among the empirically grounded assumptions that theorists of justice are supposed to take into account in their quest for adequate principles of justice. Rawls (2005, xxii–xxvii) sounds downright Hegelian when, as a seeker of reflective equilibrium, he takes political liberalism to be a justified response to the historical developments associated with the Protestant Reformation, the emergence of the modern nation-state, the search for alternatives to the violence of "religious civil war," and, finally, the realization that "reasonable pluralism" is a "permanent" and desirable feature of modern democratic societies. An adequate theory of justice *for our own time* needs to take account of these developments, and the conception of justice Rawls proposes is clearly meant to be responsive to them.

So the issue I am raising is not that Rawls is, generally speaking, insensitive to the attractions of a dialectical conception of reasoning. The issue is whether the public reasoning citizens engage in is, or ought to be, different, in the respects just specified, from the relatively unfettered search for reflective equilibrium recommended to theorists in *A Theory of Justice*. Rawls has a lot to say, when defending his preferred principles, about why he thinks some widely accepted judgments about justice ought to be abandoned. But arguments of the sort he gives in those passages, in the context of seeking reflective equilibrium, seem not to appeal to reasons that no reasonable person could reasonably reject, and they seem unlikely to issue in conclusions that all reasonable people would *have to* accept.

This is, of course, the very anxiety that led Rawls to write *Political Liberalism*. The question is whether his attempt there to make political theory less philosophically partisan is successful. Whenever conflicts arise between widely accepted intuitions and a theorist's principles, holistic reflection is required if we are to count the costs of resolving the tensions in one way or another. There is, however, typically room for disagreement among reasonable people on which of the costs should, all things considered, be borne. So the holistic reflection required to complete public reason does not appear to satisfy the demands of public reason itself.

For reasons that will emerge later, I am not persuaded that public reasoning does ordinarily function in conformity to the PRR. But I also doubt that public reasoning *should* operate strictly as Rawls recommends. It is not clear, in particular, that the PRR imposes a fair or workable constraint, especially if applied during periods of significant social change and in societies where differences in outlook go deep enough to give rise to social movements and initiatives demanding significant change.

Under such circumstances, it is common to find dialectical considerations of the sort that feature prominently in freewheeling debate among political theorists also turning up in what ordinary citizens say to one another publicly in their capacity as free and equal citizens. It is also common to find contestation over what counts as a reasonable person, about what reasons ought to serve as the default starting point for one's reasoning, about the content of the reasons that are widely accepted, and about how to resolve tensions among intuitions about cases and commitments at the level of principle. I strongly suspect that contestation over such things is no less pervasive than contestation over visions of the good.

As we have seen, one product of Rawls's theoretical quest for reflective equilibrium, the conception of justice called *justice as fairness*, is supposed to complete public reason from within. The citizen who adopts justice as fairness as the most reasonable political conception must be reasoning, to some extent, holistically and dialectically when evaluating the various supposedly reasonable conceptions and endorsing the Rawlsian one as the most reasonable. That determination would have to rest on a holistically comparative account of the strengths and weaknesses of alternative conceptions. There appears to be nothing to prevent the resulting process of reflection from doubling back to cast doubt on previously accepted notions of what belongs in the supposedly freestanding basis.

Doubts might even arise at that point—and do in fact arise, in my mind—about whether positing a freestanding basis is the best way to account for our intuitions about reciprocity. But if such doubts are correct and there is nothing preventing the process of reflection from reaching all the way down to the defining commitments of political liberalism, then it is hard to see how the contextual sensitivity and permissiveness of the reflective process is going to leave public reason with enough determinacy to give Rawls what *he* wants from it. The need for individual citizens to exercise discretion here appears to be far reaching. To participate in the completion of public reason, they need to make all-things-considered judgment calls on how to resolve tensions among various sorts of commitments they currently hold. It is clear how they could do so *from their own points of view as individuals*. Yet public reason constrains them from doing this. Its purpose is to delineate a singular, generalized point of view—that of the citizen as such. The relationship Rawls imagines between points of view adopted by *individual citizens* and the point of view of *the citizen* remains unclear.[9]

I can sum up the argument of this section by saying that Rawls initially appears to endorse a dialectical account of the reasoning of political theorists but a much more restricted account of the reasoning of citizens, modeled on a single kind of justificatory argument from a fixed basis of public reasons. In his dismissal of Waldron's criticism and in his discussion of the completion of public reason, however, he seems to complicate things by implying that public reasoning is more thoroughly dialectical than he had originally made it seem and thus is capable of doubling back to unsettle even the supposedly freestanding basis of public reason and the distinction between public and nonpublic reasons itself. I shall argue that the complications just mentioned point us in the right direction, beyond public reason as Rawls conceives of it.

We ought to pursue a thoroughgoing and explicit dialectical pragmatism when discussing public reasoning. This means viewing public reasoning as an evolving equilibrium in which theorists and citizens alike are caught up.[10] The considerations against accepting an overly restrictive model of public reasoning are considerations in favor of developing a somewhat more permissive, explicitly dialectical alternative to it. But once we have that alternative in hand, there seems to be no way of vindicating either the distinction between public and nonpublic reasoning as Rawls has drawn it or the PRR as he formulated it.

The reasoning of the theorist and the reasoning of the citizen should indeed be brought together, but not necessarily in Rawls's way. He recommends restricting theorists and citizens alike to public reason as he interprets it. I am disposed to restrict neither theorists nor citizens in this manner. If these options and their implications were fully clear, we could simply choose between them and move on. But they are not fully clear. There is more to be done.

## ACTUAL REASONING, DISSENTERS, AND CHANGE

The doctrine of public reason belongs to an ideal theory, a theory of the well-ordered society.[11] The ideal it projects is, by admission, less than fully realized. It is not intended as a utopian ideal, in the sense of being either wholly unrealized or incapable of motivating action in our society. Its purpose is to guide us toward a realizable form of reciprocity. To be well ordered, for Rawls, a society needs to have a shared justification, acceptable to all reasonable people, that settles the issue of legitimacy with respect to its basic arrangements and that also secures stability in the face of reasonable pluralism.[12]

Certainly, we do not live in a society that qualifies as well ordered by Rawls's standards. His claim about public reason pertains to how citizens *would* reason *if* they were reasonable *and* living in a well-ordered society. A natural way to interpret the practical significance of this counterfactual conditional would be to understand it in perfectionist terms. To become more reasonable and to bring our basic relationships into better order would be to make ourselves and our society more excellent in important respects. It would be to approximate a vision of civic virtue and the common good. But that cannot be what Rawls has in mind, because he is not a perfectionist. The relevance of the counterfactual conditional, for him, appears to be that it specifies a condition that must be satisfied if some important policy or constitutional provision is to qualify as legitimate, which in turn constrains a citizen's choices concerning which policies and provisions to vote for, argue for, and otherwise support.

Before going any further, we should take note of four points. The first is that the Rawlsian requirement of relying essentially on reasons that reasonable people could or would reasonably accept is a good deal more rigorous than the common practice of arguing respectfully, when one can, from widely accepted premises. The Rawlsian requirement makes use of technical philosophical notions that are themselves not widely accepted or understood. Some reasons that are public in his sense are not widely accepted. Conversely, it might well be the case that many premises widely accepted in our society do not qualify as public reasons in his sense. This is why the resemblance between public reason in Rawls's sense and the common practice of arguing from widely accepted premises is more remote than it might seem at a glance. It is important to keep in mind that this common practice is not nearly rigorous enough to satisfy Rawls's concern for legitimacy.

One thing citizens do when reasoning in public about matters of public importance is to lay down a set of premises and extract a consequence from them, thereby defending a conclusion deductively.[13] In many familiar cases, the premises are accepted by nearly everyone in the discussion. Dissenters are indeed sometimes dismissed as unreasonable. And the justification for dismissing them does sometimes involve either their unwillingness to cooperate in a free and equal society or their attempts to impose on their fellow citizens an outlook that some cooperative people reasonably reject. So something *somewhat* resembling public reason in Rawls's sense appears to be in play.

When many people casually endorse "public reason," all they appear to have in mind is that *it is good, when possible*, to defend one's political proposals with reasons that most people of goodwill—the people not disposed to *dominate* others—can accept. Rawls's doctrine is much more specific than this. Furthermore, he is not claiming simply that we should all abide by the values expressed in an existing constitution. An *actual* consensus among *most citizens* on the acceptability of an existing *constitution* differs in several respects from a *hypothetical* consensus among *all reasonable people* on a particular *conception of justice*. He thinks, whereas I doubt, that the latter is needed in order to secure stability and legitimacy.

The second point is that, even supposing there to be public reasons in Rawls's sense, it is by no means obvious which reasons those are or whether they jointly suffice to settle the public questions he wants them to settle. The importance of this point can already be glimpsed in my earlier discussion of the completion of public reason. If public reason is not completed, its results will not be sufficiently determinate to settle those questions. And yet the proposed completion of public reason appears to violate the PRR.

The third point is that arguing deductively from a set of premises that is, or ought to be, accepted by all reasonable people is only one of the things that citizens do when reasoning in public about matters of public importance. Rawls discusses several other forms of discourse that citizens engage in, but he classifies those forms as nonpublic. We need to determine whether his classification of modes of reasoning is justifiable. In particular, we need to determine whether the mode of reasoning he classifies as public can plausibly be construed in a way that quarantines it from the modes he classifies as nonpublic.

The fourth point is that widely shared assumptions about reasonableness are often employed to police dissent. Dissenters are often said to be unreasonable. They are judged uncooperative, irrational, or both. The reasons they proffer are judged beyond the pale of reasonable discussion. In many cases, I am disposed to agree with such dismissive judgments. But we need to keep in mind that the public expression of dissent is the primary engine of reasoned change in society's assumptions, including assumptions about who the reasonable people are and which reasons would be accepted by any truly reasonable person. If a prevailing consensus concerning reasonableness is used in conjunction with the PRR to disparage certain sorts of reasons as unreasonable, one likely consequence will be to promote conformism. There is a real danger that public reason's moral strictures will, in less-than-ideal practice, inhibit challenges to prejudicial conceptions of reasonableness.

To see why these four points matter, let us begin by looking more closely at the sort of reasoning Rawls deems genuinely public. It is paradigmatically of the form A, B, and C, therefore D, where A, B, and C belong to the freestanding basis and D is some proposal or constitutional provision thought to be justified by reasoning of this form. We have already acknowledged the possibility of mistaken judgments or uncertainty concerning which reasons actually belong to the freestanding basis of genuinely public reasons. Keeping this possibility in mind, we need now to confront another: What if, in a given case, the justificatory reasoning leads from previously accepted assumptions to an absurd or otherwise problematical conclusion? This additional possibility suggests that the discursive pattern being recommended to us as the public reason schema *implicitly takes for granted* that there are no considerations that would, if they were taken into account, require rejection of D.[14]

The technical philosophical name for such a consideration is *defeater*. It is noteworthy that Rawls leaves potential defeaters out of the picture when setting out his contrasts between public and nonpublic forms of reasoning. In the absence of a defeater, a person who accepts A, B, and C, and determines that D follows from A, B, and C, can safely add D to his or her commitments. But suppose there is a defeater. Then it is not enough for the justificatory argument to move from widely accepted considerations to a conclusion that follows from them.

The reasoning schema that is paradigmatic for public reason actually holds only ceteris paribus, that is, only if other things are equal. The appraisal of such reasoning is therefore always implicitly holistic, because someone can always flip the argument around in order to mount an immanent critique of the assumed premises. It is only by abstracting away from the existence of potential defeaters that public reason's approved format of deliberation and justification appears to settle what it proposes to settle, namely, the problem of legitimation.

The approved public reason schema hides an implicit ceteris paribus clause, the triggering of which by a potential defeater immediately makes considerations *other than* A, B, and C relevant to the acceptability of D. The potential range of such considerations is wide. The reasoning involved in taking such considerations into account is a central phenomenon that dialectical pragmatism seeks to illuminate. Rawls takes such considerations into account when discussing reflective equilibrium. And he should do so. He does not, as far as I can tell, take such considerations into account, for the most part, when discussing public reason. He leaves them mainly in the dark.

The problem is that public reason's preferred form of reasoning fails to resolve the problem of legitimation *except in the absence of defeaters*. Whether there are defeaters is a highly important matter, but not one that gets covered simply by reasoning of the approved sort. How, then, does it get covered?

Rawls mentions three "forms of discourse" that do not qualify, on his terms, as *public* reasoning. In each case, the speaker is a citizen, addressing his or her fellow citizens, and the topic being discussed is a matter of public concern. These three forms of discourse fail to qualify as public reasoning, in Rawls's technical sense, because they do not involve reasoning strictly from the freestanding basis to a conclusion of the relevant sort. We now need to determine whether Rawls is right to narrow the scope of public reasoning in this way.

One mode that fails to qualify as genuinely public, according to his account, is "reasoning from conjecture" (Rawls 2005, 462). This belongs to a broader practice I have elsewhere called *immanent criticism*. A speaker (e.g., Socrates or Abraham Lincoln) conjectures that at least one interlocutor (e.g., Euthyphro or Stephen Douglas) accepts assumptions A, B, and C and then proceeds to expose a problem in accepting that set of commitments, perhaps by drawing an unwelcome implication D from it. Rawls is not saying that reasoning from conjecture is an inappropriate mode of reasoning for citizens to engage in when discussing or thinking about the most important public questions. He excludes conjecture from public reason because he holds that a citizen reasoning from conjecture ultimately still needs to be able to offer reasons from the freestanding basis that suffice to justify to other citizens what is being proposed.

This exclusion ignores the kind of dialectical reasoning required for the completion of public reason, where the line between the reasoning of the theorist and the reasoning of the citizen is blurred. What the theorist of justice does, when selecting the best of the reasonable conceptions of justice, presumably involves a combination of immanent criticism of arguments on behalf of the options under consideration and holistic reflection on the relative strengths and weaknesses of such conceptions. This is like what ordinary citizens also do when an argument from widely accepted premises, or from premises widely thought to qualify as acceptable to all reasonable people, produces an apparently absurd or otherwise problematical conclusion. The problematical conclusion generates a need to consider how previously accepted assumptions might require revision, given one's other commitments, desires, hopes, and fears.

We do well to recall, at this juncture, a pair of crucial facts about dissenters. One is that their willingness to reject a conclusion reached in this way is often used to disparage their cooperativeness, their rationality, or both. The other is that the most salient instances of moral progress and conceptual change are products of such dissent. The doctrine of public reason does little to bring the process of change to light. Worse, it threatens to inhibit that process by classifying as nonpublic modes of reasoning that are essential to it.

All it takes to bring immanent criticism, the holistic appraisal of alternatives, and the need for moral and conceptual revision into play, then, is a potential defeater of D, a reason for regarding D as absurd or implausible. When introducing the approved schema as definitive of public reason, Rawls leaves potential defeaters, and thus the characteristic activity of dissenters, out of sight. This is what opens the door to Waldron's complaint. It is also an important source of the worry that political liberalism is much less hospitable to dissent and change than it takes itself to be.

In ordinary parlance, we often speak as if reasons came as prepackaged, individuated considerations for or against believing or doing something. We sometimes also speak as if the weight of these individuated considerations can be determined independently of a broader context of commitments and independently of a process in which those commitments have changed over time. Our habit of speaking in this way can give rise to an oversimplified—insufficiently holistic, insufficiently diachronic—conception of what it is to have a reason.

It is this conception that links the latter-day defenders of public reason to their Enlightenment forebears. Hegel's name for the oversimplified conception is *Verstand*. His name for the explicitly holistic and dialectical alternative conception is *Vernunft*. The doubts I have just been raising about public reason can be summed up in Hegelian terms by saying that Rawls appears to be taking the perspective of *Verstand* for granted when addressing the issue of legitimacy and when contrasting public and nonpublic modes of reasoning. He does not appear to do so when discussing reflective equilibrium or when dismissing Waldron's complaint.

That is why I once referred to Rawls as being halfway between Kant and Hegel (Stout 2004, 77–85). He appears to adopt an atomistic and static conception of reasons in some passages and a holistic and diachronic conception in others. Sometimes he sounds like an Enlightenment rationalist. At other times he sounds like dialectical pragmatist. He appears to want public reason to have a degree of holism and diachronic flexibility, but to a carefully limited degree. A great deal hangs on what this amounts to. He clearly wants public reason to be diachronically articulated, given his response to Waldron. But Rawls doesn't, as far as I can tell, work out the details. It is by no means certain that they can be worked out satisfactorily, because he has not clarified what it is for someone to have or offer a reason for something.

We are speaking elliptically whenever we treat considerations A, B, and C simply as *reasons for inferring* D, for we are leaving out of account whether D is absurd, how D comports with the rest of our prior commitments, and whether, given the broader dialectical context, we are entitled to those commitments.[15] Most of the time, there is no problem with the ellipsis. If ordinary talk of reasons were not riddled with such ellipses, we would waste a lot of time saying "other things being equal" and surveying irrelevancies in the broader epistemic landscape instead of getting on with the matter at hand. Leaving aside the possibility that D might be absurd, or might appear problematical when viewed in a larger context, usually simplifies reflection and the exchange of reasons in a beneficial way. But it can also create a static and atomistic picture of reasons. And it can reinforce a kind of conformism or complacency with regard to the status of widely accepted reasons and entrenched assumptions about reasonableness.

Once the ellipsis is filled in, the public reason schema, interpreted as a norm of commitment revision, would look something like this: If A, B, and C jointly entail or lend credence to D, and you accept A, B, and C, you should, all other things being equal, infer D. So long as the implicit ceteris paribus clause is not pushed to the surface by additional considerations against inferring D, it makes sense to speak of A, B, and C as the reasons for accepting D and to think of them as carrying whatever weight our prereflective confidence in them involves. But when the ceteris paribus clause is pushed to the surface, we had better employ an explicitly holistic notion of what it is to have a reason for something.

The pragmatist generalization of this point is that inference is always at least implicitly holistic—indeed, holistic in a way that makes it unwise to treat the logical relations between some set of accepted beliefs {A, B, C} and some D that follows from them as establishing more than a presumption, perhaps a very strong one, in favor of D. Suppose the ceteris paribus clause is pushed to the surface in a given case, because D is on its face absurd or because D is incompatible with, or in tension with, other things we believe. Then it is unclear whether we should speak of A, B, and C as *reasons for inferring* D. We would beg fewer questions by referring to them more neutrally as *considerations relevant* to the question of whether to accept D.

If D is absurd, or if accepting it produces an incompatibility or some milder form of incoherence in our total view, that would appear to be a strong reason for suspecting that at least one of A, B, and C is not a reason for inferring D at all, that it ought to have no weight in our justifications or deliberations. We might also speak of the weight of the {A, B, C} package of reasons as having been *diminished*, to employ a metaphor for our now weakened confidence in them. Either way, it no longer makes sense to think of reasons as individuated considerations with epistemic significance determined independently of a broader context. Yet that is precisely how they are spoken of, at least implicitly, in most discussions of the public reason doctrine, not least by Rawls himself.

## THE GREAT ORATOR

Let us turn now to the two remaining forms of discourse that Rawls classifies as nonpublic. In addition to "reasoning from conjecture," he refers to "declaration" and "witnessing" as forms of discourse that fall short of being genuinely public. In declaration, the speaker argues on the basis of his own commitments, some of which both fall outside the freestanding basis and are essential to the argument being made. In "witnessing," the speaker expresses "principled dissent from existing institutions, policies, or enacted legislation" but "does not appeal to principles and values of a (liberal) political conception of justice" (Rawls 2005, 465–66).[16]

To bring declaration and witnessing into the dialectical picture I have been developing as an alternative to Rawls's picture, imagine a Great Orator who combines these forms of reasoning with all of the others mentioned so far, except for the public reason schema itself. A supremely eloquent and wise citizen rises to a podium in the public forum and, in a series of debates with all comers, uses immanent criticism to reveal heretofore hidden contradictions in her opponents' outlooks (conjecture), expresses principled dissent from certain existing institutions on the basis of her own heretofore idiosyncratic commitments (witnessing), and articulates her own outlook in a surprisingly persuasive way (declaration). In declaring her outlook, she denies things previously taken for granted (assumption rejection), draws distinctions that change the look of the dialectical options and perhaps even the topics being addressed (explication), and changes the denotations and connotations of certain inherited concepts (resignification).

Imagine that you hear echoes of Gerrard Winstanley, John Milton, Mary Wollstonecraft, Henry David Thoreau, Margaret Fuller, Gandhi, and Martin Luther King Jr. in the Orator's words. She is doing the sort of thing they did at their most original. The argumentation is exquisite, the examples apt, the redefinitions of terms compelling. Suppose, further, that the vast majority of the population comes to agree with her conclusions, as a result. Now nearly everyone adopts her outlook. Yet there is one thing she has not done, which is to argue *from* the antecedently accepted "reasonable" assumptions of her audience *to* her conclusions about constitutional and legislative reform. Part of her purpose is to reject some of those assumptions and the conception of a reasonable person that is connected with them.

The reasons for converting to the Orator's outlook have to do with its recently demonstrated capacity to explain the strengths and weaknesses of its predecessor and competitor outlooks. These are dialectical considerations about which the Rawlsian model of public reason says little but about which the Rawlsian model of an evolving equilibrium says much. They are new reasons, which did not belong to the reservoir of reasons that all of the cooperative people took for granted immediately before the Great Oration. Would we, in those discursive circumstances, have reason to complain that the Great Orator has treated others unfairly? I think not, for she would have succeeded in *justifying* her conclusions respectfully *to* her fellow cooperative citizens in terms they *now* reasonably accept.

The Great Orator would not be arguing on the basis of what *had been viewed* as the approved considerations for reaching conclusions on important public questions, for this is what she has challenged and successfully overturned. Suppose that her witnessing has rightly persuaded everyone of her commitment to cooperation. Suppose, further, that she has reasoned perfectly well for someone in her social and epistemic circumstances and has fully earned entitlement to her conclusions. She herself is justified in accepting her conclusions. Finally, suppose that she has fully discharged the task of showing that her normative outlook adequately explains the strengths and weaknesses of its predecessors and competitors. Her immanent criticism of the most plausible alternative views casts grave doubt on them, while no such doubt has thus far arisen concerning the outlook she has declared. She has justified that outlook and her political conclusions *to her fellow citizens*, in the strong sense of having brought it about that they, too, are now justified in accepting the conclusions, or even are epistemically obliged to accept those conclusions. No one can think of a defeater.

It should be clear that the Great Orator has violated the PRR. Yet she has not reasoned wrongly, nor has she treated anyone unfairly. Indeed, she has justified the political implications of her normative outlook, including the implications regarding coercive enforcement of the provisions being proposed. She has done so as well as anyone could, under any circumstances. She is the Great Orator; what can I say?

A defender of Rawls might insist that the story of the Great Orator simply wishes the fact of pluralism away. And in a sense it does. It is an imaginary case, not an actual one, and it ends in a moment of utopian concord. We should be cautious when employing such cases in philosophy. But my point in introducing this story is not to suggest that the fact of pluralism is likely to pass away. The story is simply intended to make salient the *public* significance of three forms of reasoning that Rawls classifies as nonpublic, along with a few other things (including explication and resignification) that figure centrally in the dialectical pragmatism of Hegel, Dewey, and their intellectual heirs, such as Richard Bernstein, Robert Brandom, Cornel West, and Judith Butler. It should be easy to come up with somewhat similar actual cases that leave the fact of pluralism, but not a prior consensus on acceptable reasons, intact.

What it takes to justify a conclusion to someone else, by Rawls's standards, is, I have suggested, rather murky. It is clear that a citizen is, according to Rawls, ultimately obliged to offer a justificatory argument from premises of a certain sort. But how strong must the argument be to qualify as a successful justification? I suspect that few debaters in history have entirely eliminated grounds for reasonable doubt when constitutional essentials at are issue. What Lincoln did in his debates with Douglas is better described as raising the evident epistemic and moral costs of taking something like Douglas's position on slavery. To earn entitlement to the proslavery position, after Lincoln had had his say, a follower of Douglas would need to draw new distinctions and defend them against the charge of arbitrariness. But bullet biting is at least as common in political discourse as it is in philosophical discourse. Thomas Kuhn demonstrated that there is a lot of it in science as well. There is no way to eliminate it by laying down a guideline. The bullet biter restores consistency to his outlook by paying a price.

Now consider the somewhat different cases of Winstanley, Milton, Wollstonecraft, William Lloyd Garrison, Thoreau, and Gandhi, who used immanent criticism, declaration, witnessing, civil disobedience, or some combination thereof to undermine some features of an existing consensus on constitutional essentials and matters of basic justice. As in Lincoln's case, I do not know whether they succeeded in establishing beyond a reasonable doubt that their own policy proposals were correct. They did, I believe, demonstrate their entitlement to their most consequential conclusions, and they made an enormous difference to the public reasoning of their eras. They helped change which reasons could henceforth safely be treated by their fellows as a default starting point for reasoning. Their challenges to the views held by other people changed what those people would have to do in order to maintain entitlement to *their* views.

Evidently, both the default starting point for reasoning on important public topics and the related entitlements can change—and change for good reasons—without eliminating the facts of pluralism. But if this is so, it is merely arbitrary to exclude from the domain of genuinely public reasoning those forms of reasoning that can make such change happen. It makes no sense to exclude from public reasoning the forms of reasoning that are *required* to determine whether an extant consensus on reasonableness and acceptable reasons is correct.

It will be objected, once more, that Rawls does not rule out all change in the fundaments of public reason. His claim is that morally justified change of that sort must be based on public reason itself, not on anything lying outside it. The dialectical holism of public reason is present but limited, one might say. In response, I would urge that the vagaries of public reason be kept in mind—vagaries concerning what counts as a public reason, concerning how the inferences within it are supposed to work, and, most importantly, concerning the indeterminacy of what those inferences entail. These vagaries jointly make it hard to know how the PRR should be applied to real-life cases, above all to cases involving large changes in the sociopolitical order, in concept application, and in patterns of reasoning.

What the ideal of public reason requires, the objector might say, is simply that a citizen stand ready to offer reasons of the right kind, and this is something that Wollstonecraft, Gandhi, and others like them could have done or, in some instances, actually did. I suppose a Rawlsian could interpret any of these historical figures as satisfying the PRR by resolving the vagaries in a certain way, thus making public reason more permissive and dialectical than it initially appears to be. But, even assuming that we were supplied with a precise account of what the public reasons are, how would we know whether these figures *stood ready* to argue in the approved way if they did not actually do so? And if they did at times argue in the approved way, how would we know that they were not still implicitly relying, all the while, on considerations outside of public reason?

## BRACKETING

The doctrine of public reason places great emphasis on what one *would* or *could* conclude *if* one confined oneself to the freestanding basis when making inferences on one's own or when offering reasons to others. To confine oneself to the freestanding basis for some deliberative or justificatory purpose would involve bracketing beliefs and values one holds that do not belong to the freestanding basis.

It is not clear to me that the bracketing is workable or, in all relevant cases, sensible. The previous two sections put me in a position to explain why. The PRR requires you to avoid relying *essentially* on some beliefs you hold that might prove to be defeaters of conclusions inferred from premises drawn strictly from the supposedly freestanding basis of reasons taken to be public in Rawls's sense. The policy being recommended is, in the relevant circumstances, to ignore what you yourself believe insofar as that diverges from the intersection of what all cooperative people would or could reasonably accept.

A somewhat different policy would be what Ralph Waldo Emerson called *self-reliance*: Beware of any existing consensus among the supposedly cooperative people. They are mostly conformists. Like you, they are complicit in myriad injustices. Their notions of reasonableness and civility, and perhaps your own, are more likely to squelch dissent than to provide a proper basis for public discussion. Attend with care to the thoughts you have that diverge from the intersection of what everyone around you regards as reasonable. Have the courage to utter those thoughts publicly, in a spirit of freedom, and see which of them is greeted by the wise and the just as true. For that is how beneficial change transpires. Be mindful that the very thought of change is something conformity represses. Yet change is in fact happening all around us all the time.

With Emerson's warnings in mind, I wish now to pursue the following question: Why should I feel obliged to bracket beliefs and values I hold if I am *epistemically entitled* to them and they *undermine* an inference that seems correct to me *only* when viewed in abstraction from the bracketed beliefs and values?[17] The Rawlsian answer will be to repeat that such bracketing is, at day's end, a requirement of fairness to one's fellow citizens. But is it fair to expect one's fellow citizens to restrict themselves in this way, given the inferential difficulty this would cause for them in cases where other things are not equal, from their point of view?

Rawls is clearly made anxious by this question, although his answer to it does not obviously amount to something better than a reassertion of the link he envisions between reasonableness, or reciprocity, and a putative need for a basis of shared reasons. As Gerald Gaus argues:

> To say that [individuals] have strong reason to endorse such shared rules only when they reason on the basis of shared concerns and are unaware of their divergent conceptions [while bracketing them] is not an especially compelling conclusion. In reply to the conclusion "If you bracket most of what you care about, you will reason as others do, and will endorse the shared rules," the reasonable query is "And what will be my view of these rules when I do know what I deeply care about?"[18]

> (Gaus 2011, 39–40)

One of the great divides in contemporary political theory is that between philosophers who intuitively find this query reasonable, as Gaus, Waldron, Nicholas Wolterstorff, and I do, and philosophers who intuitively find it unreasonable in a morally charged sense. A great deal ends up hanging, in the reflective practice of Rawls and his followers, on the highly contestable decision to retain the latter intuition.

Grant, strictly for the purposes of argument, that there is such a thing as the freestanding basis. Let A, B, and C belong to that basis. Now imagine that someone reasons from A, B, and C to D, where D strikes you as either absurd or highly unlikely, given the rest of what you are epistemically entitled to believe and value. It is hard to see why the conjunction of A, B, and C would then give you a sufficient reason for accepting D.

It is not clear how the status of D—or, for that matter, the status of A, B, and C—can be determined responsibly without considering what else they might conflict with and what else they might imply. That would be a game of defeasible reasoning without the defeaters. The default starting point would be insulated from challenges. Notice how much less one would learn by playing this game than by playing the relatively freewheeling game of Socratic dialogue, in which immanent criticism, distinction drawing, resignification, and various other moves are counted as essential to the processes of discovery and justification.

Now consider a further complication. There appears to be a good deal of disagreement among reasonable people about moral principles that are thought to hold absolutely, as opposed to generally and for the most part.[19] We are not talking here about the wise and the just, who might agree on something much more substantial. (Justice as fairness makes a momentous move when it replaces the Aristotelian notion of "the wise and the just" with the liberal notion of the "reasonable" as the touchstone of political theory.) It would seem that many, if not most or all, ought-judgments that populate the freestanding basis posited by Rawls must have ceteris paribus clauses *in them*. These are relatively uncontroversial moral commitments concerning what would, *all other things being equal*, be in conformity with liberty, equality, and other publicly recognized values. But if that is largely what the freestanding basis turns out to contain, the problem of defeasibility is already present in the basis itself.

If at least one of A, B, and C is a normative proposition that includes a ceteris paribus clause, then the acceptability of normative conclusion D depends on whether other things *are* equal. The only apparent way to determine what the conjoined premises imply is to investigate whether things are indeed equal. And this, in many cases, seems bound to lead us outside the freestanding basis.

Suppose values in the freestanding basis entail that torture is, other things equal, morally wrong. The issue being debated in the public forum is whether torture should be outlawed even in cases thought to involve a supreme emergency. Public officials claim that torturing prisoners is sometimes necessary in order to forestall a terrorist attack in progress. The question is whether an existing statute and a constitutional ban on cruel and unusual punishment should be revised. If torture is wrong regardless of the consequences of refraining, the relevant statute and constitutional provision should stand. How, then, should the issue be debated?

Whether the values in the freestanding basis entail an absolute prohibition of torture is subject to interpretation. It is hard to see why reasonable people— who do not necessarily satisfy the more stringent Aristotelian standard of being wise and just—would not disagree on this matter. They might well disagree over which cases qualify as torture and over how the prohibition should be formulated. Some citizens interpret the prohibition of torture as having exceptions for emergency situations. Some citizens interpret it as a virtual absolute, meaning that the prohibition is to be enforced in cases of supreme emergency, even though a public official, burdened with responsibilities the rest of us do not have, will be morally obliged to violate it and accept punishment for having done so (Walzer 2006, 247–67, 326). And some citizens interpret the prohibition as a full-fledged absolute, straightforwardly applicable, regardless of the circumstances, with no moral leeway for public officials tempted to think of themselves as exceptional.

When I think of such a debate, I have trouble imagining *any* of the disputants *not* relying essentially on commitments outside the freestanding basis when deciding how to assess the moral significance of emergency situations.

The debate begins from reasonable agreement on some vaguely defined values, moves to agreement on a principle that includes a ceteris paribus clause, and somehow has to arrive at a determinate all-things-considered judgment about torture in all types of situations a public official might have to face. But the bracketing involved in public reason rules out taking everything one believes into consideration.

Some citizens who favor the absolute ban do so for Kantian reasons pertaining to dignity or for theological reasons concerning the sacred value of anyone created in God's image. Reasons of these kinds are outside the freestanding basis, according to *Political Liberalism*, so they are presumably supposed to be kept out of the debate occurring in the public forum. Yet they are not generally kept out of our actual debates on this topic. It strikes me as naive to think that commitments outside the freestanding basis are going to have little or no influence on how debaters in the public forum reason when reaching or justifying their conclusions. Some citizens have lost loved ones in terrorist attacks. Others meditate daily on the story of an imperial Roman official who tortured a peaceable man to death in hope of quelling a Jewish rebellion.

Life experiences, upbringing, and background beliefs do influence the political reasoning and conclusions of most people, like it or not. Anyone who tries to bracket such factors while deliberating will have trouble knowing whether she has succeeded and where to draw the line. This is because reasoning is generally more holistic than a defender of public reason might wish.

It is possible, of course, for a believer to avoid mentioning God, appealing to scripture, or employing the concept of sacred value when speaking in the public forum. The reasoning can always be recast in a somewhat secularized vocabulary. Such recasting is common. One motive for it is prudential: the recasting is meant to employ premises acceptable to a wide swath of the population. Rawls has a moral motive in view: we are all obliged, he thinks, to stand ready to supply an argument, in terms of public reason, for our votes and proposals regarding important political issues. It is not clear, however, what counts in his view as a proper recasting. Neither is it clear what the recasting actually achieves.

The debate over abortion illustrates why. Believers who favor a universal ban on abortions, when appealing to a broad audience or seeking to allay First Amendment concerns, speak of the dignity of all human life and stress the arbitrariness of excluding fetuses from protections extended to newborns. *Dignity* is meant to function as a secular translation of *sacred value*. What is it to possess dignity? There are various religious answers to this question. There is also a Kantian answer. Political liberalism holds that none of these answers, including the Kantian one, belong to public reason. While the secularized argument for the abortion ban might succeed rhetorically in winning over some secular Kantians, and perhaps others, it is not clear what dignity means here, what justifies attributions of dignity, or whether the recast argument has satisfied the PRR.

It is hardly surprising that many citizens persist in attributing religiously or philosophically partisan reasons to people offering arguments that are recast in this way. Insofar as we do succeed in recasting our arguments in maximally neutral terms, the inferential connections between premises and conclusions become weaker. This means that the premises do not fully explain either why the arguer accepts the conclusions of her arguments or why the people being addressed ought to accept those conclusions. The explanatory gap that opens up here is intimately related to the issue of public reason's indeterminacy and thus to the need for public reason to be "completed" in order to yield determinate resolutions of basic questions.

To pursue the issue of abortion a little further, let us now take up a familiar argument that proceeds from the value of liberty:

A': A woman ought to be at liberty to exercise authority over her own body.
B': What is in a woman's womb is in her body. Hence,
C': A woman ought to be at liberty to abort a fetus in her womb. Hence,
D': A woman should be at liberty to abort a fetus in her womb.

The argument appears valid. The problem is that premises A' and C' are as controversial as conclusion D' when interpreted as applying to all cases. The argument would win more widespread acceptance if it were rephrased as follows:

A*: *All other things being equal,* a woman ought to be at liberty to exercise authority over her own body.
B*: What is in a woman's womb is in her body. Hence,
C*: *All other things being equal,* a woman ought to be at liberty to abort a fetus in her womb.
D*: *In any given case,* a woman should be at liberty to abort a fetus in her womb.

Now the problem is that the conclusion no longer follows from the premises.

How, then, are we to decide whether to accept the all-things-considered judgment expressed in D*? The PRR tells us to set aside some of the considerations that might appear relevant. At first blush, at least, that seems an arbitrary and counterproductive recommendation. It might even be unfair. Clearly, the weight of the restriction falls more heavily on someone who thinks that there are relevant considerations outside the approved basis of public reasons than on someone who thinks that there are not.

Take the case of Reverend Faithful. He believes A*, B*, and C* but also believes:

E*: In God's eyes, all human beings, from conception to death, are full-fledged bearers of rights.
F*: E* overrides the ceteris paribus clauses in A* and C*.

Assume, further, that neither E* nor F* belongs to the freestanding basis. It is hard to see how Reverend Faithful can be expected to draw inferences from principles that include ceteris paribus clauses while bracketing beliefs he holds that have implications concerning whether things are in fact equal in all cases. This makes me wonder why it would be *fair* to expect Reverend Faithful to ignore E* and F* when trying to determine the acceptability of D*.

Perhaps his name and title have aroused a prejudice in your mind with regard to Reverend Faithful. To keep that prejudice from clouding the issue, let us assume that he is a cooperative fellow, in the sense that he harbors no desire to dominate his fellow citizens. He sincerely seeks a *mutually* acceptable form of social union with them. He recognizes the sacrifices that his policy proposal would entail for some people. He is prepared to make similarly weighty sacrifices on other issues in order to win a compromise on abortion. He is happy to express his views publicly, thereby subjecting them to challenge. He is committed to taking the challenges into account when revising his views and his proposal. He aims to be epistemically responsible and responsive to criticism.

I introduce these additional stipulations in order to clarify our intuitions about what is actually worrisome about fellow citizens who are said to be uncivil and unreasonable. Is it the kind of reason upon which they rely or is it something else that worries us? What confuses the matter is that the kind of reason upon which they rely is sometimes indicative of something else that is worrisome—a closed or inflexible mind, a desire to dominate, and so forth. Not so, in Reverend Faithful's case.

There are, of course, many citizens who believe what Reverend Faithful believes and who express those beliefs publicly while also desiring to dominate the rest of us. Reverend Faithful has no such desire. To clarify our intuitions further, I can further stipulate that he has voted against restrictions on birth control, public funding for church-related schools, and school prayer, all of which strike him as pushing things too far. That is why we take him not to desire domination of those who differ from him religiously.

What does the doctrine of public reason say to and about Reverend Faithful? According to the ideal of public reason, he is obliged, as a citizen, to stand ready, when speaking in the public forum about constitutional questions and matters of basic justice, to reason solely from the freestanding basis of "public reasons," while bracketing the rest of what he believes. He must bracket E* and F*.

Given that I have trouble imagining how I would avoid relying on considerations outside the freestanding basis when reaching all-things-considered judgments, I am uneasy with this outcome. Reciprocity implies that I should not place Reverend Faithful under a constraint that I cannot satisfy myself. I suspect that one of my reasons for disagreeing with Reverend Faithful about abortion, if I am honest about it, is that I *deny* what E* presupposes. If he and I, recognizing each other as free and equal citizens, each of us sincerely opposing domination, are prepared to hear each other out fully and then cast our votes accordingly, I see nothing inherently unfair in that. We will both have a chance to have our say, to influence the political outcome. We will both be free to contest the outcome afterwards.

If we conduct ourselves in this way, we will be showing respect for each other as the particular individuals we are. We also will be exposing our idiosyncratic views to public scrutiny, where Socratic challenges can be raised against them. The dialectic of public reasoning is a process in which the arbitrariness and contingency at work in each citizen's outlook can be brought into the public light of day. It is not a privileged location in logical space that has already been philosophically purified of perspectival partiality.

Rawls (1999a) argues that public reason is supported by an overlapping consensus among reasonable comprehensive views, including reasonable religious views. This means that Reverend Faithful's comprehensive view is simultaneously being called on to supply justificatory support for his commitment to the overlapping consensus but is not, in the most important political contexts, being permitted to guide his reasoning about what can be inferred from that basis or used to challenge assumptions about what the default starting point of our political reasoning ought to be.

Why should Reverend Faithful's theological convictions, or my secular convictions about dignity and the common good, be expected to play the one role while being prohibited from playing the other? There appears to be something arbitrary about this, but also something ideologically suspect. Religious or philosophical convictions are being called on to buttress a consensus while also being discouraged from troubling it, thinking beyond it in light of additional considerations, or changing it by exchanging reasons and challenges with others.

## THE DIALECTIC OF PUBLIC REASONING

Philosophers often begin with an a priori notion of how reasoning in some domain would need to go if it were to be acceptable. They then develop a rigid, synchronic model of the reasoning, without paying much attention to what the reasoning of actual practitioners is like or has been like. The model reflects an anxiety about justification that keeps some philosophers, but very few other people, awake at night. Initially, the hopes for the model are high, but the details are sketchy. It is not clear that the model *could* be followed or that following it, if that were possible, would lead to the expected good consequences. The most respected real-life practitioners turn out, ironically, to fall radically short of what the model's norms demand.

The heroes of the sciences, like the great democratic orators and essayists, are often famous for their imaginative departures from an established consensus. They do not begin as heroes but, typically, as heretics, scoffed at by their elders. What is remarkable about great scientists is the extent to which they change their minds after having been socialized to accept the views of their teachers. By publicly pursuing the implications of thinking differently, great scientists also change how their successors reason and ought to reason. The ordinary scientist's taken-for-granted starting point changes significantly in the wake of every great theoretical accomplishment in the field, and changes slightly with each new observation and experiment.

Logical empiricism failed to do justice to the likes of Nicolaus Copernicus and Albert Einstein. Its model of scientific method was too rigid to make sense of scientific change. It was able to draw a sharp line of demarcation between science and other things, but it unwittingly placed many great scientists and some emerging sciences on the wrong side of the line. For many years, some of the most brilliant philosophers in the world ingeniously revised the details of the model, hoping to make it workable and to make sense of revolutionary scientific change. In the end, the revisions came to seem ad hoc and the model gave way to self-consciously diachronic, dialectical accounts of scientific reasoning, though not without causing a lot of hand-wringing about the demise of objectivity.

Theorists of public reason have had as much trouble with Lincoln and King as the logical empiricists had with Copernicus and Einstein.[20] First came a relatively rigid, synchronic model of reasoning, driven by a philosophical anxiety about justification. Then came the counterintuitive consequences and ad hoc revisions. That, it seems to me, is where the study of public reasoning stands now—in a situation reminiscent of the philosophy of science circa 1960. The leading account of public reasoning has responded to counterexamples by amending its normative model, but not in a way that carries much conviction or shows much empirical interest in how citizens actually think and talk, especially when constitutional essentials and questions of basic justice are being vigorously contested.

I have argued that what Rawls calls public reason is not the only form of reasoning that can be essential to public deliberation and justification regarding legitimacy. In some cases, which resemble that of the Great Orator in the relevant respects, it is not *necessary*. A citizen can, in such cases, justify her political conclusions to her fellows without reasoning from premises of the kind Rawls regards as uniquely public. I have also argued that "public reasons" are *insufficient* in the most important class of actual cases. The impression that reasoning *from* a shared basis suffices for public discursive purposes is a product of neglecting the importance of defeaters and of other modes of reasoning that are needed to achieve, maintain, unsettle, and correct an evolving equilibrium among people willing to sublimate the *libido dominandi* and recognize one another as free and equal.

Public reasoning is a way of *reasoning with* other people in the hope of achieving and revising shared commitments concerning ends and means.[21] It sometimes moves *from* shared values or principles *to* shared ends and means, but it also often *forges* shared ends and means *out of* difference. That is what the Great Orator was doing with maximal effect in my idealized case, but also what many historical figures have done when moving from mere negation of an established consensus to the creation of a new one. Coalitions need such convergence, and so do the democratic polities within which coalitions struggle for influence and power.[22] The modes of reasoning that citizens employ when hammering out and revising shared commitments are numerous.

My interest in reasoned change in view derives from my interest in large-scale social and political change, another topic that receives disturbingly little attention in liberal political theory. Globalization, greenhouse gases, and oligarchy are three of the many worrisome things that cast longer shadows over political life with every passing day.[23] Our political institutions and practices are not coping well with such things. A large adjustment is required.[24] One good way of preparing the public and our students for that moment would be to inform ourselves about how significant social and political change has happened in the course of the past two hundred years. Many of the people who pushed such change along had reasons, and gave reasons publicly, sometimes impressively, for what they were doing. Our theorizing, teaching, organizing, and activism ought to be informed by what they said and did.

Dialectical pragmatism aims to bring such reasoning to light while affirming it as genuinely political. Like Hegel and Dewey, I reject an overly static conception of political reasoning, according to which the terms of political deliberation are first set, consented to in the form of a social contract, and then merely applied. That model not only consigns revolutionary shifts to darkness but also obscures how the terms of political deliberation evolve in less turbulent moments, as dominant and weaker groups jostle for position and apply concepts to cases from their distinctive points of view.

Dialectical pragmatism must also be distinguished, however, from theories that imagine democracy as fugitive effervescence, sovereignty as an assertion of mere will, revolutionary moments as absolute ruptures, or the future as the apocalyptic sublime. In such visions, reasoning has no important role to play in bringing about, justifying, or consolidating desirable change. Dialectical pragmatism, in contrast, is an attempt to get change and reasoning into focus simultaneously. As its Hegelian lineage would lead one to expect, it seeks to overcome the weaknesses, while inheriting the strengths, of both Enlightenment rationalism and romantic irrationalism.

The Enlightenment was right to value reciprocity. But reciprocity is not a matter of relying on a single privileged mode of reasoning. It often has less to do with appeal to already-shared reasons than with who *willingly* sacrifices what, for the sake of convergence, and who is finally *made to* sacrifice what, for the sake of convergence.[25] Reciprocity is made manifest in a pattern of interaction that plays out over time. When it is present, we are prepared to endure sacrifices and differences for the sake of goods currently held in common.[26] When reciprocity goes missing, we sense a threat of domination. The interactive pattern goes sour when one group, whether by *repeatedly* imposing sacrifices on another group or by imposing an *excessive* sacrifice on some group, gives the subjugated a reason to resent the basic relationship and then to decide, all things considered, whether to tolerate it, endeavor to transform it, or withdraw from it (Hirschman 1970).

For related reasons, legitimacy does not boil down to the ability to provide a single sort of justificatory argument. Real-life contestation over the legitimacy of regimes appears to have a default-and-challenge structure. An existing regime has legitimacy by default, in the absence of defects of roughly the sort listed in the Declaration of Independence.[27] While the line between legitimacy and illegitimacy is always somewhat fuzzy, the standard way to justify resistance is to cite defects of that sort. The number and seriousness of the defects jointly determine the strength of the case for resistance. As that case gathers strength, the claim to legitimacy weakens.

A dialectically updated list of paradigmatic defects would include genocide; imperial domination; the military targeting of civilian populations; the perpetration of disproportionate harm by armed force; the use of torture, mass incarceration, unwarranted surveillance, and censorship; silencing and intimidating dissenters; repeatedly requiring some groups to sacrifice for others without reciprocation; denial to some individuals of equal treatment under law; permitting some individuals or groups to exercise power over others as they please; the exploitation of one group by another; and arbitrary prevention of some individuals or groups from influencing or contesting governmental decisions. It is possible to tie legitimacy directly to the absence of defects such as these without making the issue depend on a privileged kind of positive justificatory argument. The enlightening things that Rawls himself says about many of these topics can and should, I believe, be disentangled from his doctrine of public reason.

In any event, the point of this chapter is not to defend alternatives to his accounts of legitimacy and citizenship. I do wish to make clear why someone might wish to stand back from the idea, now taken for granted by many political theorists, that reasoning qualifies as genuinely public only if it takes the form it would have to take in order to resolve the legitimacy problem as Rawls poses it. I do not consider it a serious, let alone fatal, objection to my account of public reasoning that I leave both legitimacy and the ethics of citizenship to be dealt with mainly by other means.[28]

## NOTES

1. Wayne Proudfoot, to whom this volume is dedicated, has mainly been concerned with the proper integration of pragmatism and naturalism in the study of religion. The present chapter continues a dialogue that he and I have been engaged in over three decades. I could not be more grateful to have such a friend and conversation partner.

2. Richard Rorty sides with Walter Lippmann's liberal elitism against John Dewey's preference for participatory democracy, in *Achieving Our Country: Leftist Thought in Twentieth-Century America* (Rorty 1998, 104). In an appendix to that book, "Movements and Campaigns," Rorty claims that large-scale movements of social reform are no longer needed (111–24). Jeffrey Stout (2010a), in *Blessed Are the Organized: Grassroots Democracy in America*, sides with Dewey against Lippmann and gives reasons for supposing that movements will go on being as important as campaigns.

3. A similar prejudice mars Richard Rorty's writings on religion and politics. See Rorty (1999), Rorty (2003), and Rorty's contribution to Springs (2010). My contribution to Springs (2010) includes critical remarks on Rorty's prejudicial generalizations about religious citizens. See also Stout (2004, 85–91; 2008; 2010b).

4. By the doctrine of "public reason," I mean everything that John Rawls (2005, 441–45) covers when discussing what he calls the *idea* of public reason, which specifies what public reason is, and what he calls the *ideal* of public reason, which specifies the relevant normative implications. In the first edition of *Political Liberalism*, Rawls defended a highly restrictive norm concerning how citizens may reason when speaking in the public forum on the most important political matters. In the second edition, he amended the norm so as to avoid the implication that Martin Luther King Jr., in particular, was misbehaving in his most influential speeches. I shall be discussing the amended version, which includes what has come to be known as the "proviso." The still later expanded edition cited here includes the crucial essay "The Idea of Public Reason Revisited." The proviso permits citizens to reason in the public forum on the basis of a comprehensive view, *provided that* they stand ready to argue for their proposals on the basis of public reason alone.

5. I take it that (2) is meant to be equivalent to the notion of what a reasonable person "might" accept or "might be reasonably expected to accept" (Rawls 2005, xlii, xlix, 218). But (2) is ambiguous. One wants to know whether the sort of expectation being discussed is a matter of prediction or a matter of holding someone to a standard.

6. For a sample warning, see Freeman (2007, 412).

7. See also Waldron (2010).

8. See also T. M. Scanlon (1999), especially 142–43; and Onora O'Neill (1999).

9. One question often raised about the original position is why multiple contractors are needed for the thought experiment, given that they all deliberate behind a veil of ignorance that deprives them of access to their perspectival differences as individuals. Wayne Proudfoot (1974) discusses related issues in an important early paper.

10. Gerald Gaus (2011) offers a detailed theory of public reasoning as an evolving equilibrium. See also Amy Gutmann and Dennis Thompson (2004), chapter 3. It is noteworthy that Rawls (2005, 446, note 19) declares deliberative democracy, as conceived by Gutmann and Thompson, to be dependent on a comprehensive view and hence nonpublic. No doubt, Rawls would have the same reservation about Gaus.

11. When Gaus (2011) entitles the second part of *The Order of Public Reason* "Real Public Reason," he is distancing his account of public reasoning from Rawlsian ideal theory.

12. See Scanlon (1999), 159–63. Paul Weithman also emphasizes the importance of the link between stability and public reason in Rawls's account of the well-ordered society. See his meticulously argued book *Why Political Liberalism? On John Rawls's Political Turn* (Weithman 2010).

13. For reasons that will emerge later, *defending* a conclusion deductively is not the same thing as *inferring* a conclusion deductively. In my view, only confusion results when the inferential process a person engages in when revising his or her commitments is construed on analogy with logic (in the sense of the science of deductive implication).

14. See Gilbert Harman (2002), especially section 1.2. I am drawing in more general ways on Harman (1973; 1986; 1999, part 1), and Harman and Kulkarni (2007), chapter 1.

15. See Harman (1986, 11; 2002, section 1.2).

16. What Rawls calls *civil disobedience*, in contrast with *witnessing*, appeals strictly to the freestanding basis.

17. Rawls's model for this sort of bracketing is that of a judge or juror abstracting from some of his or her beliefs when deliberating on a legal case. It seems to me, first, that we are far from having a clear understanding of what judges and jurors are doing when engaging in such deliberations, and second, that Rawls might be asking ordinary citizens to perform a much more tenuous sort of abstraction than one finds in a judicial context. Jurors are supposed to begin their reasoning from a somewhat restricted starting point, but this is not restricted in the same way that the freestanding basis is restricted. Because nothing as stringent as the notion of reasons that all reasonable persons would or could accept is involved, the sort of construction difficulty I am about to discuss does not arise.

18. Later in the book, Gaus (2011, 336–37) adds, "A theory that is grounded on the importance of evaluative pluralism can bracket some disagreement as a device within the theory to help us see where agreement is possible and progress might be made, but ultimately this agreement only provides Members of the Public with sufficient reasons to endorse a proposed rule if, given all their relevant evaluative standards, it is to be endorsed." See also Gaus and Vallier (2009).

19. Gaus (2011, 36–46) raises similar questions about the vagaries of shared principles in his discussion of the "problem of indeterminacy" in *The Order of Public Reason*. I am not, in this chapter, employing his technical distinction between principles and rules.

20. Rawls (2005, lii, 247, 250) discusses King in *Political Liberalism*. For references to Abraham Lincoln, see xxxi, 45, 232, 254, 420.

21. See Richardson (2002), 19–20.

22. In Stout (2010a), I address the practices and virtues of reciprocation in both coalitions and local polities by taking up a series of concrete examples of grassroots activism.

23. In *Political Liberalism*, Rawls (2005, xxviii) gives a surprisingly curt response to critics concerned with problems of "race, ethnicity, and gender" and with "the preservation of wildlife."

24. For an argument along these lines from within the Rawlsian camp, see Thomas Pogge (2010), *Politics as Usual: What Lies Behind the Pro-Poor Rhetoric*.

25. For accounts of the role sacrifice plays in this process, see Danielle S. Allen (2004), *Talking to Strangers*, chapters 3 and 4; and Beth Eddy (2003), *Rites of Identity*, chapters 3 and 6.

26. See John R. Bowlin (2016), *Tolerance Among the Virtues*.

27. For an illuminating account of the Declaration's list of "a long train of abuses and usurpations" and its expression of "respect to the opinions of mankind," see Allen (2014).

28. I am grateful to Matt Bagger, Molly Farneth, Eric Gregory, Gilbert Harman, Athemya Jayaram, Michael Lamb, Lou Ruprecht, Ian Ward, and Nicholas Wolterstorff for comments on earlier drafts.

## WORKS CITED

Allen, Danielle S. 2004. *Talking to Strangers*. Chicago: University of Chicago Press.

Allen, Danielle S. 2014. *Our Declaration: A Reading of the Declaration of Independence in Defense of Equality*. New York: Liveright.

Bowlin, John R. 2016. *Tolerance Among the Virtues*. Princeton, NJ: Princeton University Press.

Dewey, John. 1934. *A Common Faith*. New Haven, CT: Yale University Press.

Eddy, Beth. 2003. *Rites of Identity*. Princeton, NJ: Princeton University Press.

Freeman, Samuel. 2007. *Rawls*. London: Routledge.

Gaus, Gerald. 2011. *The Order of Public Reason: A Theory of Freedom and Morality in a Diverse and Bounded World*. Cambridge: Cambridge University Press.

Gaus, Gerald, and Kevin Vallier. 2009. "The Roles of Religious Conviction in a Publicly Justified Polity: The Implications of Convergence, Asymmetry and Political Institutions." *Philosophy and Social Criticism* 35:51–76.

Gutmann, Amy, and Dennis Thompson. 2004. *Why Deliberative Democracy?* Princeton, NJ: Princeton University Press.

Harman, Gilbert. 1973. *Thought*. Princeton, NJ: Princeton University Press.

Harman, Gilbert. 1986. *Change in View: Principles of Reasoning*. Cambridge, MA: MIT Press.

Harman, Gilbert. 1999. *Reasoning, Meaning, and Mind*. Oxford: Oxford University Press.

Harman, Gilbert. 2002. "Internal Critique: A Logic Is Not a Theory of Reasoning and a Theory of Reasoning Is Not a Logic." In *Handbook of the Logic of Argument and Inference: The Turn Towards the Practical*, edited by D. M. Gabbay, R. H. Johnson, H. J. Ohlbach, and J. Woods, 171–86. Amsterdam: Elsevier Science.

Harman, Gilbert, and Sanjeev Kulkarni. 2007. *Reliable Reasoning: Induction and Statistical Learning Theory*. Cambridge, MA: MIT Press, 2007.

Hirschman, Albert O. 1970. *Exit, Voice, and Loyalty: Responses to Decline in Firms, Organizations, and States*. Cambridge, MA: Harvard University Press.

O'Neill, Onora. 1999. "Constructivism in Rawls and Kant." In *The Cambridge Companion to Rawls*, edited by Samuel Freeman, 347–67. Cambridge: Cambridge University Press.

Pogge, Thomas. 2010. *Politics as Usual: What Lies Behind the Pro-Poor Rhetoric*. Cambridge: Polity.

Proudfoot, Wayne. 1974. "Rawls on Individual and Society." *Journal of Religious Ethics* 2:107–28.

Rawls, John. 1999a. "The Idea of an Overlapping Consensus." In *Collected Papers*, edited by Samuel Freeman, 421–48. Cambridge, MA: Harvard University Press.

Rawls, John. 1999b. "Kantian Constructivism in Moral Theory." In *Collected Papers*, edited by Samuel Freeman, 303–58. Cambridge, MA: Harvard University Press.

Rawls, John. 1999c. *A Theory of Justice*, rev. ed. Cambridge, MA: Harvard University Press.

Rawls, John. 2005. *Political Liberalism*, expanded ed. New York: Columbia University Press.

Richardson, Henry S. 2002. *Democratic Autonomy: Public Reasoning About the Ends of Policy*. Oxford: Oxford University Press.

Rorty, Richard. 1998. *Achieving Our Country: Leftist Thought in Twentieth-Century America*. Cambridge, MA: Harvard University Press.

Rorty, Richard. 1999. "Religion as Conversation-Stopper." *Philosophy and Social Hope*, 168–74. London: Penguin, 1999.

Rorty, Richard. 2003. "Religion in the Public Square: A Reconsideration." *Journal of Religious Ethics* 31:141–49.

Scanlon, T. M. 1999. "Rawls on Justification." In *The Cambridge Companion to Rawls*, edited by Samuel Freeman, 139–67. Cambridge: Cambridge University Press.

Springs, Jason. 2010. "Pragmatism and Democracy: Assessing Jeffrey Stout's *Democracy and Tradition*." *Journal of the American Academy of Religion* 78:413–48.

Stout, Jeffrey. 2004. *Democracy and Tradition*. Princeton, NJ: Princeton University Press.

Stout, Jeffrey. 2008. "2007 Presidential Address: The Folly of Secularism." *Journal of the American Academy of Religion* 76:533–44.

Stout, Jeffrey. 2010a. *Blessed Are the Organized: Grassroots Democracy in America*. Princeton, NJ: Princeton University Press.

Stout, Jeffrey. 2010b. "Rorty on Religion and Politics." In *The Philosophy of Richard Rorty*, edited by Randall E. Auxier and Lewis Edwin Hahn, 523–45. Chicago: Open Court.

Waldron, Jeremy. 1993. "Religious Contributions in Public Deliberation." *San Diego Law Review* 30:817–48.

Waldron, Jeremy. 2010. "Two-Way Translation: The Ethics of Engaging with Religious Contributions in Public Deliberation." NYU School of Law, Public Law Research Paper No. 10-84. http://ssrn.com/abstract=1708113.

Walzer, Michael. 2006. *Just and Unjust Wars: A Moral Argument with Historical Illustrations*, 4th ed. New York: Basic Books.

Weithman, Paul. 2010. *Why Political Liberalism? On John Rawls's Political Turn*. Oxford: Oxford University Press.

# PART IV

## Pragmatism and the Philosophy of Religion

In *Pragmatism* (1907), William James notes that in the few years since he first introduced the public to "the principle of Peirce, the principle of pragmatism" (in his 1898 address "Philosophical Conceptions and Practical Results"), a widespread "pragmatic movement, so-called . . . seems to have rather suddenly precipitated itself out of the air" (James 1975, 5, 29). Insisting that "there is absolutely nothing new in the pragmatic method," James attributes the mushrooming "movement" to his having inadvertently supplied a term that "applies itself conveniently to a number of tendencies that hitherto have lacked a collective name" (30, 290). Under the banner of *pragmatism*—a "new name for some old ways of thinking"—these "tendencies that have always existed in philosophy have all at once become conscious of themselves collectively, and of their combined mission" (5). Recognizable as aspects of the "empiricist temper" and readily detected in nominalism, utilitarianism, and positivism, these abiding tendencies, he explains, assume a more "radical" form when accentuated by a name (31).

More radically averse than its precursors to "abstraction . . . verbal solutions . . . bad a priori reasons . . . fixed principles, closed systems, and pretended absolutes and origins," pragmatism, James suggests, actualizes the liberatory and melioristic potential of the empiricist temper. It "means the open air and possibilities of nature, as against dogma . . . and the pretense of finality in truth" (31). Resistant to supposed necessities and orthodoxies, pragmatism focuses human energies on "the ways in which existing realities may be *changed*" (32, emphasis in original). The "general triumph" of pragmatism, James remarks, would "freeze out" the

"ultra-rationalistic" philosopher "much as the courtier type is frozen out in repub-
lics, [and] as the ultramontane type of priest is frozen out in protestant lands"
(31). These similes attest to James's antiauthoritarian conception of pragmatism.
Both the courtier and the ultramontane priest serve a superior to whose authority they must defer.[1] Like republicanism and Protestantism, pragmatism reassigns
the "seat of authority" (James 1975, 62). James depicts pragmatism as empirical
inquiry beholden to no ulterior authorities. It unseats epistemic authorities (to
which inquiry must answer), other than the human interests and social norms
informing the practice of inquiry itself. While introducing pragmatism as the
concentration and, in a sense, the culmination of empiricist tendencies, James
declares emphatically that he supports pragmatism's antiauthoritarian, progressive mission, its "conquering destiny" (30).

In certain respects, James set the pattern for future consideration of pragmatism. Many later philosophers assess pragmatism, as James does, in part by defining its place in the history of philosophy. Even John Dewey (1972, xi, xii), who
longs for a time when Americans come to think of pragmatism as a "creative
movement" rather than a "philosophical Ism," frequently presents his pragmatism
by contrasting it to prior philosophy. In *The Quest for Certainty* (Dewey 1929),
for instance, he sets the whole philosophical tradition, beginning with the
Greeks, against the intellectual revolutions that have rendered it obsolete and
that necessitate a reconstruction in philosophy. More recent advocates of pragmatism take its measure relative to similarly grand historical horizons. Richard
Rorty views pragmatism as having anticipated the final disposition of both main
styles of contemporary philosophy. Across a number of works, he argues that
"James and Dewey were not only waiting at the end of the dialectical road which
analytic philosophy traveled, but are waiting at the end of the road which, for
example, [Michel] Foucault and [Gilles] Deleuze are currently traveling" (Rorty
1982, xviii). Cornel West, Rorty's one-time student, presents pragmatism as the
"evasion" of modern philosophy's reigning paradigm (West 1989). Pragmatism,
he argues, reformulates philosophy, transforming it from an academic discipline
focused on epistemological questions into a public form of cultural criticism that
pursues the meaning and possibilities of democratic community. Not to be out-
done, Robert Brandom (2011, 36), another of Rorty's former students, argues
that because of pragmatism's full recognition of contingency and its fallibilism, it represents a "movement of world historical significance...a second
Enlightenment."

Perhaps intending to counter such triumphalism, philosophers who evince little enthusiasm for pragmatism sometimes join its champions in assessing it in
relation to philosophy's *longue durée*. If pragmatism's evangelists rehearse philosophy's historical sweep to exalt pragmatism, the unregenerate rehearse it to

diminish pragmatism. In Rorty's (1982, xvii) fitting description, they generally portray pragmatism "as an outdated philosophical movement [that] flourished in the early years of [the twentieth] century in a rather provincial atmosphere, and which has now been either refuted or *aufgehoben*." Willard V. O. Quine represents a notable case in point. Over the course of his career, Quine exhibited a marked disinclination to teach or write about the history of philosophy. His most comprehensive appraisal of pragmatism (Quine 1981), however, takes the form of an amusingly Whiggish history of empiricism since David Hume.[2] Quine imbibed pragmatist lessons from his teacher C. I. Lewis, and most scholars detect Lewis's influence in Quine's trademark semantic holism. Quine, nevertheless, composes a history of pragmatism that portrays it as cripplingly equivocal on pivotal issues as well as incidental and largely irrelevant to the progress of empiricism.

That professed pragmatists, in particular, would justify their stance, at least in part, by narrating pragmatism's relation to previous philosophy should not surprise. Pragmatism's antiauthoritarian naturalism precludes the availability of standards independent of the historically contingent norms informing human language and practice. Historicist in this strong sense, pragmatism naturally lends itself to historical narratives purporting to illustrate how it comports better with emerging intellectual and social commitments than do predecessor philosophies.

This thoroughgoing historicist, antiauthoritarian naturalism has seemed untenable to many philosophers (and not only those whom one might fairly describe as "ultrarationalist").[3] They mistrust pragmatism's social practice account of objectivity and ontology. Inquiry, they presume, must answer to *something* other than contingent norms and interests. James anticipates these misgivings in some luminous passages of *The Varieties of Religious Experience* (1902). In 1902, James had not yet acquiesced in the new name *pragmatism* to denote his radical application of the "general principles by which the empirical philosophy has always contended that we must be guided in our search for truth" (James 1961, 33). He opts, instead, to use the unassuming label *empirical method* to refer to his approach. The empirical method, he explains, bars any appeal to ahistorical dogmatic or a priori evaluative standards. The basis for any judgment of fact or value can only lie in the "prejudices, instincts, and common sense" of the current "mental climate" (262). Because James locates the "mark and criterion" of the mental in purposive behavior, the social practices that condition their participants' purposive behavior produce the "mental climate."[4] "Prejudices, instincts, and common sense" are the constituent norms of current social practices (including the practice of inquiry). These standards and values, he explains, evolve as "insight into nature and [people's] social arrangements progressively develop" in history (James 1961, 262). James acknowledges that lodging authority in historically contingent norms may seem "to throw our compass overboard, and to adopt caprice as our pilot." He insists, however, that recognizing the liability of current norms to change should not induce one "to embark upon a sea of wanton doubt" (265). One should not, in other words, mistake fallibilism for skepticism. Historical contingency is anyway inescapable. James (264) evidences the historical "drift" that has continually undermined or reshaped all manner of dogma. Despite its pretensions to timelessness, dogma's authority remains subject to historically evolving standards.

The essays in part 4 follow the precedents set by James. Not only do they focus on pragmatism's antiauthoritarianism—its radical suggestion that human attitudes answer to nothing other than themselves (as embodied in the norms constitutive of human social practices)—but also they draw on the history of philosophy (in particular, the philosophy of religion, whether ancient or more recent) to reflect on pragmatism. Neither ultrarationalist nor evangelical, the authors contributing to part 4 express sympathy for pragmatism but remain hesitant (in one respect or another) about its unqualified elimination of answerability to something independent of human practices.

## NOTES

1. To an American in the years following the First Vatican Council (1868), *ultramontane* would mean "advocating infallibility and authoritarianism."
2. It's not clear to what extent Quine is in on the joke.
3. Legion are those who have objected to the pragmatists' views on truth. To take a prominent, relatively recent example, Donald Davidson (2005), who otherwise generally concurs with pragmatist positions, found pragmatist claims about truth to be an insurmountable stumbling block. Robert Brandom (1994, 2011) and Huw Price (2003, 2004) have gone a long way toward providing a defensible pragmatist account of truth. The introduction to the present volume discusses this issue very briefly.
4. "*The pursuance of future ends and the choice of means for their attainment are thus the mark and criterion of the presence of mentality* in a phenomenon" (James 1950, 1:8, emphasis in original).

## WORKS CITED

Brandom, Robert. 1994. *Making it Explicit: Reasoning, Representing, and Discursive Commitment.* Cambridge, MA: Harvard University Press.
Brandom, Robert. 2011. *Perspectives on Pragmatism.* Cambridge, MA: Harvard University Press.

Davidson, Donald. 2005. "Truth Rehabilitated (1997)." In *Truth, Language, and History*, 3–18. Oxford: Clarendon.

Dewey, John. 1929. *The Quest for Certainty*. New York: Minton, Balch.

Dewey, John. 1972. Foreword to Philip P. Wiener, *Evolution and the Founders of Pragmatism*, xi–xii. Philadelphia: University of Pennsylvania Press.

James, William. 1950. *The Principles of Psychology*. 2 vols. New York: Dover.

James, William. 1961. *The Varieties of Religious Experience*. New York: Collier.

James, William. 1975. *Pragmatism* and *The Meaning of Truth*. Cambridge, MA: Harvard University Press.

Price, Huw. 2003. "Truth as Convenient Friction." *Journal of Philosophy* 100:167–90.

Price, Huw. 2004. "Naturalism Without Representationalism." In *Naturalism in Question*, edited by Mario De Caro and David Macarthur. Cambridge, MA: Harvard University Press, 71–88.

Quine, Willard Van Orman. 1981. "The Pragmatists' Place in Empiricism." In *Pragmatism: Its Sources and Prospects*, edited by Robert J. Mulvaney and Philip M. Zeltner, 21–39. Columbia: University of South Carolina Press.

Rorty, Richard. 1982. "Introduction: Pragmatism and Philosophy." In *Consequences of Pragmatism*. Minneapolis: University of Minnesota Press.

West, Cornel. 1989. *The American Evasion of Philosophy: A Genealogy of Pragmatism*. Madison: University of Wisconsin Press.

# 8

# The Fate of Radical
# Empiricism and the Future
# of Pragmatic Naturalism

NANCY FRANKENBERRY

Radical empiricists in religion from William James to William
Dean have taken experience as providing epistemic support for
beliefs, and naturalism and pragmatism as vital to religious inquiry.
From another direction, Alvin Plantinga and analytic Christian philosophers
have argued that certain religious beliefs can have epistemic merit not on the basis
of other beliefs, arguments, or evidence but, rather, on the basis of a kind of "divine
testimony," which is occasioned by certain of the believer's experiences. From
these unapologetic supernaturalist premises, they try to make the case against
naturalism in religious inquiry. Still others of us, represented in this chapter principally by Donald Davidson, regard both kinds of support as either problematic
or unintelligible, for reasons related to the linguistic turn in twentieth-century
philosophy. Richard Rorty (2006, 53) speaks for us when he says, "I see Davidson
as rewriting in terms of language the same things that James and [John] Dewey
did in terms of experience."

At the time I published *Religion and Radical Empiricism*, almost thirty years
ago, I was solidly in the radical empiricist camp. But then I drifted. Initially, one
of my purposes in recommending radical empiricism's broad conception of experience was to advance a religious and pragmatic naturalism that would overcome
the traditional dualisms of Western epistemology and metaphysics that are rooted
in the Cartesian dualism of mind and matter.[1] The project of ending false
dualisms depends on understanding the higher human expressions of life as
emerging naturally from more simple organic forms through increasingly greater
organization and more discriminating behavior.

Naturalism owes as much to Dewey as to Charles Darwin, on this score. It allows us to posit mind not as an outside observer of the natural world but as an emergent part of it, and to see knowledge and value not as transcendent imports but as emerging products and tools of natural interactions. In line with the project of applying the Darwinian/Deweyan naturalistic thesis of continuity and emergence to solve the questions raised by traditional dualisms, I once thought *experience* was the best general notion to bridge those different but continuous dimensions of nature. Since *experience* can span both the *what* of experience and the particular *how* of experiencing, I reasoned, it could be used to bridge the subject/object split which underwrites modern epistemology.

Under the influence of important works that were just appearing thirty years ago, such as Wayne Proudfoot's *Religious Experience* and Richard Rorty's *Philosophy and the Mirror of Nature*, I was torn between the idea that such a vital matter as religion could scarcely be said to live *without* experience and the idea that, when we consider some of the claims made in the name of experience, religion could hardly live *with* it. Today I am less torn, finding myself more and more in agreement with the philosopher Robert Brandom, whose monumental work *Making It Explicit* mentions, but never once *uses*, the word *experience* in 750 pages.

It has become customary to mark a difference between the classical pragmatists of the early part of the twentieth century and the contemporary pragmatists of our own era as a difference between those who enshrine experience at the center and those who exchange experience for language. Where once I doubted that language could really do all the work that I wanted, to theorize about experience, radical empiricism, and religion, today I have come to see that language goes all the way down. Far from entailing a dubious form of linguistic idealism, this view is perfectly compatible with pragmatic naturalism. Pragmatists of all stripes can affirm, with Charles Sanders Peirce (1935, 5:314), that "my language is the sum total of myself," provided that, by *language*, we mean what Donald Davidson's philosophy carefully elaborates. For Davidson, there is no distinction between knowing a language and knowing our way around in the world.

Even so, I have been able to appreciate both sides of the tension between John McDowell's *Mind and World*, which attempts to reclaim empiricism after the critique of the "myth of the given," and Donald Davidson's thorough disposal of that myth, along with what he called the "third dogma" of empiricism, or scheme–content dualism. To correct my previous ambivalence, I would like to offer here an unequivocal statement assessing what is living and what is dead in radical empiricism, after the work of Wayne Proudfoot, Wilfrid Sellars, Richard Rorty, Donald Davidson, Robert Brandom, and others. In the first part of this chapter, I attempt to summarize five arguments that bear upon the fate of radical empiricism. Once the import of these theses are weighed, it may very well be the case that *radical empiricism* is no longer the term we want, as the *empiricism* part has morphed into a pragmatism, thus blurring the two methods that William James regarded as distinct.

I turn, in the second half of the chapter, to the topic of the future of pragmatic naturalism in relation to religious studies. Here my focus is narrowed to a case study of Alvin Plantinga's ongoing defense of supernaturalism on grounds that I critique as unintelligible. If Plantinga's challenge to pragmatic naturalism can be rendered moot using Davidson's way of disposing of the skeptical hypothesis, it will remove what is arguably the most formidable current philosophical alternative to naturalism. Consequently, given the number of fundamentalist Christians with Plantinga's assumptions who flourish in America today, the future of pragmatic naturalism should be bright—and very busy. In conclusion, I briefly sketch two of the leading a/religious modalities that pragmatic naturalism is taking.

## WHAT IS LIVING AND DEAD IN RADICAL EMPIRICISM

It is easier to say what is dead than what is alive in radical empiricism, more than one hundred years after William James first coined the term. To see, at a glance, the main issues between radically empirical pragmatists and the new pragmatists who have taken the linguistic turn, consider William James's well-known theory of radical empiricism as consisting of a methodological postulate, a statement of fact, and a generalized conclusion (James 1970, xxxvi–xxxvii). In effect, new pragmatists, with no use for radical empiricism as any part of a pragmatist agenda, have contested each of these three. I can epitomize their difference from classical pragmatists by suggesting how they might slightly rephrase James at each point.

First, his methodological postulate that "the things debatable need to be definable in terms derived from experience" (James 1970, xxxvi) would now be glossed according to Robert Brandom's inferentialist pragmatism as "the things discussable in terms of the human ability to have and ascribe sentential attitudes." The idea here is that the sentence is the basic unit of meaning and what is not discussable sent, ially is off the radar. If radical empiricists want to argue that our radar is broader than our sentential attitudes, the burden of proof is on them to show what "broader" consists in, and showing that will, of course, naturally implicate sentential attitudes.

Second, James's (1970, xxxvi) statement of fact that "the relations between things, conjunctive as well as disjunctive, are just as much matters of direct, particular experience, neither more so nor less so, than the things themselves" would now give rise to Richard Rorty's complaint that to say relations are given immediately in experience presupposes a notion of "givenness" that is just one more dogma of empiricism. To radical empiricists, however, Rorty's suspicion smacks of confusing a phenomenological claim with an epistemological one. The Rortyan reply to that might be along the lines that the ability to have and ascribe sentential attitudes has nothing to do with experiences of a noncognitive type. James himself, as I read him, was irresolute on this point, sometimes writing phenomenologically, sometimes epistemologically.

Third, the generalized conclusion to which James's radical empiricism leads takes the form of a naturalized metaphysical position. It affirms that "the parts of experience hold together next by next by relations that are themselves parts of experience" and that "the directly apprehended universe needs no extraneous transempirical support, but possesses in its own right a concatenated or continuous structure" (James 1970, xxxvii). Pragmatists who have taken the linguistic turn see this type of statement as leading to a metaphysically muddled panpsychism that tries to bridge an imaginary gap between experience and "the world," or "reality." At the same time, however, radically empirical pragmatists regard this as the formula for ruling out supernatural explanations of natural phenomena, a methodological move that pragmatic naturalists themselves want to endorse.

Despite the fact that language gets considerable play in the texts of classical pragmatists who espoused radical empiricism, the focus on the givenness of pure, direct, or primary experience takes center stage in Peirce on qualitative firstness, in James on pure experience, and in Dewey on primary experience. What remains problematic about their radical empiricism is their oscillation between foundationalism and givenism, on the one hand, and historicism and pragmatic antifoundationalism, on the other hand. Putting aside well-known problems with James's notions of "pure experience" and "panpsychism" that make them unsustainable today,[2] I am chiefly interested in correcting radical empiricism's habit of adverting to prelinguistic or prereflective experience. In the wake of the widespread linguistic turn of the past several decades, at least five arguments, utilized by a variety of new pragmatists, cut against the grain of radical empiricism. Each can be put in the form of a positive and pithy single sentence. First, only a belief can justify another belief. Second, all awareness is a linguistic affair. Third, givenness is a myth. Fourth, we can lose the third dogma of empiricism, or scheme–content dualism. Fifth, nothing we can know can be ineffable. All are overlapping theses, but I will consider them separately.

## *Only a Belief Can Justify Another Belief*

Derived from the influential work of Donald Davidson, the chief argument in support of the statement that "only a belief can justify another belief" claims, first, that causes are not reasons, although reasons may be causes; and second, that justification is a practice of giving reasons, not causes. The causal processes involved in perception and awareness, as causal processes, are not subject to norms that can access them as right or wrong. They simply occur, one event following the next, cause and effect, though never so simply that relations to other causes and effects are absent. Inference, on the other hand, is an inherently normative activity and, as such, is capable of being correct or incorrect. Neither causation nor inference can be reduced to the other or equated with the other. Both must be understood as different but related contexts. Causes belong to the context of discovery, and inferences belong to the space of reasons.

Where then do we locate *experience*, that term that is crucial for radically empirical pragmatists and one that does so much work that, as Humpty Dumpty suggested, it ought to be paid overtime? New pragmatists locate experience already within the Sellarsian "logical space of reasons." Therefore, it cannot simultaneously reach outside the inferentially articulated space of reasons as though to offer an independent source of evidence or justification. This recognition calls for some revision to my *Religion and Radical Empiricism*, insofar as that work expressed an interest in finding religious beliefs to be justified, or not justified, by experience, in the broadest sense. After describing the radically empirical notion of experience as connective, relational, affective in its initial phase, and more physical, indistinct, and penumbral than sensation, consciousness, and language, I wanted to find in this matrix something religiously fecund.

But what could this mean? And was it motivated by an implicit foundationalist urge? However superior radical empiricism's theory of experience may seem, compared to the flawed account in traditional empiricism, it has risked resembling the very foundationalism that radical empiricists and other pragmatists have rightly rejected. Justification of religious beliefs can only be explored, decided, and defended in terms of what turn out to be—other beliefs.[3] To say, then, that "radical empiricism locates its own ... confirmability criterion ... [in the] felt qualities of lived experience" is, at best, misleading (Frankenberry 1987, 106).[4] For, in the justification of competing knowledge claims, the radical empiricist is no more able than anyone else to appeal to an experiential given, untouched by an interpretive framework that includes other beliefs. As Davidson (1980, 8) explained, "Your stepping on my toes neither explains nor justifies my stepping on your toes unless I believe you stepped on my toes, but the belief alone, true or false, explains my action."

To elaborate this point, one could also say that reasons can be conceived of as causal explanations, but not vice versa. This is because "scheme" and "content" cannot be disentangled. The most we can say about our "inputs," as Willard V. O. Quine sparingly called them, is that they impinge upon us. Peirce knew this (most of the time), with his doctrine of firstness. Alfred North Whitehead generously dubbed inputs *causal efficacy*, but his point was the same. As soon as we acknowledge inputs, we are forming beliefs or judgments, and it is then those beliefs (not the raw causal inputs themselves) that stand in justificatory relationships with other beliefs.

This point has logical implications for the role scholars of religion accord to both Peirce's firstness and Whitehead's causal efficacy. Neither can play an epistemic role in the vexed investigation of religious beliefs. Pragmatists may still want to recognize the brute resistance of real things to at least *some* interpretations of them, much like Luther insisted that the Bible is not a wax nose to be pushed by the pope into just any shape at all. Firstness resists some interpretations more than others, and it invites some but not all interpretations. Causal efficacy exerts massive influence on event-like structures in the form of vectorial energy transmission. However, it neither dictates nor justifies any particular semantic content for human language users. "Nothing can supply a reason for belief except another (or many another) belief," according to Davidson (2005a, 136), and even then, only in a tentative and fallibilistic manner.

Radical empiricists can give up the extravagant notion that a form of experience purportedly transcending the space of reasons can decide justificatory questions, without giving up the idea that our beliefs and inquiry direct themselves toward the world and aim at getting things right (Stout 2007). We can rule out correspondence, in the sense of confrontation, because a sentence-like entity such as a belief can be compared only with information already in the form of sentences or beliefs, not with nonlinguistic bits of the world. Coherence with other beliefs in the web is a good *test* of truth and justification, but coherence alone does not make a belief true or justified. According to Davidson's version of naturalism, the world—never lost—comes into play, causally, in the very determination of belief content, with the result that coherence must yield at least a rough correspondence.

An important implication follows from this for radical empiricists in religion. No argument can succeed that uses noncognitive or prereflective experience in the mode of causal efficacy as justificational "evidence" for consciously entertained cognitive claims. In asserting a general continuity between cognitive and noncognitive experience, Jamesian, Deweyan, and Whiteheadian radical empiricists should not claim that causal efficacy provides any criterion either for truth or for justification. The nonconceptual content of experience does no epistemic work itself; only the semantic *belief* that one's experience has this or that content is effective.

## All Awareness Is a Linguistic Affair

The Sellarsian thesis that all awareness is a linguistic affair underwrites the previous Davidsonian claim that the only thing that justifies a belief is another belief. However, it remains a matter of dispute between radically empirical pragmatists and neopragmatists. Radical empiricists want to preserve an element of "awareness" that is not discursively structured but that gives rise to discursive formations. Neopragmatists see no middle ground that does not wind up reinstalling representationalist models that presume a bogus dualism between the subjective and the objective. If by *awareness* we mean, with Sellars (1997, 63), "all awareness of sorts, resemblances, facts, etc., in short, all awareness of abstract entities— indeed, all awareness even of particulars," then awareness must be a linguistic affair. On the other hand, if all awareness is not a linguistic affair, and there is indeed some prelinguistic or extralinguistic depth of lived experience that exceeds anything that can be said, then to that extent nothing more *can* be said. Even those who agree with Bernard Meland's maxim that "we live more deeply than we can think" will recognize that we are at a loss to *describe* any awareness which surpasses language or thought without employing language in the very process and thus exhibiting the "more" as intralinguistic after all.[5]

"Primary experience," as Dewey called it, is simply *had*, but, as he said, it is not *known* until language discriminates and helps to constitute qualities as objects of knowledge. This recognition can be found not only in Dewey's *Experience and Nature* but also in other seminal texts, such as James's *Essays in Radical Empiricism* and Whitehead's *Process and Reality*, making it plausible for their defenders to argue that radical empiricism has always already taken the linguistic turn and acknowledged that the realm of cognitive justification must be strictly linguistic. The problem, however, is that one can equally find passages in these texts that oscillate between treating experience as something within the space of reasons and treating experience as something within the space of causes, or as within *both*.[6]

To cite just a few examples, Peirce's earliest articles deny the possibility of unmediated immediacies in experience and dispute the existence of any faculty of intuition. Yet his changing conceptualizations of quality or firstness flirt with the very intuitionism and foundationalism that his pragmatic naturalism was committed to repudiating. Similarly, James (1978, 37) never overcame the tension between defending the metaphysical notion of "pure experience," on the one hand, and declaring that "the trail of the human serpent is over everything," on the other. And Dewey has well-known difficulties in trying to steer a consistent course between the denial that knowledge rests on unmediated percepts and the more promising pragmatist view that knowledge is mediated all the way through. In the end, his distinction between primary experience as "had" and reflective experiences as "known" was a difference that did not *make* a difference pragmatically. It comes to no practical consequences unless the havings are specified, and once they are specified, they are no longer "givens" but mediated contents. Unless "primary experience" can be shown to play an epistemic role in practice, its invocation appears useless.

In view of this, how might we read such claims as "We experience more than we can analyze" (Whitehead 1938, 89) and the statement that there is, in experience, "a deeper matrix . . . too complex and rich with quality for the human mind to comprehend" (Wieman 1946, 66–67)? I suggest two ways. First, we cannot say anything about the "more than" that can be analyzed; it remains indeterminate. It supports no conclusions; it affords no inferences of any kind. In fact, there is no "it" there at all, cognitively speaking. "It" is excluded from knowledge. Consequently, there is no portentous payoff in pointing to the "excess," the "remainder," or the "ineffable." Second, the relations in which each event is embedded connect one thing to another thing and stretch out indefinitely so that, as Whitehead (1938, 9) said, "no fact is merely itself." Therefore, even to analyze a single fact is to be aware of the complex environmental coordination needed for its production as a fact, a coordination that is, for the most part, suppressed in human conscious awareness. This makes it both possible to write history and, at the same time, extremely difficult to do so. Put differently, it is why we have multiple biographies of Abraham Lincoln and more than four Gospels.

### Givenness Is a Myth

The myth of the given is the claim that there is a kind of immediate experience that does not rely on or presuppose grasp of concepts, so that the very having of such experience confers knowledge or serves as evidence for beliefs, judgments, or claims. Appeal to a nondiscursive "given" to back up claims or justify beliefs is considered a myth for the reason that the putative given could only count as justificatory or evidential if and when it is rendered rationally discursive, not just causally occasioned. The usual candidates for the given—sensations, feelings, qualities—play no epistemic role in grounding beliefs about the world because, in short, they do not participate in logical relations. The key idea, from Sellars through Brandom, is that only propositional attitudes and utterances *can* participate in logical and inferential relations, not sensations.

Why not entertain an alternative, ambidextrous theory of experience, one that encompasses and points in both directions, upstream to the nonconceptual world of causal stimuli and downstream to our conceptually structured thought? The answer, from Sellars, Rorty, Davidson, Brandom, and other pragmatic naturalists, comes to this: either the "given" data is unconceptualized and therefore does not provide *reasons*, because it lacks propositional content, or it does provide reasons in terms of specifiable propositional content but this is not *given* independently of the whole structure of beliefs and language and thus cannot vouch for any particular belief. We cannot try to have it both ways. Seeing through the myth of the given gives us another reason to endorse the claim that "nothing can supply a reason for a belief except another (or many another) belief" (Davidson 2005a, 136).[7]

The error of assuming givenness is frequently committed in the field of religious studies, but it need not be. To the extent that radical empiricists have wanted to give epistemic priority to experience and to promote a metaphysics of experience as an antidote to linguisticism, they have risked turning experience into a privileged given or a foundation every bit as problematic as positivist appeals to "raw feels." Rejecting foundational metaphysics and the myth of the given, an alternative way for radical empiricists to deploy the broad conception of experience today might be in developing the kind of direct understanding implicit in nonverbal intentional behaviors such as making music or love, dancing a tango, or swinging a baseball bat.[8]

Both the analysis and the nonverbal action are laced through with propositional attitudes, of course, and are thoroughly caught up in human practices and norms, including norms of description. Here again we are dealing with experiences that are in principle articulable (recall Ted Williams's highly detailed recounting of the way to swing a bat). This direction indicates what is still living in the legacy of radical empiricism. At the same time, radical empiricists will need to do more than *point* to an affective, somatic, emotional, nondiscursive dimension of experience. Simply to insist "It's there!" seems an empty gesture unless one also establishes the further pragmatic difference that aesthetic experiences make to our knowledge, politics, morality, or religious sensibilities. But once we can do *that*, we are no longer talking about prelinguistic or prereflective forms of experience. At that point, the difference that *makes* a difference pragmatically in adopting radically empirical pragmatism rather than any of the forms of neopragmatism has become elusive.


## Giving Up the Third Dogma of Empiricism, or Scheme–Content Dualism

Once we take into account the full force of Sellars's attack on the Myth of the Given, and combine it with Quine's erasing of any principled distinction between the analytic and the synthetic—that is, between matters of meaning, on the one hand, and matters of fact, on the other hand—we are positioned to give up what Davidson critiqued as the "third dogma" of empiricism, or scheme–content dualism. Succinctly stated, this is the dualism between empirical content waiting to be organized and the conceptual scheme, the organizing system. It is a dogma that, like the first two, presupposes an ability to make a distinction that is empirically unwarranted. We are simply unable to distinguish between changes in statements held as true due to changes in meaning and those held as true due to changes in belief.

Giving up this dualism, we then see that belief and meaning are interdependent. And we find that our causal, semantic, and epistemic attitudes are already intertwined with objects and events in the world. Self-knowledge and knowledge of others presupposes knowledge of the world of objects and events. Therefore, we can now dispense with the very idea of a conceptual scheme, and with it will go any radical form of conceptual relativism. The harmless kind of relativity to a language will remain but, as Davidson says, that is as objective as can be.

As Richard Rorty first argued brilliantly, Davidson's argument against the scheme–content distinction in his now famous paper "On the Very Idea of a Conceptual Scheme" deepens the Quinean third-person perspective on meaning and mind, with devastating consequences for the representationalist ideas that have fired up the "epistemology industry," as Dewey called it. If we cannot make sense of the idea that the mind produces representations of a given world by structuring, through operations of subjectivity, an input provided by an objective source, then questions about the adequacy of our conceptual schemes or the accuracy of our representational capacities can just be abandoned. They rest on an incoherent view of how thinking agents relate epistemically to the world in which they operate.

It is beginning to look as though there is no space through which experience might creep back into the holistic web of beliefs. Quine allowed sensations to anchor the web at its edges, as though observation statements could stand the test of experience on their own, while the inside of the web faced the tribunal of experience as a whole; revision would be made according to pragmatic criteria. Davidson, however, thought this only opened the door for skepticism. How do we distinguish between experiences that mislead us and those that do not? As long as empiricism, including radical empiricism, *both* puts experience within the space of reasons *and* treats it as a purely causal matter, it makes experience some kind of epistemic intermediary between thought and world. And the problem with this, as Rorty repeatedly pointed out, is that any intermediary may come to be doubted as a possibly dishonest broker. Better to reject the idea that causal relations constitute (norm-governed) reasons, neo-pragmatists agreed, and to recognize that all we have to go on is the linguistically articulated logical space of reasons.

I think pragmatism, in all its contemporary varieties, is what is left of the old Humean and positivist empiricism once it has shed its three dogmas. The extent to which the new, radical empiricism of James, Dewey, Whitehead, and others dipped into these three dogmas from time to time, or did not sufficiently get free of these dogmas, will probably remain a matter of debate for some time. Leaving aside the textual documentation here, I think it fair to say that various proponents of radical empiricism have assumed a picture according to which there is some kind of data that exists independently of its being worked up by an interpretive process in which the supposedly chaotic flux gets forged into stable forms. To that extent, the picture rests on a problematic scheme–content dualism.

Scheme–content dualism inevitably gives rise to doubts about whether some other species or other culture might have fundamentally different standards because they have a radically different conceptual organization. In the study of religion, this picture often leads to assertions about the "incommensurability" of different religions, all offering different frameworks or epistemes or paradigms or *cosmopoloi*. Here is how things may look to one group, but of course things might look *radically* different to those who have an incommensurably different conceptual scheme. All such arguments turn out to be either incoherent, for reasons that Davidson (1984b) has shown, or highly hyperbolic.

## Nothing We Can Know Can Be Ineffable

In stating that "nothing we can know can be ineffable," I am stating an obvious truism, intended to pluck the rhetoric of ineffability right out from radical empiricism. Several recent commentators have argued that radical empiricism is supportive of the writings of mystics in many religious traditions who claim experience of something said to be ineffable.[9] On the contrary, it is not enough, it seems to me, to give a nod to the possibility of nonlinguistic experience and then to go on to explain mystical claims of "ineffability" as arising somehow from these nondiscursive depths. This is especially problematic when it comes to addressing the nature of any cognitive claims based upon supposedly ineffable experiences. More has to be established than the bare idea that mystical experiences are properly ineffable. If scholars (or mystics themselves) want to draw any further inferences, there must be effability. To the extent that the experiences are ineffable, they are, to that extent, unavailable for cognition, understanding, or communication. To the extent that the experiences are communicable (a crucial condition for public intersubjective meaning), they are not ineffable. Until advocates of ineffability address this conundrum, they will be unable to wring much import, religious or otherwise, from the ineffability thesis. Radical empiricists would be better off endorsing Wayne Proudfoot's (1985, 125–27) entirely different assertion that ineffability is a rule that governs a certain discourse about religious experience, rather than being a phenomenological characteristic of that experience.

As if the interpretation of mysticism were not difficult enough, an important ambiguity dogs the discussion of ineffability. Is it a mark of the experience, of the alleged object, or both? Some proponents of ineffability claims have in mind future contingent events, matters of hope or aspiration or portended dread, rather than matters of settled actuality or an object or being that is said to exist but to be indescribable. The former case conforms well to analysis that suggests that we humans are most inarticulate about future contingent events. Depending on how we appropriate it, the settled past has presented at least some (to speak loosely) "facts of the matter," about which we can "eff" at least something, thus ruling out ineffability. Anticipatory feelings, vague misgivings, portentous stirrings of emotion—all these have to do with the future, immediate or otherwise, just as emotions such as guilt or pride have some previous state of affairs as their intentional object, retrospectively apprehended. In either case, past or future, these matters are in principle all describable. Language may limp, and sensitive souls may moan that "words cannot describe . . . ," yet we do, in fact, describe, and even "indescribable" is itself a description. Perhaps more linguistic struggle occurs in the case of articulating anticipatory feelings, as when we say something is just on the tip of our tongue. But here, too, nothing of a completely ineffable condition obtains.

Against the second type of claim, that the objects of religious reverence are so ineffable that nothing can be said of them literally but only symbolically, pragmatic naturalists have learned to raise the question David Hume had Philo pose to the pious Demea in the *Dialogues Concerning Natural Religion*: What is the difference between something about which nothing can be said, and nothing at all? The line between theological agnosticism and sheer agnosticism is very thin. If we turn pragmatist and ask what is the difference that *makes* a difference to practice between something about which nothing can be said and nothing at all, once again we find no difference.

Whether we retain the word *experience* for the broad sense in which radical empiricism has used it or restrict its use to a more narrow conception may be less important, in the end, than how we police our talk about "knowledge." Philosophers today are swimming upstream against a tidal wave if they try to use the word *knowledge* for anything other than the post-Kantian philosophical conception of conscious, conceptual experience. More precisely, the Davidsonian model of triangulation, which I will discuss further in the next part of this chapter, can serve to peg knowledge as something obtained by and through three-cornered transactions with a social world and a shared environment; it is what is necessary for there to be mental content in the first place.

Pragmatists caution that such knowledge is always selective, interpretive, and fallible. Some radical empiricists claim not knowledge but only "awareness" of an affective, somatic sort. William Dean, for one, advances the idea of nonsensuous perception as "imprecise, non-quantifiable, and vague," and then treats it as evidence, "but evidence that cannot be confirmed by sense data, rational proof, or testable results, so that it is, technically speaking, unknown" (Dean 2012, 179–180). In response, linguistic pragmatists would argue that, not just technically but also pragmatically, what is "unknown" can play no evidential or justificational role in adjudicating the claims we make about such things as selves, meaning, knowledge, or world. Still less can nonsensuous perception provide convincing evidence for the more abstract speculative claims that appear in religious literature. To offer any methodological advice in the study of religion, radical empiricists will need to cash out "awareness" in the mode of nonsensuous perception into the currency of propositional utterances. Once they can do that, such awareness will no longer be simply affective, or too dim and vague for words or knowledge.

All five of the corrections I have made to radical empiricism have emphasized the primacy of language rather than experience. This is the fate, I suggest, of radical empiricism—to have been overtaken by multiple developments in twentieth-century thought collectively termed the *linguistic turn*. Moreover, I see no alternative to the view that language has primacy in any construction of a language–experience matrix. While we may be reluctant to collapse either term into the other, it is hard to represent each as on a par with and requiring the other. For even to attempt to put language and experience on a par by stating that language and experience are inextricably intertwined amounts to giving primacy to language in order to assert and understand such an intertwining.

Nevertheless, even though there is no such thing as nondiscursive experience, most people want to say that experience counts in some overall important way, and we understand what they mean by that when we, too, are taking a relaxed, sensible, and pre-philosophical attitude in our judgments about the import of various things on experience—our own and that of other language users. Indeed, we can hardly do without the word. It must have been in this vein that Richard Rorty (2001, 156–57) could say, "We can agree with [Hans-Georg] Gadamer that 'being that can be understood is language' while remaining aware that there is more to life than understanding." Other times, we might just as well substitute the word *culture* for the word *experience*, a switch that Dewey was unwilling to make, on the grounds that "we need a cautionary and directive word, like experience, to remind us that the world which is lived, suffered and enjoyed, as well as logically thought of, has the last word in all human inquiries and surmises" (Dewey and Bentley 1964, 643).[10] Notice, however, that his emphasis in this statement falls on the *world*, not on *experience*. In the evolution of philosophical discourse since Dewey, the rhetoric of experience has given way to explorations of the semantics of language, our use of which has a normative grip on us.

If the rhetoric of experience now enjoys only a half-life, what is any longer living in radical empiricism? I would locate its legacy chiefly in relation to the "unconscious," a category which, after Sigmund Freud, has become a way of talking about what Jamesian radical empiricism pointed to as unknown, unacknowledged, disavowed, indeterminate, unformulated, and potential—in short, as the "more" beyond consciousness, and thus language, but abidingly at the heart of (Freudian-based) conceptions of subjectivity. Freud theorized this primordial region as the "primary process," just as Peirce, James, Dewey, and more recent radical empiricists gave quasi-foundational status to nonsensuous perception. Like Freud's concept of the unconscious, radically empirical pragmatism can help to cure consciousness of any illusion of self-sufficiency and to gesture toward what is presently unsayable. One advantage of being aware that much always drops out of the sayable is that we might then guard against foreclosure and premature articulation in our descriptions and ascriptions.

The importance, then, of radical empiricism's emphasis on the depths and shallows of experience, like Freud's attention to the unconscious, may be understood not as conferring any additional knowledge but rather as unsettling the certainties of consciousness. What exactly is it that intrudes into awareness and reveals consciousness to be partial and limited? We cannot say, except insofar as it enters consciousness, that is to say, comes linguistically shaped, and then we can only say retrospectively. Introspection is always indistinct retrospection.

Saying this, however, gives scholars of religion no particular purchase on any-thing of religious significance in any traditional sense of *religious*. All of the ways that I can see of making a (revised) radically empirical theory of experience reli-giously salient lead in the direction of religious naturalisms, such as, to take one prominent example, Robert Corrington's "ecstatic naturalism," which can be read as a poetic and psychoanalytically charged displacement onto nature of uncon-scious or semiconscious human material.[11]

William James thought that there is always "a plus, a thisness, which feeling can answer for." He went on, in *The Varieties of Religious Experience*, to say that "there is in the living act of perception always something that glimmers and twin-kles and will not be caught, and for which reflection comes too late. No one knows this as well as the philosopher" (James 1985, 455–57). In *The Principles of Psychology*, James was preoccupied with noticing the fringe, the halo, the penum-bra of relations that surround us at any moment. Unfocused and indistinct, it is a penumbra of relations that can potentially become better discriminated. Noth-ing in what James says here points to the impossibility of clearer or more distinct awareness of the "felt affinity and discord" of the primitive and unreflexive range of relations. Instead, he says that "it is one of those evanescent and 'transitive' facts of mind which introspection cannot turn round upon, and isolate and hold up for examination, as an entomologist passes round an insect on a pin. In the (some-what clumsy) terminology I have used, it pertains to the 'fringe' of the subjective state, and is a 'feeling of tendency'" (James 1950, 1:472).[12]

From the perspective of pragmatism's linguistic turn, it seems clear that the best way to read James's discussion in the *Principles* of fringes and halos and rela-tions is to interpret him as elaborating a feature of experience that is dim but not *dumb*, indistinct but not *inarticulate*. James was confident that the pragmatic movement signaled a new turn in thought, "something quite like the protestant reformation" (H. James 1926, 2:279).[13] Yet he considered his own contribution to be "too much an arch built only on one side" (quoted in H. James 1911, viii). The unfinished trajectory of James's radical empiricism, I have been saying, bends in the direction of Sellars, Davidson, Rorty, and Brandom.

## THE FUTURE OF PRAGMATIC NATURALISM

There were good reasons for Rorty (1991, 113) to call Donald Davidson "the culmination of the holist and pragmatist strains in contemporary analytic philosophy" as well as "the culmination of a line of thought in American philosophy which aims at being naturalistic without being reductionist."[14] Like pragmatism in general, Davidson's philosophy is known for its naturalism, holism, and antirepresentationalism. In my view, his best contribution to pragmatism and naturalism consists in his reconciliation of two things: the possibility that any particular belief we have may be in error, and the impossibility that all our beliefs about the world might be fundamentally mistaken.

The arguments behind this reconciliation are useful for showing that the specter of widespread skepticism is a bogeyman, and thus we can dismiss Alvin Plantinga's argument against naturalism on the grounds that, as he claims, it invites thoroughgoing skepticism when coupled with the evolutionary thesis. Although Plantinga's brand of supernaturalism is not likely to impress most readers of the present volume, his decades-long devotion to defeating naturalism and defending Christian supernaturalism is a direct rebuke to the naturalisms with which this volume is concerned, and, as such, deserves an explicit rejoinder. If that rejoinder can be made in one swift cut, as I believe it can, so much the better.

## Where Does the Science–Religion Conflict Lie?

Alvin Plantinga's overall aim, in the course of his many publications, is to show that naturalism is incoherent or self-defeating because natural selection is unlikely to favor true belief in the absence of a God to guide the process. In his recent book *Where the Conflict Really Lies: Science, Religion, and Naturalism*, based on the Gifford Lectures of 2006, Plantinga's central claim is that "there is superficial conflict but deep concord between science and theistic religion, but superficial concord and deep conflict between science and naturalism" (Plantinga 2011, ix).[15] His primary argument utilizes the recursive paradox that our brains, as biological devices constrained by the history of their origin, must be enlisted to analyze history itself. Darwinism implies, according to Plantinga, that the whole point and function of our minds is to enhance reproductive fitness, not to enable us to acquire true beliefs. But then, he charges, the Darwinian naturalist has an excellent reason to mistrust the beliefs those minds produce, including Darwinian naturalism itself! Here Plantinga is attacking the very citadel of naturalism, using the battering ram of evolution rendered as a self-defeating enterprise.

We do not need to conduct a detailed examination of Plantinga's defense of intelligent design, unsound science, or bizarre formalizations in order to follow his thesis in part 4 of *Where the Conflict Really Lies*, entitled "Deep Conflict." If naturalism is true, Plantinga reasons, then evolution follows. But if we affirm evolution, then we must extend its outcome to our own cognitive powers. Darwinian evolution, however, is all about survival and reproductive success and certainly not about maximizing truth. Therefore, there is no reason to think that our reasoning and cognitive powers tell the truth about the world. They may just be telling us what we need to believe in order to survive and reproduce, with information that could as easily be false. Hence, everything we believe about evolution could be false, including and especially naturalism.[16] It cannot be replied, Plantinga claims, that our very survival shows that our beliefs must be both adaptive and reliable, since our survival could depend on our behavior rather than on our beliefs, or even on a combination of false beliefs and additional factors that are accidentally beneficent. As he wrote in 1993, "there are indefinitely many belief-desire systems that fit adaptive behavior, but where the beliefs involved are not for the most part true" (Plantinga 1993, 229). And in any case we cannot assume that our beliefs have a causal role in promoting either our behavior or our survival (223). Thus, Darwinism undermines its own rational acceptability. The only way out of this dilemma is to assume a God who guarantees truth. The naturalistic epistemologist should therefore prefer theism to metaphysical naturalism, Plantinga concludes, theism being the one thing that can guarantee real truth and save us from the possibility of being completely mistaken about objective reality, and for good Darwinian reasons.

## Davidson's Reply to the Skeptic: "Get a Grip"

Simply put, there are good Davidsonian reasons to conclude that "belief is in its nature veridical" (Davidson 2001a, 146).[17] If Davidson is right, then Plantinga is wrong that the probability of human cognitive faculties "being reliable (producing mostly true beliefs)" must be quite low if naturalism and evolution are conjoined (Plantinga 1993, 219). It could be that simple.

I believe that Plantinga's argument can be countered by two considerations drawn from Davidson's work and shared by most contemporary pragmatic naturalists. First is the holism of meaning and belief, according to which we cannot clearly distinguish the meaning of words from the beliefs that guide our use of them. When we come to understand another's language, we also come to know what he believes about the world. Second is the holism of concepts and beliefs, according to which a concept is a position in a cluster of beliefs in which it figures, and each belief is a position in an overall system of beliefs—much like a crossword puzzle, which is linked in a web or grid of interlocking relational units. The implication of combining these considerations is that we cannot understand another's language without coming to see her as believing, by and large, what we believe about the world.

Now, in this scenario, what would it mean for all of us to be in error about most of what, by and large, we believe about the world? How could we even tell that we were in error? We could not tell, because disagreement is intelligible only against a background of more widespread agreement, false beliefs are intelligible only against a background of mostly true beliefs, and, as I parse it, "error" is only intelligible against a background of "mostly getting it right." If a background of overall agreement and mostly true beliefs must be in place when we take ourselves to understand others, then we can never encounter a scenario of the sort that Plantinga conjures up. Others' beliefs will be mostly the same as our own and, when they are not, as appears to be the case, notably, in diverse religious beliefs, they will still stand in logical relations to our own. In short, Davidsonian holism precludes Plantinga's hypothetical specter of largely false beliefs creeping insidiously over human society in the course of evolution.[18]

Overlooking the holistic nature of the mental, Plantinga miscalculates the amount of shared common ground required for the identification of any one belief, true or false. Suppose I were to say to Plantinga, "There's the window over there," and he saw that I am caused to utter that statement by and only by sightings of a window. Then he could not reasonably interpret my utterance unless he also takes me to believe many true things about windows: that they usually occupy spaces in buildings, that they are usually made of transparent glass but can also be opaque, that they can be made to shatter, and so forth. Without some such broad agreement, he could not be sure of his original interpretation, for he could not identify thoughts, distinguish among them, or describe them for what they are, except by locating them within a dense network of related beliefs. This sharing of common ground is not the *outcome* of understanding but a condition of it (Davidson 2004, 51).[19] Notice that Davidson does not say that most of the beliefs of anybody whom we can treat as a language user must accord with our own beliefs. Rather, his point is, as Rorty (2000, 374) glossed it in a rare endorsement of the word *true*, that "most of our beliefs about anything (snow, molecules, the moral law) must be true of that thing—must get that thing right."

The reason most of our beliefs about such things as windows, snow, molecules, and the moral law (under any of its construals) must "get that thing right" is that when we learned how to use sentences with these words in them, we automatically acquired lots of true beliefs about windows, snow, molecules, and the moral law. If somebody thinks that windows are made of green cheese and that they can fit in a hat, we shall judge that, whatever they may be talking about, it is not windows. And if someone thinks the moral law is a prescription pill, we shall also doubt that they are talking about the moral law (under any of its construals). There have to be many commonly accepted truths about a thing before we can raise the question of whether any particular belief about it is mistaken. Once we do raise that question, as Plantinga does with his make-believe wholesale skepticism, any of those commonly accepted truths can be placed in doubt, found to be erroneous, or modified, although not all of them at once.

It could not be the case, then, that all or most of our beliefs are false *at the same time*. A further reason why the totality of our basic beliefs and concepts is immune from massive error is because, as Davidson (2001a, 153) says, the content of these mental states is determined, "in the plainest and methodologically most basic cases," by their causes in the external world. It is therefore "impossible for all of our beliefs to be false together." To repeat, the inherent veridicality of belief does not preclude a great deal of error or false beliefs. We can all be wrong about something in particular, but not about most things. Being wrong about most things would disrupt meaning to the extent that, were such a situation to obtain, it could not even be described. We would not be able to say what we were talking about.

The widespread existence of falsehoods of the sort that Plantinga hypothesizes would threaten to undermine the claim that they are *about* anything or are *beliefs* at all. If, for example, I have a preponderance of falsehoods in my beliefs about evolutionary biology, it would undermine the claim that my beliefs are about evolutionary biology, and eventually, were we to follow through with Plantinga's radical skepticism, whether they are even beliefs at all. Rather than following out the logic of natural selection to a skeptical conclusion, as he purports to be doing, Plantinga apparently proceeds from a long-standing picture that has entrenched a metaphysical chasm between operations of the mind and events and objects in the world.[20]

To amplify what is wrong with that picture of human cognition, we can consider two other features of Davidson's philosophy: the principle of charity and the triangulation model. In our interpretations of our fellow humans, we are obliged to start with a principle of charity, making an initial presumption of their rationality and truth-believing. This is a matter of method, not generosity, since otherwise we would have no evidence with which to start. We cannot understand a belief or behavior entirely alien to us as interpreters unless we can place it against a background of assumed similarities. Then it cannot be so alien as to be incommensurable. The principle of charity invites us to maximize understanding.[21]

While *charity* is a principle widely advocated by a variety of philosophers, *triangulation* is perhaps the best way to the heart of Davidson's unique form of naturalism—and to the "sea change" in philosophy that he hoped would be forthcoming.[22] Triangulation is also, I suggest, the feature that has the most radical impact on skeptical arguments like Plantinga's. The triangular structure of knowledge and inquiry requires a causal nexus of interaction between at least two creatures as well as interaction between each creature and a set of common objects in the world. It occurs when both subjects react to that object or set of objects and then react in turn to each other's reactions. Triangulation yields a nonrepresentationalist, nonfoundational, social, practices-based model of knowledge and inquiry. It replaces any Cartesian, two-sided model of a subject and an object that leads us to imagine a gap between the two. Instead of a picture that gives rise to skepticism, this model has three corners, not just two—speaker, interpreter, their environment—all dependent on one another. Any inquiry whatsoever will require this three-sided engagement of a community of intentional, embodied, physically located agents, applying interpretations to other agents, in a common environment that forms the background. The third corner, crucially, saves communication from an imagined split between the subjective and the objective, as though human knowledge and inquiry might be a dyadic affair modeled on a subject proceeding outward toward an object.

We can surmise that Plantinga shaves off that third corner. Thus, he can only assume a representational model of perception and word–world relationships, a model criticized and abandoned by pragmatism in all of its forms and phases. Without a triangulated way in which to theorize how knowledge and inquiry are made possible, Plantinga is left only with a "content" on one side and some "scheme" on the other, with no way to guarantee a connection between our beliefs and the world. His skepticism makes (limited) sense in this dualistic picture, perhaps, but not in a triangulated one.[23]

Rather than drill down even deeper to disclose other aspects of a Davidsonian form of naturalism that would be useful in debate with supernaturalists like Plantinga, I suggest that we have seen enough to conclude that Plantinga does not in fact defeat naturalism, let alone reinstall supernaturalism, or even successfully relocate the conflict between science and religion.

This leads me to make two bald assertions about the future of pragmatic naturalism in its religious modality. The first is that we can and should make short shrift of supernaturalisms, no matter how philosophically sophisticated. They have cluttered up the ontological landscape for too long. While scholars of religion have reason to *define* religion in terms of linguistic and nonlinguistic interaction with superhuman agents, the explanatory task, as Wayne Proudfoot has taught us, needs to be conducted in entirely naturalistic terms. We cannot but trace the historical, social, psychological, and political factors at work in the phenomena we study, drawing on all we know in these areas to give the best explanation we can of data taken to be religious. We have learned to say of any beliefs about nonnatural forces, causes, or unseen moral orders what Proudfoot (2002, 85) forthrightly stated about James's nineteenth-century panpsychism: "that belief is no longer plausible." The idea that superhuman agents do not affect the world is not a competitor on an equal standing with the idea that superhuman agents *do* affect the world, as Plantinginians claim, but a conclusion born of long-standing and widespread cultural experience.

This is where what Plantinga excoriates as "metaphysical naturalism" wins.[24] He considers it an unjustifiable a priori conclusion. I would argue, to the contrary, that it is a justifiable judgment, inductively arrived at for good reasons. Metaphysical naturalism, taken together with methodological naturalism, is the most defensible position for at least four reasons: the proven success of methodological naturalism; the tremendous body of knowledge gained by it; the lack of a comparable method or epistemology for knowing superhuman agents; and the resulting lack of any conclusive evidence or plausibility conditions for the existence of superhuman agents. The link between these two forms of naturalism could be further amplified, but it is not my purpose here to elaborate a worldview.[25] It is enough to affirm the minimal contention of any notion of naturalism— that nothing exists beyond, beneath, or above the physical universe, the totality, the "Whole Shebang," in all its unimaginable dimensions and multiple transformations.

Confusion about burdens of proof often arise at this juncture. Much of my argument assumes that supernaturalists like Plantinga have the burden of proof, which they do not meet, either in connection with supernaturalist assumptions, in general, or the skeptical argument, in particular. In the back-and-forth of argument, when the issue is the reliability of human faculties aimed at truth, the burden is on Plantinginians, not Davidsonians. If I am trying to decide what my theory of reality should be like (with or without the evolutionary thesis), I should assume that unfamiliar widgets are going to be like familiar widgets until I am given a good reason to think otherwise. The antiskeptical argument I am appealing to quite cuts the legs out from under the kind of generalized skepticism by which Plantinga attempts to produce defeaters for any and all beliefs held by evolutionary naturalists. Of course, some particular beliefs can and will be found to be false, but this does not carry over to a tipping point into the faux skepticism for which Plantinga provides no justification. Bearing a heavier burden of proof for his presumed defeaters, he has not so far carried it to the general satisfaction of philosophers.

I will conclude with a second bald conclusion, that the most interesting recent thinking about religion naturalistically takes the form of a philosophy of religion without religion. Two authors in the present volume, Terry F. Godlove and Philip Kitcher, clarify two distinct options that represent this a/religious stance (if one may call it that), in contrast to more familiar forms of religious naturalism which hold that nature, broadly conceived, is the proper religious object, thus inspiring a sense of transcendence and natural piety without requiring a supernatural source for its intelligibility.[26] The key question in Godlove's contribution to this volume, and of concern to me in the first part of this chapter, is to what extent experience has an immediate nonconceptual content.[27] Is our grasp of the world exhausted by our conceptual capacities?

Godlove's proposal makes an important intervention in the Friedrich Schleiermacher–Proudfoot dispute about religious experience, but it goes beyond that. It opens out onto the larger question of whether there is a primary religious object for pragmatic naturalists to study at all. The gist of the proposal is to treat the nonconceptual content of experience as presuppositional, not experiential; this makes available (for Schleiermacher) a nonconceptual content of experience, in the form of unavoidable space-time preconditions on which we depend, and (for Proudfoot) avoids smuggling in unavailing concepts to try to reconcile immediacy with intentionality. But the most suggestive part, which Godlove (2014, 5) barely adumbrates, is the idea that there may be no properly religious object at all, only "unavoidable questions, unacceptable answers."

Here, Immanuel Kant's space-time preconditions, on which we depend, and Schleiermacher's sense of absolute dependence coincide—as presuppositional conditions, not experiential purchases. In this territory, we are not after empirical availability but, rather, a logical order of dependence. What conditions must we presuppose in order to have experience at all? Kant called this a transcendental inquiry, but since I am not bold enough to take on board the burden of German idealism, I prefer to think in terms of unavoidable constraints. It is, for example, an unavoidable constraint on the nature of our experience that empirical objects must strike us as being at some distance from where we are, and that tomorrow's sea fight cannot occur now.

I see this as the same dynamic at work in Dewey's "enveloping whole, the totality," in Whitehead's "extensive continuum," and in a variety of other conceptions that do not make explicit religious associations but instead explore aesthetic, scientific, or epistemological problems. Perhaps we could even make naturalistic sense of James's "unseen moral order" as something more than what we have put there, if we think of it simply as the way our concepts must refer to the only world that conforms to the conditions under which human understanding is possible. The order in question is a priori, and it is moral in the sense that we are obliged to conform to its conditions in space and time.

Pragmatic naturalists will be careful to note that the notion of the whole of space-time conditions on which human life is dependent is not the notion of an overarching consciousness, in the fashion of a Ralph Waldo Emerson or a Josiah Royce, nor an all-inclusive divine mind, in the formula favored by Charles Hartshorne. Nature's unity is "ever not quite," as James always reminded his readers. We do not and cannot experience the whole as such, for the whole never appears as a really existing object. At best, humans experience a certain complex of conditions, which can either be described as a sense of the whole or rendered transcendentally as a presupposition for any experience at all. On this basis, we then construct particular interpretations or imaginative construals. The early pragmatic naturalist John Herman Randall Jr. (1958, 198–99) summed it up this way: "We never encounter 'the Universe,' we never act toward, experience, or feel being or existence as 'a whole' . . . There is hence no discoverable 'ultimate context,' no 'ultimate substance.' . . . 'The Universe,' or 'Nature,' is not 'a process'—a single process."[28]

In addition to Godlove's Kantian modesty, we have Philip Kitcher's (2014) recent defense of "secular humanism," an old-fashioned term he redeploys and explicates with great sensitivity. Breathing new life into those old bones, Kitcher's secular humanism descends directly from Dewey's 1933 Terry lectures, updated to consider arguments by advocates of "refined religion" who still seek some non-supernatural semblance of transcendence. Kitcher finds refined religion wanting, for reasons I need not spell out here. A version of Kitcher's a/religious stance can be found in Richard Rorty's distinctly humanistic valorization of maturity and freedom, coupled with disdain for any suggestion of humans' "answerability" to some transcendent nonhuman reality. One might say that Kitcher's *Life After Faith* helps to tweak Rorty's Promethean tendencies in a less romantic but still humanistic direction. Neither Rorty nor Kitcher, however, links his vision to an ecological imperative to care for Earth, the most proximate "whence" upon which we humans depend.

Alternatively, we have what Godlove calls the unavoidable "imprint" on our cognitive processes of a world we have not made, a world that forces itself upon us, not in the form of the myth of the given but as "the grip of the given."[29] Our dependence on the world, in this sense, is as much ecological as epistemic, in my view. While it is important to see, as Godlove splendidly conveys, that something about our basic cognitive connection to the world invites religious ideas—which are, however, in tension with those very cognitive capabilities, so that, as Kant showed, religious illusion has its roots in the very nature of human reason itself—it is also possible to tweak Godlove's description of Kant's humanizing project toward an a/religious stance that cultivates a feeling of dependence and directs commitment to the natural world. One can enlarge the extension of *world* to mean "universe of space-time" as well as contract it to indicate answerability for the care of Earth, as I am doing. In this way, we could emphasize what secular humanists like Kitcher and Rorty might well agree with but what their anthropocentrism risks masking: our intricate human dependence on and answerability to planet Earth's ecosystem.

Kitcher and Rorty want us to understand that we are only answerable to ourselves—a humanist message about self-assertion and social cooperation—and to see that the illusion of a wholly mind-independent world is simply a philosophical substitute for the transcendent God of religion. An alternative option lies open, however, that would embrace the natural world as the only home humans have, the one thing to which we human beings are ourselves answerable because we are of its very warp and woof. For pragmatic naturalists who follow this second path, Rorty's strategy of merely exchanging the epistemological project and its discourse of objectivity for a new political discourse about human solidarity will not suffice without an understanding of humankind's solidarity with the natural environment—a world never in danger of being lost epistemologically but now facing disaster ecologically. "Answerability to the nonhuman world," in our time, takes the urgent form of striving for ecological repair and environmental justice, among other measures. For a/religious naturalists of this stripe, human answerability to a nonhuman source upon which we depend has never been more imperative, if we are to avert planetary disaster in the face of climate change, carbon emissions, population growth, vanishing species, and depleted natural resources.

We now have the makings of a serious tension between two broad alternatives for developing the ethico-religious meaning of pragmatic naturalism. The future of pragmatic naturalism in an a/religious key will no doubt play out between them. The choice hinges on one's preference either for an anthropocentrically committed orientation or for answerability and responsibility to the natural, non-human environment, inclusive of other creatures, other species, and, more controversially, possible other forms of nonhuman life in the cosmos. Of the two, I prefer Earth-centered a/religion over humancentric a/religion, perhaps because answerability and a feeling of dependence are residues of Western religions that still seem to me worthwhile. Though I am suspicious about placing too much of a halo around humankind, I see nothing abject about understanding our social practices and forms of solidarity as dependent on a larger, nonhuman context in which "we live and move and have our being" (Acts 17:28).

Provided we do not try to trace any of this to a mysterious transcendent reality or convert what is strictly unknowable (the Whole Shebang on which planet Earth itself depends) into something known, we can be animated by a sense of answerability and responsibility to a world we never made, something "more than" and semi-independent of our forms of human solidarity. Walking a very fine line between a purely epistemological project and pragmatic naturalism in an a/religious key, one hesitates to take tweaking to the point where it shades into transcendental illusion, even as one acknowledges an ineluctable human tendency in that direction. Epistemologically, positing Nature or the Whole or the Totality as the proper object of religious devotion is devoid of inferential content. A philosophy of religion without religion, however, cannot help but respect the all-too-human urge that gives rise to inferentially rich religious questions.

It has been the ironic fate of Jamesian radical empiricism, as I have portrayed it, to assert that lived experience is not exhausted by the scope of our conceptual-linguistic nets, but neither is it possible to *say* anything about the "more." There is a certain pathos to this impasse. In parallel fashion, I find pragmatic naturalism's best a/religious option to consist in cultivating a sense of dependence on and answerability to the whole—but that whole, in the most general sense, is neither immediately experienced nor, strictly speaking, knowable. More than a little pathos accompanies this last impasse.

## NOTES

1.  Cartesian dualism itself may be rooted in the even more primal dualism of male and female, according to feminist critics. In *Sexism and God-Talk: Towards a Feminist Theology*, for example, Rosemary Ruether (1983) contends that male–female dualism was the original model for the projection of mind–body dualism.
2.  I think there are good arguments against both notions, but I do not consider them in this chapter. The best defense of both "pure experience" and "panpsychism" is the nuanced interpretation in David Lamberth (1999).
3.  Therefore, I should not have written that "justification terminates ultimately not with beliefs about felt qualities of experience but with the felt qualities themselves," as if these experiences could be separated from the beliefs that we hold about them (Frankenberry 1987, 188). Neither should William Dean (1989, 87, 93) have maintained that radical empiricism enables one to ground pragmatism on empirical judgments and to offer reasons for one's normative judgments, as if radical empiricism

produces some experience-based criteria that, in Dean's view, Richard Rorty and the new historicists need but stubbornly refuse to adopt.

4. I appreciate Delwin Brown's point to this effect (Brown 1994, 170, note 103). As J. Wesley Robbins (1999) correctly noted, I accepted Donald Davidson's argument by the time of writing "Pragmatism, Truth, and the Disenchantment of Subjectivity" (Frankenberry 1999).

5. I made much the same point in *Religion and Radical Empiricism* (Frankenberry 1987, 138–44).

6. This is less clear in the case of Alfred North Whitehead, and perhaps accounts for his comment in the preface to *Process and Reality* that one of his aims was to rescue the thought of William James and John Dewey from the charge of anti-intellectualism. For more, see Frankenberry (2015).

7. John McDowell (1996, 11), a critic of Davidson on this point, thinks this idea only generates belief systems that resemble "a frictionless spinning in a void." He wants a minimal empiricism such that belief systems have *some* empirical content and are to that extent constrained "from the outside." See also McDowell (2008).

8. Inspired by Dewey's aesthetics, Richard Shusterman (2008, 2012) has invented the term *somaesthetics* to designate a range of such intentional gestures or movements, which can be understood and appropriately responded to by a partner, teammate, or audience without being articulated into words. James Gibson (1986) attempts a transformation of James's radical empiricism into an ecological psychology. See also Harry Heft (2001). Nathaniel F. Barrett and Wesley Wildman (2009) have presented original related research.

9. See, for example, Hood (2008) and Blum (2012, 2014). I offer a reply and related reflections in Frankenberry, "Naturalisms, Ineffability Claims, and Symbolic Meanings," in *The Question of Methodological Naturalism*, ed. Jason N. Blum (forthcoming).

10. See John Dewey and Arthur Bentley (1964), 643, as well as appendix 2 in Dewey (1981), 372.

11. For an excellent rendering of Robert Corrington's work in relation to radical empiricism and process metaphysics, see Demian Wheeler (2014).

12. In such cases, it makes sense to speak of a certain "wisdom of the body."

13. Letter to Henry James, May 4, 1907.

14. He explains, "These motifs, in turn, are the culmination of a long struggle (which extends far outside the boundaries of 'analytic' philosophy) against Platonic and religious conceptions of the world" (Rorty 1991, 117).

15. The chief argument that Alvin Plantinga takes to be the most significant defeater of naturalism first appeared in *Warrant and Proper Function* (1993) but is updated in *Where the Conflict Really Lies* (2011). In the latter, especially, his presentation of evolutionary biology is ill-informed, but that is not my concern here.

16. By *naturalism*, Plantinga means not only what is often called *methodological naturalism* (bracket out God, so long as you're doing science), but also *metaphysical naturalism* (bracket out God because God does not exist and therefore cannot guarantee truth).

17. See also Ramberg (2001).

18.    Terry F. Godlove (1999, 459) calls attention to "an elegant feature of this argument" by explaining that its grip tightens as the skeptic or "conceptual schemer squirms harder," claiming to discover more allegedly alien concepts only to find that "the areas of known agreement will continue to outstrip areas of known difference by an ever-increasing proportion, making the ascription of even a preponderance of otherness a self-defeating activity."

19.    See also Davidson (1984d), 169.

20.    It is a separate question whether Plantinga even understands the logic of natural selection in the first place. That new mutations are random is an essential claim of evolutionary theory. But Plantinga seems to think that God could simply direct the mutations from time to time, making sure that humans, who would otherwise be adventitious, did evolve. As I understand it, this is precisely the position of "theistic evolution" adopted by the Harvard botanist Asa Gray and critiqued by Charles Darwin, in their correspondence, on the grounds that it skidded right off the scientific tracks.

21.    Davidson appears to have moved from "agreement" to "understanding" between "Radical Interpretation" (Davidson 1984c), originally published in 1973, and his introduction to *Inquiries Into Truth and Interpretation* (Davidson 1984a, xvii), where he made it clear that "the aim of interpretation is not agreement but understanding."

22.    For "sea change," see Davidson (2001c). For the triangulation metaphor, a striking feature of his later writings, see "Rational Animals" (Davidson 2001d), "Epistemology Externalized" (Davidson 2001b), "Three Varieties of Knowledge" (Davidson 2001f), "The Second Person" (Davidson 2001e), and "The Social Aspect of Language" (Davidson 2005b). The first four papers are reprinted in *Subjective, Intersubjective, Objective* (2001), and the fifth paper is reprinted in *Truth, Language, and History* (2005).

23.    This may be too generous. Would not his reasoning be subject to the tu quoque effect of making false all of Plantinga's own beliefs, including the make-believe belief that most of the beliefs he holds are false? There is also the charge of incoherence, for in order to assign a truth value of *false* to one or several of his own sentences, or those of others, it is logically necessary for Plantinga to presuppose that most of the other ones he is prepared to utter under appropriate conditions, as well as those uttered by others, can be presumed to be true. For it is only against such a background that he can accuse naturalists and evolutionists of particular errors. Given such a presupposition, it is incoherent for him to imagine that his words could slip off the radar of all the various events, processes, social practices, and cultural politics that make his beliefs the way they are by setting the truth conditions for his statements.

24.    Recall Rorty's (1991, 117) statement, "These motifs, in turn, are the culmination of a long struggle (which extends far outside the boundaries of 'analytic' philosophy) against Platonic and religious conceptions of the world."

25.    For a more amplified account of the link between the two, see Forrest (2000).

26.    I have in mind such authors as Donald Crosby, Ursula Goodenough, Jerome Stone, Charley Hardwick, and Loyal Rue. For a helpful discussion and classification of types of religious naturalism, see Hogue (2010).

27. Using different language, I wrestled with this same question in comparing David Griffin's process notion of religious experience with Wayne Proudfoot's constructivism and Ann Taves's attribution theory, in Frankenberry (2013). I now am inclined to agree with Godlove that the difficulty in formulating an account of receptivity, and thus of a subject's basic cognitive relation to the world, is due to construing it only in causal or inferential terms.

28. Dewey's "sense of the Whole" later became the theme of the Chicago School of religious naturalism, of which William Dean is the best advocate today. The Columbia School of naturalism, on the other hand, represented by John Herman Randall Jr., Justus Buchler, and others, cultivated a more austere view of nature, and its chief representative today is Robert Corrington.

29. The phrase comes from Robert Hanna, quoted in Godlove (2014), 100. Godlove presents this as purely epistemological reflection and, like Immanuel Kant, declines to press in a religious direction that would invite transcendental illusion.

## WORKS CITED

Barrett, Nathaniel F., and Wesley Wildman. 2009. "Seeing Is Believing? How Reinterpreting Perception as Dynamic Engagement Alters the Justificatory Force of Religious Experience." *International Journal for Philosophy of Religion* 66:71–86.

Blum, Jason N. 2012. "Radical Empiricism and the Unremarkable Nature of Mystical Ineffability." *Method and Theory in the Study of Religion* 24:201–19.

Blum, Jason N. 2014. "The Science of Consciousness and Mystical Experience: An Argument for Radical Empiricism." *Journal of the American Academy of Religion* 82:150–73.

Brown, Delwin. 1994. *Boundaries of Our Habitations: Traditions and Theological Construction*. Albany: State University of New York Press.

Davidson, Donald. 1980. "Actions, Reasons, and Causes (1963)." In *Essays on Actions and Events*, 3–19. Oxford: Oxford University Press.

Davidson, Donald. 1984a. Introduction to *Inquiries Into Truth and Interpretation*, vii–xx. Oxford: Clarendon.

Davidson, Donald. 1984b. "On the Very Idea of a Conceptual Scheme (1974)." In *Inquiries Into Truth and Interpretation*, 183–98. Oxford: Clarendon.

Davidson, Donald. 1984c. "Radical Interpretation (1973)." In *Inquiries Into Truth and Interpretation*, 125–40. Oxford: Clarendon.

Davidson, Donald. 1984d. "Thought and Talk (1975)." In *Inquiries Into Truth and Interpretation*, 155–70. Oxford: Clarendon.

Davidson, Donald. 2001a. "A Coherence Theory of Truth and Knowledge (1983)," reprinted with "Afterthoughts (1987)." In *Subjective, Intersubjective, Objective*, 137–58. Oxford: Clarendon.

Davidson, Donald. 2001b. "Epistemology Externalized (1990)." In *Subjective, Intersubjective, Objective*, 193–204. Oxford: Clarendon.

Davidson, Donald. 2001c. "The Myth of the Subjective (1988)." In *Subjective, Intersubjective, Objective*, 39–52. Oxford: Clarendon.

Davidson, Donald. 2001d. "Rational Animals (1982)." In *Subjective, Intersubjective, Objective*, 95–106. Oxford: Clarendon.

Davidson, Donald. 2001e. "The Second Person (1992)." In *Subjective, Intersubjective, Objective*, 107–22. Oxford: Clarendon.

Davidson, Donald. 2001f. "Three Varieties of Knowledge (1991)." In *Subjective, Intersubjective, Objective*, 205–20. Oxford: Clarendon.

Davidson, Donald. 2004. "The Objectivity of Values (1995)." In *Problems of Rationality*, 39–51. Oxford: Clarendon.

Davidson, Donald. 2005a. "Seeing Through Language (1997)." In *Truth, Language, and History*, 127–42. Oxford: Clarendon.

Davidson, Donald. 2005b. "The Social Aspect of Language (1994)." In *Truth, Language, and History*, 109–26. Oxford: Clarendon.

Dean, William. 1989. *History Making History: The New Historicism in American Religious Thought*. Albany: State University of New York Press.

Dean, William. 2012. "Even Stevens: A Poet for Liberal Theologians." *Journal of Religion* 92:177–98.

Dewey, John. 1981. *John Dewey: The Later Works, 1925–1953*, vol. 1, *1925: Experience and Nature*. Carbondale: Southern Illinois University Press.

Dewey, John, and Arthur Bentley. 1964. *A Philosophical Correspondence, 1932–1951*. New Brunswick, NJ: Rutgers University Press.

Forrest, Barbara. 2000. "Methodological Naturalism and Philosophical Naturalism: Clarifying the Connection." *Philo* 3:7–29.

Frankenberry, Nancy. 1987. *Religion and Radical Empiricism*. Albany: State University of New York Press.

Frankenberry, Nancy. 1999. "Pragmatism, Truth, and the Disenchantment of Subjectivity." In *Language, Truth, and Religious Belief*, edited by Nancy Frankenberry and Hans H. Penner, 507–32. Atlanta: Scholars' Press.

Frankenberry, Nancy. 2013. "The Vagaries of Religious Experience: David Griffin's Reenchantment in Light of Constructivism and Attribution Theory." In *Reason and Reenchantment: The Philosophical, Religious, and Political Thought of David Ray Griffin*, edited by John B. Cobb Jr., Richard A. Falk, and Catherine Keller, 111–29. Claremont, CA: Process Century.

Frankenberry, Nancy. 2015. "Contingency All the Way Down: Whitehead Among the Pragmatists." In *Thinking with Whitehead and the American Pragmatists*, edited by Brian G. Henning, William T. Meyers, and Joseph D. John, 97–116. Lanham, MD: Lexington.

Frankenberry, Nancy. Forthcoming. "Naturalisms, Ineffability Claims, and Symbolic Meanings." In *The Question of Methodological Naturalism*, edited by Jason N. Blum. Leiden: Brill.

Gibson, James. 1986 [1979]. *The Ecological Approach to Visual Perception*. Hillsdale, NJ: Lawrence Erlbaum.

Godlove, Terry F. 1999. "In What Sense Are Religions Conceptual Frameworks?" In *Language, Truth, and Religious Belief: Studies in Twentieth-Century Theory and Method in Religion*, edited by Nancy K. Frankenberry and Hans H. Penner, 450–72. Atlanta: Scholars' Press.

Godlove, Terry F. 2014. *Kant and the Meaning of Religion*. New York: Columbia University Press.

Heft, Harry. 2001. *Ecological Psychology in Context: James Gibson, Roger Barker, and the Legacy of William James's Radical Empiricism*. Mahwah, NJ: Lawrence Erlbaum.

Hogue, Michael. 2010. *The Promise of Religious Naturalism*. Rowman and Littlefield.

Hood, R. W., Jr. 2008. "Theoretical Fruits From the Empirical Study of Mysticism: A Jamesian Perspective." *Journal für Psychologie* 16:1–28.

James, Henry. 1911. "Prefatory Note." In William James, *Some Problems of Philosophy: A Beginning of an Introduction to Philosophy*, vii–viii. New York: Longmans, Green.

James, Henry. 1926. *Letters of William James*, 2nd ed., edited by Henry James. 2 vols. Boston: Little, Brown.

James, William. 1950. *The Principles of Psychology*. 2 vols. New York: Dover.

James, William. 1970. *The Meaning of Truth*. Ann Arbor: University of Michigan Press.

James, William. 1978. *Pragmatism* and *the Meaning of Truth*. Cambridge, MA: Harvard University Press.

James, William. 1985. *The Varieties of Religious Experience*. Cambridge, MA: Harvard University Press.

Kitcher, Philip. 2014. *Life After Faith: The Case for Secular Humanism*. New Haven, CT: Yale University Press.

Lamberth, David C. 1999. *William James and the Metaphysics of Experience*. Cambridge: Cambridge University Press.

McDowell, John. 1996. *Mind and World*, 2nd ed. Cambridge, MA: Harvard University Press.

McDowell, John. 2008. "Avoiding the Myth of the Given." In *John McDowell: Experience, Norm, and Nature*, edited by Jakob Lindgaard, 1–14. Oxford: Wiley-Blackwell.

Peirce, Charles Sanders. 1935. *The Collected Papers of Charles Sanders Peirce*, vols. 1–6, edited by Charles Hartshorne and Paul Weiss. Cambridge, MA: Harvard University Press.

Plantinga, Alvin. 1993. *Warrant and Proper Function*. New York: Oxford University Press.

Plantinga, Alvin. 2011. *Where the Conflict Really Lies: Science, Religion, and Naturalism*. New York: Oxford University Press.

Proudfoot, Wayne. 1985. *Religious Experience*. Berkeley: University of California Press.

Proudfoot, Wayne. 2002. "Religious Belief and Naturalism." In *Radical Interpretation in Religion*, edited by Nancy K. Frankenberry, 78–92. Cambridge: Cambridge University Press.

Ramberg, Bjorn. 2001. "What Davidson Said to the Sceptic." In *Interpreting Davidson*, edited by Petr Kotatko, Peter Pagin, and Gabriel Segal, 213–36. Stanford, CA: Center for the Study of Language and Information.

Randall, John Herman, Jr. 1958. *Nature and Historical Experience*. New York: Columbia University Press.

Robbins, J. Wesley. 1999. Review of *Language, Truth, and Religious Belief*. *American Journal of Theology and Philosophy* 20:281–85.

Rorty, Richard. 1991. "Non-Reductive Physicalism." In *Objectivity, Relativism, and Truth*, 113–25. Cambridge: Cambridge University Press.

Rorty, Richard. 2000. "Response to Bjorn Ramberg." In *Rorty and His Critics*, edited by Robert Brandom, 370–77. Malden, MA: Blackwell.

Rorty, Richard. 2001. "Response to Richard Shusterman." In *Richard Rorty: Critical Dialogues*, edited by Matthew Festenstein and Simon Thompson, 155–57. Cambridge: Polity.

Rorty, Richard. 2006. "Toward a Postmetaphysical Culture." In *Take Care of Freedom and Truth Will Take Care of Itself: Interviews with Richard Rorty*, edited by Eduardo Mendieta, 46–55. Stanford, CA: Stanford University Press.

Ruether, Rosemary. 1983. *Sexism and God-Talk: Towards a Feminist Theology*. Boston: Beacon.

Sellars, Wilfrid. 1997. *Empiricism and the Philosophy of Mind*. Cambridge, MA: Harvard University Press.

Shusterman, Richard. 2008. *Body Consciousness: A Philosophy of Mindfulness and Somaesthetics*. New York: Cambridge University Press.

Shusterman, Richard. 2012. *Thinking Through the Body*. New York: Cambridge University Press.

Stout, Jeffrey. 2007. "On Our Interest in Getting Things Right: Pragmatism Without Narcissism." In *New Pragmatists*, edited by Cheryl Misak, 7–31. New York: Oxford University Press.

Wheeler, Demian. 2014. "American Religious Empiricism and the Possibility of an Ecstatic Naturalist Process Metaphysics." *Journal for the Study of Religion, Nature and Culture* 8: 156–81.

Whitehead, Alfred North. 1938. *Modes of Thought*. New York: Macmillan.

Wieman, Henry Nelson. 1946. *The Source of Human Good*. Carbondale: Southern Illinois University Press.

# 9

# Nonconceptualism and Religious Experience

## *Kant, Schleiermacher, Proudfoot*

TERRY F. GODLOVE

I n recent years, we have seen increased interest in a range of disciplines
on the topic of nonconceptual content. As a first approximation, the
central question is whether our grasp of the world is exhausted by our
conceptual capacities. Conceptualists say yea; nonconceptualists, nay. Until
recently, Immanuel Kant's place seemed clearly with the conceptualists. If we read
Kant's famous slogan "Intuitions without concepts are blind" as "Intuitions without concepts are nothing," then the issue would appear to be settled. On this
reading, long-dominant, especially among Anglo-American commentators, Kant
comes out a champion of conceptualism—as defending the claim that the content of perception is determined by our conceptual capacities. John McDowell
(1996, 25), for one, reads Kant in this spirit, as holding that "experiences themselves are already equipped with conceptual content." But thanks to recent work
by Robert Hanna and others, the issue of Kant's allegiance now appears more
complex.

The prospect of a Kantian nonconceptualism makes a compelling connection between Kant and Friedrich Schleiermacher, for, of course, in his *On Religion: Speeches to Its Cultured Despisers* and *The Christian Faith*, the connection
between piety and generally prereflective experience has an important role. Just
how important a role remains controversial. In *Religious Experience*, Wayne
Proudfoot (1985) accuses Schleiermacher of enlisting nonconceptualism in the
service of a protectionist strategy; by making religious experience essentially
nonconceptual, he effectively immunizes it against the criticism that it reflects

this or that conceptual shortcoming. Proudfoot's work has occasioned a large and productive literature and has gained a wide enough currency to be recently labeled the "standard interpretation" (Dole 2010b, 20). At the same time, a countervailing current of scholarship has tried to place Schleiermacher's interest in individual feeling, subjectivity, and the nonconceptual within a wider context of language, community, and causal explanation (Gerrish 1988; Dole 2010b; Vial 2010). Proudfoot (2010) himself has lately been more tentative about the details of Schleiermacher's nonconceptualism.

In what follows, I want to put the focus back on nonconceptualism. I will try to show that some familiar themes from *On Religion* and *The Christian Faith* take on new life if, with Kant, we take seriously the thought that experience reflects a nonconceptual element. I have no light to shed on the wider issues of Schleiermacher scholarship and, in particular, nothing to say about the relative importance of nonconceptualism in Schleiermacher's wider thought. I am taking it that Schleiermacher is committed to a form of nonconceptualism and that he is, to some extent, deploying Kantian materials. With these two assumptions, the questions that interest me then emerge: How close is Kant's nonconceptualism to Schleiermacher's? Can Kant's nonconceptualism be put to use, if not on Schleiermacher's behalf, then on behalf of issues with which Schleiermacher is occupied? We will see that following this trail leads us to a position in which it becomes difficult to distinguish between epistemological and religious reflection.

## KANT'S NONCONCEPTUALISM

When put in a very general way, we all are probably nonconceptualists.[1] When a child first learns to say *dada*, she is reacting to what is in front of her, to what is affecting her. She is not aware that this dada is one of many dadas, much less that dadas are enduring physical objects and not event histories or time slices or undetached dada parts, and so on. There probably are no concepts in play whatsoever. She is simply reacting to having been affected in a certain way. In later life, as she passes through a familiar room, lost in reverie, she is in some sense aware of the bookcase in the corner and the lamp on the table, though, again, perhaps not in a conceptual way. Thus, the point is not confined to early language learning, and it holds even when questions of ontology have been settled.

In the contemporary literature on nonconceptual content, this point is often framed in terms of belief. Thus, one finds the claim that the content of a mental state is conceptual if and only if it draws on the relevant belief or beliefs—say, that dada is before her or that the bookcase is in the corner. In this view, it is the failure to draw on or even to hold these beliefs that makes for the nonconceptuality in these cases. Or, again, the claim has been made that we cannot possibly be applying concepts tailored to all aspects of the rich detail presented to us in perceptual experience—for example, to each of the different shades of color we perceive. This is the so-called fineness-of-grain argument for nonconceptualism.[2]

Kant's nonconceptualism is of a different sort than either of these. Notice that both the child and the adult must locate the objects in question at some distance from where they find themselves. The force of *must* here does not seem to be that of physical necessity. It seems, rather, to be presuppositional. If subjects like us are going to cognize dadas or bookcases or lamps at all, we must presuppose an expanse in which objects of cognition are located with respect to where each of us is. Notice, too, that the presupposed expanse does not stop with the edges of the objects of cognition, with the walls of the containing room, with the boundaries of the house or the solar system or whatever. The presupposed expanse is continuous and therefore singular; in this case, the whole, as Kant says, precedes the parts.[3]

By contrast, in discursive representation, the parts precede the whole in the sense that the subject draws on concepts composed of what may be "common to different things" (A656/B684). Since concepts are composed of what may be common to more than one thing, they are all general. Thus, they cannot be directly related to individuals, since, in the nature of the case, more than one object may fall under any given concept. Gareth Evans (1982, 75) captures this feature of Kant's view with what he calls the "generality constraint":

We cannot avoid thinking of a thought about an individual object x, to the effect that it is *F*, as the exercise of two separable capacities; one being the capacity to think of x, which could be equally exercised in thoughts about x to the effect that it is *G* or *H*; and the other being a conception of what it is to be *F*, which could be equally exercised in thoughts about other individuals, to the effect that they are *F*.

The distinction Kant wants is between the generality of F, G, or H (their potential applicability to more than one object), as contrasted to the singularity of the spatial (and temporal) expanses in which we must locate x, the object to which those general concepts apply (if they do). Since conceptual representation depends on generality, and since space (and time) are singular, we cannot give them conceptual representation; when we speak of spaces and times we are abstracting them out of a single expanse. In this way, we arrive at the full sense of experience as it is portrayed in *Critique of Pure Reason*: the cognition of objects in space and in time-relations to which general concepts are applied. Thus, when we apply general concepts to objects, the field of possible application is already narrowed to that of spatiotemporal somethings (ignoring for the moment reference to my own internal states). Since, for Kant, experience is the activity of applying concepts to objects, we can say that all experience incorporates a nonconceptual aspect.

Such considerations as these lead Robert Hanna to dispute the standard, conceptualist interpretation of Kant's famous remark that "thoughts without content are empty, intuitions without concepts are blind" (A50–51/B74–76). Wilfred Sellars and John McDowell, for example, deny the cognitive independence of intuitions—they either are fictions or are meaningless. Instead, Hanna proposes:

> Nonconceptual content can provide rational human animals with an inherently spatiotemporally situated, egocentrically-centered, biologically/neurobiologically embodied, pre-reflectively conscious, skillful perceptual and practical grip on things in our world. Call this fundamental normative fact *the Grip of the Given*, with due regard to the two-part thought that *to stand within* the Grip of the Given is also thereby to *have* a grip on things in our world. More precisely: To stand within the Grip of the Given is to be so related to things and other minded animals in our world, and thereby to have a grip on the positions and dispositions of things and other minded animals in our world, via essentially nonconceptual content, that we are poised for achieving accurate reference, true statements, knowledge, consistency and valid consequence in logical reasoning, effectiveness in intentional performance, goodness of means or ends, rightness in choice or conduct, and consistency and coherence of motivation in practical reasoning—in short, we are poised for achieving any or all of the highest values of our cognitive and practical lives.[4]
>
> (Hanna 2013, 76, emphasis in original)

The main burden of this paragraph is to turn the "myth of the given" on its head. In the Sellars/McDowell reading, Kant has us in immediate contact only with sensation, on the basis of which we reconstruct the world of spatiotemporal objects. But that reading does not fit with the arguments sketched above, according to which the objects to which we apply general concepts—say, *white*, *cold*, and *round*—have already conformed to the (nonconceptual) modes under which we can be affected, space and time. We are, as Hanna puts it, already poised for success; we already have a grip. The object is presented through empirical intuition by its two defining features, immediacy and singularity. We then judge of the object that it is, say, a snowball.

In the first instance, then, what puts Kant on the side of nonconceptualism is the thesis that our forms of sensibility introduce a formal, structural element of nonconceptuality in all those judgments that depend on empirical intuition. Putting the point in this way leaves open the question of whether we can isolate the nonconceptual aspect of empirical cognition in the sense of entertaining it itself as a conscious state. Can we "have" a Kantian nonconceptual experience? Does Kant think we can? We will have to come to some clarity about at least the first question in order to illuminate the comparison with Schleiermacher.

For the moment, I will simply note a passage emphasized in this connection by Manley Thompson.[5] For Kant, a perception is mere sensation insofar as it relates "solely to the subject as a modification of its state" (A320/B376). Here there is no question of awareness, no conceptual or nonconceptual structure—a mere sensory manifold. A next step involves the subject apprehending the object as "something given in space and time—of a spatiotemporal something—it is an empirical intuition, an objective perception, and a species of cognitive representation" (Thompson 1992, 87). Finally, we can speak of the subject applying concepts so that the object now has sensory qualities; it is an object of possible experience in the full sense. The question whose treatment I am postponing is whether Kant's view is that we do or at least can actually experience the middle stage for itself; whether we can experience objects as mere spatiotemporal somethings without implicating conceptual representation.

The passage Thompson emphasizes seems to suggest that Kant thinks we can. Kant writes that only with the application of concepts do "we first obtain knowledge [cognition] properly so called" (die Erkenntnis in eigentlicher Bedeutung) (A78/B103). Thompson (1992, 87) comments that Kant's "phrase 'first obtain knowledge properly so called' suggests that he was prepared to recognize something which occurs prior to conceptual synthesis and which may be called 'knowledge' in some sense." The question is whether this takes us beyond nonconceptual content to nonconceptual experience.

## RECEPTIVITY

Human subjects are open to being affected by the world; any plausible account of empirical knowledge must take account of that fact. Much of the issue between

Kant and Schleiermacher turns on whether that affection is analyzable in purely causal terms.

On the Kantian side of this question, Thompson is again helpful. He points out that, in summarizing the transcendental deduction in the second edition of the *Critique*, Kant calls it a *Darstellung* (B168), and that, later, in the "Analytic of Principles," he uses *darstellen* as the verb to indicate how an object "is to be exhibited immediately in intuition" (A156/B195). Later still, in the "Methodology," the basic contrast between mathematics and transcendental philosophy turns out to be a difference in the way we exhibit an object in each. In mathematics, we exhibit an object by a priori construction in pure intuition. For example, in arithmetic, we cannot find "12" in "7 + 5" simply by applying the principle of noncontradiction; rather, we have to carry out the operation by constructing seven strokes in the imagination and continuing on, adding five more (B15). In geometry, to consider whether the internal angles of a triangle equal 180 degrees, I must, again, construct a figure in the imagination; I cannot find 180 degrees simply by inspecting the bare concept *triangle* (B65). In transcendental philosophy—so the claim goes—we have a priori rules to which we must conform in the course of experience, rules seeing to the unity of thought (those of "general" logic) and rules seeing to the unity of experience ("transcendental" logic).

Now, the point I want to take from these remarks is not the *difference* between mathematics and philosophy but the *sameness* in the mode or manner in which, in each of them, we exhibit an object. The objective necessity in both mathematics and transcendental philosophy is an exhibited necessity—exhibited, on the one hand, in mathematical constructions and, on the other hand, in arguments for the unavoidability of conformity to the rules determining the formal conditions of empirical truth.

By contrast, Kant tells us that causal necessity in natural science holds between objects of possible experience and is an inferred necessity—inferred inductively and therefore known only a posteriori (see, for example, A766/B794). The point extends to those regions of cognitive psychology that take the human subject as a biological organism causally interacting with its environment. We compare input of various sorts against the subject's verbal and nonverbal output; in this context, the notion of input and output is unproblematic. Here, as elsewhere in the natural sciences, we infer a connection between objects of experience, one known inductively and a posteriori.[6]

But, in philosophy, when I ask about the legitimacy of conformity to these rules of general and transcendental logic, that very conformity is in force in the activity of asking this question. I must follow the rules in inquiring whether I have the right to follow them. There is, then, no room for the kind of causal inferences we make in the natural sciences—no room for the sifting of evidence, the consideration of alternative explanations, and so forth. Sifting and considering, no less than any other form of discursive activity, will require conformity to the rules whose justification we are considering. Under the circumstances, Kant thinks all we can do is display or exhibit this conformity as unavoidable. A *Darstellung*.

Let us take an example. Suppose I claim to have cognized an effect before its cause. Kant learned from David Hume that, as a matter of logic, my claim is unproblematic. It is not self-contradictory. It can at least be thought. But when I subject my claim to the rules of time determination, it must then pass a stricter test. If I am to cognize a series of events as a series, my cognitions must occur in one temporal stretch—otherwise the notions of *before* and *after* make no sense and, without them, the very idea of a sequence of events falls apart. But then, each moment must emerge out of the preceding one, and so each successive event in time arises out of prior events.

In outline, thus argues Kant in the "Second Analogy." But this two-stage arrangement—that is, requiring that a piece of purported empirical knowledge pass both logical tests (e.g., is it self-contradictory?) and epistemological tests (e.g., does it conform to the rules of time determination?)—brings us back to Kant's distinction between general and transcendental logic. General logic, overseeing the unity of thought, is indifferent about whether I claim to have cognized the cause before the effect or the effect before the cause; because neither claim is self-contradictory, both satisfy its requirements. But in extending my thinking beyond mere objects of thought to existing objects outside of me, I draw into play the synthetic a priori rules—among them, those of time determination—that make possible the unity of experience. This is the domain of transcendental logic.

Note that I do not exhibit these rules by offering an explanation of how, in the present example, "the nature of time" orders human cognition. That would be to again fall back on a causal, naturalistic, inferred necessity—an explanation rather than a *Darstellung*. I can only exhibit my cognition as in conformity with the rules of the unity of experience, and thereby establish contact with objects of experience and not merely with objects of thought. I do not, of course, establish that what I say about them is true, but, as long as I exhibit my conformity to the "formal conditions of empirical truth," I am assured that my empirical inquiry will at least remain in contact with those objects. I take it that this is what Hanna means by having a "grip on things in our world."

In his discussion of receptivity in *On Religion*, Schleiermacher does not follow Kant in distinguishing between an exhibited and an inferred necessity. He cannot follow Kant on this point because—to my knowledge—the notion of a priori constraint has no place in his thinking. Without such constraint to display, Schleiermacher has to construe the fundamental relationship between a thought and its object in causal terms. This picture comes out clearly in a familiar passage from the first edition:

> I entreat you to become familiar with this concept: intuition of the universe. It is the hinge of my whole speech; it is the highest and most universal formula of religion on the basis of which you should be able to find every place in religion, from which you may determine its essence and limits. All intuition proceeds from an influence of the intuited on the one who intuits, from an original and independent action of the former, which is then grasped, apprehended, and conceived by the latter according to one's own nature. If the emanations of light—which happen completely without your efforts—did not affect your sense, if the smallest part of the body, the tips of your fingers, were not mechanically or chemically affected, if the pressure of weight did not reveal to you an opposition and a limit to your power, you would intuit nothing and perceive nothing.[7]
>
> (Schleiermacher 1996, 24–25 [2:213–14])

Schleiermacher is commenting on the physical interactions between an organism and its environment. The account is naturalistic in that sense. In the recent literature, much emphasis has been put on the middle sentence in the above passage: "All intuition proceeds from an influence of the intuited on the one who intuits, from an original and independent action of the former, which is then grasped, apprehended, and conceived by the latter according to one's own nature." Theodore Vial (2010, 47) thinks that the last clause shows a departure from Kant in that "intuition is shaped by our culture and language." And Proudfoot (2010, 29), agreeing with Vial, takes it to show that "neither intuition nor feeling is prelinguistic for Schleiermacher."

In the line of thought I am developing, the real point of divergence between Kant and Schleiermacher lies elsewhere. In fact, Kant is happy to admit that our reaction to sensory impingement is concept-laden—so that, for instance, someone who has never seen anything remotely duck-like will be unlikely to see Ludwig Wittgenstein's duck/rabbit as a duck. As far as I can see, such an admission does not, for either Kant or Schleiermacher, call into question the status of the impingement itself as prelinguistic and nonconceptual.

The real divergence here between Kant and Schleiermacher is over what the subject of the impingement is entitled to say about its source. Schleiermacher portrays the subject of the impingement as able to make inferences about the origin of the affection ("mechanical" or "chemical"). In Kantian terms, we have here to do with an inferred and not with an exhibited necessity. It is not a *Darstellung*.[8] It cannot be, since, to get an exhibited necessity, you need unavoidable rule-governed constraints on thought and experience available for exhibiting—if not those rules favored by Kant then ones that play a parallel structural role. Without them, you have a causal naturalism.

Other critics, more persuaded than Vial and Proudfoot of the Kantian pedigree of Schleiermacher's treatment of intuition, tend to put much weight on the prominence Schleiermacher gives to the passive aspect of experience. For example, Manfred Frank (2005, 28) notes that, in *On Religion*, "in contrast to concepts . . . intuitions are maximally 'passive.'" But, from a Kantian point of view, this unqualified passivity will make trouble—in the form of Proudfoot's original criticisms—for Schleiermacher's broader account of receptivity. What is crucial to Kant's picture of intuition is not simply the passivity inherent in being open to affection by the world—so much we could construe, with Schleiermacher, in causal terms—but passivity under a priori, partly nonconceptual constraint.

Because, in the first edition of the second speech in *On Religion*, Schleiermacher transplants the Kantian notion of *Anschauung* (intuition) into a causal context, the topic of nonconceptual content or nonconceptual experience does not arise there as it does for Kant. Ironically, it is only with Schleiermacher's well-documented move, in the later editions of *On Religion* and *The Christian Faith*, away from the first edition's more Kantian-sounding talk of intuition that we come to a deeper encounter between him and Kant over the sense in which experience reflects nonconceptual content. When Kant speaks of the "passivity" or "receptivity" of the senses, he is trying, as Thompson (1983, 36) puts it, "to capture something of our sense of being in a world we never made, of having to cope with a reality outside and independent of our consciousness." The contact with reality at stake here is more basic, more primitive than can be captured by appealing to causation. It is not the result of observing an organism interacting with its environment, and so it does not mark an inferred necessity. With this Kantian orientation comes a fundamental sense of dependence as well as an immediacy and independence from concepts and beliefs that, at the same time, carries a reference to the pre-individuated world pressing itself upon us. We are, I take it, heading into Schleiermacher's dialectical neighborhood.

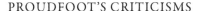

## PROUDFOOT'S CRITICISMS

These issues form the context in which I would like to consider Proudfoot's criticisms of Schleiermacher in *Religious Experience*. Proudfoot's general theme is that one cannot support or legitimate a representation or feeling by pointing out that one has been caused to have it. He remarks, "The 'object' of the feeling might be only a grammatical object and have no independent existence" (Proudfoot 1985, 22)—the real cause might be something else altogether. To put the point in more general terms provided by McDowell (1996, 24 and elsewhere), causation in this context supports exculpation, not justification.[9] I take the criticism to be that Schleiermacher's reliance on a purely causal connection between mind and world leaves him outside the realm of justification and so unable to specify the object of the state of consciousness that interests him.

It is important to note that Proudfoot is writing of the later editions of *On Religion*. Many critics have noted that, in the first edition, Schleiermacher displays a certain disinterest in specifying the object of religious consciousness. Thus, we have Van Harvey's (1971, 449) well-known remark that "so far as the concept of God is concerned, Schleiermacher seems to have regarded it as almost irrelevant to religion in the first edition." But, in the later editions, Proudfoot's remark has a more vivid target, for there, as Richard Crouter (1988, 65) observes, Schleiermacher "reveals a deliberate effort to give the earlier argument a more theistic interpretation"—that is, he is more concerned to specify the object of religious consciousness.

The initial criticism, then, is that an account of receptivity that relies solely on sensory impingement cannot make sense of justifying a belief or experience. This criticism brings us into the thick of a contemporary discussion in the theory of knowledge. Thus, McDowell (1996, 133) has pressed this objection against Willard V. O. Quine's program of naturalized epistemology: "The only connection he countenances between experience and the acceptance of statements is a brutely causal linkage that subjects are conditioned into when they learn a language.... Quine conceives experiences so they can only be outside the space of reasons, the order of justification."

McDowell might as well have been writing of Schleiermacher. But Quine has open to him an initial move that is not available to Schleiermacher. Quine is happy to adopt a third-person point of view, that of the cognitive psychologist who is charting, in someone else's case, the input of experience as against verbal output. In that sense, as Quine (1969, 83) says, epistemology becomes "contained in natural science, as a chapter of psychology." This move, whatever its prospects, is not open to Schleiermacher because he follows Kant in casting his reflection in the first person—as reflection on the nature of his own experience. This first-person orientation is, I take it, crucial to Schleiermacher's purposes. That is, he is inviting religion's cultured despisers to reflect not on the nature of others' experience but on their own. McDowell's point—and, I take it, Proudfoot's—is that knowing that an experience has been caused does not by itself allow me infer its cause. That knowledge—and, in Schleiermacher's picture, that is all the knowledge available—makes for exculpation, not justification.

One strategy for avoiding this entire set of issues would be for Schleiermacher somehow to incorporate reference to or identification of the object of religious experience into the act of cognition itself, thereby avoiding the need both for a causal explanation of the cognition and an inference about its origin. I take it that Proudfoot reads Schleiermacher as pursuing just this strategy in the following passage: "Your feeling is piety in so far as it is the result of the operation of God in you by means of the universe" (Schleiermacher 1958, 45 [12:63]).[10] Proudfoot (1985, 14) comments, "Reference to a belief about the cause of the experience is built into the rules for identifying the experience." He is alleging that Schleiermacher is trying to slip justification in through the back door.

In the later editions of the work, Schleiermacher calls upon the notion of *immediacy* to take up precisely this slack. *Immediacy* is present in the first edition, but there it is typically paired with *intuition* and contrasted with general, "abstract thought."[11] In the later editions, and, as we will see, in *The Christian Faith*, immediacy plays an additional role. It modifies *consciousness*, as in the new definition of religion: "the immediate consciousness of the universal existence of all finite things, in and through the Infinite, and of all temporal things in and through the Eternal" (Schleiermacher 1958, 36 [12:53]). By "immediate consciousness," Schleiermacher apparently means the awareness of an object of perception unaccompanied by self-awareness—and that usage of *immediate* is, as Vial (2010, 49) points out in connection with *The Christian Faith*, unobjectionable. No doubt we do often find ourselves experiencing this or that without inferring that we are experiencing this or that. We just experience it. In recent work, Proudfoot (2010, 37) agrees that this sense of immediacy carries no suspicion of protectionism or special pleading, as indeed it does not. But Vial (2010, 49) goes on to remark that "it is this [use of *immediate*] to a large extent that leads to interpretations in the English secondary literature that Schleiermacher intends a prelinguistic, nonconceptual, and mystical point of contact with the divine." That is far from clear.

I am not in a position to make a counterclaim about the English secondary literature, but this unproblematic use of *immediacy* is not Proudfoot's target in *Religious Experience*. In fact, Schleiermacher retains, alongside the new one, the earlier use of the term, in such passages from the second edition as the following: "All is immediately true in religion . . . But that only is immediate which has not yet passed through the stage of idea, but has grown up purely in feeling" (Schleiermacher 1958, 54 [12:73]). Here *immediate* is not modifying *consciousness* but is describing a variety of cognition that clearly seems designed to carry a general sense of nonconceptuality. The trouble, as Proudfoot points out, is that Schleiermacher needs *feeling* here to include an element of recognition—and that requires the experience to have passed through the stage of idea. It requires an inference. When I judge that an object is this or that (say, "the universal existence of all finite things"), I have to bring into play the relevant concepts. This is so, even if the consciousness is, in Schleiermacher's second, new sense, immediate—that is, even when I judge the object to be this or that without attaching my own self-recognition to the judgment (Proudfoot 1985, 11).

When taken together, Proudfoot's criticisms, as I understand them, present Schleiermacher with an unhappy choice: either he makes the object of piety cause the feeling, in which case the object cannot be identified by the subject *as* the cause, or he builds it into the experience of piety itself, in which case the experience can no longer carry the desired sense of immediacy. In the next section, I will argue that Schleiermacher fares better against these criticisms in *The Christian Faith*. But first let us look more closely at what can be said on Schleiermacher's behalf at this point.

Underlying Proudfoot's criticisms is a claim about Schleiermacher and nonconceptual experience. Writing of *On Religion*, Proudfoot (1985, 11) claims that Schleiermacher is mistaken in thinking that "he has identified a moment of consciousness independent of thought and yet still having cognitive significance." This strikes me as the right thing to say. But it is important for my purposes here to measure the distance between Schleiermacher and those Kantian resources that could be brought to bear on his behalf. Consider this passage from the second edition of the second speech. Schleiermacher is working up (and working us up) to the famous "love scene," in which the distinctive moment of piety is portrayed as incapable of being given conceptual expression: "Your thought can only embrace what is sundered. Wherefore as soon as you have made any given definite activity of your soul an object of communication or contemplation, you have already begun to separate. It is therefore impossible to adduce any definite example, for, as soon as anything is an example, what I wish to indicate is already past" (Schleiermacher 1958, 41–42 [12:59]).

I take it we are familiar with the phenomenon that Schleiermacher has in view, or at least a close relation. Suppose I react to a bright light and then judge that the light is bright. We would, I think, want to say that the reaction is immediate in the sense that it is unavoidable. But we might also want to say that the judgment, too, is immediate in that same sense; I might find myself judging that the light is bright in a way that has nothing to do with conscious volition. Still, there is the difference that, for Kant, the judgment, but not the reaction, is composed of general concepts and can be true or false. But what can we say about the reaction? Not an easy question, for answering seems to require us to give linguistic representation to something which, by its nature, is intuitive and nonconceptual. This is the brightest thread connecting Kant and Schleiermacher on the subject of nonconceptual content.

Have we hit upon, then, a proper sense of nonconceptual experience? I think we must answer in the negative. As I am reading him, what Schleiermacher has in view in the love scene can be elucidated by making explicit a fundamental distinction in Kant's epistemology, namely, a distinction between the intuitive representation that I must presuppose (the intuition, the brute reaction) and the discursive representation that I create (the judgment). Schleiermacher is right to take the former as immediate, and he is right that it is impossible to adduce an example. But he is mistaken to think that we have to do here with a transition from one kind of experience (pre-sundered, pre-separated) to another (ordinary, discursive).

The immediacy and nonconceptuality at stake has the status not of experience at all; rather, it has the status of a presupposition. In judging that the light is bright, I apply general concepts to what I presuppose as immediate and nondiscursive: an intuition. Thus, what blocks nonconceptual experience in the sense that Schleiermacher wants—that is, the experience of an intuition—is just what Kant has in view in his theory of concepts. Reference to this or that object will be by way of general terms, even when I cannot avoid coming to the judgment to which they contribute, even when the judgment is immediate in that sense. When, as in the passage from Schleiermacher, we reflect on this presupposition, it is tempting, but misguided, to think that we are reflecting on a form of nonconceptual experience. In the end, Proudfoot is right that Schleiermacher has not "identified a moment of consciousness independent of thought and yet still having cognitive significance." In Schleiermacher's terms, all cannot be immediately true in religion for the reason that nothing can be immediately true, whether in religion or elsewhere.[12]

I have tried to put this point in the positive, to say what real phenomenon Schleiermacher has in view, that is, the unavoidable presupposition of an intuitive, nondiscursive representation to which we apply general concepts. To put the point in the negative, I am portraying Schleiermacher as having fallen victim to the myth of the given, as assuming the impossible burden of connecting concepts up with brute sensory stimulation. That, as McDowell (1996, 20) says, is "fraudulent." Schleiermacher assumes the burden of making this connection when he takes the transition from pre-sundered to ordinary experience as a move from one kind of experience to another. The challenge for Schleiermacher, in all editions of *On Religion*, is to give an account of what pre-sundered experience might come to, using as materials nothing more than the "mechanical and chemical" stimulation of our sensory receptors, while maintaining the point of view of one who reflects on the nature of his or her own experience.

In the later editions, the difficulty is sharper because the subject must recognize the affection as directed toward a certain specified object—God, the infinite, the whole—and that manifestly requires the use of concepts. But what are the bearers of that content? It is hard to see what recourse Schleiermacher has, except to answer that the content is just, as Hanna (2013, 14) puts it, "the unstructured causal-sensory 'given' input to cognitive faculties, passively waiting to be carved up by concepts." But if, as is required by Schleiermacher's nonconceptualism, identifying concepts are not to be supplied by the subject (we can only help ourselves to that "which has not yet passed through the stage of idea"), then they will somehow have to be generated by the sensations themselves—and that would seem to require a bit of magic. To put the point in the idiom of Sellars and McDowell: to the extent that we place the workings of receptivity outside the space of concepts, it is not clear how it can become available for awareness. At this point, Schleiermacher's insistence on an extreme form of nonconceptualism—again, admitting only that "which has not yet passed through the stage of idea"—is working hard against him.

At the same time, I want to emphasize that, in one important respect, Schleiermacher is working with a better picture of our basic cognitive connection to the world than is McDowell. Schleiermacher is at least trying to make room for immediacy within his account of experience, that is, contra McDowell, for the boundedness of the conceptual. According to McDowell (1996, 41), "spontaneity is inextricably implicated in deliverances of receptivity." Furthermore, "the impressions on our senses that keep the dynamic system in motion are already equipped with conceptual content. The facts that are made manifest to us in those impressions, or at least seem to be, are not beyond an outer boundary that encloses the conceptual sphere, and the impingements of the world on our sensibility are not inward crossings of such a boundary" (45–46).

I am taking Kant and Schleiermacher to be united in the view that, on the contrary, the deliverances of receptivity are immediate and nondiscursive—that it takes a related bit of magic to see what strikes me as "already equipped with conceptual content."[13] What makes Schleiermacher vulnerable to the myth of the given is his treatment of this immediacy as itself a mode of experience, as, in fact, the location of piety. This commitment, in turn, requires him to produce a story about how immediacy and concepts could cooperate to produce any such form of experience—a cooperation that McDowell and Proudfoot so persuasively diagnose as impossible.

For Kant's part, the deliverances of receptivity are presupposed as immediate and nondiscursive, that is, intuitive. As I argued in the first section of this chapter, what prevents Kant from falling into the myth of the given is the nonconceptual content supplied by the spatiotemporal context of all conceptual determination. As Kant sees it, in being open to affection by objects, I must locate myself—and, so, locate the source of what strikes me—in one temporal and one spatial expanse. As we have seen, the arguments for these claims are not naturalistic. That is, they do not appeal to the nature of time and space. Rather, they are designed to exhibit our unavoidable conformity to rules—in this case, rules dictating that I must locate the source of whatever strikes me in one unidirectional sequence of events and at some distance from me. Thus, what strikes me has already conformed to the forms of receptivity. This, in turn, means that I apply concepts not to an unstructured, immediate "given" but to individuals with Kantian-style nonconceptual content, that is, with spatiotemporal location. They are already equipped, contra both Schleiermacher and McDowell, with nonconceptual content.

I have said that the temptation for Schleiermacher is to view the immediacy of intuitive representation as itself a form of experience. In our explication of Kant's view, the parallel temptation is to locate a Kantian sense of nonconceptual experience in the fact that I must cognize objects of experience as spatiotemporal somethings, to which conceptual determinations are added. This would be to reproduce Schleiermacher's error—as though, again, this were a matter of moving from one kind of experience (nonconceptual) to another (discursively structured). Rather, as Thompson (1992, 95) points out, *spatiotemporal something* applies equally to the object of any intuitive representation, just as *apple* can be applied to more than one object, and so the movement on which we are reflecting is carried out within the realm of general, discursive representation.

From Schleiermacher's point of view, Kant's nonconceptualism offers a mixed bag. On the one hand, it promises a way out from under Proudfoot's objections. Because Kant is trying to exhibit the unavoidability in the following of certain rules, he cannot be accused of tying the experience in question to any particular object in an arbitrary or unsupported way; because he rejects giving a causal, naturalistic explanation of nonconceptual content, the question of how to advance from exculpation to justification does not arise. While Kant does invoke a rich array of concepts in analyzing the immediacy and nondiscursivity of receptivity—for example, the notion of something being forced into awareness is, by itself, concept-laden—he is merely using concepts (what else?) to reflect on the necessity of this presupposition.

By contrast, as I have been arguing, Schleiermacher's problem is that he has committed himself to a form of experience (pre-sundered, pre-separated) that cannot be had without drawing on our conceptual capacities. Kant's strategy is to put the workings of receptivity outside the space of general concepts (and outside the spatial theory of concepts), but not outside the space of reasons. The judgment that what strikes me as a spatiotemporal something is "an objective perception and a species of cognitive representation" (Thompson 1992, 87)—I may be mistaken about it, laboring under some form of illusion, and so forth. This means that nonconceptual content is no longer "raised above all error and misunderstanding," which, for Schleiermacher, would be a bitter pill. On the other hand, by accepting the Kantian identification of thought with general concepts, Schleiermacher acquires what Proudfoot (1985, 11) rightly points out he has not purchased for himself, namely, "a moment of consciousness independent of thought and yet still having cognitive significance."

## THE CHRISTIAN FAITH

A long line of commentators has noted Kantian elements in Schleiermacher's new definition of piety in *The Christian Faith*. I will not rehearse them here. The question is whether our emphasis on Kant's nonconceptualism brings out anything new in these familiar lines: "However diverse they might be, what all the expressions of piety have in common, whereby they are at the same distinguished from all other feelings—thus the selfsame nature of piety—is this: that we are conscious of ourselves as absolutely dependent or, which intends the same meaning, as being in relation to God" (Schleiermacher 2016, section 4).[14]

As Schleiermacher develops this passage in the next several paragraphs, we may identify several respects in which he makes contact with Kant's nonconceptualism. Part of the sense of dependence comes from our recognition that we do not make the empirical objects toward which our thoughts are directed; we must be affected by them. Furthermore, Schleiermacher says the sense of dependence he has in mind cannot be pegged to the affection of any individual object, and, as we have seen, that is also true for Kant. To speak of individual objects is to already have applied concepts to what strikes us; by contrast, our awareness that we have not made the world, that we must cope with its affection, is prior to judgments about this or that object, and prior even to settling questions of ontology. To the extent that Schleiermacher writes in this spirit, he can justly speak of what we presuppose as immediate and nonconceptual and, reflecting on it later, can describe it as involving a fundamental sense of dependence.

Although this is not Schleiermacher's line of thought, neither does he explicitly reject it. What he rejects, consistently and with eloquence, is the thought that the sense of dependence he wants can be traced to the physical thrust of empirical objects on our sensory surfaces—the very naturalistic context he had developed in *On Religion*. This, says Schleiermacher (2016, section 4.4), "permits only a feeling of limited dependence but excludes the feeling of absolute dependence." The idea seems to be that, in a naturalistic context, we are aware of our own spontaneity in applying concepts to what strikes us, and this activity by the subject renders the sense of dependence less than absolute.

To this point, he is thinking along Kantian lines. The rules of thought that Kant tries to exhibit are, Kant tells us, *selbstgedachte* (B167)—self-thought, spontaneous. But instead of pursuing a *Darstellung* of these rules, Schleiermacher (2016, section 4.4) seeks an object suitable to the feeling of absolute dependence: "In our proposition 'absolute dependence' and 'being in relation to God' are made equivalent. This affirmation is to be understood in such a way that precisely the *whence* composited in this self-consciousness, the whence our receptive and self-initiated active existence, is to be designated by the term 'God' and for us 'whence' holds the truly primary meaning of the term 'God.'"

We can appreciate the logic: if the world and its objects prompt "a limited feeling of dependence," then prompting a sense of absolute dependence would seem to require going further, that is, outside the world. We can also appreciate the burden this move imposes. We have seen how difficult it is to explicate the relationship between finite objects and the subject; in what does the relationship between the subject and God consist? From section 4.4 of *The Christian Faith* forward, Schleiermacher is apparently reaching for an explication of the feeling of absolute dependence that does not require the concept of causation. What is it?

This is, of course, one of the knotty points of Schleiermacher interpretation. My interest in it is limited to its connection to Schleiermacher's nonconceptualism. The overriding consideration is clear: whatever the relationship between the subject and God turns out to be, it must preserve Schleiermacher's basic claim that religious feeling is "neither a knowing nor a doing but a distinct formation of feeling or of immediate self-consciousness" (Schleiermacher 2016, section 3). Robert Adams (2005, 38) has recently suggested that the connection is inferential. The idea of God "is *inferred* from the description or interpretation of the essential religious consciousness as a feeling *of* absolute dependence" (emphasis in original). This would allow a distinction between the feeling of absolute dependence and its nonconceptuality, on the one hand, and the inference that delivers God as the content of the "whence," on the other hand. As an interpretation of the text, Adams's suggestion fits with Schleiermacher's insistence that God is not given in the feeling itself. Of course, there have been other suggestions, including the thought that religious feeling comprises "a different faculty or capacity that mediates God, or the absolute" (Titans 2006, 136), and there is Schleiermacher's (2016, section 52.1) own eventual recourse to "God's absolutely timeless causality."

Other creative solutions have been proposed. However, at this point it becomes hard to resist the thought that what's called for is not so much ingenuity as diagnostic insight. What to say about extraworldly inferences, ad hoc faculties, and timeless causation? Proudfoot's assessment, in *Religious Experience* and more recently, is to say that Schleiermacher is stuck with ordinary causation whether he likes it or not (Proudfoot 1985, 32; 2010, 31). We might even say that Schleiermacher invites this verdict by his refusal to entertain any alternatives to his own *except* a causal naturalism. That is, when he tries to entertain alternative explications of dependence, he can only imagine someone who means "the dependence of finite beings on the entirety and totality of all that is finite and, consequently, would affirm that what is coposited therein, as well as what is referred to, would not be God but the world. However, we cannot regard this explanation as anything but a misunderstanding" (Schleiermacher, 2016, section 32.2).

Kant, too, thinks the defender of nonconceptual content should regard this as a misunderstanding, but not because he insists on confining his explanations to this world. Rather, Kant wants us to see causal naturalism and causal supernaturalism as making the same mistake, that of failing to take seriously the rule-governedness of experience, which, in turn, as I have been saying, would invite a *Darstellung*—a presentation or exhibition of that rule-following in action, in, say, my inability to hear tomorrow's thunder today or to locate an object anywhere except at some distance from me. Because he has nothing to play the structural role of conformity to a priori rules, Schleiermacher has no way to formulate the Kantian notion of receptivity and therefore no way to construe the basic cognitive relationship between subject and world, except in causal or inferential terms.

The point is not that Kantian nonconceptualism succeeds as an explication of Schleiermacher's notion of absolute dependence. The point is that the sense of dependence at the heart of Kant's doctrine of receptivity is closer to Schleiermacher than any alternative construal he considers in *The Christian Faith* or, as far as I know, elsewhere in his corpus. Writing of Schleiermacher's sense of absolute dependence, Adams (2005, 39) remarks, "Introspectively, then, you should be able to find it in yourself; look for a feeling of not having made yourself to be as you are [of *Sichselbstnichtsogesetzthaben* (sections 4.1 and 4.3)] with respect to your whole condition." At this point, Adams is strikingly close to Thompson's (1983, 36) characterization of Kantian receptivity as "intended to capture something of our sense of being in a world we never made, of having to cope with a reality outside and independent of our consciousness." Apparently, we have reached a point at which the trajectories of religious and philosophical reflection are rather close.

One of the contested questions concerning *The Christian Faith* has been whether Schleiermacher's introduction of God as the intentional object of the feeling of absolute dependence undercuts his claim for the nonconceptuality of religious experience. Commenting on this question, Adams (2005, 38–39) writes, "That deserves, I think, to remain a controversial issue. The question is whether there can be, and indeed are, states of consciousness that are not conceptually structured but are best understood by us by analogy with the intentionality of conceptual thought. More than one influential philosophical movement is committed to a negative answer to this question, but it is not obvious that the negative answer is correct."

In the line of thought I have been developing, it may well be that Kant's nonconceptualism answers Adams's question in the positive—and does so without having to rely on an analogy with conceptual thought. Following out Adams's implication, we must now feel the full weight of the resources Kant's nonconceptualism can offer Schleiermacher against Proudfoot's criticisms: a sense of dependence that cuts deeper than the individuation of objects and is more basic than questions of ontology; a construal of the "whence" that need not be explicated in bogus causal or inferential terms and that floats free of cultural and linguistic practices; an intuition of the universe that encompasses, as Arthur Melnick (2004, 11) puts it, "the full scope of the only space and time that there is" and that does not carry with it the threat of arbitrariness or protectionism; and a form of consciousness that may justly be said to be "immediate, raised above all error and misunderstanding," because it is prior to the distinction between subject and object.

Now, we may readily grant that no item on this list matches up precisely with what Schleiermacher has in mind. But, equally, I do not see how to avoid the conclusion that we are confronted with deeply coincident diagnoses of our basic cognitive position in the world. At the same time, notice how little room Kant leaves Schleiermacher for theological purposes—that is, how the slightest deviation from the posture of philosophical anthropology threatens to bring transcendental illusion in its wake. If, for example, Schleiermacher proceeds with the derivations of the divine attributes (eternity, omnipresence, omnipotence, and omniscience) and Christian doctrines (sin, grace, Christ, regeneration, and so forth), then illusion follows immediately. Schleiermacher is quite clear that, since all of these attributes and doctrines "are meant simply to explicate the feeling of absolute dependence, all of them must somehow be traced back to divine causality" (Schleiermacher 2016, section 50.3). But, as Kant sees it, to take causation out of the realm of possible experience is the very nature of transcendental illusion (A609/B637).[15]

Alternatively, Schleiermacher can emphasize the strain of theological modesty running throughout *The Christian Faith*, the leading idea of which is that the divine attributes "correspond to nothing that is real in its nature within God" (2016, section 50.3)—in which case we will want to ask about the difference between modesty and skepticism. To be sure, Schleiermacher has open to him at least two familiar lines of reply. He can point out that, in his view, divine and natural causation "are the same thing, only regarded from different viewpoints" (section 46.2). Then we will want to know what real work divine causation is doing in the world. The threat here is epiphenomenalism. Granted, we can describe events around us as sustained by divine preservation, but if all the explanatory and interpretive work can be done by appealing only to natural causation—as, indeed, Schleiermacher himself insists can be done—then why should we view these events in any other light?[16] If Schleiermacher answers that the feeling of absolute dependence gives us a reason to do so, then he leaves theology behind for speculative metaphysics.

Second, Schleiermacher can argue that the Kantian critique confuses theology with speculative metaphysics—that, now emphasizing the second clause in Schleiermacher's quote, theology contents itself with "elucidating the feeling of absolute dependence." But then it becomes unclear what to make of such apparent assertions about divine causation as, for example, that divine preservation sustains (*Erhaltung*) the entire system of natural causation. Is this not an assertion after all? Does it really only express a feeling? Theologically, this line leaves Schleiermacher ripe for the neo-orthodox critique that was not long in coming. This problem is not Schleiermacher's alone but, rather, must be faced by any account of cognition that takes as its starting point the passivity or receptivity of the senses: How, then, to build a story about our ability to represent those objects that affect us and that are independent of our senses?

In developing his pragmatism, Peirce (1935, 6:95) embraced this starting point through what he called "that Secondness that jabs you perpetually in the ribs." He grappled throughout his authorship with the problem of finding objectivity in an epistemology that begins with nothing but items of consciousness. Kant's solution is to remind us that these jabs are governed by a priori and, in some cases, nonconceptual rules. Whether that puts Kant's transcendental philosophy at an advantage over Schleiermacher's theology or Peirce's pragmatism is, of course, a further question.

## NOTES

1. For a guide to the broader literature, see Gunther (2008), beginning at 8. For the Kantian literature, see Heidemann (2011). In these paragraphs, I am following Melnick (1985).
2. For discussion, see Gunther (2008), beginning at 8.
3. These arguments are contained in the so-called Metaphysical Exposition of the concept of space in *Critique of Pure Reason* (A22/B37–A25/B40). I discuss the arguments of the Metaphysical Exposition in greater detail in Godlove (2009). As is well known, Kant runs together the question of whether space is an a priori form of intuition with the question of whether there are a priori constraints on its applied geometry. In particular, he wrongly thinks he can give a priori arguments to show that the geometry of space must be Euclidean. In this essay, I join others in pointing out that the arguments of the Metaphysical Exposition can be split off from what Kant wrongly takes to be their Euclidean consequences.
4. See Heidemann (2011) for a survey of the broader landscape.
5. The discussion here follows Godlove (2011).
6. See Thompson (1983), 47, note 19.
7. Quotations from the first edition of *On Religion* follow the Richard Crouter translation (Schleiermacher 1996). References in the text are followed by the *Kritische Gesamtausgabe* (Schleiermacher 1984) volume and pagination in brackets.
8. Several sentences later, we come to the famous line, "To accept everything individual as a part of the whole and everything limited as a representation of the infinite is religion" (Und so alles Einzelne als einen Theil des Ganzen, alles Beschränkte als eine Darstellung des Unendlichen hinnehmen, das ist Religion) (Schleiermacher 1996, 25 [2:214]). Peter Grove (2010, 111), commenting on Schleiermacher's use of *Darstellung* in this passage, recommends replacing Crouter's *representation* with *presentation*, but this does not affect the present point, which is that Schleiermacher gives *Darstellung* a causal context and, thereby, a usage foreign to Kant.

9.  As we have seen, a Kantian *Darstellung* is not supposed to provide justification for particular claims about particular objects in the world. It is only supposed to legitimize our continued contact with objects of experience as inquiry proceeds. In Robert Hanna's terms, we are poised, but not more than poised, for success.

10. Quotations from the 1831 edition of *On Religion* follow the John Oman translation (Schleiermacher 1958). References in the text are followed by the *Kritische Gesamtausgabe* (Schleiermacher 1995) volume and pagination in brackets.

11. For instance, "Intuition is and always remains something individual, set apart, the immediate perception, nothing more. To bind it and to incorporate it into a whole is once more the business not of sense but of abstract thought. The same is true of religion; it stops with the immediate experiences of the existence and action of the universe, with the individual intuitions and feelings; each of these is a self-contained work without connection with others or dependence upon them" (Schleiermacher 1996, 105 [2:215]).

    Theodore Vial (2010, 46) argues that Schleiermacher's use of *intuition* is not prelinguistic, but passages such as this one are hard to square with that claim. The problem is that natural language seems to require general terms. We do not need to subscribe to Kant's spatial theory of concepts to recognize that command over the English word *apple* brings with it the knowledge that the word is in principle applicable to more than one object; "connection with others" is then required of linguistic representations. Such passages as this seem to be denying this function to intuition. In that narrow respect, Schleiermacher follows Kant's usage.

12. It is of course open to Schleiermacher to abandon the first-person point of view for a thoroughgoing naturalism. And, in fact, Andrew Dole (2010b, 115) ably documents what he calls the "social dimension of Schleiermacher's thought on religion." Dole points out that, later in *On Religion* and also in subsequent work, Schleiermacher "offers an account of religious socialization that locates the origin of *inward* religion ... in *outward* religion" (113, emphasis in original). Dole apparently sees, as I do not, a way to harmonize the irreducibly first-person form of the second speech with the third-person (social) form of the fourth and fifth speeches. In any case, with the loss of the first-person point of view goes any compelling connection between Kant and Schleiermacher on the subject of nonconceptual content, as well as the force of Wayne Proudfoot's original criticisms in *Religious Experience*.

13. Writing of John McDowell's suggestion with this criticism in mind, Michael Friedman (2002, 46) asks, "Are we not here very close indeed to the traditional idealist doctrine that the world to which our thought relates is a creature of our own conceptualization?" In his response to Friedman, McDowell (2002, 272) remarks, "I do not need to say anything about Kant's idea that our sensibility has its own a priori form." I am arguing in this chapter that, in fact, decisive emphasis should go on Kant's claim that sensibility has its own a priori form.

14. Quotations from *The Christian Faith* follow the Terrence N. Tice, Catherine L. Kelsey, and Edwina Lawler translation of the second edition (Schleiermacher 2016).

15. For discussion, see Dawn DeVries and B. A. Gerrish (2005, 193). Dole (2010a, 18) comments, "Because the divine causality is simple and eternal, it does not operate

at discrete locations within the natural order, but rather operates upon that order as a whole." Kant's point is that the last clause takes us away from the only context in which we can attach any sense to *operates*.

16. In contemporary terms, Schleiermacher appears to be articulating a "property dualism" in theology, along the lines of Donald Davidson's in the philosophy of mind. Divine causality (mental events) is (are) irreducible to natural causality (physical events), but neither are they two different things. Jaegwon Kim, among others, brings the charge of epiphenomenalism against Davidson.

## WORKS CITED

Adams, Robert. 2005. "Faith and Religious Knowledge." In *The Cambridge Companion to Friedrich Schleiermacher*, edited by Jacqueline Mariña, 35–51. New York: Cambridge University Press.

Crouter, Richard, ed. 1988. Introduction to *Friedrich Schleiermacher, On Religion: Speeches to Its Cultured Despisers*, 1–73. Translated by Richard Crouter. New York: Cambridge University Press.

DeVries, Dawn, and B. A. Gerrish. 2005. "Providence and Grace: Schleiermacher on Justification and Election." In *The Cambridge Companion to Friedrich Schleiermacher*, edited by Jacqueline Mariña, 189–207. New York: Cambridge University Press.

Dole, Andrew. 2010a. "Schleiermacher and Religious Naturalism." In *Schleiermacher, the Study of Religion, and the Future of Theology: A Transatlantic Dialogue*, edited by Brent Sockness and Wilhelm Gräb, 15–26. Berlin: Walter de Gruyter.

Dole, Andrew. 2010b. *Schleiermacher on Religion and the Natural Order*. New York: Oxford University Press.

Evans, Gareth. 1982. *The Varieties of Reference*. New York: Oxford.

Frank, Manfred. 2005. "Metaphysical Foundations: A Look at Schleiermacher's *Dialectic*." In *The Cambridge Companion to Friedrich Schleiermacher*, edited by Jacqueline Mariña, 15–34. New York: Cambridge University Press.

Friedman, Michael. 2002. "Exorcizing the Philosophical Tradition." In *Reading McDowell: On Mind and World*, edited by Nicholas H. Smith, 25–57. New York: Routledge.

Gerrish, B. A. 1988. Review of *The Nature of Doctrine: Religion and Theology in a Postliberal Age*. *Journal of Religion* 68:87–92.

Godlove, Terry. 2009. "Poincaré, Kant, and the Scope of Mathematical Intuition." *Review of Metaphysics* 62:779–806.

Godlove, Terry. 2011. "Hanna, Kantian Non-Conceptualism, and Benaceraff's Dilemma." *International Journal of Philosophical Studies* 19:447–64.

Grove, Peter. 2010. "Symbolism in Schleiermacher's Theory of Religion." In *Schleiermacher, the Study of Religion, and the Future of Theology: A Transatlantic Dialogue*, edited by Brent Sockness and Wilhelm Gräb, 109–20. Berlin: Walter de Gruyter.

Gunther, York H., ed. 2008. *Essays on Nonconceptual Content*. Cambridge, MA: MIT Press.

Hanna, Robert, 2013. "Beyond the Myth of the Myth: A Kantian Theory of Non-Conceptual Content." In *Kant and Non-Conceptual Content*, edited by Dietmar H. Heidemann, 11–86. London: Routledge.

Harvey, Van A. 1971. "On the New Edition of Schleiermacher's *Address on Religion*." *Journal of the American Academy of Religion* 39:488–512.

Heidemann, Dietmar. 2011. "Introduction: Kant and Nonconceptual Content—Preliminary Remarks." *International Journal of Philosophical Studies* 19:319–22.

Kant, Immanuel. 1999. *Critique of Pure Reason*, translated by Paul Guyer and Allen W. Wood. New York: Cambridge University Press.

McDowell, John. 1996. *Mind and World*, 2nd ed. Cambridge, MA: Harvard University Press.

McDowell, John. 2002. "Responses." In *Reading McDowell: On Mind and World*, edited by Nicholas H. Smith, 269–305. New York: Routledge.

Melnick, Arthur. 1985. "Kant's Theory of Space as a Form of Intuition." In *The Philosophy of Immanuel Kant*, edited by Richard Kennington, 39–56. Washington, DC: Catholic University of America Press, 1985.

Melnick, Arthur. 2004. "The Consistency of Kant's Theory of Space and Time." In *Themes in Kant's Metaphysics and Ethics*, 3–20. Washington, DC: Catholic University of America Press.

Peirce, Charles Sanders. 1935. *The Collected Papers of Charles Sanders Peirce*, vols. 1–6, edited by Charles Hartshorne and Paul Weiss. Cambridge, MA: Harvard University Press.

Proudfoot, Wayne. 1985. *Religious Experience*. Berkeley: University of California Press.

Proudfoot, Wayne. 2010. "Immediacy and Intentionality in the Feeling of Absolute Dependence." In *Schleiermacher, the Study of Religion, and the Future of Theology: A Transatlantic Dialogue*, edited by Brent Sockness and Wilhelm Gräb, 27–37. Berlin: Walter de Gruyter.

Quine, W. V. 1969. "Epistemology Naturalized." In *Ontological Relativity and Other Essays*, 69–80. New York: Columbia University Press.

Schleiermacher, Friedrich. 1958. *On Religion: Speeches to its Cultured Despisers*. Translated by John Oman. New York: Harper.

Schleiermacher, Friedrich. 1984. *Kritische Gesamtausgabe I Schriften und Entwürfe Band 2: Schriften aus der Berliner Zeit 1796–1799*. Edited by Günter Meckenstock. Berlin: Walter de Gruyter.

Schleiermacher, Friedrich. 1995. *Kritische Gesamtausgabe. Schriften und Entwürfe I/12: Über die Religion (2.-)4. Auflage. Monologen (2.-)4*. Edited by Günter Meckenstock. Berlin: Walter de Gruyter.

Schleiermacher, Friedrich. 1996. *On Religion: Speeches to Its Cultured Despisers*, 2nd ed. Translated by Richard Crouter. New York: Cambridge University Press.

Schleiermacher, Friedrich. 2003. *Der christliche Glaube nach den Grundsätzen der evangelischen Kirche im Zusammenhange dargestellt*, 2. Auflage (1830/31). Edited by Rolf Schäfer. Berlin: Walter de Gruyter.

Schleiermacher, Friedrich. 2016. *The Christian Faith*, 2nd ed. Translated by Terrence N. Tice, Catherine L. Kelsey, and Edwina Lawler. Louisville, KY: Westminster John Knox.

Thompson, Manley. 1983. "Things in Themselves." *Proceedings and Addresses of the American Philosophical Association* 57:33–49.

Thompson, Manley. 1992. "Singular Terms and Intuitions in Kant's Epistemology." In *Kant's Philosophy of Mathematics: Modern Essays*, edited by D. J. Posey, 81–107. Dordrecht: Kluwer.

Titans, Normunds. 2006. *Overcoming Metaphysics as a Problem in the History of Philosophy: The Contribution of Friedrich Schleiermacher*. Lewiston, NY: Edwin Mellen.

Vial, Theodore. 2010. "*Anschauung* and Intuition, Again (Or, 'We Remain Bound to the Earth')." In *Schleiermacher, the Study of Religion, and the Future of Theology: A Transatlantic Dialogue*, edited by Brent Sockness and Wilhelm Gräb, 40–50. Berlin: Walter de Gruyter.

# IO

# The Oracle and the Inner Teacher

*Piecemeal Naturalism*

JAMES WETZEL

*"You can't hear God speak to someone else, you can hear him only if you are being addressed."—That is a grammatical remark.*

—Ludwig Wittgenstein, *Zettel* (717)

I need to begin by acknowledging a debt. The message has sunk in. I am no longer tempted, having studied in my formative years with Wayne Proudfoot, a philosopher of great patience and discretion, to travel down the rabbit hole of special experience and seek there the key to the mystery of human separateness, or the difference that makes one person a mystic and another a skeptic. And the skeptic and the mystic can, of course, be the same person at different times, or even different aspects of the same person at a single time. If we stand opaque to one another and to ourselves, on different sides of an apparent divide of reverences, there is no substitute for having to study the language of self-description that we have yet, and may never yet, come to hold as our own. This is a matter of living with those we want to know, and they with us, and certainly we can live with the dead as well as the living, as anyone with a genealogy and a sense of time will eventually come to realize. In any pragmatics of religious inquiry, broadly construed, we fold the claims of special revelation into an investigation of how other people are choosing or refusing to describe themselves and their experience. Such an investigation has as much potential to disorient us and resettle our certainties as it does to confirm our science, and therein lies a good part of its value.

On a more narrow construal of what religious inquiry is—or perhaps I should say, here, "inquiry into religion"—the object can be either to test the limits of naturalism, limits not simply of our current science but also of our very concept of a science, or to bring putative claims about supernatural objects or states of consciousness squarely within the domain of naturalistic explanation. I think we are in murky territory here, and while I believe that a pragmatics of inquiry into religion need not, and should not, presuppose the truth of naturalism (whatever that may turn out to be), I am suspicious of our intellectual culture's over-fascination with the issue.

In this chapter, I offer three reflections that collectively aim to ease whatever compunction we may feel about being less than a consistent naturalist or less than the fiercest of naturalism's antagonists. In the first reflection, I treat naturalism as a chastened reverence—a post-tragic realism—rather than as a fully comprehensive framework of inquiry. In the second, I bring this reverence into conversation with the reverence that is often taken to be its clear alternative. In the last section, a short coda, I add an element of confession.

## ABANDONED SON

When the young Oedipus, stung by the suggestion that he is a *plastos* (πλαστός, a fake), goes looking for reassurance at Delphi, we already know that matters are not going to turn out well for him. He is, for us, as much a complex as a character, a cipher for the dark forces of desire that bind the psyche from within. Oedipus the character wants to know whether he is truly his father's son, and he clings myopically to one framework, the simplest one, for couching the answer: either he is the son and rightful heir of Polybos, king of Corinth, or he is some lowborn nobody, a common son of fortune (τύχη).

As it turns out, the Pythia at Delphi will speak more to the complex than to the character and his cherished ambitions. She tells Oedipus that he is fated to replace his father, wed his mother, and bring into the world children the sight of whom no one such as he will be able to bear. In other words, he is indeed his father's son, albeit not as he imagines. He is like any patriarch's true heir. He lacks a good, working sense of the natural forces that keep sons from becoming their fathers and that offer them sane ways of reconnecting with their mothers.

Oedipus, in his ignorance, assumes that the Oracle has changed the subject. She is telling him secrets about what he may do, if he does not act quickly and decisively, to Polybos, the man he presumes is his father. Apparently, Oedipus no longer needs the Oracle to check his presumption. He just needs to get out of town:

> After I heard all this, I fled Corinth,
> measuring my progress by the stars, searching for a place
> where I would never see those words, those dreadful predictions
> come true. And on my way
> I came to the place where you say King Laios was murdered.
>
> (Sophocles 1978, 59)

It is the older Oedipus, having already made the dreadful predictions come true, who speaks here. He cannot avoid his fate because he confronts it, unbeknownst to him, in retrospect. There is nothing more for this Oedipus to do, fate-wise, than to add new awareness to old deeds: the man he kills on the road from Corinth to Thebes proves to have been Laios, his father, and the widowed queen he wins, having solved the riddle of the Sphinx, is Jocasta, his mother. When Oedipus sees what he has unknowingly done, years after the doing, he blinds himself with Jocasta's brooch pins and claims this as his one unfated act. Blame his life's agonies on the god Apollo, but not the self-blinding. That, Oedipus insists, he did all on his own: "I, nobody else, *I*, I raised these two hands of mine, held them above my head, and plunged them down; I stabbed out these eyes" (85).

Oedipus seems not to realize that he has preempted himself. His defiant use of brooch pins falls within the legacy of a prior self-blinding, one that casts its long shadow forward. He first blinds himself at Delphi, where as a young man he ignores a call to self-knowledge and turns a god's offering into a disturbing piece of news. Even if Apollo, the oracular god of illumination, is, as Oedipus suggests, responsible for his subsequent agonies, if not his self-blinding, we would still have to add this qualification: that the aim of an illuminating god is to illumine and not to cause suffering. The suffering that Oedipus endures has as much to do with his self-blinding as with some inscrutable power of light.

While I doubt whether the impulse to sort out fate from freely willed human folly helps us much to understand Sophoclean tragedy, I concede that the impulse, when reading Sophocles, is hard to resist. Bernard Williams, in the part of his Sather lectures that finds him discussing "supernatural necessity," does not resist the impulse, but it remains clear to him from the start where it leads: to nothing illuminating (Williams 1993, chap. 6, especially 130–31). "Let us take the large step," invites Williams, "of wrenching the Oedipus story out of myth and tragedy and asking questions about it as though it were an item of *faits divers* (questions that, needless to say, it would be absurd to ask about the play)" (142).

In keeping with his invitation, consider a couple of scenarios. One: When Laios is told that his infant son is going to grow up to kill his father and marry his mother, he refuses to believe this and keeps Oedipus at home. The boy grows up to live out a grotesque Oedipal fantasy. This is less tragedy than farce, but there it is. Two: Return now to the exiled Oedipus, stirred by the question of his origins. This time the Delphic oracle is given to explication. Oedipus is told that he is destined to kill his father and wed his mother, but also that Laios of Thebes and not Polybos of Corinth is his natural father. When he researches the issue of how he has come to live in Corinth, with pierced heels, he learns of his father's unnatural cruelty and plots a murderous revenge. The part that has him fathering his mother's children I will here gladly leave to someone else's imagination.

There are myriad imaginings that slip Oedipus back into his Oedipal fate. It is also possible to imagine, in a slightly different key, how the various ways in which Oedipus would have been kept from his fate are themselves prevented. The overall impression is the same. The supernatural agent—in some ways personal (Apollo), in some ways not (fate)—has no particular means to get to a particular end. One way or another, Oedipus will be made to act, well, Oedipally; it does not matter how.

But what does this way of thinking about supernatural agency really tell us? That supernatural agents are essentially miraculous technicians, never lacking the means for doing what they want to do? How much credit do we want to give our imaginations here? We seem to be on the verge of imagining an absolute cause, unconstrained by any context of application, a creativity ex nihilo. Williams (1993, 145) himself opts for a more down-to-earth point of view: "The special feature of supernatural necessity," he writes, "is that there is nothing relevant to be said about the ways in which things might have gone differently—either about other routes by which the inevitable outcome might still have come about or about routes which *if* they had been taken (though inevitably they were not), the outcome would have been prevented."

Where we might be tempted to imagine an absolute cause, Williams sees a literary artifact. There was never any real illumination to be gained from moving Oedipus from drama to history and subjecting his fated life to counterfactual speculation. The exercise shows us only how ridiculous the gods become when they are made to play the role of natural causes. Supernatural necessity, for Williams, has to remain fictional if it is to remain what it essentially is: an artful reminder, if done well, of the element of inscrutability in historical consciousness. When the fiction is confused with the history it is meant (always somewhat ironically) to represent, we are more apt to get the *bad* fiction of a supersensible intelligibility that makes everything make perfect sense, albeit never to finite minds. And Williams clearly does not want to buy into that one.

For the remainder of what follows, I will be following Williams in the thought that supernaturalism is, from our human point view, more naturally bound to a narrative imagination than to our penchant, in distracted moments, for positing an unsituated cause, forever eluding representation (the God behind the curtain). I say "from our human point of view" as if to imply that there is some other point of view, radically foreign to the evolution of our own, that would better explain ourselves to us, if only we could, *per impossibile*, inhabit it. I don't deny the truth of this thought, but only because I can't make it out well enough to assess its possibility. When I bother to speak about the humanness of our human point of view, I am not trying to draw a line in what would be, as far as I can tell, metaphysical sand; I am simply underscoring the fact that talk of things beyond nature and natural understanding has much, if not everything, to do with the connections human beings feel they have with one another—or fail to. In terms beholden to Ludwig Wittgenstein, I am hoping to exchange a fascination for the quasi-scientific regulation of supernaturalism (theoretically permissible or not) for something more "grammatical" (see *Zettel* 717, quoted earlier). I want to look at the way a way of talking about the divine—as, say, being accessible to one individual but not another—can bring out latent possibilities for both alienation and new insight in an evolving form of life.

All of this, no doubt, sounds very down-to-earth; it sounds like I am rejecting metaphysical speculation and all of her bastard children and embracing a more naturalistic approach to religious phenomena. But I am not so down-to-earth, and my naturalism, such as it is, is more pragmatic than principled. And so, before I venture into a lesson in philosophical grammar, in this case a lesson in divine illumination, I should sketch in some detail where I diverge from Williams, whose naturalism does seem more principled than my own. Otherwise, my own claim to naturalism cannot help but be misleading.

At the end of his great study of the ancient Greeks, the overall effect of which is to make fifth-century tragedians into better interlocutors for us, Williams (1993, 166) describes the knowingness that we, who live "not only beyond Christianity, but beyond its Kantian and Hegelian legacies," bring to our side of the conversation: "We know that the world was not made for us, or we for the world, that our history tells no purposive story, and that there is no position outside the world or outside history from which we might hope to authenticate our activities." Wayne Proudfoot, an avid of reader of Williams, finds in this sentiment an apt characterization of what a naturalist fundamentally believes—or, in this case, knows: that it is up to us, the accidental students of our mortal condition, to give or deny the world we share a meaning; there is no imposition of meaning that comes from elsewhere.[1] I find, in my own case, that I am able to affirm the pragmatism that goes along with a certain kind of tragic wisdom, the sort that Williams is expressing, but I am more reluctant than either Proudfoot or Williams is to move from tragedy to naturalism.

Let me explain. When we remove Oedipus from the context of Sophoclean drama and proceed to entertain alternative scenarios of his fatedness, Williams wants us first to notice that we are progressively evacuating supernatural agency, which has here become too plastic in its operation to be meaningfully personified, of all meaningful content. But there is a profounder point that he wants to make. It is not as if supernatural agency has had an abundance of content to begin with, in the context where the anthropomorphic gods of Homer have largely ceded their authority to murkier, more impersonal divinities, like Delphi's Apollo. For Williams (1993, 151), Sophocles is a great dramatist precisely because he is so deft at concealing the emptiness of agency that is all "purpose and power" and no skin and bones, nothing, that is, that is truly situated. The haunting effect is to make human inscrutability seem like a divine mystery.

But what for ancients is a tease of inaccessible wisdom is for moderns, living after the boon days of moral orders, a mere fact of finitude. We don't need a divine oracle to tell us that our ethical relations to the world and to one another are less than fully transparent; we also no longer expect full transparency to be other than dehumanizing. Our gods haven't failed us; we have just lived and suffered long enough to begin to take in the sobering, but not essentially tragic, facts of our situation. We are Oedipus on the couch, far from Mount Kithairon, and we have traveled, at not inconsiderable cost, all the way from tragic consolation to post-tragic realism. "I am not suggesting," cautions Williams (1993, 166), "that we should feel sorry for ourselves because we are not Homeric or tragic or Periclean people."

I resist this post-tragic realism, not because I hope to linger with Oedipus on Kithairon (it is indeed too late for that) but because this kind of realism is blind to what compels Oedipus to want to return there and sort out the meaning of his suffering. For the post-tragic realist, there is nothing to sort out. Sophocles has been drawing dread and promise out of the empty well of a supernatural cause—really a sophist's trick. But I think of Sophocles differently. His gift is not for concealment but for discretion. He discerns the fineness of the difference between self-deception and seeking to know. Oedipus goes to Delphi to solve the riddle of himself, but when he encounters a further riddle, he retreats to a familiar self-image and seeks his sanctuary there. He flees the god.

The Oedipus who lives to suffer the consequences is not especially interested in the workings of divine power. He senses that he has done as much to cause his own suffering as the god has. If there are agonies that reach beyond his self-inflicted blindness, then he will take them as birth pangs of a new aware-ness. He will go back to sacred Kithairon, once the place of his abandonment, and see. The god is offering him a good that is, from his current point of view, inscrutable. Perhaps Oedipus is himself that good. The prospect keeps him from suicide and gives him hope of real self-knowledge. Not everyone, of course, will want to follow him into this possibility. The Chorus Leader looks down at the broken, bleeding, eyeless man and counsels suicide: "How can I say that what you did was right? Better to be dead than live blind" (Sophocles 1978, 86). Ironi-cally, Oedipus is in a position to agree.

There are many goods that are good because we posit them to be such. If, as one version of naturalism would have it, the posits are all the goods there are, then human beings, it seems to me, would have an essentially technological relation to their values. There is no end here, nothing of value, apart from the successful application of a means to an end. It takes more than a passing fancy to posit a good; it requires an intentionally directed, often collaborative, activity of mate-rialization. Say that I value my daughter's education. I will be positing the good of that, and thus finding that good in the world I help create, as I work to keep my daughter in a demanding but also nurturing school. And there would be no such school for her were no one but me positing the education of a child as a good of great value.

Again, many goods are good because we collectively posit them to be such, but I still see no reason to think that the posits are all the goods there are. Often a materialization does not go so well. Take the case of my daughter's education. Sup-pose that I run out of money and family allies, or that my daughter hates school, or that I find that I just lack the resolve to prioritize her schooling. Does it clearly follow that I do not value my daughter's education or, even worse, that I do not love her?

My awareness that I am not always in a transparent or easily realized relation-ship to my own values is precisely what encourages the thought in me that I am sometimes relating *to* a value. When I relate to it, the value seems, in some way, independent of my will to posit its existence. And while I readily concede how difficult it has been for theorists of value to specify what manner of independence this might be, a murky objectivity is still a better hypothesis than a creation ex nihilo. Values, to be sure, are not straightforwardly material objects, like food and medicine, but they admit of some kind of materialization or no one would ever be tempted to think of food and medicine as goods.

Akeel Bilgrami, a theorist with a gift for parsing, renders values as properties that inhere in the world and convey to an agent (whose power of agency is first and foremost *responsive*) the world's normative demands.[2] That is certainly not your average naturalism speaking. "To say values are properties in the world (including nature)," Bilgrami (2010, 29) notes, "is to make the world (including nature) not comprehensively surveyable by the methods of natural science." Bilgrami is prepared to accede to the antinaturalism of his view of values, but his antinaturalism, he insists (by way of another ingenious parsing), is not unscientific. Science still rules in its own domain.

In the story that tells us how thinking types came to accommodate themselves to the death of God—or, more prosaically, to the death of explanatory theism—where Williams puts post-tragic realism, Bilgrami is more inclined to speak of a secular version of enchantment (48). The difference between the two notions turns on how reasonably the world itself may be imagined, in the intimacy of its being, to resist being reduced in value to an object of use. I myself prefer the notion of a *piecemeal naturalism*. The term has as its complement the *piecemeal supernaturalism* that William James (2004, 445) both coins and favors in his postscript to *The Varieties of Religious Experience*: "It admits miracles and providential leadings, and finds no intellectual difficulty in mixing the ideal and the real worlds together by interpolating influences from the ideal region among the forces that causally determine the real world's details."

Since I have not stopped following Williams in the thought that supernatural agents are better suited to stories than to theories, I don't hold out much hope for the intelligibility of a causal intervention from outside "the real world." Piecemeal naturalism cedes the domain of causes to nature, but without making too much of causes. Quite naturally, we speak of *goodness* as falling within the causal order and as something we can, in piecemeal ways, effect. There is still a goodness that we don't make good and that does not make us good, and yet without it there would be no meaningful talk of goodness or its lack. I don't mean to imply here the existence of a supergood, some unitary and (from our point of view) inscrutable end, in contrast to which all other goods are a mere means. If there were such a good, it would be the posit of a perfectly tyrannical but still quite natural being, dedicated to the business of *making* us good. We have no reason to believe that such a being exists.

The best way to be a piecemeal naturalist is to be a pragmatist. Give up on the world-behind-the-world fantasy, at least when it comes to knowing, and accept that the world is not designed to make you good or to smooth out the wrinkles in your soul. You are a working knower, required to bring some of your own materials—your values, your interests, your history—to a work in progress. You are also the work in progress, liable to be worked on, in ways good and bad, by what is around you. You emerge and reemerge an altered knower, sometimes the worse for wear, sometimes more supple. There is no end to this, other than by willful ignorance or death.

My rather unsentimental characterization of pragmatism is superficially similar to the knowingness that Williams lays out at the end of *Shame and Necessity*. But where Williams sees a world naturally devoid of purpose, I wrestle with the inscrutability of the good. I am less in a position than Williams is, given the divergence in our points of view, to leave tragedy to the Greeks. But my piecemeal naturalism is not essentially tragic. It is not particularly secular, either. I illustrate both points in the lesson that follows.

## BELOVED SON

When I claim that there is a goodness that lies beyond our human capabilities to make things good or become good ourselves, I am aware that I am apt to be sounding as gnomic as the Delphic oracle itself, and with less excuse. But I am not deriving my sense of the sublime good from any source more basic than my own attempt, though one hardly unique to me, to share a life with others. I can speak intelligibly of this goodness, which is never *just* a function of my sociability or anyone else's, in the way that I can speak intelligibly of the grammar that governs my possibilities of sense-making. In both cases, I have no choice but to make use of the very thing I am attempting to explicate, and that use, seen in a certain kind of light, is the explication. The qualification about light is important. Not all uses of language are revelatory of what grammar is, even as grammar, if only in some mangled or loosely implied form, is always operative in language use. What is true of language is all the more true of the good. Attempts to be good or make good mostly fail, sometimes spectacularly, to be revealing of what goodness is. (Ask Oedipus, or Adam.) But it does not follow that there is a goodness that can be revealed apart from those attempts.

Imagine a father–son relationship better than the wounding one that Laios and Oedipus suffer through, mostly as total strangers to one another. A great leap forward in time and imagination takes us to Augustine, the West's premier theologian of the Fall, and Adeodatus, his beloved son. Adeodatus is the child of his father's tumultuous passion for a woman he famously leaves unnamed.[3] Augustine will speak of Adeodatus—whose name means "God given"—as born of his father's sin (*natum carnaliter de peccato meo*), but he is unreservedly admiring of his son's precocious intellect and refined sensibilities. In the dialogue *De magistro* (The

Teacher), an exchange between father and son on the possibility of shared under-standing, the gifts that Augustine admires in Adeodatus are much in evidence. Augustine insists that, though he is the author of the dialogue (written circa 389), he is not the author of his son's voice. He reassures us of this in the passage of the *Confessions* (9.6.14) where he is marking the death of his son, at seventeen, less than a year after the remarkable exchange that would come to serve as the boy's memo-rial: "My memory of him," Augustine eulogizes, "is more than untroubled; I fear nothing from his boyhood or adolescence, nothing at all for that man."[4]

For my purposes, it is not necessary to assume that *De magistro* is an actual transcription of a conversation between Augustine and Adeodatus. The assump-tion would, in any case, do nothing to help us understand what the dialogue is driving at. Augustine starts things off with the question "What is your sense of what we want to do when we speak?" The likely answer, "to communicate," Adeodatus parses into two parts: "to teach" (*docere*), which here means, very basically, to inform, and "to learn" (*discere*), to be informed (*De magistro* 1.1).[5] Augustine then engages in the rather strange tactic of arguing at length for a conclusion he is quite convinced is false, the inverse, in fact, of what is true. (It is strange mainly because he is insistent that their conversation, as far as he is concerned, is no game of rhetoric but a preparation for blessedness.)[6] Augustine presses Adeodatus to concede that speaking is all about the "teaching" part of communication—the business of making one's meaning perfectly conveyable to someone else. The "learning" part, the receptivity to meaning, is not a proper part of speaking at all.

On this view of language use, we ask questions not to be informed but to inform others of what we want from them in the way of information. That is certainly a tight squeeze of a distinction. When Adeodatus tries it on for size, he seems uncomfortable with the fit, but he trusts his father. There must be some point to all this bending over backwards to embrace an absolutist point of view. Augustine then proceeds to "teach" Adeodatus that no one ever teaches anyone anything. The attempt to teach, to inform, is for embodied beings always an act of signification—the use of a sign, often a word, to convey a meaning—and successful signification is a movement from meaning to sign, not sign to meaning.

To use Augustine's example: I read in the book of Daniel that when three pious young men of Israel are thrown into King Nebuchadnezzar's furnace, they are still wearing their *sarabarae*. I am at a loss as to what a *sarabara* is, until someone better versed in the *Vetus Latina* (Old Latin Bible) tells me that it refers to a kind of headgear or covering.[7] But the translation of one form of signage to another only helps, of course, if I already know what a "head" is and what a "covering" is from my prior sense of the things that can come up for signification. There is an evident, albeit not uncontroversial, moral that Augustine wants to draw from this kind of example: "that a sign is learned more from its object than an object is from its sign" (*De magistro* 10.33).

But he does not leave the moral there, where sense and reference call for some sorting. He pushes on to the mysterious inner teacher who illuminates his mind directly, without mediation from signs, and who invests his thinking with significance. Augustine has no doubt that the inner teacher is doing the same for Adeodatus and all the other way stations of God's image—or this, at least, is what he is learning. The work of the inner teacher, in and between us, is what the *De magistro* exchange has been driving at.

Augustine's identification of the inner teacher as Christ, "the unending wisdom and changeless virtue of God" (11.38), is not likely to diminish the impression of his more naturalistically inclined readers that he has lapsed into religious enthusiasm (again). It can seem as if he is overreacting in *De magistro* to the limitations of any attempt to secure a meaning ostensively. Again, to use one of Augustine's examples, suppose I want to know what *walking* means while you and I are walking together. You speed up your gait in an effort to showcase your act of walking, and I end up thinking that *walking* means "hurrying" (3.6). It is possible to imagine all kinds of cases where the desire to fix a meaning is frustrated by an unintended or unforeseen reading of the intended fix. In the *Philosophical Investigations*, which opens with a passage from the *Confessions* (1.8.13) on language learning, Wittgenstein is especially good at conjuring up such interpretive possibilities and using them to deflate an unnaturally sublimed logic.

But of course it does not follow from latent possibilities and the indeterminacy of ostension that language learning never takes place. Maybe when you speed up, I get what you are getting at; you are trying to indicate, through a bit of dramatic exaggeration, what *walking* means. Or perhaps you just stop the two of us, signal me not to budge, and then, while pointing at your legs, begin to walk on your own (*De magistro* 4.7). Or perhaps just forget about this fanciful hypothetical. I know what *walking* means. So do you. Only small children (for the most part) need to be introduced to walking and what it means (and usually it is a wondrous introduction). In *De magistro*, Augustine is making himself understood to his grown son in all kinds of ways. He doesn't need to avail himself of a supernatural means of communicating. And even if he thought he did, there would be no particular way for this means to work (recall Williams on "supernatural necessity"); Augustine would soon be finding himself in the ad hoc business of having to sanctify apparent agreement.

A closer reading of *De magistro* suggests that Augustine has little interest in the skeptical implications of teaching that has to make use, as all teaching does at root, of ostensive definition. The implication that lends itself to the most drama is the one that relativizes understanding: while it may look as if we can define what many words mean simply by pointing (wordlessly) to their referents, how would we ever really know, in these baptisms of meaning, that all parties have the same referents in mind? Perhaps it is only a matter of time before our apparent consensus about what things mean unravels and we become refugees of Babel.

Augustine counsels Adeodatus not to "fall into fear and loathing of reason" when a good argument renders doubtful the things he has been prone to accept without question and "wrenches them from his hands" (*De magistro* 10.31). But is this what has happened? Has an argument come along in *De magistro* to discredit the reliability of ostensive definition and, by extension, the agreement that makes meaningful discourse possible? Augustine seems confident that it has not. He recounts to Adeodatus, as if this would obviously settle the matter, the hypothetical case of a bird catcher who shows a curious onlooker, unfamiliar with the craft, how to catch a bird. Our bird catcher doesn't utter a single word; he just gets to work with his reeds, his rod, and his hawk. Augustine (10.32) invites Adeodatus to confirm the appropriate moral: "Hasn't this man taught the onlooker what he desired to know, not by using a sign but by way of the thing itself?"

Adeodatus hesitates. There was, after all, that case about the walking and the hurrying. Why think that the art of bird catching, which is a more complex activity than an afternoon walk, can be captured in a single display? Augustine's answer basically comes to this: let's just assume that it can. Imagine that the imagined observer of the bird catcher's art is a quick study. When Adeodatus points out that this kind of stipulation can just as readily be applied to other cases as well, like that of the walking demo, Augustine is only too happy to agree. "For the matter at hand," he tells Adeodatus, "it is enough that some people can be taught some things, even if not all, without use of a sign" (10.32). In other words, it is not the occasional failure of an ostensive definition that is going to move Augustine to invoke Christ, the inner teacher, and leave all the real teaching to him.

In the essay that has done more than any other to bring *De magistro* to the attention of contemporary analytic, naturalistically minded philosophers, Miles Burnyeat (1999) brings Wittgenstein and Augustine into a tighter affinity and tries to resolve the puzzle in Augustine of how mimetic teachers, like the bird catcher, can be in the same conceptual space as Christ, whose rights to teaching are exclusive.[8] Most of Burnyeat's essay is on Augustine; Wittgenstein is there largely to lend contemporary gravitas to a distinctively ancient understanding of

THE ORACLE AND THE INNER TEACHER

*understanding*, one that Augustine takes over from Plato and gives a theological twist. Since this mode of understanding, as Burnyeat conceives of it, makes much of irreducibly first-person insight and can't seem to get enough of ocular metaphors for knowing, it is going to need some added heft before it can make its way back into an intellectual culture that has come to prize objectivity and prefers logic to inner light. As if to reassure modern types, who probably aren't reading nearly as much history of philosophy as Burnyeat is, Burnyeat ends his essay with a speculation about why Wittgenstein removes the confession from *Confessions* 1.8.13: "To leave out God and the Platonic mind for the beginning of the *Philosophical Investigations*," he writes, "was to accept Augustine's problem as his own and to declare that it must now be solved in naturalistic, purely human terms" (Burnyeat 1999, 300).

It is far from clear what Augustine's problem is in *De magistro*. He basically wants to know, from the outset, what the point is of having a conversation with his son. That is an odd conversation starter, to be sure. It certainly wouldn't work for Laios and Oedipus, or for any father and son whose relationship is mostly one of distrust. And then comes Augustine's dogged insistence on a notion of teaching that he will soon concede is a misconception of what we humans do when we speak. Is there a kind of confession here in Augustine's striking turnabout? Is his problem that he often wants to forget what true teaching is and that this forgetfulness tends to rob even his closest conversations of their point? We would know better, of course, if we knew more of what motivates him to call upon the inner teacher, whose manner of teaching (if *manner* is even the right word here) no human is able to emulate. But here is where the naturalists, hoping to excise this part, tend to get sidetracked.

In his reading of *De magistro*, Burnyeat has very little to say about the inner teacher. Mostly he develops the notion that Augustine, like Plato before him, thinks of understanding as both synoptic and essentially tied to a first-person perspective. I will attempt an illustration of this that is not Burnyeat's. Imagine Augustine and Adeodatus in the midst of a difficult conversation. The topic is whether it was good thing for Augustine to have sent the boy's mother away, effectively divorcing her, when Adeodatus was about fourteen. Certainly it was a painful thing for Augustine to do. In the *Confessions* (9.15.25), he speaks of having his heart bloodied (*trahebat sanguinem*) when she was torn from his side. The passage also manages to disguise the uncomfortable truth that it was Augustine himself who was doing the tearing. At the time, he felt the need for a marriage more upwardly bound than the one that could be had with the low-born mother of his only child. She left Augustine at his request, vowing never to be with another man.

In the conversation I am asking you to imagine, Adeodatus has become the sensitive young intellect of his father's affection, and Augustine is a contemplative, no longer looking to climb the social ladder. The two men are anxious to understand each other; they each have had their separate experience of what their lives together, without her, have been like. To the extent that understanding is essentially a first-person affair, nothing that either can say to the other necessitates mutual understanding. The gap between being on the inside of an experience and being without is categorical, and while understanding across the gap remains possible and even common, it is never entirely explicable. So let's just stipulate that, in this case, Augustine and Adeodatus come to a mutual understanding.

But now father and son will want to do more than understand the meaning of each other's words. They will want to know the truth of their situation, the actual good of it. For this, they will need to have what Burnyeat (1999, 299) calls "the complete synoptic vision that embraces all partial understandings." This is the vision that would allow them to see how one partial good relates to another and how all partial goods relate perfectly to the good itself. Short of having this sublime synopsis of things, Augustine and Adeodatus can more or less understand each other, but in the fullest sense of the word, they cannot *understand*. This fulsome sense of understanding is the ancient view that Burnyeat attributes to Plato and Augustine and gives credit to Wittgenstein for reviving, albeit in "naturalistic, purely human terms." Plato, I gather, has too disembodied a notion of a knowing mind (*the* knowing mind) to be naturalistic. Augustine ventures even further into supernaturalism when he insists on construing the Platonic mind as a divine agent. His creator God shines the eternal light of the synopsis into the darkened minds of his synopsized creatures and somehow relieves their perspectives of their partiality: "Hence the dictum," surmises Burnyeat, "that Christ is the only Teacher, the one source of illumination." Other purveyors of teaching—bird catchers, bishops, and boys of great learning—teach wholly out of borrowed light; they all do the inner teacher's bidding.

That is really all Burnyeat has to say about the inner teacher in *De magistro*. If he is right, then Augustine's modification of Platonism is to wed the notion of supernatural necessity, or fate, to having a transcendent perspective: many are called to know and understand, but few are chosen (only one, in fact, and he is already God). We are back to the murky metaphysics that prompts Williams to trade in the arbitrary will of an oracular god for the natural opacities of historical existence. But I see no reason for thinking that Augustine's invocation of the inner teacher has anything to do with a hankering after synopsis. If anything, Augustine is hoping to be free of that particular idol of knowledge. Adeodatus hits the right notes about the inner teacher at the dialogue's end: this teacher, which he also refers to as "that secret oracle" (*secretum illud oraculum*), teaches him that words are the occasion but not the cause of learning and that learning, thus freed from manipulation and fate, is a matter of giving and receiving love (*De magistro* 14.46).

It matters to our understanding of *De magistro* that Augustine and Adeodatus are not Laios and Oedipus; it matters that the two of them, unlike their tragic shadows, wish for each other's good. They wish this more than they wish to be one. Let's return to Augustine's insistence in the *Confessions* that Adeodatus speaks in *De magistro* in his own voice. There is perhaps a bit of incidental vanity here. Augustine is assuring us that he is not the only person in the world with the gift of intellectual brilliance. But more fundamentally, I think, he is taking delight in his son's distinctiveness and lending his memory to it. Augustine will always want to recall the goodness that was never his to determine—or corrupt. But the most fundamental thing of all for him may well be that God's gift, or what the name Adeodatus can be taken to signify, is all there is to the good.

Here we need to be less anxious to settle accounts with nature than is the case with many pious naturalists. Augustine's God is not a supernatural cause. And a supernatural *cause*, as far as I can make it out, is not very supernatural. It is best cast as the tyrannical power to synopsize parts and fit them wholly within one, jealously singular perspective on the good—a freak of nature, if there ever were one. Augustine's inner teacher is not even one with himself. Christ is God's eternal wisdom, the second person of the Trinity, but also Jesus of Nazareth, born of a woman. The two are not the same, except for the love that flows between them—and really not even then.

And so it goes with Augustine and his son Adeodatus, whose name signifies both the beloved son and all there is to the good. The temptation in reading Augustine (I tend to think of it as the naturalist's temptation) is to assume that all of Augustine's beloveds lose out in the end to the original goodness that has no further use for them but use. This is to bring to his God a mind obsessed with willpower and ways to cash in on goodness. But Augustine does not find it a liability that his words cannot command his love, and he does not expect his God to be a more effective tyrant than he is. His inner teacher keeps reminding him that his primary relationship to goodness is inscrutable and so not fundamentally one of use. It is a reminder as natural as it is strange: a father loves his son beyond reckoning.

## A SHORT CODA: *ELOI, ELOI, LAMA SABACHTHANI?*

Augustine's father was nowhere near as bad to him as Laios was to Oedipus. There was no mutilation, no binding, no abandonment. But the portrait of his earthly father that Augustine gives us in the *Confessions* is still far from uniformly endearing. We get a Patricius who loved his son for what his son's natural gifts—his skill with words, his lust for life—could bring to Patricius: greater wealth and grandsons, both common vehicles of a patriarch's self-aggrandizement. Augustine is especially sensitive to, and resentful of, his father's treatment of his mother. Patricius drank to excess and had sex with other women; he also had a temper. Were it not for his mother's patient resolve to wait out his anger and to answer his infidelities with only a show of quiet dignity, she no doubt would have been subjected to the beatings that the other women in her town, with similarly intemperate husbands, were enduring.

When Augustine marks the death of Patricius, not far into the *Confessions* narrative, he has no more than a parenthetical phrase to spare: "with my father having died (*defuncto patre*) two years earlier" (3.4.7). In the surrounding sentence, into which this ablative absolute has been unceremoniously inserted (or perhaps buried), Augustine has been describing his budding adolescent interest in philosophy, prompted by his reading of Cicero's *Hortensius*; it is the beginning of his long turn away from the ambitions his father had set for him. When he marks the death of Monica, at the end of the *Confessions* narrative (the stretch of time that has taken him from infancy to his mother's death), he is on the inside of a grief that is thoroughly transforming—and breaking—his heart.

In Augustine's mind, his mother's death is closely associated with the ecstatic experience that the two of them enter into together at Ostia.[9] Mother and son have been living the past several years in Italy, along with Adeodatus, and now they are all on their way back home to Africa. Ostia, near Rome, is their port of departure. While waiting to depart, Augustine and Monica settle into the quiet of their temporary abode and look out upon its garden. They begin to speak intimately of the life of the saints, not in time, among still-alienated creatures, but at the still point of eternal beginning. They soon imagine themselves transported to the summit of being that extends beyond even the mind's reach, and there they are able, somehow without losing awareness of each other, to encounter changeless Wisdom apart from the mediation of signs. Perhaps they get a small taste of the love that lies beyond and before the possibility of misreading.

It doesn't last, whatever it is that they experience. They soon return to familiar earth, albeit with the feeling that they have had to leave a part of themselves—the first fruits of spirit (*primitias spiritus*)—in that heaven of heavens. Five days or so later, Monica lapses into a delirium and dies of fever. In a moment of lucidity before the end, she sees Augustine's horrified look, knows that she is going to die, and implores him not to carry her body back to Africa. She is well beyond the desire, once dear to her, to be buried next to her husband, Patricius, in a marital grave.

When I think of the Ostia ecstasy and its untidy implications for a post-tragic realism (or naturalism, by another name), I am put in mind again of the piecemeal supernaturalism that William James was abashedly peddling to his Gifford auditors, many of whom would have been most at home with impersonality, spiritual or otherwise, as a bottom line. For James, Augustine is a venerable witness to the intrusive genius that bursts unbidden into the human scene and, for a time, utterly suspends the priorities of the natural order, where the positing of goods is the normal business of the day. There is nothing further to posit when the day is God's; eternity is the Sabbath of all things. And yet time continues.

When Monica returns to her senses and finds herself, once again, a creature of time, she matter-of-factly tells her son that her business with life is done, that she is ready to die. With a son's tact and discretion, Augustine confesses that he doesn't remember his reply. What he allows himself to remember is the grief that soon follows. At first grief, he resolves to tuck himself into the memory of his sublime elevation with her, where all relatings are seamless. But there is no room for grief in eternal memory, and grieving is what Augustine is. He finally gives in to his giving in when he is heart-struck by the thought of his mother's peculiar generosity to him in life, her unfeigned patience with his will to wander—Monica, the prodigal's mother. His tears flow freely into the release of his grief and, with a buoyant heart, he finds rest. He is, in a way he was wholly unable to anticipate, home. Augustine ends his memorial to his mother with a loving remembrance of her marriage to Patricius, a man in life who had his own will to wander. No longer does the son resent his mother's forbearance. It has become a generous thing, not only in her but also in Augustine. In burying his father and mother together in his confession, Augustine unites them more profoundly than could any mound of dust and clay.

I am aware of my human tendency to see harmony where there is none, to project reconciliation into a place where conciliation is not prior or even conceivable. I am too sentimental. I shouldn't believe so readily in Augustine's forgiveness of Patricius. I shouldn't expect or want a mediation, likely maternal, that undoes the wounding between Laios and Oedipus. I read too much fiction, too much theology. And before I have reckoned much with the calculation that puts supernatural entities into their properly liminal place, I wonder whether these dying words of a beloved son can possibly betoken forgiveness: "My God, my God, why have you abandoned me?" Luke seems to think so; the other gospel writers are less clear.

If naturalism is the reminder that some opacities are not mysteries to be fathomed but bricks in the edifice of humility, then I am grateful for naturalism. But I am also, it must be said, equally aware of my human tendency to confuse a lack of sentimentality with the virtue of objectivity and to forget that it is the unsentimental heart that (thankfully) breaks. I don't care much for the grand synopsis that makes everything come out all right. I don't think that the synopsis, as we are given to conceive of it in this life, can possibly be the vision we want, even if we would prefer, quite understandably, to live in a world less mortgaged to the offerings of heartbreak. All things considered, I will take my naturalism piecemeal.

## NOTES

1. See Wayne Proudfoot's essay in the present volume, "Pragmatism, Naturalism, and Genealogy in the Study of Religion," sections 3 and 4. Compare this with his statement, "Many religious thinkers and scholars of religion who reject supernaturalism nevertheless continue to shy away from the naturalistic alternative, that whatever there is in the universe that is shaped to our moral lives, or continuous with the higher parts of ourselves, is what we, collectively, have put there" (Proudfoot 2002, 89).

2. See Bilgrami (2010); his full-blown argument for the objectivity of values can be found in Bilgrami (2006).

3. She is invoked, but not named, in *Confessions* 4.2.2 and 6.15.25.

4. I am using James J. O'Donnell's (1992) edition of the Latin text of *Confessions*.

5. I am using the *Corpus Christianorum Series Latina* edition of *De magistro* (Augustine 1970). For useful remarks on the translation of *docere* in the context of the dialogue, see Madec (1999), 535–36.

6. In *De magistro* 8.21, Augustine says to Adeodatus, "Indulge me if I play with you at first; I do so not for the sake of playing but of cultivating mental strength and focus, those means by which we not only endure but love the heat and light of the place where the blessed life is lived."

7. According to Lewis and Short, *sarabara* is neuter plural, not feminine singular, and it refers to wide trousers, not to headgear. Apparently, Augustine was genuinely unclear about the meaning of this particular word.

8. Miles Burnyeat's now classic essay "Wittgenstein and Augustine *De magistro*" first appeared in *Proceedings of the Aristotelian Society*, supp. vol. 61 (1987), 1–24. It has since been reprinted in *The Augustinian Tradition*, edited by Gareth B. Matthews (Burnyeat 1999). The Matthews volume is part of the prestigious Philosophical Traditions series, under the general editorship of Amélie Oksenberg Rorty, and it marks Augustine's coming of age in Anglo-American philosophy.

9. I will be glossing the material that begins at *Confessions* 9.10.23 and goes through 9.13.36; my assumption is that the ecstasy at Ostia is of a piece with the memorial for Monica that is to follow.

## WORKS CITED

Augustine. 1970. *De magistro*. In *Corpus Christianorum Series Latina*, vol. 29, edited by W. B. Green and K. D. Daur, 155–203. Turnholt: Brepols.

Bilgrami, Akeel. 2006. *Self-Knowledge and Resentment*. Cambridge, MA: Harvard University Press.

Bilgrami, Akeel. 2010. "The Wider Significance of Naturalism: A Genealogical Essay." In *Naturalism and Normativity*, edited by Mario De Caro and David Macarthur, 23–54. New York: Columbia University Press.

Burnyeat, Miles. 1999. "Wittgenstein and Augustine *De magistro*." In *The Augustinian Tradition*, edited by Gareth B. Matthews, 286–303. Berkeley: University of California Press.

James, William. 2004. *The Varieties of Religious Experience*. New York: Barnes and Noble.

Madec, Goulven. 1999. "Note complémentaire 2." In *Oeuvres de Saint Augustin*, vol. 6, *Dialogues Philosophiques III*. Paris: Institut d'Études Augustiniennes.

O'Donnell, James J. 1992. *Augustine* Confessions, vol. 1, *Introduction and Text*. Oxford: Clarendon.

Proudfoot, Wayne. 2002. "Religious Belief and Naturalism." In *Radical Interpretation in Religion*, edited by Nancy K. Frankenberry, 78–92. Cambridge: Cambridge University Press.

Sophocles. 1978. *Oedipus the King*. Translated by Stephen Berg and Diskin Clay. Oxford: Oxford University Press.

Williams, Bernard. 1993. *Shame and Necessity*. Berkeley: University of California Press.

Wittgenstein, Ludwig. 1967. *Zettel*. Translated by G. E. M. Anscombe. Berkeley: University of California Press.

# Contributors

MATTHEW C. BAGGER teaches in the Department of Religious Studies at the University of Alabama.

SCOTT DAVIS is the Lewis T. Booker Professor in Religion and Ethics at the University of Richmond.

NANCY FRANKENBERRY is the John Phillips Professor in Religion, Emeritus, at Dartmouth College.

TERRY F. GODLOVE is Professor of Philosophy and Senior Associate Dean for Curriculum and Personnel at Hofstra University.

JONATHON KAHN is Professor of Religion at Vassar College.

PHILIP KITCHER is the John Dewey Professor of Philosophy at Columbia University.

WAYNE PROUDFOOT is Professor of Religion at Columbia University.

MICHAEL L. RAPOSA is Professor of Religious Studies and the E. W. Fairchild Professor of American Studies at Lehigh University.

JEFFREY STOUT is Professor of Religion at Princeton University.

JAMES WETZEL is the Augustinian Endowed Chair at Villanova University.

# Index